MANAGING CAREERS
& EMPLOYABILITY

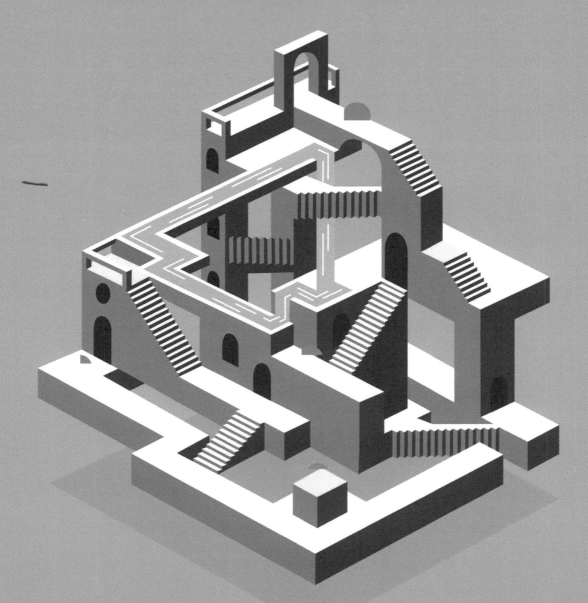

Sara Miller McCune founded SAGE Publishing in 1965 to support the dissemination of usable knowledge and educate a global community. SAGE publishes more than 1000 journals and over 800 new books each year, spanning a wide range of subject areas. Our growing selection of library products includes archives, data, case studies and video. SAGE remains majority owned by our founder and after her lifetime will become owned by a charitable trust that secures the company's continued independence.

Los Angeles | London | New Delhi | Singapore | Washington DC | Melbourne

MANAGING CAREERS & EMPLOYABILITY

YEHUDA BARUCH

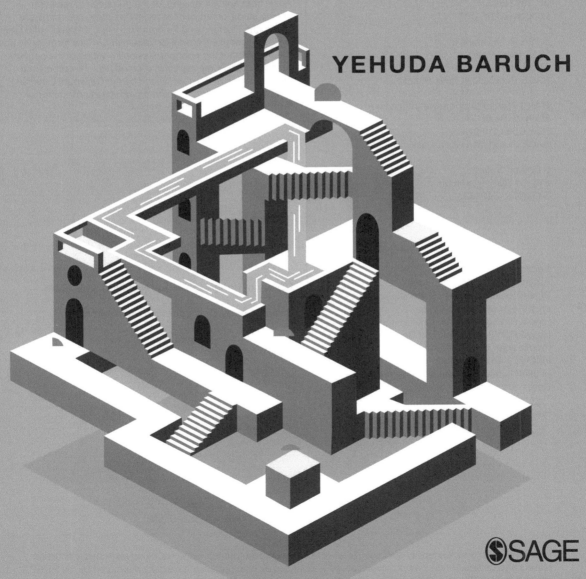

$SAGE

Los Angeles | London | New Delhi
Singapore | Washington DC | Melbourne

Los Angeles | London | New Delhi
Singapore | Washington DC | Melbourne

SAGE Publications Ltd
1 Oliver's Yard
55 City Road
London EC1Y 1SP

SAGE Publications Inc.
2455 Teller Road
Thousand Oaks, California 91320
SAGE Publications India Pvt Ltd

B 1/I 1 Mohan Cooperative Industrial Area
Mathura Road
New Delhi 110 044
SAGE Publications Asia-Pacific Pte Ltd

3 Church Street
#10–04 Samsung Hub
Singapore 049483

Editor: Ruth Stitt
Assistant editor: Jessica Moran
Digital content assistant/Editorial assistant,
digital: Mandy Gao
Production editor: Sarah Cooke
Copyeditor: Solveig Gardner Servian
Proofreader: Bryan Campbell
Indexer: Silvia Benvenuto
Marketing manager: Lucia Sweet
Cover design: Naomi Robinson
Typeset by: C&M Digitals (P) Ltd, Chennai, India
Printed in the UK

Library of Congress Control Number: 2021945298

British Library Cataloguing in Publication data

A catalogue record for this book is available from
the British Library

ISBN 978–1-5297–5185–7
ISBN 978–1-5297–5184–0 (pbk)

At SAGE we take sustainability seriously. Most of our products are printed in the UK using responsibly sourced
papers and boards. When we print overseas we ensure sustainable papers are used as measured by the PREPS
grading system. We undertake an annual audit to monitor our sustainability.

Dedicated to the career scholarly community

Contents

Detailed Contents

List of Figures

List of Tables

Abbreviations

AA   Affirmative action

ACAS   Advisory, Conciliation, and Arbitration Service

AI   Artificial intelligence

CAST   Career active system triad

CPM   Career planning and management

EEO   Equal employment opportunities

EDI   Equality, diversity, and inclusion

EU   European Union

HR   Human resource

HRM   Human resource management

SHRM   Strategic human resource management

IHRM   International human resource management

ILM   Internal labour market

IT   Information technology

M&As   Mergers and aquisitions

MBA   Master of Business Administration

MBO   Management buy-out

MCC   Mass career customization

MNCs   Multinational corporations

MPT   Multiple part-time

OCM   Organizational change management

PA   Performance appraisal

PRP   Performance-related pay

PWDs   People with disabilities

RBI   Repetitive brain injury

RBV   Resource-based view

RCS   Reverse culture shock

RSI   Repetitive strain injury

TCN   Third-country national

TINS   Two incomes, no sex syndrome

TM   Talent management

UBI   Universal basic income

UK   United Kingdom

USA   United States of America

VUCA   Volatility, uncertainty, complexity, and ambiguity

About the Author

Yehuda Baruch (DSc *Technion*, Israel, PostDoc at *City University* and *London Business School*) is a Professor of Management at Southampton Business School, the University of Southampton, UK, and Affiliated Professor, Audencia, Nantes, France. His research covers a broad range of topics, with a particular focus on careers and global HRM. He has published over 160 refereed papers, including in *Journal of Management, Academy of Management Annals, Human Resource Management, Organizational Dynamics, Journal of Vocational Behavior, Human Relations, Research Policy* and *Organization Studies* among other journals, and over 50 books and book chapters. His work is widely acknowledged. Dr Baruch is Fellow of the Academy of Social Sciences and the British Academy of Management. Formerly he served as Vice-president Research of EURAM, Associate Editor of *Human Resource Management* (USA), Editor of *Group & Organization Management* and *Career Development International*; Chair, Careers Division, Academy of Management.

Preface

One slogan that for me represents organizational truism is 'Our people are our most important assets'. It came to be the most cited motto for a multitude of organizations; many enterprises adopt it as their credo. I believe that the difference between using it as an empty slogan or lip service and the case of an organization that really takes it as its leading philosophy, will be manifested in the actual way organizations treat their employees, at all hierarchical levels. This, in turn, will be reflected in both individual and organizational success.

Career management is a clear way to develop and reveal the bond between the organization and the employees. The practice of career planning and management (CPM) is concerned with one of the two primary roles of HRM in any organization: to obtain and to retain employees. From the organizational perspective, this book is dedicated to the second one, retaining the human talent, utilizing career systems that fit contemporary trends.

In my years of teaching HRM and careers I have found that a growing number of students develop an interest in taking a course/module or an elective in the career area. These students and their professors should be able to benefit from a textbook that is dedicated to this field. I could not find a similar book to use for such an elective for my own teaching, and that served as the initial impetus for writing the first version of the book in 2004, and now developed it further. The career area is increasingly gaining recognition as a crucial part of HRM, but for which the standard HRM textbooks would usually devote no more than a single chapter.

The purpose of the book is to present the reader with the concepts and principles of CPM in light of contemporary developments. At the individual level it would help self-development, career competence and employability. Many current concepts suggested by scholars and management gurus are relevant and have strong implication for career systems. In contrast, many of the readings in the area still refer to the traditional type of careers. This book focuses on career systems and the way they are managed by individuals and organizations, reflecting the diversity which exists in management studies – both in practice and in theory. Each chapter ends with a list of thought-provoking questions for students and managers alike.

An attempt was made to integrate traditional concept on one hand, and contemporary innovative inspirations on the other hand. It is written from a global perspective, though most cases are from developed countries. The book should appeal to both academics and practitioners. It is directed for the readership of managers and the academic community in the management area – both students and scholars.

I hope the reader, mostly students, but also consultants, HR managers, and anyone who has a career and wishes to develop it further, will benefit from the book.

Yehuda Baruch

Acknowledgements

To the scholars whose work has inspired me to create the book.

To the students who used my first book (Managing Careers, 2004a) and gave me rich feedback.

To SAGE Publishing and the supporting team – for commissioning it, for the dedicated continuous support, and the delivery of the final product.

Online Resources

Lecturers can visit **https://study.sagepub.com/baruch** to access a range of online resources designed to support teaching. *Managing Careers and Employability* is accompanied by:

- A **Teaching Guide** containing teaching notes for each chapter
- **PowerPoints** that can be adapted and edited to suit specific teaching needs

Foreword

Managing Careers and Employability
by Yehuda Baruch

Denise M. Rousseau
Carnegie Mellon University

Who really *manages* a career? As Yehuda Baruch makes clear in this thoughtful book, there are several answers to this question. Workers can make choices, pursue education, build networks, and navigate the demands of work, family, and their own well-being. But some workers face precarity from unstable employment or distressed economies, having far fewer choices and resources than the high-flyers with boundaryless careers. Precarious workers do still try to "manage" toward a better future with career goals diminished by the obstacles they face. This book calls attention to such differences because managing a career takes many forms predicated not just on individual attributes but on organizational and societal factors too.

Historically organizations did manage careers, with classics texts describing the career paths mapped out at AT&T (Bray, Campbell & Grant, 1974) and other large corporations in the decades immediately after WWII. Going further back in time, older texts describe careers managed by "placement," where the company kept moving a worker around until finding a job that person could do (Viteles, 1932). Contemporary organizations generally are less active in career management than was once the case. Instead, they more *selectively* manage careers. Some offer internal mobility and privileged resources for workers they value most, while striving to retain for a while longer those they won't keep long-term, and largely ignoring the career interests of others.

As *Managing Careers and Employability* makes clear, the net result is a differentiated picture of career management as engaged in by employers, workers, policy makers, and institutions. The differentiated ways of managing careers described in this book challenge stereotypical notions of career management often based on boundaryless careers or central planning.

Instead, as Baruch makes clear, we need the lens of a multi-level ecosystem to understand how careers are shaped, the resources available, and dynamics that emerge as the actors, human, communal, organizational, and institutional attempt to pursue their goals.

As in any multi-level phenomenon, careers and employability are likely to be best understood through the regular practice of thinking "one-level up and one-level down" (first advocated by Richard Hackman (2003) for thinking about behaviour in groups and organizations). This thinking in levels goes something like this. To understand how an organizational practice operates in the domain of careers and employability (let's say, up-or-out promotions or high-potential-development-programs), we need to identify

1. the *organizational* activities each entails and the supports required;
2. the mix of *workers* involved and how each practice affects their willingness to join the firm, remain there, and work hard for it;
3. the *environmental* implications of each practice.

Organizationally, both up-or-out promotions and high-potential programs require well-developed internal career paths and substantial investments in training. From a worker perspective, these practices tend to draw different kinds of people as those attracted to a competitive up-or-out system are likely to differ from those attracted to developmental opportunities. Environmentally, these two practices are predicated on distinct labor market assumptions, the former presumes talented new entrants are always available, while the latter does not. And as noted above, contemporary organizations are selective regarding which employees engage in these career practices or don't, with implications for when and where such practices are used.

As you read Yehuda Baruch's *Managing Careers and Employability,* be prepared to think in levels and in doing so expand your understanding of the dynamics of employment and careers present and future.

References

Bray, D. W., Campbell, R. J., & Grant, D. L. (1974). *Formative years in business: A long-term AT&T study of managerial lives.* Wiley-Interscience.

Hackman, J. R. (2003). Learning more by crossing levels: Evidence from airplanes, hospitals, and orchestras. *Journal of Organizational Behavior, 24*(8), 905–922.

Viteles, M. (1932). *Industrial Psychology.* Norton.

Introduction

1

LEARNING OBJECTIVES

After reading this chapter you should be able to:

- Define careers
- Distinguish between individual and organizational career perspectives
- Identify contemporary careers
- Understand the meaning and role of employability
- Understand the impact of environmental factors on careers
- Explain how organizations can work alongside individuals to match their mutual needs
- Understand career system management within the general HRM framework

Chapter outline

Introduction

Over the past and into the present, careers have taken various forms and their meanings change. The X, Y and Z generations' perception of *career* is different from that of the baby boomers, for example. Our generation witnesses a sea change in the shape of careers, moving from the concept of lifelong career as an archetype model, quite often fulfilled, to a world of work where stable employment with the same organization is not only the exception but also not even aspired to. Within organizations, we witness fluidity of structures and reshaping of configuration on a continuous basis, which is reflected in dynamic career systems. Both people's and organization's perspectives of CPM have been altered.

The change in the career's realm is not a singular phenomenon and has not occurred in isolation. It is just one aspect of changes that are taking place, at a seemingly ever-accelerating pace, in society in general and in management in particular. Businesses and public organizations are experiencing rapid developments in many areas – economy, technology, society, politics, and relationships. These have wide implications for the planning and management of careers. Many careers have become global, and globalization influences most careers. Global events like the 2008 financial crisis or the COVID-19 pandemic had a powerful impact. New types of careers are enabled by technology alongside changing norms of behaviours and practices. New professions and vocations emerge whereas others decline or disappear.

The development of people can be self-imitated or externally prompted. Individuals plan and manage their careers, but at the same time the planning and managing of employees' careers has always been considered an organizational role, part of the Human Resource Management (HRM) department within organizations. Organizations must invest in and develop their assets, and the statement that 'people are the most important asset of the organization' may now be seen as a cliché, but any cliché was once a novelty and this one remains true today. Human capital is a worthy investment for individuals, organizations and nations. Individuals who acquire valuable human (and social) capital gain employability: the ability to obtain employment if and when needed. Organizations invest in their people – their assets – to gain competitive advantage, and nations invest in education to gain global advantage and avoid a 'brain drain' (migration to other countries of their highly educated workforce). With concurrent changes in individual perspectives, organizational management and the wider society, the notion of *career* and subsequently its management has been transformed.

Career perspectives: Individual versus organizational

The meaning of CPM depends very much on whether an individual or organizational perspective is taken. Many viewed career management as a process by which individuals develop, implement and monitor their career goals and strategies (Gutteridge, 1986; Hall, 2002). Much of the literature on careers has indeed focused on the individual perspective. However, already in the early 1990s it was suggested that 'The focus of career development has shifted radically, from the individual to the organization' (Gutteridge et al., 1993). Still the pendulum seems to be shifting back to an individual orientation of managing careers, which follows a general trend of the modern age that emphasizes individualism rather than collectivism, in particular in Western societies (Pervin & John, 1999). This book takes a more balanced approach, arguing that organizations can and perhaps should take a lead role in planning and managing careers; also that this role would be different from that prescribed in the past by those who have studied the field of careers. Much of the book examines the organizational side of careers and considers the wider career system as a general career eco-system (Baruch, 2015; Baruch & Rousseau, 2019).

What is the meaning of career?

The answer to this depends on the viewpoint of the questioner. A career belongs to the individual but in much, if not most, employment the career will be planned and managed for the individual by the organization. The organizational structure forms the (internal) 'road map', providing identifiable positions, interrelationships between these positions, the qualities necessary to fill them, and moreover, mechanisms to enable people to navigate this road map. This way organizations can take a leading role and have control over CPM.

The origin of the word 'career' came from the Latin word *carrus* (a wheeled vehicle) which moves through a track, providing the metaphor for a movement in a path through which people progress during their lifetime. In Italian it became *carriera*, and then in the 16th century *carrière* in French.

Psychologists from the USA defined career as 'The pattern of work-related experiences that span the course of a person's life' (Greenhaus et al., 2019). Arthur et al. (1989) regard career as 'an evolving sequence of a person's work experience over time'. On the other side of the ocean, Arnold (1997) defined career as 'the sequence of employment-related positions, roles, activities and experiences encountered by a person', and Baruch and Rosenstein (1992) consider career as 'a process of development of the employee through a path of experience and jobs in the organization/organizations.' Careers can indeed be seen as a sequencing of an individual's life, work roles, and experiences, if one limits one's perspective to that of the individual. Nevertheless, careers take place in specified social environments, and in particular in organizations – a crucial point missed by many scholars who analyse careers from psychological perspective only. The normal or typical professional career usually follows a sequence of developmental phases, each of which is delineated by a distinct shift in the individual's sense of self, but each is shaped and influenced by the organization in which the person works.

The variety of definitions, only a few of which are presented here, re-emphasizes that *career* involves a process of progress and development of individuals, which is sometimes described as the 'life stories of people'. Nevertheless there is in the careers domain a substantial overlap between individual and organizational roles.

A pause for reflection

How far ahead have you planned your career?

Do you have an idea about the profession, the job, or the sector you will work in next year? In five years?

Did you have career counselling to help you plan ahead? With whom?

What is the area of study?

The concept of a career builds on several theoretical disciplines, but as the formulation of career theory was quite individually focused, its development was traditionally dominated by psychologists. However, careers are also, to a certain extent, a 'property' of organizations, and managed by them as part of human resource management (Campbell & Moses, 1986).

They take place in and are influenced by environmental contextual factors – in particular economy, politics, technology, social, and cultural. An approach that takes into account in the wider sense is *career ecosystem* (Baruch, 2015). Yet the two major actors in the system are the individual and the organization. Within organizations, career management is part of HRM. The basic roles of HRM are to obtain and retain employees, and career systems deal with the latter role of retaining (and sometimes releasing an excess of) employees.

Research has put into focus the changing meaning of careers. Many have examined the shift from long-term relationships to transactional, short-termism (Adamson et al., 1998). At one time people would have expected to serve an organization for their entire working life. Now people expect the organization to serve them, and over a timespan that could easily be only two to three years. The average time people spend in a single job is less than 5 years and job loss is an increasing phenomenon, in particular in the private sector (Farber, 2010), though others suggest 10 years (Rodrigues & Guest, 2010). Contemporary career thinking suggests that career systems have become more dynamic and fluid, but also more volatile (Groysberg et al., 2019).

Planning horizons have shortened, and the future needs of organizations have become less clear.

Subsequently, both individuals and organizations struggle to redefine careers and the role each should play in their management. The main shift is from careers that offer secure employment for all, to careers that provide 'opportunities for development'. This development means that managing careers has ceased to be merely an organizational obligation, and rather rests with the individual. Similarly, in reviews of the literature on career writing during the last years of the 20th century and early 21st century, Sullivan (1999) and Sullivan and Baruch (2009) identified two prominent streams of research in career studies: developmental stage theories and the boundaryless career, emerging at the end of the 1990s. Another core stream in the study of careers is career choice theories and the meaning of career success (see e.g., Spurk et al., 2019).

Another distinction that is sometimes made in the study of careers is between the concepts of the individual focus and those of the organizational/cultural focus. However, convergence is better than distinction as a way of understanding careers. Balancing individual and organizational needs is the goal of many career models (Herriot, 1992; Baruch, 2006a; Lips-Wiersma & Hall, 2007). The need to satisfy and comply with individual needs and organizational requirements has been long established (Herriot & Pemberton, 1996; Schein, 1978), and individual aspirations are developed within organizational contexts and career systems. A broader perspective would place the wider environment – professional, organizational and cultural – as the reference for individual career aspiration. A comprehensive view of careers sees it as a specific eco-system with multiple players (individuals, organizations, nations, cultures, professions, to name the prominent ones) working together in local and global labour markets (Baruch, 2015).

Why employability?

In the contemporary labour market, one cannot and should not rely on the idea that one's job or career is stable and secure. Job and career progression requires people to move and change, thus being employable. Employability was defined by Hillage and Pollard (1998):

Employability is about the capability to move self-sufficiently within the labour market to realize potential through sustainable employment. For the individual, employability depends on the knowledge, skills and attitudes they possess, the way they use those assets and present them to employers and the context (e.g. personal circumstances and labour market environment) within which they seek work.

Employability is critical for fulfilling the individual need for work. Work offers meaning for life, self-worth and esteem, and, of course, provides tangible benefits of income. Work also relates to societal worth and contribution to the wellbeing beyond that of the person. Employability is an essential ingredient for a successful career. Employability should be considered and studied from several perspectives, in particular the individual level, the organizational level and industry level (Van der Heijde & Van der Heijden, 2006). Different careers require different mixtures of competences and characteristics, starting with physical and cognitive ability as well as the aptitude to be flexible, adaptive, agile and, in particular, having the right mindset (e.g. a global mindset for those looking for a global career, or general career resilience and flexibility).

Until not long ago, 'employability' was considered a 'buzzword' (Baruch, 2001a; Thijssen et al., 2008), but it has become the most studied construct in recent career studies (Baruch et al., 2015). In Chapter 4 we will focus further on employability and its role in career development.

Long-term expectations of mutual loyalty and commitment from either the individual or the organization is a thing of the past. It is the responsibility of the employee to make sure that they have the required competence to perform the job, and if the worst comes to worst (i.e. being made redundant) to use their competences, skills and capabilities to gain a new job. That is the essence of employability. While it is still necessary for organizations to invest in their employees, providing them with 'employability' is not taken as a primary role (Baruch, 2001a). It is in the interest of the individual to remain employable.

Employability does not necessarily mean being an employee of an organization. Entrepreneurial careers are of increasing importance and relevance to the labour market. Self-employment can be a worthy sustainable and and lasting career choice for those that have the drive and ability to be independent. To succeed in an entrepreneurial career, one needs specific qualities and attitudes (Douglas & Shepherd, 2002; Liguori et al., 2020). Previous experience of entrepreneurship is beneficial in deciding whether one is suitable for such a career, and a family and social support network is essential.

Graduate employability

Globally there is an acceleration of tertiary education, with more people attending universities to the extent of some half of the population of the young age group in developed countries. For these students, the first point of entry to the labour market is following graduation. Thus, graduates look from their education and degree not merely gaining knowledge, but also employability. For organizations, graduates will form the source for future talent, and will require talent management (McCracken et al., 2016). Employability for graduates depends on many factors. For example, a degree in music or philosophy may not lead to a career in that field (e.g. Dobrow Riza & Heller, 2015). Other factors in graduate recruitment are national levels of unemployment, timing of entering the labour market (most notably during both the financial crisis of 2008 and the COVID-19 pandemic), support from career advisors and services at the university, and graduate recruitment agencies (see Case study 1.1) to mention a few.

A pause for reflection

In their measures for graduates' employability, Rothwell and Arnold (2007) included items such as 'I will easily find a job with an employer after completing my degree course' and 'I am confident that I could quickly get a job related to my degree course'.

How do you feel about your employability – what would your answer be? How much of your answer is due to your personality, knowledge, confidence and esteem, compared with the university and the degree course you undertook?

CASE STUDY 1.1: GET THE CAREER YOU DESERVE: HOW GRADUATE RECRUITMENT WORKS

Graduate Recruitment Bureau, or GRB, was established by two business graduates in 1997, and grew organically, employing 65 members of staff in 2020. Under the slogan *Get the career you deserve*, they pride themselves as 'the go-to platform for high caliber University students, graduates and recruiters'.

The firm is a major UK graduate recruitment consultancy. It offers a Career Matchmaking service for students and graduates. Their business model is a free service for students and graduates, building on a client base of some 2,000 employers across all sectors, whom they charge a percentage of the graduates' remuneration. Amongst GRB clients are the Post Office, IBM, Unilever, Ocado and several fast-growing SMEs.

GRB's recruitment experts have successfully matched over 8,000 graduates with full-time, graduate-level jobs. The following quotes demonstrate how both sides benefited from the service provided by GRB in the transition from university to the workplace.

(Continued)

Feedback from students and graduates

'GRB is the only recruitment agency that connected me to a legitimate company and actually found me a job. I tried a couple of them, with zero success. ... I'm happy with my job now and it's thanks to GRB, and specifically James, the consultant that was responsible for me – he really was amazing!' *Maths graduate*

'A great recruitment agency! The recruitment process was very smooth, fast, with constant updates and communication and the staff was very extremely helpful and supportive. I would definitely recommend!' *Computer Science graduate*

'A superb facility for students who don't have time during their final year to spend filling out a million identical forms while jobhunting. ... GRB did support me particularly well both before and after I had been offered a role she found for me and remained a contact with both me and my new workplace to ensure a smooth hiring process.' *Electronic Engineering graduate*

Feedback from employers

'The service was excellent. GRB engaged with us throughout every stage of the process through detailed weekly reports and regular conference calls ensuring we were fully informed at all times. We feel they went over and above with their support including attending and supporting us with our assessment days at very short notice. They are a great team who are a real pleasure to work with. The caliber of the candidates that they provided to us were of an extremely high standard. ... This increased the number of graduate placements we intended to make.' *Head of Talent, Post Office*

'With professionalism from the very beginning, [the GRB team] have allowed us to increase our interview output from 10 to over 50 interviews per week, shortening our lead times and providing a great candidate experience whilst doing so. Communication was excellent throughout the campaign. ... Overall, [we] would recommend GRB to any organization looking for support with volume recruitment campaigns.' *HR & Graduate Scheme Recruitment Advisor, National Audit Office*

'... we felt that the *GRB* team offered a completely personalized service and that they actually became a part of our extended team throughout the whole process.' *Group Talent & Development Advisor, Story Homes*

'A digital assessment day solution delivered a more efficient process for our recruitment team, a better candidate experience and some excellent feedback from our assessors and hiring managers. A very worthwhile investment – one I'd highly recommend to other recruiters.' *Early Careers Talent Acquisition Manager, Fidelity International*

For further details about GRB, see www.grb.uk.com

Source: This case was kindly provided by Dan Hawes, GRB

A pause for reflection

Who is responsible for your employability?

What are the pros and cons for the student and graduate for opting to look for a job with the help and support of graduate recruitment agencies?

Would it be wise to ignore this route? Would it be wise to count only on this route?

Balancing individual and organizational needs

Herriot and Pemberton (1996) offered the model presented in Figure 1.1. They outline four properties they feel an established career model should posses. These are:

- Conceptualization (i.e. taking into account not merely the organization, but also the business, political and economic environment).
- Cyclical and processual nature of the model.
- Subjectivity (rather than normativity) for the meaning of career success.
- Interactive nature in the sense of relationship between the organization and the individual.

Let us examine the model from both the organization and individual perspectives.

The first proposition of the model associates the business environment with the organization in terms of strategy, structure and processes. As will be shown later (Chapter 4), these correspond with philosophy, policy and practice. This conceptualization means that factors such as the sector of operation, national culture, business activity or prosperity of the market influence the strategic goals set by organizations, how organizations are designed and structured, and the practices they apply for managing people and processes. The model argues that the internal labour market (ILM) is an ideal archetype, that is, that promoting from within is the best approach to career management, but that absolute ILM never occurs in practice, and in extreme cases might block innovation and creativity.

From the individual perspective, proposition 2 suggests that the social context in which people grow and develop influences their values, norms and beliefs. These, in turn, influence their career aspirations, career choice, and progress. Propositions 3 and 4, respectively, argue that organizational strategy, structure and processes will determine what organizations need and expect from people and their careers, whereas people's identities will determine what they wish to gain from the organization. Similarly, propositions 5 and 6 reflect the ways in which organizations and people conclude their contractual relationships.

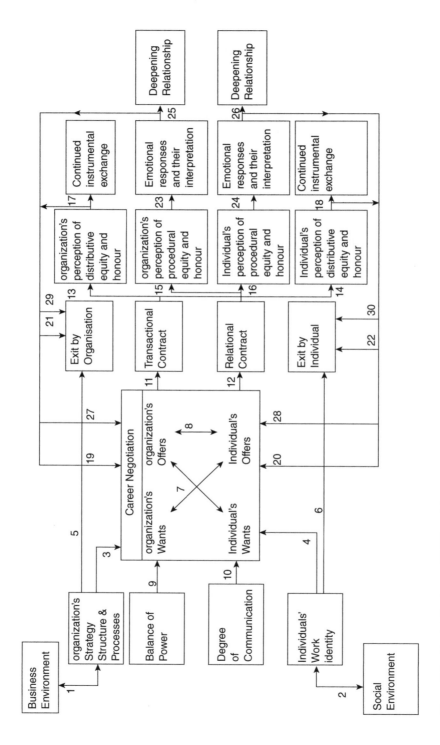

Figure 1.1 Herriot–Pemberton (1996) model

At the core of the Herriot and Pemberton's model lies the element of mutual recognition, negotiation and agreement about the 'give and take', the psychological and contractual agreement organizations and individuals consent to (or believe they have agreed upon). It is the point of equilibrium between what people offer to the organization and what they expect in return, and vice versa. Other influential factors on this core process are the balance of power (proposition 9) and communication between the parties (proposition 10).

The intermediate outcomes of the core process are manifested in two types of relationship between the individual and the organization. These can be transactional, calculated 'deals', on the one hand (proposition 11), and relational, even emotional, bond relationships (proposition 12) on the other. The transactional relationship is instrumental (in that services are provided in exchange for compensation). The relational relationship reflects mutual commitment. In practice both types exist in any employment relationship. There is then the perception of distributive justice (propositions 13 and 14) and of procedural justice (propositions 15 and 16). On distributive and procedural justice, see Box 1.1.

Box 1.1: Procedural and distributive justice

Procedural justice: Perception about justice or fairness that occurs when the process used to set work outcomes and benefits is seen as fair and reasonable.

Distributive justice: Perception about justice or fairness that occurs when the actual work outcomes and benefits are seen as fair and reasonable.

Source: Greenberg and Cropanzano (2001)

Many studies identified the positive impact of organizational justice on careers within organizations, and this impact was stable across cultures (Suifan et al., 2017).

As a result of the perception of organizational justice, people and organizations will continue to exercise instrumental exchange if they perceive that there is adequate distributive equality (propositions 17 and 18). They will not do so if they believe there has been a breach of the 'contract' – in such a case they will try to re-negotiate the contract (propositions 19 and 20) or leave the organization (propositions 21 and 22).

In a primarily relational contract, the impact of organizational justice will be mainly on the emotional element, and if the contract is perceived as fair the positive interpretation (propositions 23 and 24) will be reflected in a deepening relationship (propositions 25 and 26). Breach of a contract would similarly lead to an attempt to try to renegotiate the contract (propositions 27 and 28) or to leave the organization (propositions 29 and 30).

A pause for reflection

Think about your latest career move (this can be your first job search, an internal move within an organization, a move to another organization, or starting your own enterprise). How can you analyse that move in light of Herriot and Pemberton's model? How significant was your perception of both procedural and distributive justice as a factor in making your decision?

Herriot and Pemberton's (1996) model places at its core the traditional conception of requiring a match between individual and organization in terms of needs, wants and provisions. It is a dynamic model in the sense that, in line with the 'open systems' approach (Katz & Kahn, 1966), events are cyclical. The model views an organizational career as a continuous sequence of renegotiations of psychological contracts (see later chapters for a more detailed discussion). The contracts are 'signed' between the employee and the organization. This leads to the question of whether a psychological contract can exist with an entity that is not a person. In practice the contract is agreed with people that represent the organization (managers, HR department). All in all, the model is reinforced by evidential support suggested by Herriot and Pemberton, and fits well with the evolving nature of organizational careers.

Labour markets

Employers' requirements from the labour market are complex. They face a highly competitive, global market, in which flexibility is essential to cope with continually changing trends and positions. As a result, when seeking staff, they look for people with multiple competencies, high skills levels and those who are capable of high performance. At the same time they also need a highly flexible workforce. Commitment is still important, as is loyalty, but such sentiments now tend be towards the profession, the team or the project, and not necessarily towards the organization. Non-traditional workers (people who work in alternative arrangements such as on-call workers, independent contractors, temporary workers or agency workers, as well as contingent workers called in to work in emergencies) form an increasing proportion of the workforce. Some may opt for the non-traditional career route from choice whereas others are forced into this path by the lack of other opportunities. Another phenomenon is that people who wish to work full time but cannot find a single full-time job are opting instead for multiple part-time jobs. All of these alternative contractual work arrangements are part of the general flexibility that companies need to apply in their operational practices.

In addition to the acquisition and maintenance of knowledge and capabilities, one element crucial for organizational competitiveness is 'to know what you know' – whom these competencies reside with. For example, in a large project, different people will be needed at different stages. The organization should be able to detect where these people are, what they are occupied with, and further, how to utilize the newly gained knowledge. If there is a lack of resources, the organization needs to know where they can buy them, or how to outsource these activities. Some industries' work and staffing evolve around projects rather than specific firms (e.g. construction and film making). Networking relationships with the wider business environment are necessary in such a case.

CASE STUDY 1.2: THE TEMPTATION OF TEMPING ...

In October 1946, with an office in Detroit, Michigan, and two employees, William Russell Kelly started a new company to meet the office and clerical needs of Detroit-area businesses. The company was staffed by housewives and students – people who had flexible schedules. Growth was fast, and involved with lending employees to customers. Kelly's development of this new type of service – creating a pool of people with a variety of office skills to provide temporary help for offices – marked the beginning of the modern temporary staffing services industry.

Companies realized that using reliable temporary employees (commonly referred to as 'temps') made good business sense. Temporary work facilitates flexibility and may enable business agility. Temps, especially women, discovered a good way to find work for short periods of time. Soon it became apparent that the relationships with the 'mother company' can be long term, and that the services need not be restricted to low-level skills jobs. The next stage was internationalization.

The business community recognized that such temp agencies offer flexibility, diversity, quality, and above all, delivery of performance.

They are not the only ones in temping...

Kelly Services entered the Fortune 500 list in the late 1990s (ranked 384 in 2001, 503 in 2020). With some 8,000 employees, the firm generates over $5 billion in revenue each year, by providing employment to more than 800,000 people annually. A much stronger competitor is Manpower, with some 30,000 employees, generating some 3 million staff (2017 data), operating in 80 countries. Manpower was ranked 141 in the Fortune 500 list in 2020 (182 in the 2001).

In short, temping is a thriving business.

Box 1.2: Temping from the perspectives of different actors in the labour market

The question for individual: Should I temp or should I not?

The question for employer: Should I use temporary workforce, and if so, what share of my workforce should it be?

Temporary work lacks the stability of a single workplace, but offers variations and fast learning experience. Temping, if successful, may lead to a permanent job with the employer of choice after experiencing different options. It offers flexibility, and uncertainty, for both actors. If the individual is happy to tolerate these factors, temp work may be a great career option. The more flexibility employers look for, the better it is for them to use temping services.

Business growth is a characteristic of the temp service sector. Good news for these companies. But what about their staff? Generally, temporary employees tend to have less training, lower payment, no stability, and ambiguous job security as compared with permanent employees. (That is, they have no secure role, implied from their status, and only a low level of job security from their employing temp agency.) They do, however, gain diverse experience and flexibility to manage their work–life balance.

Since the Industrial Revolution, the organizational career has become the norm. Of course, the traditional organizational career was never applicable to all: redundancy was not devised until the late 1980s, which soon became so frequent and on such a large scale (Osterman, 1996) due to the global competitive market and financial instability. Entrepreneurial careers such as in small businesses and sole traders have always existed. Even in Japan, lifelong employment was promised and provided only by large firms, which employed just one-third of the workforce.

However, the organizational career was the role model for a 'proper' and desired career. Career success has been defined in terms of progression through the hierarchy (Townsend, 1970) in a 'career tournament' mode (Rosenbaum, 1979). Derived from this definition is expectations – what each person would expect from their career, and in particular from the employing organization, in relation to their career. If individuals see it as solely their own responsibility to manage their career, the organization is neutralized from its role as partner in the management of careers.

The level of involvement is diverse, ranging from irrelevant, through to a supporting role, a directive role, and up to a controlling or managerial role. Two cases illustrate the extremes of involvement. The first is the portfolio career person, who manages his or her own career, and who has no need of organizational mechanisms to manage, direct or support their career development (Comfort, 1997). Portfolio careers are not merely for consultants or professionals; they can be found in medicine and music, for example (Bartleet et al., 2019). The other extreme can still be found in large bureaucracies (e.g. army systems), where new recruits are set on a clear career path, planned and designed, at least for their first few years of service, and managed from the top until they reach the higher ranks (e.g. when they become officers). In most organizations, however, there is a certain degree of freedom, but the amount depends very much on the sector, the profession, the size of the organization and the state of the economy. Medical doctors still have to invest some seven years in their basic training, and further time in their specialism. To change career, even within the profession, would mean a further investment in time and effort, and is neither popular nor usual – one rarely finds medical specialists changing to another specialism, for example, a general practitioner or a surgeon becoming an orthopaedic surgeon or an anaesthetist, and so on. Moreover, people from outside the profession cannot embark on a career in the medical field. The same is true in any chartered profession, but even for others, long-term investment is needed to start making a living in a new career. However, the opposite route is available. Many medical doctors can opt to leave the role of active practitioner to become managers in the health service, combine consultancy with other activities (as a form of portfolio career), or move to academia or politics, and so on. Other professions, especially in the information technology (IT) sector, are more likely to witness career transitions.

The changing nature of careers

Arthur et al. (1989) have indicated that the concept of a career is not the property of any one theoretical or disciplinary view. They presented eight viewpoints on the career concept (those of psychology, social psychology, sociology, anthropology, economics, political science, history and geography), mostly within the boundaries of the behavioural sciences. New trends in this framework are manifested in the need to fit contemporary changes in culture and economic conditions. These lead to different shapes of career. The theoretical framework encompassing them started with the boundaryless career theory, suggesting that individuals can now cross career boundaries that were not easy or possible in the past (Arthur, 1994, 2014). This was followed by individual perspectives such as the protean career (the concept of the individual as the agent of self: Hall, 1976, 1996; Hall & Moss, 1998) (see Chapter 3 for elaboration) and the perspectives of the organization and the wider society such as the post-corporate career (Peiperl & Baruch, 1997) and the career ecosystem theory (Baruch, 2015) (see Chapter 4 for elaboration). These approaches to the management of careers have developed as a result of the deterioration of order and the relative simplicity associated with clear, stable and open organizational structures and procedures. With the turbulence and lack of structure and order evident in the realm of careers, even chaos theory may well prove useful in this regard (see Bird et al., 2002; Pryor & Bright, 2011).

Organizational careers: The rumours of their death have been premature

While rumours of the death of organizational careers may have been premature, there is certainly a change, a transformation, and a transition. The notion of career and the meaning of career success have moved, perhaps been upgraded. Climbing the hierarchy is no longer the sole criterion. Inner satisfaction, life balance, autonomy, and freedom have entered the formula (for further elaboration see Chapter 3). Many would recognize the true nature of the situation as being analogous to the following statement:

'Growth for the sake of growth is the ideology of the cancer cell.'

Edward Abbey

Similarly, climbing up the organizational ladder just for the sake of being higher in the hierarchy does not make sense. Realization of this notion has enabled significant changes to the meaning of career advancement. Many contemporary scholars view the changes in structure (and restructuring) of organizations, together with economic turbulence, as the factors which have forced significant shifts in the paradigm of careers. The traditional career has dominated industrial employment for decades, because most organizational structures supported it. Such structures were bureaucracy based, and the many managerial layers created a metaphorical ladder for climbing up the organization. Traditional systems were fit for bureaucracy (Wilensky, 1964), but current career systems are dynamic and volatile (Groysberg et al., 2019; Baruch & Rousseau, 2019).

Box 1.3: The use of metaphors in career studies

Metaphors can be a powerful way to understand careers. Inkson et al. (2015) suggested using metaphors as a lens to explore careers. Many career concepts used to develop career theory employed metaphors as their label (Baruch et al., 2015). Examples (apart from the leading theories of boundaryless and protean careers) are kaleidoscope careers, butterfly careers, and intelligent careers, to name a few.

With the flattening of organizations and the elimination of entire managerial layers, career paths have become blurred since the 1980s and the 1990s (Drucker, 1999). Nevertheless, there may be other factors, probably a combination of economic forces and the way in which people perceive their career, that enable the flattening of organizations.

Whichever is the cause and which the effect, these changes mean that a different approach to the management of careers should be sought, one that can fit in with the new realities of work, and the new characteristics should be derived from the nature of change in working life. The transformation of careers in general, and of psychological contracts specifically, is due to large economic, demographic and cultural forces, combined with business globalization and competitiveness. One aspect is the short horizons of career planning. 'Just-in-time' and business process re-engineering (mostly in manufacturing) and the privatization of many services are translated into limited options for long-term career plans at organizational level due to competitive pressures. Careers in China have changed significantly with the creation of 'new capitalism' with many private and state-owned enterprises.

An example of transformation in both the social and economic realms is the decreasing level of involvement of the state in life. There is less support for the deprived in society, and Socialism has ceased to be the ideal. Governments have reduced subsidies for lagging sectors (see the cases of the steel and textile industries in the UK or the car industry in Sweden, for example). A free-market, individualistic-oriented approach has come to dominate capitalist governments and has also contributed to the transformation of careers.

New psychological contracts: The evolution of employment relationships

Today's organizational structures, and hence career systems, are characterized by continual change. To keep the right people, organizations and employees need to develop new psychological contracts in line with contemporary business culture (Rousseau, 1995; Baruch & Hind, 1999). The idea of the psychological contract was originally suggested by Levinson and his colleagues in the early 1960s. It was re-introduced to organizational studies and developed later by scholars such as Kotter (1973), Schein (1980), and Nicholson and Johns (1985). It is still very topical, in particular within the context of transition into the new psychological contract (Baruch & Rousseau, 2019; Robinson et al., 1994; Rousseau, 1995).

In lay terms, the psychological contract is 'the unspoken promise, not present in the small print of the employment contract, of what [the] employer gives, and what employees give in return' (Baruch & Hind, 1999). Such a contract is fundamentally different from the formal, legal employment contracts in their context and expected impact (Spindler, 1994).

The evolution of the new psychological contract has led to a situation where there are no long-term contracts of loyalty and no mutual commitment. In the past, organizational commitment was commonly accepted as the desired norm, for both organizations and employees. As a result, the downsizing process has had very negative outcomes (Groysberg et al., 2019; Kets de Vries & Balazs, 1997). It is not only a common belief, but also a widely verified conjecture, that organizational commitment, motivational levels, and satisfaction are associated with each other, and a high level of these will lead to improved performance and a tendency to remain in an organization (Sullivan & Baruch, 2009). However, since mutual commitment has diminished or ceased to exist and the trust-based relationship has deteriorated in the industrial world, the relevance of the construct of organizational commitment has declined (Mercurio, 2015). Others argue for the need to maintain organizational commitment even in such times for the benefits it generates to organizations (Watson Wyatt, 1999). Moreover, it is argued, proper HRM management improves employees' organizational commitment (Veld et al., 2010).

Instead of the traditional concept of developing and gaining commitment, new ideas need to be introduced to compensate for the loss of balance in the relationship equation. We can now find ideas based on employability, with the organization being expected to invest in the training and development of its employees, and the employee being expected to exert effort and be flexible.

Through the concept of employability, employees will be able to find good jobs if the company has no further need for their services, and the company will be released from a lifelong obligation to employees (Handy, 1989; Waterman et al., 1994). This means a new deal, which is different from that of mutual commitment, and is not necessarily the one employees would prefer, nor the one that organizations would easily adopt (Baruch, 2001a). The organization seems to have abandoned traditional thinking. For example, there is a clear decline in traditional collective bargaining with unions, and instead more individual dealing with employees, under the concept of idiosyncratic deals or 'I-deals' (Rousseau, 2015).

Let us look at the roots of career theory: Hughes (1937) argued for the importance of ordering work experience and logic to the linkages between successive positions occupied over time. Thus his 'moving perspective of time' means, for organizational career management, that the career concept implies a relationship between employer and employee over time. A career is more than a single job, a single position, or a single role. It is a developmental process of progression. The individual and the organization share duties and responsibilities; both are equal partners in the game.

The last decades saw a significant change in the nature and notion of the psychological contract (e.g. Baruch & Bozionelos, 2011; Rousseau et al., 2018), as these contracts are based on the interactive process of an exchange relationship. Robinson and Morrison (1995) studied the impact of such changes to discover the role of trust in mediating the adverse impact of breaking former psychological contracts. In the new deal, it is difficult to create trust in the traditional sense.

Employees do not always welcome such a transformation. It means no more lifetime employment (or a promise of such), no more mutual loyalty. The typical traditional deal was: employees offer loyalty, conformity, commitment; employers offer security of employment, career prospects, training and development, and care when in difficulty. The archetype was a full-time career with a single employer, with both sides basing the relationship on 'trust'. To a certain extent, employees can easily understand and accept this type of relationship.

Under the new deal, employees offer long hours, assume added responsibility, provide broader skills, and tolerate change and ambiguity, whereas employers offer high pay, reward for performance, and above all the fact of having a job (Herriot & Pemberton, 1995). There is no single archetype model that fits all – diversity and flexibility are the new rules. When there is readiness for changes and adjusted expectations there will not be a process of disillusionment and a feeling of betrayal on the part of employees. This leads to a dynamic labour market with various career moves. DeFillippi and Arthur (1994) were among the first to use the term 'boundaryless career', an idea that developed alongside the concept of the boundaryless organization (see Box 1.4).

Box 1.4: The Boundaryless Organization (Ashkenas et al., 1995)

1. The Boundaryless Organization presents a framework for better understanding the way in which organizations undergo both structural and psychological transitions. Even traditional bureaucracies try to adjust to a rapidly changing business environment. Flexibility is a key to gaining competitive advantage, including adaptation to the change, leading change, being both responsive and proactive. Ashkenas et al. suggest that breaking down barriers is one of the ways in which organizations can employ personnel to survive and flourish.
2. There are different types of barriers to be overcome: vertical, horizontal, external, and geographical. Breaking down vertical barriers is crucial since hierarchical bureaucracies tend to restrict the flow of information, are reluctant to respond to changing environments, and are inflexible in both their thinking and their actions. The question, of course, is how to break down these barriers and maintain established procedures, stability, keep organizational memory and sustain strong organizational identity.
3. Breaking down horizontal barriers means eliminating the traditional barriers between the conventional functions and operations or organizations.
4. Breaking down the barriers between the organization and the environment or other organizations is complex, but working with joint ventures, suppliers, customers, government agencies, and so on blurs the boundaries. Factors like mergers and acquisitions, restructuring, delayering are intended to lead to better agility, though do not always deliver.
5. Breaking down geographical boundaries is reflected at both the national level (in terms of alternative work arrangements, within-country migration, and 'virtual organizations') and the international level (in terms of globalization). Global events, in particular the COVID-19 pandemic, have forced many organizations to rethink their institutional logics and consider different ways of operation to survive.
6. From our point of view, the boundaryless organization is the site of the boundaryless career. The four 'deviations' – vertical, horizontal, external, geographical – from the traditional type of organization have a direct impact on individuals and, in particular, on organizational career systems.

The blurring of boundaries will be dealt with further in Chapters 4 and 5.

Terms and metaphors other than 'boundaryless career' have been used. Examples include Arthur, Claman and DeFillippi (1995) suggested the phrase 'intelligent careers' (see later in Chapter 2). Mainiero and Sullivan's (2006) kaleidoscope career used different wording, but all these terms reflect a similar trend. There has been a change from what we knew in the past. The concept of a rigid ladder which people move up, as long as they do the right thing, was the basic building-block of the management of people. (Of course, certain moves have always depended on one's social background: e.g. slaves had very limited opportunities for promotion; aristocrats frequently filled top managerial positions.) These days have passed. It will take less than a generation for people to get used to the 'new deal' (Herriot & Pemberton, 1995) and the new psychological contracts. At the turn of the last century and the first decades of the 21st century, the industrial world found itself in the middle of a transition process, and the question is how organizations should handle the transformation to cause as little harm as possible. Industrial relations systems have changed too, reducing the power and relevance of unions in many sectors. Collective bargaining has been replaced by individual contracts, following the I-deals concept (Rousseau, 2015 – for further discussion see Chapter 7). Global events such as the 2008 financial crisis and the 2020 COVID-19 pandemic have added to the equation. How can such new contracts be agreed upon and be 'signed'?

Table 1.1   Traditional versus transformed deals

Aspect	Traditional deal	Transformed deal
Environment characteristic	Stability	Dynamism
Career choice made	Once, at early career age	Series, at different age stages
Main career responsibility lies with	Organization	Individual
Career horizon (workplace)	Single organization	Several organizations
Career horizon (time)	Long	Short
Employer expects/Employee gives	Loyalty and commitment	Long time working hours
Employer gives/Employee expects	Job security	Investment in employability
Means to sustain stable employment	Secure a job in large corporation	Invest in employability
Progress criteria	Advance according to tenure	Advances according to results and knowledge
Success means	Winning the tournament i.e. progress up the hierarchy ladder	Inner feeling of achievement
Training	Formal programs, generalist	On-the-job, company specific, sometimes ad-hoc
Employment relations	Focus on legal contract; collective bargaining for unionized environment	Focus on psychological contract; move to I-deals

There are exceptions to and deviations from Table 1.1. It appears that scholars arguing for the existence and the changed meaning of the psychological contract have ignored certain facts. While many, in particular managers, work longer hours, the overall tendency in Europe is to shorten the legal weekly working hours. Investment in employability has always been present, but new types of training mean *less* employability, for example if they are firm-specific only. Organizations' claims to promote employability via the new deal are perhaps exaggerated (Baruch, 2001a). For the individual, of course, having employability is very positive. Full-time employment in one organization was never the rule for many, but it usually represented the desired option. Nevertheless, there are certain occupations and organizations where this was and is still the norm. Money (income) was and continues to be a definite criterion for career success evaluation, as are other extrinsic outcomes such as advancing up the ladder. Of course, fewer options were available when organizations became flatter. At the same time, the inner feelings of achievement and satisfaction have always been important, and they are even more so now. All in all, the new deal does not represent a full revolution, but rather a widespread evolution.

Changing the rules of the game

The massive restructuring of the economy has had a fundamental effect upon peoples' careers. There is not merely a new psychological contract, there is also a shift from a skill-based to a knowledge-based labour market. The portfolio of competencies needed for success continues to evolve, and includes 'career competencies', in particular employability, as the factor needed to reach career success (Akkermans & Tims, 2017).

The fact that these major changes have occurred within one generation has left us with insufficient time to adapt easily to all the changes involved (De Vos & Van der Heijden, 2015). In terms of the economy, the hyper-turbulent environment as reflected in the labour market does not allow the conventional process of supply and demand to dictate the rules of the game for the economy. Sometimes the behaviour of the market (and also career opportunities as reflected in the labour market) resembles chaos theory (Bailyn, 1993; Glieck, 1988; Pryor & Bright, 2011) rather than traditional processes. Reaching a 'steady state' in terms of balance, stress, and performance, for example, may require more time than modern conditions allow.

The impact of the COVID-19 pandemic has been influential, as this global crisis has created a career shock for many (Akkermans et al., 2020). For the majority it was negative, with many unable to work at all, a significant number of people having to rely on governments schemes to survive, and others working under inappropriate conditions as not all homes are suitable for working from home (in particular for parents of school-age children).

The pace and the magnitude of change are accelerating continually, and have a profound global impact in many areas of change. It is not just that there are specific changes in the areas of technology, the economy, politics, demography, society and psychology, the family, and knowledge, but the fact that all of these changes happened simultaneously. There is not space here to look at developments in each of these areas, so we shall consider just some of them.

We look first at demographic change. After the baby boom generation that followed the Second World War, a decline in the birth rate characterized the industrial world. At the same time, developing countries enjoyed the benefits of improved medical treatment, lower death rates, and a substantial increase in their population. One result of these changes is that the most sought-after jobs tend to be mainly in the industrialized societies, notably the USA, Europe, and Japan. China has developed too under specific conditions that makes career management highly demanding for individuals, employers, and authorities (Yao et al., 2020). Another factor is that more and more people live longer in retirement age, and deserve to enjoy this stage of life. A person's career does not need to end at formal retirement. Many work after retirement, sometimes in part-time jobs, while many choose to engage in voluntary work in the community (such as for charitable bodies). This is a career change from which organizations can benefit, for example by using former employees, now retired, when extra personnel are needed.

However, the more fundamental demographic change is within the working population, and is concerned with massive moves across sectors. If we use three categories – primary (agriculture, mining, utilities), secondary (manufacturing and construction), and tertiary (services, business and professionals) – we can analyse historical trends and their relevance for the creation of new career opportunities alongside a decline in traditional ones. In the past, the primary sector accounted for some 80–90 per cent of the population, but since the Industrial Revolution this sector has declined sharply, to less than 4 per cent of the population. At the same time the secondary sector has grown rapidly, up to the middle of the 20th century. Since then the tertiary sector has flourished, causing the manufacturing sector to decline to about one-fifth of the workforce by 2020. These shifts in labour market constituencies mean that there are far more professions and career options available than in the past. Moreover, such change processes are still taking place, and it is likely that in future people will have to be prepared to change career and adapt to new circumstances as a norm. A second career was the exception even in the 1970s. A succession of careers had become the new norm by the beginning of the 21st century.

Changes in the occupational sector from a historical perspective

---

Box 1.5: Can we learn from history?

'The only thing we learn from history is that we don't learn from history.'

Woody Allen

Western Europe's population almost doubled in the second half of the 18th century, mostly as a result of the use of new food crops (such as the potato) and a decline in epidemic diseases. A population growth of this magnitude compelled change: peasants and craftsmen by that time had too many descendants for the former system of inheritance to work, which had once ensured continuity of income. People had to seek new forms of labour to survive. Similarly, the families of businessmen and landlords had to innovate to provide for their families, more of whom were now surviving. These demographic pressures, coupled with the fact that both industry and trade were developing rapidly, and on a global scale, resulted in the availability of human resources for the Industrial Revolution. The other two elements that enabled the Industrial Revolution to take place were technological developments and an increase in the available capital (partly due to access to global markets as a result of colonialism). The same triad – people, technology, and capital – is operating in the present revolution.

Table 1.2 indicates the contribution of these factors in the major eras of the history of mankind.

Table 1.2   The roles of people, technology, and capital over time

Historical era	Human added value	Technology	Dominant Capital
Hunter-gatherer	Instinct	Primitive	Fruits, vegetables, wild animals
Agriculture	Tradition	Simple	Land
Industry	Process	Heavy	Finance
IT revolution	Knowledge	High-Tech	Creativity and innovation
Industry 4	Ingenuity	Artificial intelligence	Critical thinking

We now look at an example from a totally different careers era: the project-based industry.

In some sectors, careers development is not associated with an organization, but involves floating from project to project. The construction industry is mostly project based. Within the industry people move from project to project, either within their own firm or across projects. The role of networking is highly instrumental for gaining and maintaining employability and a prosperous career within such sectors. It is the same in the film industry, and more sectors may move to this type of employment relationship and career progress as time goes on.

Different career patterns have been created throughout history. Probably the first profound change was from the prehistoric hunter-gatherer to an almost fully agriculture-based society (Giddens, 1997). It should be remembered that even in ancient Rome and early China, less than 10 per cent of the people lived in urban areas. This status was stable for generations, until the growth of mostly manufacturing societies in the industrial world following the Industrial Revolution in the 18th and 19th centuries, and in turn the move to mostly services-based economies in the 20th century. Note that the pace of change has accelerated even more in the 21st century. Table 1.3 presents rough percentage of segments of the workforce population across time. One possibly emerging new status for the 21st century is those permanently unemployed: people who have been made redundant because their skills are no longer needed, who will be able to claim universal basic income (UBI) to tide them over whilst they have no permanent job income. Such ideas are not without shortcomings and challenges (Hoynes & Rothstein, 2019), but gaining momentum as a possible type of future 'career' or even a new social class.

The future will see more knowledge-related work and knowledge-based careers. Some acquisition knowledge and knowledge maintenance is technology led, some via system-embedded knowledge, but much is knowledge that resides within people. Data and information are highly valued, not for their intrinsic worth but via human capital which enables their effective use. Knowledge management is being constantly revolutionized through innovation by inspired and inventive human beings using state of the art technologies. The knowledge

Table 1.3 Occupational groupings across time

	Hunter-gatherer	Agriculture	Public-governance	Production	Service	Unemployed (job)	Unemployed career
Pre-history	100	0	0	0	0		
Early age		90	10		0		
Industrial revolution		10	20	50	10	vary	
The late 20th Century		2–3	20	20–	50–	10	
The 21st Century		2–3	20*	15	40+	10	?

*This percentage varies considerably, even within the OECD countries it can be between some 10% to 35%.

industry creates innovative types of careers and leads to greater creativity (Dubina et al., 2012). Knowledge can be captured through Internet connections, and shared through smart phones, video conferences and e-mails. Networking has become more crucial than ever for personal progress. Within traditional industries too, the growing need for knowledge management requires the establishment of specialist positions. IT support as a specific organizational unit has been incorporated in the organizational structure of most enterprises. These new occupations have emerged and gained recognition and remuneration while other vocations have been declining, some becoming obsolete. At the same time, being technology savvy has become a crucial competence for success in most occupations.

Different contemporary career competencies are required. The concept of 'intelligent careers', for example, introduced in the mid-1990s, focuses on the three types of knowledge: know-how, know-why, and know-whom (Arthur et al., 1995, 1999, 2016; Jones & DeFillippi, 1996) (see Chapter 2 for elaboration). There exist a long timeframe and extreme conceptual differences between the sociological contract of J.-J. Rousseau (1792) and the new psychological contracts of D. Rousseau (1995), presented earlier in this chapter. J.-J. Rousseau, a philosopher from the 18th century, coined the term 'social contract' to reconcile what rights permit us to do and what our interest prescribes. His famous phrase, 'Man is born free, and everywhere he is in chains', relates to the rule of laws, regulations, and customs. For the purpose of this book, these can be reflected in individuals, organizational, and national realities. Individuals may benefit or suffer from their socio-economic status, their gender, age, education, and so on which may ultimately influence their career. Within an organizational context these would be the strategy, policy, and practices that will generate what Rousseau called 'conventions', which serve as the basis of all legitimate authority. Organizational policies and practices may improve the level of inclusiveness, for example. At the wider level, each participant in society gives trust to that society and its consensus, and in return receives the right and obligation to participate in, and contribute to, that general consensus or general will by which each is governed.

Career systems and their multi constituencies: Who brings what, who does what

The main four constituencies of careers are the individual (and his or her family), the organization, society, and public bodies (which range from local bodies and professional associations to national governments and international organizations such as the United Nations).

Figure 1.2 depicts the different elements that each participant brings into the system and participants' responsibilities (with Figure 1.2a examining who *brings in* what, and Figure 1.2b looking at who *does* what).

The following section will discuss both figures and the system they represent in career management. Each segment of the figure will be accompanied by a Box in which a case example will illustrate the way the system works. The example focuses on the issue of women in the workplace and in management, and the role of the various constituencies.

Public bodies

The government is responsible for employment legislation (e.g. equal employment opportunities (EEO); applicability of collective bargaining), and is also involved with behavioural norms (mostly through the education system). An example is the reduction in working hours for

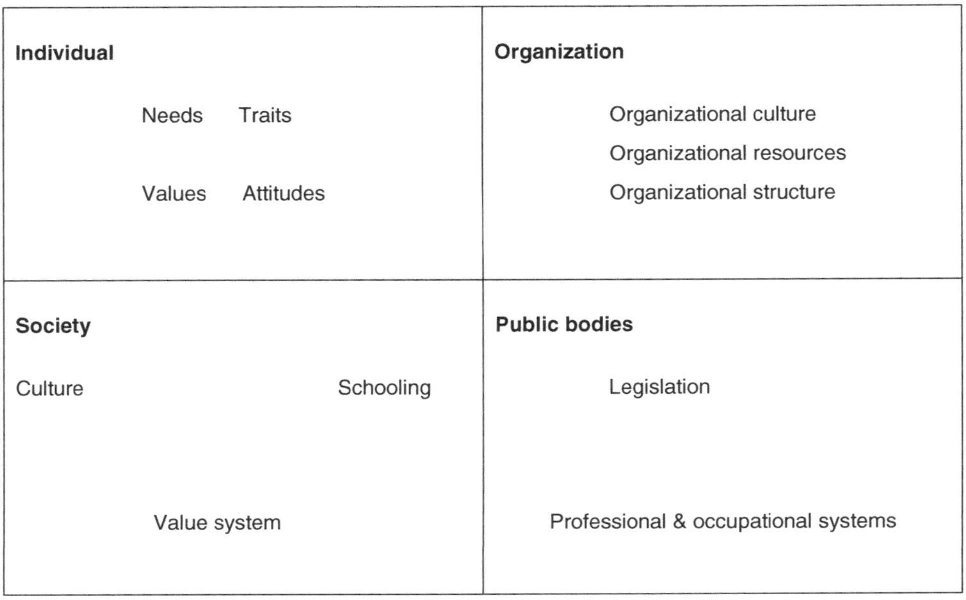

Individual	Organization
Needs Traits	Organizational culture
	Organizational resources
Values Attitudes	Organizational structure
Society	**Public bodies**
Culture Schooling	Legislation
Value system	Professional & occupational systems

Figure 1.2a   Who *brings in* what

Individual	Organization
perform plan (set target) in search of employability learn negotiate feedback	inspire support offer control train negotiate
Society	**Public bodies**
family support unions educate disciplinary associations	legal jurisdiction, courts public support mechanisms (e.g. career & job centre)

Figure 1.2b   Who *does* what

employees. In Europe, the average working hours per week have declined sharply in the last few decades. In the early years of the 19th century, people worked 12 hours a day (including lunch break), six days a week (some 60 working hours a week). By the end of the 20th century, the average was below 40 hours per week in most of Western Europe. Currently, the average in Europe is 40 hours, with Denmark, Norway, and Sweden having a 30-hour week, and 32-hours per week in the Netherlands (see Figure 1.3 for 2016 data). Globally, working hours decline, but there is variety, even within the OECD: In Turkey, Mexico and Colombia the level is still above 45 hours per week. For individuals, reducing working hours per week improves work–life balance, and for nations it can be a factor to keep unemployment low.

Another aspect of contemporary life, including working life, is the trend towards the 'litigious society'. This global trend follows the American lead in increasing the involvement of the legal system in employment (as well as in other facets of life), moving the boundaries of what conventional thinking regarded as a management prerogative. Employers are increasingly seen as liable for any ill-treatment their employees might suffer (or perceived to suffer) during their work. Many relate to discrimination, harassment, and occupational health (especially stress related) and all are concerned with career management and development. People can be discriminated against (e.g. by not being selected to a job, by being paid less for similar work, or by being laid off) simply for their demographic background. The implications can be significant, mentally and financially. Job termination can cause low self-esteem as well as

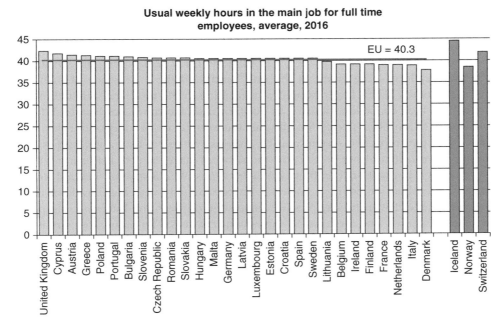

Figure 1.3   Weekly working hours (Eurostat, 2018)

persistent economic damage due to the loss of earning capacity. If an employee can prove that they were discriminated against due to gender, ethnicity, disability, and so on, then they will be entitled to compensation. This impact can last for a prolonged period (Kennedy, 2019). If the issue affects a group of employees, the financial implications can be severe for the employer – see Box 1.6. More on the issue of inclusion, discrimination and equality will be discussed in Chapter 9.

Box 1.6: On work discrimination

In 2000, a San Francisco court ruled that United Airlines, a leading American airline, was guilty of sexual discrimination against some 16,000 stewardesses, reversing an earlier judgment. United Airlines stipulated that staff members must maintain an 'attractive' weight to keep their job. There was a difference between men and women, the assumption being that men were of a heavy build whereas women had medium body frames. This decision cost the company hundreds of millions of dollars (see Warhurst & Nickson, 2020).

Governments have a major interest in the maintenance of a stable progressive society in a flourishing economy. The new model economy does not provide enough full-time jobs. The last occasion on which there was such a shift in the pattern of employment was the massive move from agriculture to industry at the time of the Industrial Revolution. The salvation in that case was the creation of big cities on the one hand, and the emergence of manufacturing industry on the other. When fewer people were needed in the food and agricultural industry, they moved into the production industry. In our time a similar move has occurred: fewer people are needed to produce goods for all, and the surplus of producers transfer to service industries. Now, the impact of system and IT, coupled with ever-increasing improvements in the quantity and quality of both production and services, have created a situation where fewer people are needed in traditional employment. New types of 'industry' are needed to make use of the talent unleashed, otherwise a society with permanently very high levels of unemployment will be created. Diversity may provide some solution, with the Internet a big player, and e-business, e-commerce, and e-education the new buzzwords. The leisure industry is growing, as more people work fewer hours. But many have no work, and the available statistics are misleading. The official unemployment level is around 10 per cent in most European countries, and higher in Japan and the other Tiger Economies of Asia. Actual figures, especially for young people, are higher. Many have opted to work in the black economy, a development of great concern to society.

Those predominantly affected by changing employment patterns fall into two age groups. The first is those aged 50–55 and older who have been made redundant, with no realistic prospects for alternative employment. The second is young people with inadequate education and no qualifications that will help them gain employment. For the young people, governments have been establishing new initiatives. In the UK there is the New Deal programme, under which the government pays employers a subsidy for a certain period at the start of the young person's employment. Germany has developed a programme to encourage young unemployed people to join business start-up projects. For the older age group, there are opportunities in non-traditional areas (e.g. volunteering). However, to make such work a viable alternative, governments should provide a proper budget for such initiatives that would yield further career options. Other people can opt for part-time or multi-part-time employment arrangements.

Society

The role of society is wider than that of government, and is concerned with setting and establishing the values and attitudes that provide norms for behaviour (and inhibit deviations from the norm). Values towards work can be associated with education, as indicated earlier, and at home, in the community, or in religious institutions. Values such as power distance or collectivism versus individualism (Hofstede, 1980, 2011; Triandis, 1995) have an impact on work attitudes and career perspectives.

A variety of clusters of work attitudes have been identified within different geographical regions, and the implication of these are relevant to career systems (Ronen & Shenkar, 2013).

For example, in an individualistic and a high-achievement-oriented society we should expect an environment of career competition (see Chapter 3), while in collectivistic-oriented societies slow career progress, coupled with the ability to reach consensus, may be the preferred choice.

Another realm with an impact on values is that of religion. Max Weber's article, 'The Protestant Ethic and the Spirit of Capitalism' (1905) cited the Protestant work ethics as an example of how religion can encourage people to invest effort in work (Levitt & Dunber, 2014). In contrast, a fatalistic approach to life would not encourage great investment in work and career, and is associated with an external locus of control (Rotter, 1966).

Box 1.7: Women in management

In women's careers, the role of society is strongly associated with values attached to and attitudes towards working women. These values, attitudes, and norms are affected by the way working women are portrayed in the media – in newspapers, films, and advertisements. The education system also may offer mechanisms for combating discrimination, and in this context one may note the professionalization of management via the Master of Business Administration (MBA) degree and the effect this has had on helping to reduce discrimination.

Also the family, as the part of society which is closest to the individual, has a crucial role in enabling and encouraging women to work. For example, even if the government provides the option for fathers to take paternity leave, it is up to the family to decide whether he will or will not take this option.

Note: See Chapter 9 for a full discussion of diversity and equality in the workplace.

The individual

The individual's characteristics and values strongly determine a person's career choice and means of progress and the way that person manages their career. Most people work in organizations, while others prefer to start their own business or be self-employed. Career systems in organizations require people to be able to manage their careers, and in most cases encourage them to help others (subordinates, and sometimes colleagues too) to manage theirs. People negotiate career options, and actively progress towards their career goals. Individuals bring into the career world their inner needs and values. Maslow's hierarchy of needs can still provide a strong, though somewhat simplistic, explanation for people's career choices. A career can fulfil needs for recognition, self-esteem, and self-actualization (Maslow, 1943). Chapters 2 and 3 will elaborate on the individual perspective.

Values

> Value in the sense of *good* is inherently connected with that which promotes, furthers, assists, a course of activity, and ... value in the sense of *right* is inherently connected with that which is needed, required, in the maintenance of a course of activity.' (Dewey, 1939, p. 57)

Values, whether at the individual, organizational, or national level, form the basis for attitudes and behaviours (Rokeach, 1973). His empirical work shows that values may also be measured. This adds a practical dimension to the management of careers: the ability to fit systems to match not only the inner needs, but also the values of employees. Values form the foundation stone for company philosophy and hence must be useful in developing a strategy for career systems.

A pause for reflection

What would you consider your main values, and how are they reflected in your career aspiration?

How has your local culture influenced your values (e.g. in what way would your values be different if you had been raised in another place. For example, if you are from New York, what if you had been born in Utah, or in another US state? Or what differences are possible between people from Paris and Marseille? From Shanghai and Guangzhou?

Many of the values and perceptions of the career world are learned through observation, and the first impact is largely due to experience within the family. Individual family background affects children's values, attitudes, and behaviours, and as a result will influence the future career choices of children (Stewart & Barling, 1996).

Traits

Many traits, most obviously the physical ones, are due to inheritance. Our genes determine our bodily dimensions and appearance, which are important for career choice and success at work. More important (for most jobs), however, are our intellectual capacities, and again, these are determined by our genes as well as by environmental influences and educational inputs. Studies of leadership have not been conclusive about the impact of traits on leadership (Lord et al., 1986; Zaccaro et al., 2018), but they are certainly associated with the career choice, the career aims, and the career strategy that people follow. However, if we look beyond demographic and inheritance traits, we can see that personality traits have much to do with career choice and career success. Judge et al. (1995, 1999, 2015) have noted the role of personality factors (in particular the Big Five) on career success (see Chapter 2 for an elaboration of the Big Five personality traits).

Attitudes

Fishbein and Ajzen (1975) provided a model that is based on the general behavioural approach, which ascertains that values, norms, and beliefs are antecedents to attitudes that subsequently lead to intentions, inclinations, and tendencies, which in turn generate actions. In addition, attitudes (as well as values and norms and beliefs) are affected by individual personality (and demography) and by culture and environment. Fishbein and Ajzen's theory of planned action can serve to explain the 'why' of career choices (see Figure 1.4).

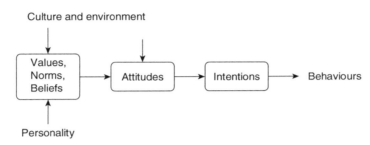

Figure 1.4   Fishbein–Ajzen model of planned action (1975)

People's attitudes towards different career patterns can be affected by the general culture of their society, the media to which they are exposed, the education system they experienced, and of course, the career advice and direction provided to them. For students, this may be provided by university career advisors, for employees, by the organization for which they work, and for the unemployed, by governmental and other authorities.

Box 1.8: Women's attitudes

The careers of many women differ from those of men. For example, career breaks after the birth of a child are not uncommon, and do not necessarily indicate a lower level of commitment on the part of women. The great importance attached to having a career means that a growing number of women in Western societies choose now to delay the arrival of children as long as possible, or not to have children at all. Nevertheless, modern developments and lifestyles enable women to shorten significantly the length of their career breaks, with minimal interruption to their careers.

Another trend is that on reaching the higher ranks of organizations, some people leave to start their own businesses. This tendency to 'opt out' of the traditional career structures, in particular for women, was described using the kaleidoscope metaphor by Mainiero and Sullivan (2006), as will be discussed in Chapter 9.

Kolb's framework of individual experiential learning (Kolb, 1984) is applicable to career management. His stages of experience, reflection, conceptualization, and experimental loop can be translated to the steps of career development. The later addition of a retention stage (which follows the conceptualization phase) by Popper and Lipshitz (2000) makes sense in this perspective.

Box 1.9: Inclusion or exclusion?

Individual values towards women's equality have a mostly implicit rather than explicit impact, in a litigious society where people are obliged to behave in a politically correct manner. Nevertheless, different people and different cultures pose a wide range of approaches to women's work. At one extreme is the total exclusion of women from the workforce (e.g. no female expatriate can work as a manager in Saudi Arabia); at the opposite extreme we find full equality, as in Scandinavia. The attitudes towards women in managerial positions influences the spectrum for women's career choices, the types of organizations and professions they try to enter, and their career aspirations.

Organization

Organizations are where careers occur and develop. Moreover, organizations *are* career systems. Organizations plan careers and manage them. In this sense organizations have multiple roles in the world of careers. In view of the organizational focus of this book it should be emphasized that an organization may be an entity, but its representation to the employee in relation to career issues can be done via several layers.

A basic distinction should be made between the HR function and line management. Even within these different providers of career management there are subgroups. In line management there is always the individual's direct manager, but also higher-level managers, mentors, and so on, up to the Chief Executive Officer/Managing Director/President. Within the HR function there may be a central or headquarters HR department as well as the HR function of the specific unit (either a departmental, a plant, a subsidiary, or a divisional HR unit).

Technology impact

Breakthroughs in mechanical technology and the energy generation methods that followed preceded the Industrial Revolution. Another technological breakthrough has had a significant impact on the creation of our information age: the IT revolution.

Technological innovation can end in de-skilling for many, as happened in the car industry at the beginning of the 20th century. The trend towards efficiency at the time meant a division of labour. This concept originated with the thinking of Adam Smith (1776, 1982) and was further developed with the 'discovery' of *scientific management* (Taylor, 1911). Scientific management and Fordism stripped employees of their knowledge and de-skilled work in the conveyer-belt industries. A further development in this direction came when robots started to replace employees in mundane areas of work. Simultaneously the service sector grew enormously. The 'white-collar' knowledge jobs had overtaken 'blue-collar' jobs long ago.

The developments with artificial intelligence (AI) accelerated this trend and may release a significant number of employees from the labour market, which will cause substantial concerns for current employees (Brougham & Haar, 2018). This could possibly create a new wave of people that will be destined to continuous unemployment, and will require the use of support such as UBI – see Box 1.10 (Hoynes & Rothstein, 2019).

Box 1.10: Universal basic income (UBI)

The idea of UBI (or simply basic income) – also referred to as 'citizen's basic income' or 'basic income guarantee' among others – emerged from the idea (and ideology) that in the future it may be appropriate to guarantee a basic income that would enable any person to live comfortably without working.

So far, it is a theoretical or conceptual idea, suggesting that all members of society will benefit from a kind of social insurance.

Contemporary ideas move further because many countries are wealthy enough to afford such a scheme. A major contributing factor that changed the original idea is that due to technological progress, it may well be that significant proportions of a population will not need to work. The reason is similar to the case when the improvements in agriculture efficiency enable the world to rely on just about 2% of the population to grow enough food for all, compared with some 85% centuries ago. AI, robotics, and automation may release much of the current workforce used for manufacturing and services. Some scenarios suggest that all those people will have no alternative employment.

The UBI means that governments will set and finance public programmes for a periodic payment delivered to all citizens of a given population without a means test or work requirement. Work would not be essential to be a worthy citizen.

Discuss:

1. What do you think about the idea of UBI – its ideology and practicality?
2. Would it be feasible to implement this now in your country?
3. May be feasible in the future?
4. How would you feel about living without working?

Box 1.11: Call-centres, the sweatshops of the modern age

Many call centres operate along the lines of the plant conveyor belt. Employees have pre-scribed messages that they are expected to read from their computer screens. Each answer will lead to the following question the computer tells them to ask, using prescribed wording. There is no room for variation or initiative, and the work is usually conducted under tightly con-trolled conditions, with continuous monitoring, leading to high level of stress.

Yet with the right approach and creation of family-like association between employers, employees, and customers, working at call centres can be a favourable option. Levitt and Dunber (2014, p. 128–130) manifest this for the case of Zappos, where employees gain more power and can consider their work as fun too.

Technology can affect or enable the creation of a different culture. This can be due to the opportunities opened up by new technology. Just as the technology of shipbuilding enabled European countries to become explorers and colonists, new frontiers have been opened in the cyberspace. Technology can influence individual characteristics too: Tapscott (1998) suggested that young people have the following qualities: curiosity, self-reliance, contrariness, smartness, focus, ability to adapt, high self-esteem, and possessed of a global orientation. They are also at ease with digital tools. Cultures characterized by openness, immediacy, and an emphasis on results suit them well. They use e-mail for communication (some 20 years later, e-communication took over for all, but mostly younger generation, with smartphones enabling smart applications to replace most other communication methods). They prefer flat organizations, and would not hesitate to become entrepreneurs. This observation became the base for generational studies, with Generation X (born in 1960–79), Generation Y, also known as Millennials (born 1980–95), and Generation Z (born 1995+) are significantly different from the baby boomer generation on several accounts, in particular career related (Culpin et al., 2015). Whatever the differences across generations, employers need to harness these qualities otherwise they will lose or mis-manage this pool of talent. The issue of generational variations will be explored in greater depth in Chapter 4.

The so-called Generations X, Y, and Z are believed to be obsessed with the electronic media. For them, e-business poses a positive challenge, not only as customers or to fill their leisure time, but also as an employment domain. On the labour market front, the tech industry generates a variety of new jobs and roles. Some are totally new and innovative, like forecasting trends – either in business, like financial markets, or in nature, like predicting natural disasters. Others represent a reduction in the type of skills and abilities required: alongside those who initi-ate new sales points online, there is the return of what might be termed 'milk-round drivers' – after all, even if goods are sold virtually, someone needs to pack and deliver them to the customer's home or office. The competencies of others are upgraded too. Online fraud has developed considerably since those early days, and cyber crime became a new threat to society – and at the same time provides new career opportunities – to criminals, to police, and to IT firms specializing in security.

As a result, there are new challenges: what alternatives are there for people in the middle levels? Technology can help individuals to move up, to use their other higher skills, but more frequently to get down to the ordinary, simple and not so challenging jobs, or, as suggested above, to become a generation when having no job is a regular, accepted 'career path'.

Box 1.12: Mind exercise: Generational differences

Consider your current career, or your anticipated future career. How different it is from the career your parents have had? From the careers of your grandparents?

Looking into the future – if you have children, what do you think their career might look like?

How much of those differences is due to technology, and how much is due to other factors?

Career ecosystems

The phenomenon of careers and their management can be depicted as part of a wide ecosystem which operates across internal and external labour markets. Ecosystem is a scientific concept, originally developed as part of the ecology discipline. Within business and management settings, the ecosystem concept is concerned with the management (self and organizational) of people, knowledge, and talent as fit for overall efficiency and improvement. The application of ecosystem theory to careers was suggested by Baruch (2015) and extended later (e.g. Baruch & Rousseau, 2019). An ecosystem is 'a system that contains a large number of loosely coupled (interconnected) actors who depend on each other to ensure the overall effectiveness of the system' (Iansiti & Levien, 2004, p. 5). The system has multiple actors, each with their own agenda. Individuals move in various directions, and there is a significant 'flow of talent' across organizations, sectors, and nations. An example is how one organization, a leader in its field, generates a pool of future leaders for the wider sector: Baxter, the pharmaceutical firm, was known to develop talent and let many of their executives move and lead other constituencies, including rival firms in this sector (Higgins, 2005).

The career ecosystem operates in a constellation that is not merely economical but also part of a social political phenomenon in a global environment (Gunz et al., 2011). Eco-system mechanisms of adjustment, expansion and decline, and flow of talent, to name a few processes, are at constant evolution. Amongst the characteristics of the labour markets as eco-system are:

- a constant flow of human capital, prompted and influenced by push/pull factors
- spiral learning processes, required for continuous adjustments and adaptation to new situations

- ongoing change processes influencing the directions and magnitude of human capital flow
- labour markets being global, and influenced by factors at many levels.

The main actors are:

- individuals (competence, needs, values and attitudes)
- organizations (nature of career system – traditional or dynamic, stage of globalization, sector and product type, knowledge management)
- nations/societies (economy, culture, politics, legal).

Successful Career Systems

Successful career systems depend on the process that takes place between the individual and the organization. Later in this book we will consider what we mean by individual career success, and the role of the organization in this. At this point it is sufficient to indicate that the essence of what a career is has changed, and with it the meaning of career success (Spurk et al., 2019). The meaning of career success differs, of course, according to various dimensions:

- internal – how a person sees the development of their own career in terms of inner values, goals, aspirations
- external – how career success is perceived by the external environment, such as in terms of status, hierarchy, income and power
- organizational – in terms of organizational power and influence; these were once measured by position on the career ladder, and now in different, more subtle ways
- society – the labour market, professional development, globalization.

From the organizational viewpoint, much of the substance of career management is reflected in the career practices for planning and management of careers. The importance and prominence of organizational career practices as part of HRM has been recognized by many scholars, as will be discussed and elaborated on in Chapter 6. To better understand organizational context, let us look at Figure 1.5.

Vertical integration is the basis of integrating HRM into the strategic management of the organization, rather than holding the minor supportive role of an administrative function. At its 'highest' level it comprises strategic alignment (Holbeche, 2009; Stewart & Brown, 2019). Vertical integration starts with an organization's business strategy (or its general strategy, for non-business organizations). Out of this strategy are derived the requirements of resources, and in particular of human resources – human capital. To achieve this strategy the HR function has to apply career practices, the vehicle through which the actual, practical management of people is conducted. These, in turn, should target individual needs, values, and behaviours.

Horizontal coherence refers to a more specific, professional aspect of HRM, the integration within the organization of all HRM practices, which starts with acquiring the right people, and continues up to the time of their departure. Recruitment and selection are only the first stages

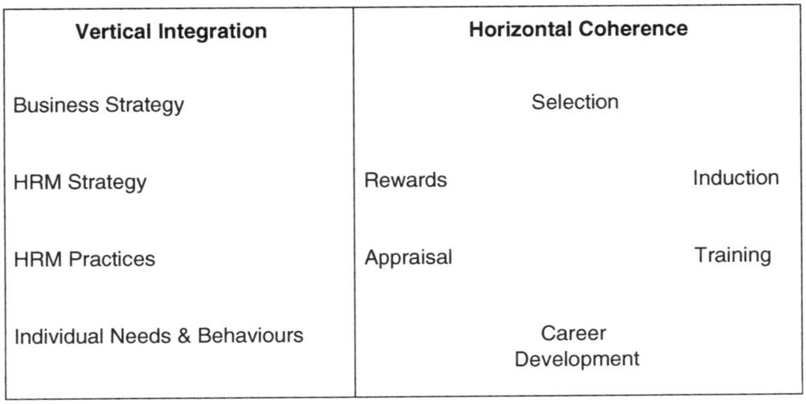

Vertical Integration	Horizontal Coherence	
	Selection	
Business Strategy		
HRM Strategy	Rewards	Induction
HRM Practices	Appraisal	Training
Individual Needs & Behaviours	Career Development	

Figure 1.5 Vertical integration versus horizontal coherence

in the management of people. Once the people are selected, the process to make them effective organizational members begins. For the HRM function this requires putting into operation a comprehensive array of career practices to plan and manage the retention of the members of an organization. Moreover, as will be presented in Chapter 6, there is a need to integrate the practices to achieve a harmony of operations, which I term 'horizontal coherence'. The art of career management requires the combining of vertical integration and horizontal coherence.

Career management as part of the HR matrix

The HR matrix reflects two aspects of HRM: the practical aspect, which is manifested through the operational element of HRM practices, and the level of strategic alignment, which is expected to form the base for strategic human resource management (SHRM) (Fombrun et al., 1984; Hendry, 1995; Kaufman, 2015). Highly strategic management of human resources is important for the overall competitive advantage of an organization. Aligning HRM and organizational strategy is important to the attainment of organizational goals, ultimately organizational performance, as suggested by several meta analyses (Combs et al., 2006; Jiang et al., 2012; Tzabbar, 2017). Yet, the HRM function can utilize practices very professionally, or not at all professionally. At the same time, the level of strategic alignment with other business or operational units of the organization may be low, even abandoned altogether, or consequential. The quality of the HRM function can be evaluated in terms of the strength of its operational practices (Baruch, 1997).

In the low-low quadrant of the HR matrix (Figure 1.6) there are organizations with poor HRM practices, and those which lack strategic planning and management. In the high-low quadrant there are organizations which manage to apply best practices (and later in the book we will deal with the option of outsourcing some or all of these practices). In the low-high quadrant there are organizations that have developed strategic thinking and aligned HRM with business planning and management. These organizations achieve high strategic vision, but lack the practical ability to apply this in day-to-day activities, the building blocks of HRM. These organizations are more inclined to outsource HRM activities, and later on we will examine the common pitfalls they can encounter in doing so. The high-high quadrant is the archetype ideal model of an organization that achieves what I would call 'HR excellence'. This is the type of organization that manages to combine both strategic alignment and best practice.

Therefore, if organizations apply best-practice HRM, they have achieved only half of what they should achieve. Similarly, applying highly integrated strategic management at the top tier without backing it up with the right practices is insufficient. As represented in Figure 1.6, a schematic differentiation can be made, using a two-by-two matrix, where organizations can be classed as either high or low on either practices or strategy.

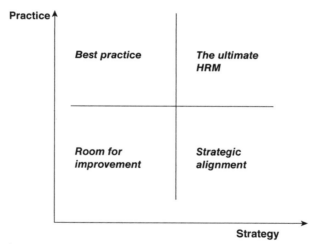

Figure 1.6   The HR matrix

Organizations should incorporate a strategic approach into the management of people. At present, organizations are subject to changes in both the external and the internal environment. These alter the conventional HR systems and call for different strategic thinking. New realities require strategic direction, such as a move away from hierarchical structures to new models of organizational architecture (e.g. flexibility, core versus peripheral employees, outsourcing business functions and the 'virtual organization'). The case of COVID-19 exemplified how an external significant event, such as a pandemic, can be addressed by organizations in many different ways. Special attention needs to be devoted to the issues of globalization and the international management of people (e.g. expatriation). Accordingly, new practices should be applied to transform the strategic vision into practical management issues, finding new ways to maintain the relationship between individuals and their organizations.

From strategic HRM to strategic career systems

Taking a further step, from general HR management to CPM, the rest of this book focuses on career issues. It takes a strategic approach to the management of careers, in line with the conceptual framework of Sonnenfeld and Peiperl (1988), which refers to career management as a strategic response and requires a fit with strategic organizational management (their model being based on the Miles and Snow (1978) framework). On the other dimension of the HR matrix, the practical level, best practice should be applied for the creation and maintenance of career practices portfolio to match the operational needs of the organization in terms of people management (Baruch, 1999). Organizational and national level benchmarking can be useful for the latter.

Apart from the organizational perspective, it is recognized that individuals play a crucial role. Thus, the following chapters will investigate and analyse the individual perspective, and the remainder of the book will be organization oriented.

A pause for reflection

What positive and negative practices applied by managers to retain people have you encountered in the past? If you have not yet acquired work experience, ask a friend or a family member to tell you what positive and negative practices applied by managers to retain people. Write down at least one example of a positive and one example of a negative approach.

Summary

This chapter defined, compared, and contrasted several career perspectives, in particular the individual versus the organizational, the balance between them, and the environment in which they take place (such as labour markets). The chapter focused on the changing nature of careers, employment relationships (and the new psychological contract) and career systems and their multi-constituencies: who brings what and who does what, with emphasis on the impact of technology. Last, we looked at the strategic role of careers within the wider HR context.

KEY TERMS

Boundaryless career

Career

Career constituencies

Career ecosystems

Employability

Intelligent careers

Internal labour market

Labour market

New deals

New psychological contracts

Procedural and distributive justice

Temporary work

The HR matrix

Values, attitudes, and behaviours

Vertical integration and horizontal coherence

DISCUSSION QUESTIONS

LESSONS AND FOOD FOR THOUGHT

1. *For the student*: What do you make of this chapter when planning your own career strategy for the future? Look at Figure 1.2b – what does 'In search of employability' mean for you?
2. *For students in part-time or full-time employment*: How have changes in the external environment – economic, social, technological, and political – influenced the management of people in your organization? How did your HRM department react to them in terms of its organizational career system? Do you think the HRM department was also proactive in anticipating changes and preparing for the future?
3. *For the student wishing to serve as a consultant*: What would be your advice to your employer about ways to satisfy the need for updated career systems? What would be the main points and issues you would discuss with HR managers when asked for advice on developing a career system for an organization? What would be the impact of geography, sector and demography on your advice?

REVIEW QUESTIONS

1. Which individual characteristics would provide an advantage for 'the new careerist'?
2. Show how the Fishbein–Ajzen model translates into actions in terms of career related behaviours for you.

3.   In what ways does new technology influence your career aspirations? Your practical job search?

CRITICAL THINKING

1.   How would you create your own online job profile in a way that will get you job offers?
2.   What would you change if you wish to have an international career rather than a career in your own country?
3.   Is 'fluidity' or perceptual motion in the realm of careers 'good' or 'bad'? In what sense?

EXERCISES

EXERCISE 1

In groups of 2–4 students: Plan your next two career moves: (a) assuming these will take place within the boundaries of your employing organization; and (b) assuming these will be external to the present employer. What are the main actions that will be needed in order to successfully fulfil these plans?

Compare and contrast your aspirations with those of your group members.

EXERCISE 2

Which would be the more beneficial first step to your career – starting in a small organization or in a large one? Debates within the group can lead to further debates between groups with different views.

Individual Careers

2

After reading this chapter you should be able to:

- Define an individual career
- Identify the meaning of career choice
- Understand how individual properties influence career choice
- Recognize a variety of career stages models
- Identify future direction and paths available to lead careers

Chapter outline

Introduction: Career – individual perspective

To understand careers and their management, it is important to start with understanding individual careers. Without realization of the antecedents, processes, and outcomes of careers for individuals we will not be able to develop an appropriate organizational system to deal with them. Another significant factor to be recognized is that major changes are taking place in the environment, the society, and in organizations. The second half of the 20th century witnessed a shift from career systems relying on bureaucracy, when careers were depicted as climbing up a clear organizational hierarchy, to a new dynamic and apparently boundaryless system. The traditional system was depicted by academics (Wilensky, 1961) and practitioners alike (Townsend, 1970) as upward oriented, bounded, and rigid, taking place within organizational structures. The career was assumed to comprise a long procession of climbing up the ladder. On a different dimension, that of diversity, the labour market and world of career was single oriented, single mindedness – career was for white males only. Women were allowed to work as secretaries, support staff, and in manufacturing, to conduct a repetitive work of low skill level. People of colour were bound to the rank-and-file jobs.

Careers aspired to started and ended in the same workplace, working for a single employer, and although performance was assumed to decline with age, in particular in production roles, experience would be assumed to compensate for such deficiencies. Thus, experience and tenure were principal factors in making promotion decisions. Most people would work till their retirement age. This type of environment and culture lends itself to strong organizational control of careers.

However, even traditional literature on careers views the individual as the main 'owner' of the career. Some take it to the extreme by suggesting that the individual is the *only* one in charge. This might be true for merely a few cases, albeit increasingly recently and notable, such as independent consultants, portfolio career people (Comfort, 1997; Gold & Fraser, 2002), typical to professions like medicine (Fahami, 2018) and music (Bartleet et al., 2019), not just consultants, self-employed, interim managers (Clutterbuck & Dearlove, 1999; Inkson et al., 2001), and so on. Nevertheless, most people work in and for organizations. As a result, the majority share the career responsibility with their employing organization.

This chapter does not deal solely with the individual, it also looks at other aspects of individuals' careers. Apart from the employing organization and the individual, other people and bodies play crucial roles in people's careers. The family, the partner, close friends, professional bodies and trade unions – all are important. Moreover, in both career choice and career development, much is subject to chance. In many cases it seems that the direction careers take has much to do with luck and random choice, and many career choices are at least partially unintentional. Unplanned events at certain critical points in one's life and career can lead to an unexpected change of direction. Such incidents include meeting a member of a particular profession, reading a book or seeing a film that glorifies a specific type of job or role, or even accidental browsing through web-page job offers sections while unemployed when on a boring train journey or during an enforced lockdown period.

The two major career issues for the individual that are covered in this chapter are 'career choice' and 'career development'. Amongst the topics covered are theoretical frameworks of career choice, the early career, the career plateau, obsolescence, leaving the labour market, career and other life interests, quality of working life, stress and careers, demography, including individual and gender differences (though diversity will be fully covered in Chapter 8), dual-career couples, international careers, career aspirations, the new psychological contracts, and innovative career concepts such as the protean career.

In the 1920s and 1930s, the Chicago School of Sociology studied the life histories of the local communities in an attempt to understand how people viewed their lives (Barley, 1989). When the Chicago sociologists used the term 'career', therefore, they were referring to a heuristic concept, applicable to a wider range of situations than contemporary usage in management circles would imply (Davis, 2017; Hughes, 1958). Only later was the concept of careers restricted to the organizational domain. Present-day approaches have returned to the original wider framework embracing all aspects of a person's life, not just the individual's organizational and professional life.

Career choice

Work is an essential and mostly a desired part of our lives. Its role goes far beyond the need to provide food, shelter, and other essentials for life. Work provides people with a sense of purpose, challenges, self-fulfilment, and development, as well as the essential income to enable them to participate in other spheres of life. Work is a source of identity as well as of creativity and mastery (Foster, 2012; Jahoda, 1982; Wille & De Fruyt, 2014). Work provides us with status and offers opportunities for social networking. Many find love and affection and meet their partners during and through work. Work helps us to pass the time and gives our lives structure. A different, 'positive', aspect of work is that for many, work may even serve as a shelter and sanctuary from home and family (Hochschild, 1997). Hochschild argued that in order to avoid home-related issues and challenges such as relationship matters people absorb themselves in work, sometimes for long hours. In sum, in terms of the 'hierarchy of needs' suggested by Maslow (1943), work provides the basic needs as well as opportunities for achieving the higher needs. His theory is still considered relevant (Abulof, 2017), though there is no strong empirical evidence to back it up with data.

Many of the outcomes of work and career that people face will depend on why they do what they do; this is not merely a matter of which vocation, profession, job, or career they choose. It is how important work is for them, as a facet of their lives. The 'acid test' for the centrality of work and career choice can be found in 'the lottery dilemma': what would you do about work if you had won a lottery or inherited a large sum of money that would enable you to quit working and still enjoy a comfortable lifestyle.

Before turning to Table 2.1, try to answer the question honestly. As a student you may not be working now, but if you were faced with the lottery dilemma after working for a year or two, what would you choose?

- Stop working.
- Continue working in the same job.
- Continue working but under different conditions.

Now, consider how you think other people from your country would answer the question above, and how these responses would compare with other nations. Then compare your answer with the data presented in Table 2.1, which ranks the answers of an international sample in 'The Meaning of Working' survey (MOW, 1987) to the question 'What would you do if you were financially secure?'.

Table 2.1   The lottery dilemma in various countries

Stop working		Continue working in the same job		Continue working but under different conditions	
Country	%	Country	%	Country	%
Britain	31	Japan	66	Britain	53
West Germany	30	Yugoslavia	62	USA	49
Belgium	16	Israel	50	Belgium	47
Netherlands	14	Netherlands	42	Netherlands	44
USA	12	USA	39	West Germany	39
Israel	12	Belgium	37	Israel	37
Japan	7	West Germany	31	Yugoslavia	34
Yugoslavia	4	Britain	16	Japan	27

Source: MOW, 1987

Table 2.1 clearly indicates that people are committed to work and employment, although not necessarily to their current job or their original career choice. The level of commitment is influenced by several factors. Clearly the status and type of one's present job have an impact, as well as individual characteristics, but to these we need to add national and cultural background. In Britain, for example, less than one in six would stay in the same job, compared with two out of six in Japan. Noon et al. (2013) elucidate this phenomenon, giving a variety of explanations, the first of which is the moral necessity to work. This may be the case in cultures where work is seen as a 'duty', where work is viewed as an activity central to one's life (Bothma et al., 2015; Mannheim & Dubin, 1986), where the role of work is conscientious endeavour or disciplined compliance (Noon et al., 2013).

Career calling – a unique choice

Some people make their career choice at a very young age, often in response to an inner 'calling' to follow a certain career (Hall & Chandler, 2005), which they pursue though not all of them successfully. Other people choose a career later, while some never really make a definite choice of career. Many have to modify their career aspirations due to changes in the environment, recognition of their own limitations, changes in their values and attitudes, and transformation of life realities. Life realities can take place due to a minor change, like disappearance of a certain profession, or a major change, like the impact of COVID-19. The choice of a career may be unintended, but even when planned, people do not necessarily achieve their goals.

Box 2.1: Unintended careers

In this Box we will see how people may end up in an unintended career by introducing the cases of the two people who have different and unintended career trajectories.

M.C., male, in his 60s

M.C. was the national IT manager of a large professional association. This job was one in a succession of senior positions he held in the IT sector, another step in a successful career. He benefitted from a strong professional reputation and fair income. M.C. also had an interest in food, and was developing a hobby of making butters from nuts – not the standard peanut butter, but more adventurous nuts (e.g. pistachio, pecan, pine nut, etc.). His family and friends loved his products, and he start selling them in weekend street markets in London. Demand continued to grow, and eventually he realized that he could turn his hobby

(Continued)

into a full-time job. He decided to resign from his IT position and become a fully-fledged food entrepreneur. The company, Nutural World, has grown steadily and become a success (www.nuturalworld.com). Nutural World products continue to gain success with customers, with steadily increasing orders from Ocado, Amazon, and selected independent shops and delicatessens around the UK.

J.L., female, in her 40s

When she has just finished her high-school, and before taking on further studies (either vocational or university), J.L. wanted to earn some money to go travelling. She opened the newspaper and saw an ad for a job in an insurance firm where they promised training and fair work conditions and terms. Following an interview, she accepted the job offer. Twenty years later, she progressed to a middle-level manager position in that same large insurance firm. Although she had not previously envisaged a career in insurance, and had planned just short-term employment, it seems to suit her well.

These real-life examples show extreme cases of unintended careers. Nevertheless, one must assume that unless M.C. had liked food, and J.L. had preferred job security, they would not have ended up in their present careers. In many other instances there is certain amount of luck or an unintentional element in career choice, though a more spiritual approach may see it in another way: 'Luck is God's way to stay anonymous' (Tim D. Hall, citing Tom Cavanagh). Whether luck or a planned career, a set of individual propensities and qualities are required for following and succeeding in particular vocations and professions.

A pause for reflection

When did you choose the university where you are now studying? Was it a rational choice? Was it your first choice, the one you wished for and had planned for over a period of a few years? Or did you choose it on the advice of a friend, or because you read about it online?

To what extent are people prepared for their future career? What motivates people to choose a specific career direction? In what ways do experience and individual background influence decisions? How and why are different choices made at different stages of life? To better understand these issues, let us start by looking at some case studies.

Case study 2.2 presents two typical cases of career choice dilemmas.

CASE STUDY 2.2A: TREVOR'S CAREER CHOICE DILEMMA

Trevor studied for a first degree in Mechanical Engineering at a well-known university. Soon after graduation he started his first job in industry, working on a research and development project for a high-technology firm, part of a larger company. After he had been working on a project for two years, the manager of his department left the company and Trevor was asked to take over his role. In his new position he had responsibility for three technicians, one young engineer, and several support staff. He did well, but felt he was 'wasting' his time managing the department rather than being involved in engineering work. A year later the project was completed, and the mother-company decided to produce the subject of the project on a commercial basis. Trevor was asked to move to another subsidiary of the company, which focused on production.

At this point he felt that such a managerial role required further training in management. He completed an in-house course in management, and started working as deputy to the head of the production department. The most difficult area for him in his new role was the financial management of projects. After discussions with his wife and friends, he enrolled in an evening course in financial management at the local business school.

Trevor found the course very interesting, and in due course undertook a Master's degree. This proved a great success, and after two years, now with two children, and with the prospect of replacing his own manager and head of the production unit, Trevor should have been happy. However, he felt he might have chosen the wrong career. Even his subsequent promotion did not satisfy him. After only one year as head of department, Trevor decided to embark on an academic career in the area of financial management.

His strong mathematical competence and enthusiasm for his studies convinced a well-known professor in a prestigious university to accept him as a PhD student. He left his fairly well-paid job for a student bursary and joined the programme. During his three years of study his wife was supportive, and Trevor enjoyed his studies immensely. He even managed to get few consultancy projects that helped him financially. Publishing parts of his dissertation in a top management journal helped him to gain a post as a lecturer in a good university, the only disadvantage being that he had to relocate to a different city.

One of his research projects required him to work with one of the top consultancy firms. He enjoyed working on two research ideas and developed a model that was adopted by the company. However, one thing bothered him. He was now in his early 40s, and realized that his partners in the research projects earned about twice as much as he did. He had a mortgage to pay, three children, and the combined salaries of himself and his wife were not enough to enable them to have the lifestyle

(Continued)

they desired. At this point one of his research projects on financial models took him to a company that asked him to undertake some consultancy work concurrently with his academic work. The benefits were enormous compared to what he earned from his salaried work. He knew there were good prospects for him to earn much more in consultancy, and he thought carefully about ending his academic career. He asked himself whether he should opt to work for a large company such as one of the leading consultancy firms, or open his own start-up consultancy.

CASE STUDY 2.2B: LYNNE'S CAREER CHOICE DILEMMA

Lynne studied for a first degree in art and languages. At the end of her studies she took a year off to travel, and while in Australia met a girlfriend, Terry, who had graduated in art and business management. Together they started to talk about their dreams and realized they had a common wish – to design clothes and fashion items. On their return to the UK via India and Hungary, they established contacts with several local textile manufacturers.

Back home they applied for a start-up loan from the Department of Trade and Industry (DTI), and received a moderate sum that enabled them to open a small boutique in Brighton. Within three years Lynne and Terry expanded the business, and then opened another branch and enjoyed a fair income. However, Lynne realized that much of her work involved either dealing with financial matters or communicating with suppliers, tax collectors, and a few unhappy customers. The artistic element of her work had been reduced to a minor fraction and she felt frustrated. She took an evening class in pottery where her distinctive decorative style was highly appreciated. In fact, at the end of the course she managed to sell more of her work than any other student. As a result, Lynne persuaded her business partner to open a new section in one of their shops, for pottery and other artistic objects. This success planted new ideas in her mind. She was 30 by now, and had a partner with whom she wanted to share her life.

Both Trevor and Lynne faced a career choice dilemma. Today such career and life stories are quite common, but this was not the case before the last few decades of the 20th century. Before that there would usually be one point in life when a person would choose a career, a certain specific career, that is (and up to some 50 years ago it would be *his* career rather than 'his or hers'). Before the 18th century, life was even simpler, of course. A man's career was usually determined by the career of his father. Women had no occupational career (with a few exceptions such as nuns). For most of the 20th century, career choices similar to those faced by Trevor and Lynne were very unusual. Even after the Second World War only a minority of people studied for a university degree. Most people did not hop from job to job, and certainly second or third careers were the exception. By the turn of the last century, about one-third of the population of the relevant age group in industrial nations have studied for a first degree, and this trend continues – the UK government has set a target of 50 per cent of high-school leavers to study for a university degree. Moreover, people are expected to continue learning, not merely while of university age, but throughout their working life. People have second and third careers. The fourth career change Trevor was contemplating was unheard of even as recently as the 1970s. Starting up a business would not have been an option for Lynne's mother or aunt.

Questions regarding these cases

What is the best career advice for Trevor? What is the best career advice for Lynne? Does 'best advice' exist at all?

What is the purpose of career counselling and what is it based on? (There is more on career counselling in Chapter 3.)

Think about your own career pattern up to the present. Have you known from an early age what you wanted to do? Are you still following that original aspiration?

Have you changed your career path? What caused the change – internal motives or external circumstances?

Let us try to gain a better understanding of the needs of individuals and the requirements of organizations and their roles in CPM.

Internal, external, and organizational careers

In defining what career is, we should distinguish between internal, external, and organizational careers. They are distinguished from each other, and can be evaluated in different ways (Heslin, 2005; Spurk et al., 2019). Abele et al. (2011) discuss the many ways career success can be measured. It is never easy to identify how successful a person is, and they open their paper with this:

> *Imagine that somebody asks you the following question: 'How successful has your occupational career been so far?' Would it be easy for you to answer this question or would you need considerable time to think about it?* (2011, p. 195)

For a student this question may be too early, but should make them consider how they would define what success in career means for them.

The internal career is a person's self-perception about his or her own career: its development, advancement, and fulfilment of goals. This self-perception involves setting subjective career goals and evaluating one's own achievement in reaching them. An internal career is subjective, and therefore the definition of internal career success depends on the inner feelings and values of the person, and is relative to the career aims set by the self for the self.

The external career concerns how other people and organizations perceive a person's career – the development, advancement and fulfilment of the person's goals. Evaluating career success by means of external evaluation is more objective than internal career measurement, but it still depends on the particular observer's viewpoint. Success in an external career is assessed mainly in terms of hierarchy level and pace of progress on such a ladder, social status (e.g. occupational status), professional qualifications, and financial success (i.e. income and other monetary rewards).

The organizational career is a path people move along, in terms of the positions and the roles they fill during their working life. Career progress or advancement can be quite objective and measurable within a single organization or between organizations with equivalent promotion scales (e.g. army versus navy). However, such comparisons are less clear or may even be meaningless for dynamic careers, as moves involve multiple transitions. Here, comparisons might be impractical or irrelevant. For example, is the CEO of an organization employing 1,000 people 'higher' than a Vice President who manages 3,000 employees in a company of 10,000?

While organizations retain career systems through which they plan and manage people's careers, it is people who *have* careers. People will plan and manage their careers, not always according to an organization's plans and schemes. It may be most appropriate to consider careers as being under 'mutual ownership' – that of people and organizations. We now look at individual career choice models.

Individual models of career choice

Many of the career theories dealing with the individual refer to career choice. Osipow (1990) summarized the leading theories of career choice and development, and concluded that the most prominent career choice theories are Holland's RIASEC model (Holland, 1959; Nauta, 2010) and social learning (Krumboltz et al., 2013). Let us explore these theories in turn.

Holland's RIASEC model

One of the most widely used and academically validated models of career choice is Holland's RIASEC (1958). Developed many years ago, but still relevant and in wide use, Holland's model identifies people's vocational or occupational preferences, and helps also in determining a fit between a person's choices and organizational characteristics (and sometimes even team characteristics) that can be expressed in similar terms. These six categories of people and six models of occupational environment are: *Realistic, Investigative, Artistic, Social, Enterprising,* and *Conventional.* There is an association among the six types, most commonly depicted as a hexagon as shown in Figure 2.1.

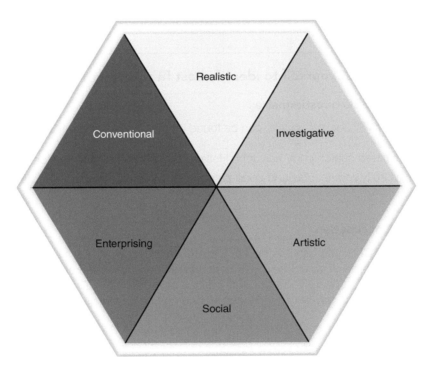

Figure 2.1 Holland's RAISEC hexagon (1958)

Holland's theory follows the three basic elements of Parsons' (1909) concept of career choice: the person, the occupation and the fit between the two. It has the advantage of good face validity and years of corroborative empirical evidence for the theory and its practical derivatives (Spokane, 1996). Consistent though moderate correlation (ranging from r = 0.15 to r = 0.54) was found between person–environment fit (to use Holland's term) and job satisfaction. Research evidence shows that finding the right work to match with career interests is related to performance and persistence in work as well as in academic settings (Nye et al., 2012). Such a fit means that there is a certain level of similarity or a match between individual vocational preferences and the characteristics of the work environment in which the person works, using the RIASEC terminology.

The Dictionary of Holland Occupational Codes (Gottfredson & Holland, 1996) contains a vast variety of occupations and vocations, many of which did not exist in the past. A more updated but more general is a set of occupations available on O*NET (2020) – see Box 2.3.

The person–environment congruence has been the subject of much recent research. Even though the person–environment fit is a fundamental issue in the behavioural sciences, its prescription cannot be accurate. The Holland theory fits well with earlier work, such as a meta-analysis that found a close relationship between person–environment congruence and measures of wellbeing (satisfaction, stability, etc.) (Armstrong et al., 2008; Assouline & Meir, 1987).

Box 2.2: Test yourself to identify best fit with your future work

The Holland RIASEC questionnaire

The Holland RAISEC questionnaire can be found on the following websites:

www.self-directed-search.com/ has John Holland's original test (available for a fee).

https://www.truity.com/test/holland-code-career-test is one of the sites that offers the text for free.

Find the right occupation

Based on Koys (2017), you can use the US Department of Labour's 'My Next Move' (https://www.mynextmove.org/). It would help you understand your career interests using Holland's typology. It will further enable you to explore various occupations in O*NET (at https://www.onetcenter.org/), so you may be able to focus on one (or just few) target occupation(s).

Koys' exercise helps to:

- increase career awareness
- increase ability to identify opportunities
- increase career preparedness skills.

Many factors may be considered regarding career choice. Figure 2.2 suggest you explore four factors to help lead your career decision: what you love or enjoy; what your community needs from you (that you have the capacity to provide); the practical element – remuneration for your future career; and what you are good at – your competence. These can be positioned across four dimensions: passion, mission, the type of job you may encounter along the specific career; and your professionalism.

Career choice

Figure 2.2 Career choice factors

Matching internal and external entities to enable career success

Each individual has their specific personality, and possesses a portfolio of abilities, skills, and competencies, as well as their own set of values, norms, and beliefs. The personality, abilities, skills, and competencies are important for reaching a person–job fit. The Holland RIASEC (1959) framework exemplifies how a person can identify jobs, profession, or vocation that will fit for them. When there is good fit, individuals will better perform and be more inclined to have a high level of satisfaction – from job, work, and life in general. In a complementary way, the values, norms, and beliefs of the individual may fit (or otherwise) the specific organization they may work for (e.g. the organizational culture, what the organization stands for) and if there is a good fit, there is much higher propensity that the individual will be able to better identify and engage with their organization (Edmans, 2012). If the vision one has for his or her future corresponds with the vision the organization has set to reach, the stronger the chances are for strong future mutual benefits.

The above discussion indicates a need for a fit between the personality of a person and his or her job. There are also other factors relevant for the career–job fit, in particular abilities and competence – cognitive, physical, emotional abilities – without which job performance will not be reached. It is the role of the organization's HRM to look for such a fit, first when selecting an applicant to join the organization, and then when promotion or other career decisions are at stake. There is more on this topic in the second part of the book.

Person–job fit is just one aspect required for a successful career. The person–organization fit (e.g. to the organizational culture) is paramount, and without such fit people who may be able to perform certain jobs will fail or leave the organization. On the wider perspective, person–environment fit is important for making optimal career choices at both the individual and organizational level.

Career choice in academe

Since the Industrial Revolution, the number of areas of knowledge and associated jobs and vocations has expanded enormously, and large numbers of new specialties have developed. This expansion accelerated even further in the last decades. Basic education has become mandatory in most developed societies. More and more occupations require specific qualifications, hence extended periods of formal training. Institutions of higher education have arisen that provide the training called for by the higher levels of knowledge work.

Totally new vocational areas have emerged (most notably Internet-related jobs such as web design). Even in relatively traditional occupations there is divergence. Describing psychology main sub-disciplines, Danziger (2013) refers to developmental psychology, social psychology, and industrial psychology – and points out the proliferation of sub-disciplines. Indeed, even within psychology, there are several sub-disciplines, each quite distinct and requiring different knowledge: academic, clinical, counselling, engineering or human factors, industrial or organizational, marketing, military, psychometric, school, or consulting (Sternberg, 1998). Even this list can be expanded by adding occupational psychologist, social psychologist, and other sub-professions. Each of these has a different focus, and requires different academic training.

As a result, the academic sector has grown substantially in most industrial societies, and has become a career field for more than just the elite few of the past (Baruch & Hall, 2004; Angervall et al., 2018). Many embark on an academic career while others who study for a PhD have to accept underemployment due to the competitiveness of this area (Larson et al., 2014). Underemployment is not unique to the academic labour market, and is a phenomenon growing in relevance, albeit not a new phenomenon (McKee-Ryan & Harvey, 2011). As far back as the early 1970s, the British academic labour market comprised only 33,000 employees (Williams, Blackstone and Metcalf, 1974), and there was a high similarity between the UK and US academic labour markets. However, unlike the US academic labour market, that of the UK is tightly regulated (e.g. all universities have fixed salary scales, and there is a high level of unionization). In 2016, the number of UK academic employees was 420,000 (HESE, 2020). The basis for the calculation varies according to the definition of 'higher education'. The numbers in the USA for 2018 represent a larger population of 1.5 million faculty members in degree-granting, post-secondary institutions compared with some 850,000 in the 1980s (Metzger, 1987). Overall, there has been extensive growth of the academic sector in the USA, and the trend has continued in this direction. Moreover, the academic career system is becoming a role model for many occupations due to its knowledge-based and boundaryless nature (Baruch & Hall, 2004).

Social learning

Social learning (Bandura, 1977) is concerned with feedback from the environment, in particular from career counselling and the development of self-efficacy as a result of reinforcement (Bandura, 1997; Reed et al., 2010). People learn from their environment and tune their career aspirations based on the feedback and role models they have in family and friends. This can explain, for example, the relationship between socio-economic background and later participation in tertiary education (Tomaszewski, Perales, & Xiang, 2017). External intervention can help to facilitate high self-efficacy via learning that affects people's attitudes and behaviours. Self-efficacy has repeatedly been shown to be an antecedent of performance in organizational settings. In general, the literature provides strong evidence of a high degree of correlation between efficacy perceptions and subsequent performance (Sitzmann & Yeo, 2013). Both feedback from the wider environment (i.e. not just from the parents) and reinforcement of successful performance help people in choosing professions and careers that would suit them best.

To make a 'proper' choice, that is, to optimize their career prospects, people need first to realize their own vocational inclination, and second to acquire knowledge of the occupational environment associated with various professional options. In the example above of academic roles, to succeed one needs either to be keen to create new knowledge (i.e. research), or to educate and develop future generations of graduates (i.e. teaching), or both. Vocational inclination depends on the motivation, knowledge, personality, and competence of a person. Occupation is much more than a collection of activities and functions. It is the culture, the reputation, the status, and the associated lifestyle of a particular discipline.

Different choice – entrepreneurship

Many do not wish to follow the organizational career route, but are inspired to create their own venture, perhaps a small company, sometimes just a one-person entity, or they aspire to build a large company from scratch. Such people are entrepreneurs, and their careers mostly involves a struggle, and sometimes deep frustration – for every one that has 'made it', there are many who have had to give up their dreams or accept that their business will never grow as they had hoped. Yet, every large corporation was once a small enterprise, and not every person is willing to walk the beaten path. Also, some entrepreneurs aim simply to create a small business that will satisfy their needs and ambitions. Entrepreneurship is not just about the personal traits such as the 'right' personality, the knowledge, sometimes appearance and style. Entrepreneurs use their creativity and innovation to develop their business (Drucker, 2014). They use their competence to identify opportunities and benefit from them (Eckhardt & Shane, 2003), thereby contributing to the economy (Parker, 2018).

One characteristic that distinguishes entrepreneurs from managers is their risk propensity (Stewart & Roth, 2001). Using a psychometric meta-analytic review of literature concerning the comparative risk propensities, Stewart and Roth pointed out the importance of the role personality plays in entrepreneurial career choice. The McClelland (1985) theory of needs (e.g.

the need for achievement, the need for control) also provides a relevant basis for understanding entrepreneurs' careers. Today, successful entrepreneurs become the role model for new generation of young aspiring people who wish to establish a business and make name for themselves (Anderson & Warren, 2011). Many biographies of entrepreneurs (see, e.g. the Dyson biography by Coren, 2001) account for such differences. Interested individuals are offered advice about 'how to make it' in many books, academic and practical (Blundel, Lockett, & Wang, 2017).

Individual models of career stage and development

Many view career as a developmental process that comprises several stages. Most notably is Super's developmental theory (1957), one of the well-known career stages models. Some maintain there are distinct stages, and have argued for specific boundaries between them. Each stage influences the next, and together they form a continuum.

The first impressions people have about careers, career roles, and the world of work emerge from the individual family background. According to the social identity theory presented above, this will affect children's behaviour, and as a result, will influence their future career choice (Stewart & Barling, 1996). It is not merely the family. Early work experience also helps to set the social identity of young people (Esters & Retallick, 2013).

Several scholars have developed career stage theories. Two of the eminent theories are those developed in the past by Super and by Levinson. Super's (1957) theory of career stages reflects how, during the lifespan of a person, individuals implement their inner being and self-concept in one or more career (or vocational) choices. Levinson (1978, 1986) distinguishes between transition stages (each lasting for a period of five years) and stability stages (each of which may last some five to seven years). Later in this chapter we will examine both Super's and Levinson's frameworks in light of contemporary developments. One problem with suggesting a specific timespan for either the chronological age or the duration of a stage is that there is no empirical support for any of the suggested figures (Sullivan & Baruch, 2009).

Levinson's (1978) theory of the 'seasons of man's life' suffers from the notion of determinism, almost fatalism, inherent in the title of the concept. That is, the use of the seasons metaphor implies that these career stages are fixed, unchangeable, and that each person has to experience the same sequence throughout life. Another criticism concerns the title of the theory, namely the gendered element. However, at the time of Levinson's earlier writing, managerial careers were mostly male dominated. Even now managerial careers, in particular at the most senior levels, still are, though the gap is narrowing. There are also sector-specific reasons for lack of gender balance, such as under-representation of women in engineering (Powell et al., 2012). More about the gendered side of careers in Chapter 8.

In the past, after a turbulent period in their early career – a period of discovery and exploration – individuals would arrive at a point at which both their own self-concept and the organization's concept of them had reached harmony. At this point they would typically have achieved a balance between work and family/social life, and their employers would begin to reap a return on their investment in the individual (e.g. training, mentoring). In the 21st century that equilibrium has ceased to exist. Both individuals and organizations are creating new cycles. These can be either vicious or victorious cycles, that is, sometimes such a cycle represents a spiral of ongoing development and achievements for both individuals and their employers, but in other cases there are cycles of deterioration in self-perception, self-esteem, and contribution, ending in long-term unemployment or poor performance, usually coupled with a poor quality of life. Individuals can be trapped in mundane roles in the gig economy (Page-Tickell & Yerby, 2020). Organizations can exploit individuals via policies such as zero-hours contracts – a questionable practice that is nevertheless growing in scope (Farina et al., 2020).

A pause for reflection

Think about what can and should organizations do to help and prompt positive development, and at the same time identify and prevent negative deterioration? Later on in the book we will examine this phenomenon from the organizational point of view and see what practices may be useful for such treatment.

Super's lifespan, life space theory (1980) combines the psychology of individual development during life and social role theory in order to understand multiple-role careers via the life-career rainbow (see Figure 2.3).

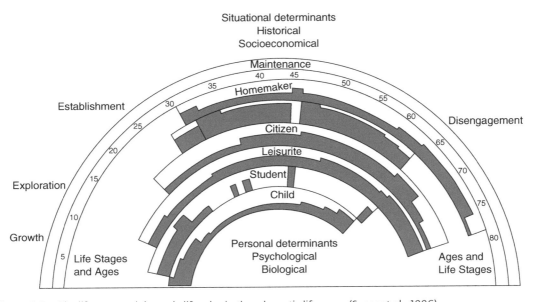

Figure 2.3   The life-career rainbow: six life roles in the schematic life space (Super et al., 1996)

Chronological age and career age

Super (1957) indicated the parallelism between people's chronological age and state of development and their career stage. Super's rainbow stages are: (a) childhood growth (up to the age of 14); (b) search and inquiry (up to the age of 25); (c) establishment (up to age 45); (d) continuity or maintenance (up to age 56); and (e) decline or disengagement. The other dimension of the rainbow is concerned with life space, and the social roles of: the child, the student, the leisure seeker, the citizen, the worker, and the home-maker. It is of interest to note that working life comprises just one part of the career, as was shown in early studies of the Chicago School mentioned earlier. These roles interact, and can benefit from each other, but they also create conflicting commitments.

The following description of Super's stages is based on Super et al. (1996). The growth stage includes dealing with the tasks associated with becoming concerned about the future, increasing control over one's own life, committing to school and work, and acquiring competent work habits and attitudes. During the exploration stage individuals encounter crystallizing, specifying, and implementing occupational choice. The establishment stage occurs at the beginning of one's career and the tasks are stabilizing, consolidating, and advancing in one's occupational position. Maintenance is concerned mainly with the issue of midlife crisis and includes the tasks of holding on, keeping up, and innovating. This stage can be associated with a career plateau. It can involve becoming more firmly entrenched in one's chosen occupation, or transition to a different occupation. The last career stage of disengagement is all about phasing out – deceleration and retirement.

The description fits well the stable type of career people experienced in the years between the beginning of the Industrial Revolution and the late 20th century. The changes elaborated upon in Chapter 1 have altered the framework of reference for Super's concept, although much of it is still relevant. A summary of the theory's propositions (Super et al., 1996) bring some basic factors: for example, that people differ in abilities, personalities, needs, values, interests, traits, and their self-concept, or that development can be guided by external facilitation. Similarly, expecting that work and life satisfaction depends on finding adequate outlets for one's own qualities.

Other propositions are relevant and applicable to the understanding of individual careers, for example:

- People are qualified, by virtue of these characteristics, for a number of occupations.
- Each occupation requires a characteristic pattern of personal abilities, traits, and so on, with a certain degree of tolerance to allow varieties of occupations for each individual and a variety of individuals for each occupation.
- Vocational preferences and competencies and life and work situations change with time and experience, but the self-concept is relatively stable since it derives from social learning.
- Career development is about the development and implementation of an occupational self-concept.
- The process of synthesis or compromise between individual and social factors is one of role playing and learning.

Other propositions may need re-evaluation, like a suggestion that the career pattern is determined by parental socio-economic background, mental ability, education, skills, personality, career maturity, and opportunities. This proposition undervalue the individual agency in self-management of careers.

All in all, the propositions, put together, comprise a comprehensive approach to the study of individual careers.

Question

Which proposition of these propositions would you find most relevant to your own career?

The Levinson model

Daniel Levinson's work was based on traditional American men (women being added to his analysis later), and identified four basic career stages: childhood and adolescence, which is really a pre-career stage; early adulthood; middle adulthood; and late adulthood. Within each stage there is an inner stage of transition. Early adulthood starts with entry to the labour market. At the time of Levinson's study the typical age for starting work was 17, while in the first half of the 20th century it was even lower, age 14, as few people continued on to higher education. The early years (up to the age of 28, according to Levinson) are the time for a person to establish a direction and try to gain a certain stability. At about the age of 30, though, people may reappraise their life, moving on to a stable stage of identifying what they are seeking from life and work, establishing a role in society, in the organization, and in the family.

The early adulthood stage ends with midlife transition or crisis, which takes place at around the age of 40–45. This is the time when people tend to reflect on their life so far, and contemplate the future. Levinson identified three factors that contribute to the fact that most people have such a crisis or re-evaluation of their career in their early 40s. First, by the age of 40, people have enough feedback to contemplate their achievements, their fulfilment of their childhood dreams, or their failure to do so. Second, this is coupled with a feeling of becoming 'older': the age of 40 seems something of a threshold. Third, people might begin to feel a decline in their physical strength even if it is only minor.

Then, according to Levinson, when they reach middle adulthood, people come to terms with their career and their inner feelings, and have a stable stage between about the ages of 50 and 55. This stage is followed, again, by an unstable phase of transition, in which they set new goals. Then comes the last career stage of late adulthood, when a combination of bodily decline and sometimes illness, and rapidly approaching retirement, causes people to end their working career and prepare themselves for retirement.

Several major changes make the Levinson model in need of redefinition and restructuring. His model is based on, and was established within, the context of the American economy.

Moreover, in general, there have been major changes in the nature of careers, elaborated in Chapter 1 (e.g. that many have second, third, or more careers, that people sometimes have to take early retirement at the age of 55 to 60, etc.). To this we must add other developments, such as general improvements in individual health and the fact that people at the age of 65 should no longer feel that they must prepare for decline and death, but rather to a long period of active enjoyment of leisure. Retirement may not be a preferred, desirable, or even a possible option (Baruch, Sayce, & Gregoriou, 2014).

Other career stage models

Several other models offer a similar idea of association between age or life stage and career development, usually in terms of career progress. There are minor variations in the ages of the groups or the names of the stages in these models, such as those of Hall and Nougaim (1968), and Form and Miller (1949). Schein's (1978) model is also similar, but offers eight stages: growth and search (up to 21); entry to the world of work (16–25); basic training (16–25); starting full-time career (17–30); mid-career (25+); late career (40+); decline (50+); and retirement. Here there is an overlap in the age groups, but there is still an attempt to retain age boundaries. A different type of career stage model is offered by Evans (1986), who argued that there are fluctuations in the early working stage (15–35/40), then stable growth, followed by the last stage, which starts at the age of 50. This last stage can be either further growth, plateau, or decline.

Others wisely refrained from attaching specific ages to the stages. Such are the Baird and Kram (1983) and Dalton et al. (1977) models. The latter focuses on professional growth and managerial development (and was validated by Thompson et al. in 1986). Dalton et al. suggested a four-stage model of career development. Their model is based upon a longitudinal study of academic scholars and professional engineers, which aimed to find out why some individuals continued to contribute and be productive throughout their careers, while others' productivity and contributions diminished over time. According to Dalton et al., a career can be conceptualized as a progression through developmental stages that are independent of organizational structure or hierarchy. In the first stage, the individuals or protégés take on the role of apprentices, learning to perform fairly routine tasks and taking direction from more experienced mentors. In the second stage, the protégés have developed specific competences and start to demonstrate their own initiative and creativity. By the time the individuals have reached the third stage, they have become mentors to others and have broadened their interests by contributing through others. In the fourth stage, the individuals have been able to shape the practices, policies, and even the culture and direction of the entire organization. They guide and represent the organization, either as a senior manager, or an expert, or via resource acquisition. The employee follows an individual route and makes an autonomous search for self-responsibility. The problem with this model is that many never develop into the third stage, and even fewer reach the fourth.

Most researchers refer to career stages as a given. However, several characteristics influence the number and sequence of stages. Most notable is gender. In a further variation of his own 1957 model, Super revised it, distinguishing between men and women. Four types of career path were suggested for men: stable, conventional (with some advances till stability is reached), unstable, and multiple paths. For women, seven options were presented: housewife, stable (usually in low-skilled labour), stable, dual (alongside the housewife role, sometimes via part-time jobs), disrupted (due to maternity leave), unstable, and multiple paths. Such gender differences were also identified by Sullivan (1999). Other differentiating characteristics include profession, culture, size of organization, and type of employment, to mention just a few. Table 2.2 summarizes the major career stage models.

Table 2.2 Several well-known career stage models

Scholar	No. of stages	Use of age	Stages labels
Baird & Kram (1983)	4	no	Establishment; Progress; Maintenance; Retirement
Dalton, Thompson & Price (1977)	4	no	Work under guidance (apprentices) Autonomous work Mentoring others Direction, representation, sponsoring
Form & Miller (1949)	5	Yes	0–15: Orientation to the world of work 15–18: Beginning stage, sometimes part time work 18–34: Entry to labor market stage 34–60: Stable stage 60–65: Retirement
Greenhous (1987)	5	Yes	0–25: Entry to labor world 18–25: Entry to organization world 25–40: Establishment and achievements 40–55: Plateau career 55–retirement: Late career
Hall & Nougaim (1968)	5	Yes	0–25: Pre-work 26–30: Establishment 31–45: Progress 46–65: maintenance 65+: Retirement
Levinson (1978)	4+3/5*	Yes	0–17: Childhood & adolescence 17–22: Transitional: early adult 23–40: –28, entering; –40, settling down (with age 30 transition) 40–45: Transition: mid life 45–60: middle adulthood and culmination (with age 50 transition) 60–65: Transition: late adult 65+: Late adulthood

(Continued)

Table 2.2 (Continued)

Scholar	No. of stages	Use of age	Stages labels
Schein (1978)	8	Yes	0–21: Growth and search 16–25: Entry to the world of work 16–25: Basic training 17–30: Starting full time employment 25+: Mid career 40+: Late career 40+ Decline ?: retirement
Super (1957, 1980)	5	Yes	0–14: Childhood growth 0–25: Search and inquiry 25–45: Establishment 45–56: Continuity or maintenance 56+: Decline or disengagement.

* five transitional stages, three of them major between the childhood/adult/late-adulthood.

Using specific age groupings is inadequate in today's dynamic environment, and when people have multiple careers. Even in the past such rigidity would not fit variations among professions and their disciplinary accreditation (the training period can be very long, e.g. in medicine or accountancy), nations (if a period of military service is compulsory the starting age of a career moves accordingly), and educational background. At the beginning of the 21st century we have witnessed a hyper-turbulent business environment, which has meant changes in the norms of behaviour, and even in value systems, and has reduced the relevance of age as a measure of career stage.

Similarly, to use a specific number of career stages is inadequate. People with multiple careers or who experience career break(s) will have a different number of stages. Some professions have no stages (e.g. class teacher). Others have multiple career paths with different stages (e.g. military careers). What is important is the qualities associated with the different career stages people find themselves in. Amongst other aspects, career stage is important for understanding and interpreting job satisfaction. Feldman (1988) argued that there is ample empirical evidence that young workers are somewhat dissatisfied with pay and relationships with supervisors, but happy with learning opportunities. Satisfaction increased later in life, and then reduced towards the 'mid-life crisis' in the early 40s, which is usually overcome by a proper approach, and rectified in the final stages of the career.

Table 2.3 offers an integrated model, which has neither a definite number of stages, nor specific age boundaries. Still it encompasses and captures the common nature and notion of the various career stage models.

While the basic model comprises seven stages, stages (b) to (e) can, and in most cases will, be repeated several times. And similarly, while no specific ages are suggested, some indications can be given for most stages. The first stage will usually end with the completion of formal school education, which is about 18 in most industrial nations. The entry and acquiring a profession stage can be very short: if one decides at the age of 16 or 18 to be a delivery driver, within a few days or weeks one can start working. If one wishes to become

Table 2.3 Integrated model

Stage	Description
(a) Foundation	Childhood and adolescence experience and education help in planting the seeds of career aspiration
(b) Career entry	Usually through attainment of profession. Can be done via being an apprentice, training on the job, and attending college, university or other professional training. Usually even for qualified people, the first stage of work will include further professional establishment.
(c) Advancement	Both professional and hierarchical development within organization(s) or expanding own business. This stage can be characterized with either continuous advancement or reaching a plateau. In today's career environment and concepts, this stage will typically be associated with several changes of employer.
(d) Re-evaluation	Checking match between aspiration and fulfillment; re-thinking job/role/career. Can emerge from internal feeling or need (e.g., bored due to lack of challenge, life-crisis), or external force (redundancy, obsolescence of the profession). May end with decision to stay on the same path or to change career direction, returning to stage (b).
(e) Reinforcement	If making a decision to stay on the same path, the person should reinforce the present career but otherwise, career change calls for a returning to the stage (b) for re-establishment of the new career.
(f) Decline	Most but the few (who have full life of advancement till the latest moment) will start at a certain stage to envisage a withdrawal from working life, which can be swift or long term, spreading over few years.
(g) Retirement	Leaving the labor market (not necessarily at age of 65)

a lawyer, it usually takes about five years to complete the basic training. Certain life crises tend to come at a similar age (such as the mid-life crisis, which could be associated with the biological rhythm of life). The age of retirement is, which typically was 65, then moved to 67, but for many who are made redundant at a mature age, typically after 50, it may be too difficult to find an alternative job at the same status, therefore early retirement is more commonplace.

Personality and career

From the individual viewpoint, career has much to do with psychology. To understand careers – career targets and aspirations, career satisfaction, career perception, and so on – we need to recognize psychological issues. These include motivational and behavioural theories, for example, the 'self-fulfilling prophecy' (Eden, 1984) and Festinger's (1957) 'cognitive dissonance' frameworks, and new concepts in the psychology of individual traits, in particular 'the Big Five' (Goldberg, 1993; Oshio et al., 2018). (These frameworks are presented in most organizational behaviour textbooks.) These measures are more sophisticated than the traditional Myers–Briggs type indicator, which builds on Cattell's 16PF (Cattell & Kline, 1977). Nevertheless, Cattell's 16PF is quite a basic tool, and the exercise in Box 2.3 is a useful aid to understanding the role personality plays in shaping one's career, and helps to understand individuals and their differences (Schermer et al., 2020).

Box 2.3: Personality profiling exercise

How can your personality be described and characterized?

Stage 1

Use Figure 2.4 as a rapid self-assessment of your own 16 personality factors. Evaluate, for each question, for each pair, where on the continuum you lie. Mark it with a pen. (Be honest – there is no such thing as a good or bad profile.)

Join up the 'dots' to construct your 'profile'.

	1 2 3 4 5 6 7 8 9	
Reserved, detached	* * * * * * * * *	Outgoing, easygoing
Concrete thinker	* * * * * * * * *	Abstract thinker
Emotional	* * * * * * * * *	Emotionally stable
Mild, accommodating	* * * * * * * * *	Assertive, aggressive
Serious, reflective	* * * * * * * * *	Lively, happy-go-lucky
Flexible, rule-breaker	* * * * * * * * *	Conscientious, preserving
Shy, restrained	* * * * * * * * *	Venturesome, bold
Tough-minded	* * * * * * * * *	Tender-minded
Trusting, adaptable	* * * * * * * * *	Suspicious, self-opinionated
Practical, conventional	* * * * * * * * *	Imaginative, creative
Forthright, unpretentious	* * * * * * * * *	Astute, worldly
Confident, complacent	* * * * * * * * *	Worrying, insecure
Conservative, traditional	* * * * * * * * *	Experimenting, free-thinking
Group-dependent 'joiner'	* * * * * * * * *	Self-sufficient, resourceful
Less controlled	* * * * * * * * *	Controlled, exacting
Relaxed, tranquil	* * * * * * * * *	Tense, frustrated

Figure 2.4   Personality profiling: Cattel's 16PF

Stage 2 (class or group exercise)

Compare your choices with one or two students who sit next to you – note and discuss differences.

Stage 3

Choose three factors where you gave yourself 'extreme' ranks (i.e. 1 or 2 or 6 or 7).

Think of a recent event, case or incident in which you have recently been involved.

Did your behaviour on that occasion offer a good illustration of these personality characteristics?

Again, if this is done as a class or group exercise, compare your case with that of a fellow student. Look at his or her profile. Will he or she make a good policeman? A good copywriter?

Can you try to draw the profile for the present prime minister/president/head of state? How different it is from the profile you would draw for the ideal candidate for this job (of leading and managing your country)?

Stage 4

Critical thinking – don't take anything for granted.

While the 16PF measures look valid, they have their specific problems:

1. Are all the pairs mutually exclusive or might it be that the extreme options represent two different dimensions?
2. What happens when a person behaves differently under different circumstances?
3. How does one's evaluation compare with another's, for these relative terms? (That is, some people tend to give moderate ratings whereas others would tend to vote for the extreme.)
4. What would your resulting profile be if you re-evaluated yourself next week? Next month? (Test–retest fit.)
5. Are these measures objective? What will happen if you compare your self-rating to a rating done by a group of people who know you well?

Many inventories of personality exist, but the Big Five framework is updated and comprehensive, and will be discussed here not as a representative concept but as a leading current approach to the study of personality in the context of work. The Big Five factors were introduced to the literature of personality and careers by Goldberg (1990, 1993). Measures for the Big Five factors were developed later and proven robust (Oshio et al., 2018). Their implications for practice in both psychology and HRM receive wide attention (Leutner et al., 2014). Can the Big Five produce a profile of what is needed for a successful career? Like the Cattell 16PF, they are presented as a set of pairs of opposite characteristics and qualities.

The five factors are: (a) neuroticism versus stability, (b) extroversion versus introversion, (c) openness to experience, (d) agreeableness, and (e) conscientiousness. Empirical evidence suggests associations between some of these factors and performance. For example, in international careers, the impact of certain factors will depend on the culture of operation (Schmitt et al., 2008). In Western culture, extroversion is positive and important characteristic for managers. Conversely, such a quality will be less highly valued in Eastern culture. Openness to experience may be the one factor that can help in the identification of suitable candidates for global managers. However, both agreeableness and conscientiousness (or a tendency to be efficient, organized, and prudent) are commonly considered desirable traits, essential to the success of any manager. All in all, the Big Five can help to explain career success, but attention must be given to the environment of operation as a contingent variable (Judge et al., 1999).

While the Big Five factors are considered very important, their use can be problematic, not only for their simplicity (five dimensions compared to Cattell's 16), but especially since they are mostly perceived as 'positive'. For this reason, direct measurement will not reveal wide differentiation among respondents (e.g. the majority of people will tend to describe themselves as positive – stable, somewhat extrovert, open to experience, agreeable, and highly conscientious).

Another stream of work about the essential ingredients for career success stems from the ideas of Howard Gardner, as expressed in his book *Frames of Mind* (1983), on multiple intelligence. This was taken further by Goleman's *Emotional Intelligence* (2006). Empirical studies provide some support for the notion that it is the combination of competencies that is needed for success: Dulewicz (2000) identified the crucial roles of combining the three Qs – emotional intelligence (EQ), intelligence quotient (IQ), and management competencies (MQ) – to explain successful careers. He identified that IQ (27%), EQ (36%), and MQ (16%) explains advancement or career success (see Chapter 3 for an elaboration of the meaning and nature of career success). Although statistics can never be accurate when people's minds and the perception of advancement are under evaluation, these findings lend support to the importance of multiple intelligences in studying individuals' careers. Along the same lines, Kanfer and Heggestad (1997) coined the term 'motivational fit', which indicates that there are outcomes in the form of either anxiety or achievement when using both emotional and motivational perspectives.

Final note: In the past, when most jobs and careers were highly dependent on physical properties, the physical attributes of people were a decisive factor in career choice and development. This was coupled with stability and hereditary – many took the same employment as their parents. As most jobs and careers now depend on mental and personality factors, these have become the most crucial factors in determining one's career. Social developments enable social mobility and diversity, with more openness and new options for people from all facets of society to pursue their desired career. The following chapter, then, takes us further into the understanding of career and the meaning of career success.

Summary

This chapter summarized the concept of career as perceived from the individual perspective. It covered several aspects and research directions, in particular career choice, career stages, and the role personality plays in making career choices and in interpreting careers. This prepares the reader for the next chapter, where the focus will be on innovative career concepts (such as intelligent careers, the post-corporate career, and boundaryless careers).

KEY TERMS

Career choice

Career stage

External career

Internal career

Organizational career

Personality factors

The Big Five

DISCUSSION QUESTIONS

LESSONS AND FOOD FOR THOUGHT

1. *For the working student:* Does your present career fully or partially match your original career choice?

   Does your organization offer a career system that recognizes the different career choices of people? That offers diverse options for people at different stages of their career?

2. *If you aim to become an HR consultant:* What career advice could you, as a consultant, offer organizations or individual people, managers and executives, about associating their present career stage with their future prospects?

   How prepared are you to provide advice based on career choice models, to people seeking to change their career?

3. *For the student:* At what career stage are you at present? Analyse this stage according to at least two different career-stage models. In what ways have your parents influence your needs, aspirations, competencies? In what way have you been influenced by the other students you know?

Individual Careers and Career Models

3

LEARNING OBJECTIVES

After reading this chapter you should be able to:

- Identify the meaning of career success
- Critically analyse individual career models
- Understand how individual properties influence career choice
- Recognize future directions and paths available to careers

Chapter outline

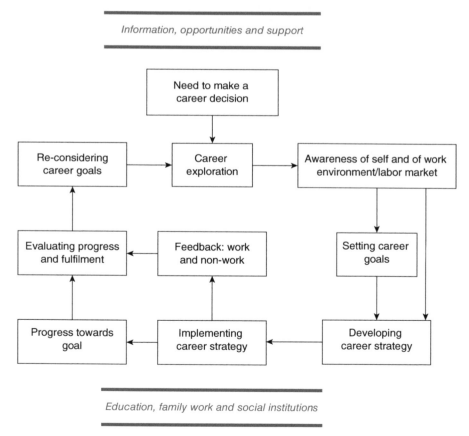

Information, opportunities and support

Education, family work and social institutions

Figure 3.1   Greenhaus et al.'s model of strategic career planning (adapted from Greenhaus et al., 2019)

Models of individual career development and the protean career

There are several individual career models. Most notable are the individual development stages and career choice models (discussed in Chapter 2), and general models of individual CPM. One innovative and comprehensive model at the individual level of analysis, Greenhaus et al.'s model (2019), focuses on individual management as a problem-solving process (see Figure 3.1).

This model focuses on the individual as the one who needs to make a decision, a need that leads to a career search and into a process of setting career goals, developing strategies and tactics to fulfil them, making progress, together forming a process that requires career evaluation. The organization is only an external player in the system, according to this model, along with environmental influences. The major criticism of this framework is that it undermines the role organizations play in planning and managing careers. (There is further discussion of this aspect of CPM in the following chapters.)

One problem with most of the individual career models is that they originated, in or derive from, a psychological perspective rather than having management science in view. To rectify that, Gunz (1989) offered a model of individuals' perceptions of their careers within an organizational context. Gunz described the organizational context as generating a 'career climbing-frame', but his model, unlike earlier hierarchical models, has an optional orientation form (see Figure 3.2).

		Non-deviant	Deviant
Future oriented?	No	Subsisting	
	Yes	Building	Searching

Figure 3.2 Gunz's model of orientation to organizational career climbing-frame (adapted from Gunz, 1989, p. 241)

Gunz proposed a theoretical framework, which recognizes the duality of managerial careers by distinguishing between organizational and individual levels of analysis. For Gunz, at the organizational level, careers can be seen as part of a process of social reproduction, by inducting newcomers into the internal culture, norms, and behaviours of the organization. This process links organizational forms and behaviour with comparatively stable career patterns that characterize particular firms or certain types of firms. At the individual level, Gunz perceived careers as a sequence of work role transitions, representing choices between opportunities offered by organizations. Each level of analysis illuminates a different aspect of managerial careers, but it is equally important that each should be seen in the light of the other levels. Later works called for the recognition of both individual and organizational roles in the process of career management (Baruch, 2006a; Lips-Wiersma & Hall, 2007). The organizational management of career should be aligned with the individual aspirations to allow a successful career path to be established (Bagdadli & Gianecchini, 2019). While in this chapter we focus on individual agency, the organizational side will be presented later in the book (see Chapter 6 for further elaboration).

Among theories focused on the individual, one innovative approach is the 'protean career' (see Figure 3.3). The idea of the protean career was first offered by Hall (1976), but it was not until later that it was recognized as reflecting real-life experiences (Hall, 2004). Hall and Mirvis (1996) described the protean career as a new form (at the time) in which the individual, rather than the organization, takes responsibility for transforming their career path. Moreover, the individual is capable of changing himself or herself according to need. The term 'protean' is taken from the name of the Greek god Proteus, who could change his shape at will. Hall describes the process as follows:

> The protean career is a process which the person, not the organization, is managing. It consists of all the person's varied experience in education, training, work in several organizations, changes in occupational field, etc. ... The protean person's own personal career choices and search for self-fulfilment are the unifying or integrative elements in his or her life. (1976: p. 201)

---

1. The career is managed by the person, not the organization.

2. The career is a lifelong series of experiences, skills, learning, transitions, and identity changes. ("Career age" counts, not chronological age.)

3. Development is:

   ➢ Continuous learning
   ➢ Self-directed
   ➢ Relational, and
   ➢ Found in work challenges

4. Development is not (necessarily):

   ➢ Formal training
   ➢ Retraining, or
   ➢ Upward mobility

5. The ingredients for success change

   ➢ From know-how to learn-how
   ➢ From job security to employability
   ➢ From organizational careers to protean careers, and
   ➢ From "work self" to "whole self"

6. The organization provides:

   ➢ Challenging assignments
   ➢ Developmental relationships
   ➢ Information and other developmental resources

7. The goal: Psychological success.

Figure 3.3 Elements of the new 'protean' career contract (Hall & Moss, 1998, p. 26. Reprinted by permission.)

The protean career is essentially a contract with oneself, rather than with the organization. Hall used the metaphor of the career fingerprint to describe the individual nature of the protean career, which is outside the structures and traditional boundaries of the organizational hierarchy, professional progress, or a stable direction. It is not restricted to the realm of paid work or work and non-work domains. The protean concept alters the relationship between the organization and the employee. The person takes on the role of his or her own agent, instead of leaving that to the organization (where either the line manager or the HR department has traditionally served as 'agent' for employees' careers).

Taking such personal responsibility for their own career may be difficult for people who have spent a considerable part of their working life in the traditional organizational career system (see the discussion later in this chapter of the concept of the desert generation). Hall and Mirvis (1996) describe the changes in the careers cycle in the new model of career stages: people will have several careers, each of which will comprise the inner stages of exploration, trial, establishment, and mastery. However, following mastery will come a new cycle of exploration, ending with the discovery of a new path, a different profession, role, or organization. This cycle corresponds to that identified by Cascio (2000), that is, that people now have several careers and therefore have to manage several career cycles.

In practice, when millions of jobs are lost in the industrial world, mostly from large firms, the individual has no option but to take responsibility, to manage their own career and, at best, to make good use of organizational support mechanisms and career facilities. This was the background against which ideas such as the protean career and the post-corporate career (see below) developed. Under such circumstances, the protean career and career resilience (Waterman et al., 1994; Seibert et al., 2016) are fully explicable. Both the financial crisis of 2008 and the COVID-19 pandemic of 2020 were external events that influenced the wider career system, but different individuals reacted to them in different ways, indicating that career sustainability depends not only on external circumstances but also on individual qualities.

Evaluation of the protean career

There are two measures widely used to evaluate the level to which a person holds a protean career orientation. Both were developed for the same purpose. One, that of Briscoe et al. (2006), included 14 items, and identified two major sub-dimensions of the protean career:

> 'values-driven', in the sense that the person's internal values provide the guidance and measure of success for the individual's career; and 'self-directed' in personal career management—having the ability to be adaptive in terms of performance and learning demands. Studies using these two sub-scale had mixed statistical support for it. (Gubler et al., 2014)

The other one is by Baruch (2014), measuring the protean orientation as a single construct. It was also used by a number of studies. Both measures were found useful and related to other career outcomes (Gubler et al., 2014). Table 3.1 presents the items for both measures.

Table 3.1 Protean career measures

Briscoe et al. (2006) measure	Baruch (2014) measure
The self-directed career management scale	***Protean career orientation scale***
I am in charge of my own career.	For me, career success is how I am doing against my goals and values.
Ultimately, I depend upon myself to move my career forward.	
I am responsible for my success or failure in my career.	I navigate my own career, mostly according to my plans(s).
Where my career is concerned, I am very much "my own person."	If I have to find a new job, it would be easy.
Overall, I have a very independent, self-directed career.	I am in charge of my own career.
In the past I have relied more upon myself than others to find a new job when necessary.	I take responsibility for my own development.
	Freedom and autonomy are driving forces in my career.
Freedom to choose my own career path is one of my most important values.	For me, career success means having flexibility in my job.
When development opportunities have not been offered by my company, I've sought them out on my own.	
The values-driven scale	
I'll follow my own guidance if my company asks me to do something that goes against my values.	
In the past I have sided with my own values when the company has asked me to do something I don't agree with.	
What I think about what is right in my career is more important to me than what my company thinks.	
It doesn't matter much to me how other people evaluate the choices I make in my career.	
I navigate my own career, based upon my personal priorities, as opposed to my employer's priorities.	
What's most important to me is how I feel about my career success, not how other people feel.	

Individuals and career counselling

Telling people they are in charge may be easier said than done. People need support, and do not always have the knowledge or the mental strength to direct themselves without advice and guidance. This is where career counselling comes in. Career counselling may help people to identify a suitable vocation and career path. It can identify the environment in which a person is most likely to flourish. It is typically taken at an early stage in a person's career, by school leavers, sometimes alongside 'self-managed' counselling based on books providing practical guidance (particularly popular and useful is *What Color is your Parachute?* by Bolles and Bolles, of which a new edition is published every year). However, many take career counselling at different stages of their lives. People at a crossroads in their career, people who encounter a career crisis, and people who realize that they have made a poor career choice may all find career counselling useful. By adding an objective perspective, career counselling can reveal the full picture, and may show people their 'blind spots' and so can provide fresh insights and new directions, unleash hitherto unknown properties, reveal competencies that can be developed, and unveil hidden qualities. (Career counselling is discussed in more detail in Chapter 7.)

Box 3.1: Individual careers counselling

There are now numerous individual counsellors and small counselling agencies who specialize in offering career advice and direction, providing a personalized career counselling service. Individual career counselling needs to be tailor made, as advice is provided to each person according to their needs, and first and foremost, their personality. In addition to one-to-one counselling, firms typically do offer some form of psychometric or psychological assessment to guide clients through career choices.

For those interested in becoming an accredited career counsellor, see http://www.career-counselling-services.co.uk/.

If you are in the USA, for example, you can select a counsellor from https://www.global careercounsellor.com/

Other countries will have similar agencies, some focusing on early career, others on career change for a later career stage.

Typically, career counselling will offer a dual service – to individuals and to companies. Services for individuals will include: career guidance and career development programme for all ages; self-marketing support for people seeking their first job or for a job change; coaching in job search techniques; and workshops to increase personal effectiveness.

Services for employers may comprise: recruitment support (psychometric assessment services, staffing interviewing teams, etc.); career development, personal development, coaching and mentoring programs; solutions for 'square peg in round hole' situations; support during organizational restructuring; redundancy counselling and outplacement programmes for individuals or groups.

Some agencies are specific to certain parts of the population. For example, Career Transition Partnership is the official provider of the UK Armed Forces resettlement, servicing armed forces leavers with the transition to civilian life. In a complementary service, they support thousands of organizations looking to employ ex-service personnel. See https://www.ctp.org.uk/about-us/the-ctp.

For the student, an easy (and probably cheaper) choice of career counselling would be the local university career centre; most universities today have career centre or careers service, with options for career counselling and advice.

Studying individual careers

By the end of the 1990s, new career systems had appeared: boundaryless, multidirectional, and flexible (Sullivan & Baruch, 2009). Osterman (1996) said it all in the title of his book: *Broken Ladders*. Psychological contracts concerning the career one may expect to aspire to are agreed upon between organizations and employees. Diversity has ceased to be a slogan and has become a reality. Women have entered all types of jobs, but very soon discovered a glass ceiling, which was a strong phenomenon in the past (Morrison, 1982), but changed significantly (Sahoo & Lenka, 2016). Already by the end of the last century, however, that ceiling was showing signs of cracking, but only that (Altman et al., 2005). Similarly, there is much greater racial and ethnic diversity in the white-collar labour market than in the past. This change has occurred against a background of increased awareness of political correctness and equality issues, legislative sanctions and legal challenges to discrimination. On the other hand, age discrimination is still prevalent in many professional and occupational areas. Chapter 9 of this book provides an in-depth exploration of these issues.

Much of the current research on individual careers focuses on identifying what is a career from the individual view-point and how people approach their careers in the wider context of life. Each person has a career, a life story, a continuum of work and non-work experiences. Work experience is interwoven with other facets of life. Developmental processes take place along this road. People look for advancement, development and progress. The simplest and the most visible way is still via promotion through the organizational ranks.

The model proposed by Greenhaus et al. (2019; see Figure 3.1) offered a career management model, an individual-oriented approach. Greenhaus et al. put the individual at the centre of the model. They see the individual as needing to make a career choice (influenced mainly by family, and by educational and social institutions) and to conduct a career search, which presumably includes formal training. This stage is followed by the development of self-awareness, setting career goals and developing a strategy to reach these goals. Employing the strategy and a feedback loop provides the person with an evaluation of the suitability of the goal for their own needs and aspirations, and the level to which they can achieve the goals. As a consequence, people may revise their career goals, embark on an entirely new career, or even abandon a career completely. In this model the organizational role is very limited, and is restricted to the provision of information and support systems. An essential element for individuals is career goals – the terms in which they are set, the values they represent and the means to reach them. This old-style classical approach to careers focused on external measures, such as status and financial reward.

However, by the 1970s it was felt that career goals and the meaning of career success were much wider. Already some 50 years ago, it was suggested that a good manager is one who can balance role, home, and personal needs (Tranowieski, 1973). Five role characteristics were long associated with significance to individual careers: (i) conducting meaningful assignments, which would result in better inner feelings; (ii) achieving something of worth; (iii) learning new skills; (iv) developing competencies; and (v) freedom in the job (Renwich & Lawler, 1978). Along the same lines, career development may be lateral (Baruch, 2004b), and may not necessarily lead to higher authority and control (Guan et al., 2019). In this respect, the academic career model was one of the first to enable people to develop in their profession, gain recognition, reputation, and general career success, irrespective of their hierarchical progress (Baruch & Hall, 2004). The academic hierarchy scale is flat. Moreover, career progress does not follow a series of 'upward' movements. In a typical career progression in academia we may find a professor or a senior lecturer becoming a dean, research director or head of an examination board, and then returning to his or her research and teaching role after few years in the position (Baruch & Hall, 2004). Becoming an academic is a highly sought-after career for PhD graduates, but the field is very competitive with limits to growth in permanent positions (Etmanski, 2019).

Continuous learning and career adaptability

Learning and development at the individual level will have implications for and will be reflected at the organizational level. However, there is a difference between individual learning and organizational learning, where the latter is mediated by the former. In this respect, Kolb's work, as well as criticism of it, is useful for understanding the learning process (Kolb, 2014; Popper & Lipshitz, 2000). As Kolb posits, learning is a cyclical process. Organizational learning is not simple the aggregate learning of the individuals. In organizational terms, it is what is left in the 'organizational memory' and reflected later in practices and policies as a result.

Experiential learning was defined as 'the process whereby knowledge is created through the transformation of experience. Knowledge results from the combination of grasping and transforming experience' (Kolb, 1984, p. 41). Later, Kolb and Kolb (2005) offered a collection of six propositions to manifest the principle of experiential learning and its relevance and importance in learning, in particular within higher education. These are:

1. Learning is best conceived as a process, not in terms of outcomes.
2. All learning is relearning. Learning is best facilitated by a process that draws out the beliefs and ideas about a topic so that they can be examined, tested, and integrated with new, more refined ideas.
3. Learning requires the resolution of conflicts between dialectically opposed modes of adaptation to the world.
4. Learning is a holistic process of adaptation to the world.
5. Learning results from synergetic transactions between the person and the environment.
6. Learning is the process of creating knowledge.

All in all, learning, either within the education system, the workplace, or elsewhere, is critical for the individual in order to gain knowledge, understanding, and insights that will be instrumental for their career development. In particular, learning is critical for successful career adaptation (Tolentino et al., 2014). Career adaptability is a psychosocial resource required for managing career-related tasks, transitions, and events, and is a central construct in career construction theory (Savickas, 2013). The changing nature of careers requires individuals to adapt, develop, sometimes self-regulate their capacities, and adjust to new circumstances in order to sustain their career. A meta-analysis studying the four career adaptability dimensions (concern, control, curiosity, and confidence) identified the impact of career adaptability and outcomes such as job performance, job satisfaction, and turnover intentions (Rudolph et al., 2017). Career adaptability is strongly related to employability (Maree, 2017) – in order to be employable, one should be ready to and capable of adapting to new circumstances and life events – planned or unplanned.

Career success

'There are two tragedies in life. One is to lose your heart's desire. The other one is to gain it.'

G. B. Shaw

'There are two things to aim at in this life; first to get what you want; and, after that, to enjoy it. Only the wisest of mankind achieve the second.'

Logan Paersall Smith

We all want to achieve success, but the meaning of success is different for different people, and varies according to the circumstances. This section discusses the nature of career success, how it can have different meanings, and how it can be evaluated and measured.

To evaluate career success from the personal viewpoint one can refer either to objective, 'hard' measures (rank, income), or to subjective, 'soft' measures, mostly concerned with personal feelings of achievement and values (Ng et al., 2005; Spurk et al., 2019). The meaning of success will always be associated with personal, professional, and organizational objectives, and how far these have been accomplished. Following Marx's contention that the social circumstances in which the activity of individuals occurs condition their perception of the world in which they live, it is clear why career success will never be similar for all.

Objectives are derived also from the choice of career and the assumed progress in a particular vocation. As shown earlier, this starts with the general selection of the individual's life interests which are critical to career choice (Chapter 2). Making vocational choices depends on individual inclinations, aspirations, interests, and competencies, but this choice is also influenced by the family, education, and social institutions (Greenhaus et al., 2019). The criteria for evaluating success can be, first, reaching what you aimed for, and second, how far doing so helped to fulfil your needs. This takes us back to Shaw again: obtaining entrance to the profession, organization, or specific job you have always dreamed of does not necessarily mean that you will be happy or even satisfied with your career once you have achieved it (Berkelaar & Buzzanell, 2015). This sobering process is most apparent in jobs such as nursing, with a high proportion of nurses leaving the profession due to a combination of individual and organizational issues (Brunetto et al., 2016).

A pause for reflection

Objective or subjective career achievement

Think of two young men opting for a career in the army. One has set himself the goal of becoming a Captain. In the end he manages to reach the rank of Major. His friend set himself the target to become a Lieutenant-General. In the end he is promoted to Colonel.

The rank of the first is lower than that of the second, but the first one has exceeded his target whereas his friend has failed to achieve his.

Who has the greater success, the one who reached the higher rank or the one who surpassed his goal? Should success be measured externally or internally?

Derr's (1986) framework identified five measures for career success, contrasting with, or at least adding to, the traditional measures of career success. The three traditional measures are formal education, life-long employment with job security, and hierarchical progress. Derr's five dimensions are getting ahead, getting secure, getting high, getting free, and getting balanced.

Derr's dimensions may be illustrated as follows:

1. *Getting ahead*: motivation derives from the need to advance both in professional standing and up the organizational ladder.
2. *Getting secure*: having a solid position within the organization.
3. *Getting high*: being inspired by the nature and content of the work performed.
4. *Getting free*: being motivated by a need for autonomy and the ability to create one's own work environment.
5. *Getting balanced*: attaching equal or greater value to non-work interests.

A pause for reflection

How important are each of Derr's dimensions for you?

Try to put them in order of relevance for you.

How will these preferences manifest itself in the career you have chosen or will choose to pursue?

Novel contemporary careers frameworks presented later in this chapter, such as the *boundaryless*, the *intelligent*, the *kaleidoscope*, and the *post-corporate* frameworks, distinguish between individual and organizational elements, putting more emphasis on the individual role (and the *protean* career takes this trend to the extreme of placing the entire responsibility of career management on the individual). Later in the book we will see how the career ecosystem framework (Baruch, 2015) integrates individual, organizational, and contextual levels in a comprehensive manner.

The individual, as well as having the traditional need to be promoted, can perceive career success as a multi-level set of self-development targets. Examples are: gaining employability (replacing the security of the traditional 'job for life' concept); making lateral transitions for enrichment, rather than following the traditional route 'up the ladder'; undertaking self-management and entrepreneurship for those who wish to try new ventures outside the organization; and achieving a better and richer quality of life, reflected in the availability of alternative work arrangements and improved work–family balance. When the new psychological contract is 'signed', it confirms the mutual expectations of individual and organization, and enables people to look for higher meaning in life and employment.

For the organization, indications of an appropriate career system include the empowerment of people to become active participants in managing their careers. These indications are relevant in terms of career management (though not to the extreme where the organization withdraws from its roles; see Baruch, 1999 and Bagdadli & Gianecchini, 2019), investment in people (e.g. training, developmental processes), new career paths to replace the traditional pyramid type, flexibility in the management of people, and providing a better quality of life at work and in the wider context, reflected in work–family policies, a shorter working week, flexible working hours, and so on. The new psychological contract establishes the transition. Under such conditions a new partnership arises, based on a mature trust relationship. Table 3.2 presents the traditional, the 'new careerist', and the contemporary concepts for both individuals and organizations, against the related indicators of career success. It is important to balance individual and organizational perspectives when planning and managing careers (Baruch, 2006a).

> *'All men seek one: success or happiness. The only way to achieve true success is to express yourself completely in service to society. First have a definite, clear, practical ideal – a goal, objective. Second, have the necessary means to achieve your ends – wisdom, money materials, and methods. Third, adjust your means to that end.'*
>
> Aristotle, 384–322 BC (cited in Handy, 2007, p. 30)

Contemporary changes in individual thinking have caused many to distance themselves from this sociological, altruistic approach. Individual consciousness rather than belonging to the collective whole rules people's search in life (Wolfe, 1998).

Table 3.2   Career enablers – different perspectives

Traditional concepts	The 'New Careerist' (Derr's framework)	The Kaleidoscope's ABC	Contemporary-Individual	Contemporary-Organization
Formal education	Getting ahead	Authenticity	Self-development competencies	Empowerment
Lifelong employment, job security	Getting secure	Balance	Employability	Investment in people
Climbing up the ladder	Getting high	Challenge	Lateral transitions spiral movements	New or no career paths
	Getting free		Self-management; entrepreneurship	Flexibility

Traditional concepts	The 'New Careerist' (Derr's framework)	The Kaleidoscope's ABC	Contemporary-Individual	Contemporary-Organization
	Getting balanced		Quality of life, work-family balance	Alternative work arrangements, work-family policies, etc.
			New psychological contracts	
			Search for spiritual meaning based on individual consciousness	True, open partnership

Career success is a desired outcome for most individuals. However, for each individual the outcomes desired are different. In addition, people develop a set of desired outcomes, not a single aim. The measures that can be used to assess such desired outcomes and the extent to which they are reached are complex.

Commonly accepted measures are:

- *Advancement*: hierarchy, power, professionalism, reputation (status), but also autonomy, entrepreneurship, self-control.
- *Learning*: gaining new skills, abilities, competencies.
- *Physiological and survival*: money making (buying power), employability.
- *Psychological*: satisfaction, recognition, self-esteem, and self-actualization. To these we may add career resilience, in both meanings of resilience – toughness of spirit in confronting career crisis – and flexibility or pliability in adapting to ever-changing labour markets.

The reader will probably now recall the chapter on motivation in their organizational behaviour textbook. Indeed, the need to succeed in a career is a great motivator. The relative importance of motivators depends also on a variety of antecedents, such as demography (e.g. gender, religion) and attitudes (e.g. work role centrality – how important and central work is for one's life).

To evaluate an individual's progress or advancement within organizational boundaries, one starts from their first role in the organization. In analysing career success it was recognized that the entry stage has a strong impact on further career progress – in terms of time in the job, in the organization, and the highest position the individual is expected to reach (Forbes, 1987; Stuth & Jahn, 2020). This may be because individuals discover their unique aptitudes, abilities, and values, and these, in conjunction with socio-environmental influences, help them to establish their career goals. This influences their choice of employment, for example, type and culture of organization. Once employed, the degree to which employees fit in their new firms and the type of socialization used by those employers deferentially affects the implementation of their goals (Royle, 2015). Timing is also a factor, and the economic condition of society may influence future careers. Entering the labour market in a time of prosperity or recession can be influential too, though for high earners it is less critical (Altonji et al., 2016).

The first role is, however, only the first step in a long and winding road.

Ideal versus reality

To reach effective career resilience and employability, people need to acquire and maintain over time a set of competencies (abilities, know-how, skills) required for finding a job when necessary, wherever it may be (Blokker et al., 2019). Boundaries such as the firm, the profession, and international borders should play no significant role in the job search. Nevertheless, in practice, the idea is quite illusive, and it should be recognized that the idea of boundarylessness is metaphorical rather than absolute. Much occurs in internal markets, that is, lateral job moves within organizations are much easier to manage than cross-organizational moves, and organizations do not view job hopping favourably. Changing one's profession takes time and effort, and the formalization of qualifications means that it is not simple to swap jobs that require specific qualifications. (The litigious society in which we live forces organizations to hire people with the right qualifications, even though such qualifications do not necessarily guarantee that those who possess them have the right qualities). Notably, national borders pose real problems for people. Whereas some borders have become less crucial (the most vivid example is the EU borderless employment region), people from outside such larger communities, in particular those from less developed countries, face severe barriers to finding a job outside their own country. The UK suffered major upset in the labour market following Brexit, because it posed restrictions on the free movement of prospective employees in necessary occupations. For example, a person from outside Europe, even from the USA or Canada, has no automatic right to a work permit in European countries, and vice versa. People from less-developed countries may find their national qualifications are worthless or irrelevant in Europe. Thus the boundaryless ideal can rarely be utilized, being in part an oversimplification of a nice idea, replete with impractical terms.

Reality of serendipity

It should be remembered, though, that in many instances the career path people follow does not necessarily stem from their initial aspirations and career plans set in advance. As indicated earlier, unexpected events may force people to make unintended career moves. March and March (1977) went so far as to claim that career progress is (almost) random, that is, people progress according to opportunities which happen to be placed in their way (using the metaphor of career as a journey – *see* later in this book for the use of metaphors in career studies). This view should be taken as too one-sided – there is a role for planning, goal-setting and management of careers – for both individuals and organizations (Baruch, 2006a).

While serendipity does occur in life, it would be hard to base a theory solely on this factor. Nevertheless, in some occupations luck and chance may play a part. Political careers are highly susceptible to chance events according to individual and national circumstances. Serendipity plays a major role in other careers too (Bright et al., 2005), both managerial careers (Grimland et al., 2012) and rank-and-file jobs like drivers (Baruch, Wordsworth, Mills, & Wright, 2016). A combination of chance events and career stage can significantly influence certain professions, such as in academic careers when entry to the profession can coincide with a political chance event that will determine their prospect for the future (Kindsiko & Baruch, 2019).

Individual career concepts

Whyte's concept of an 'organization man' (1956), although outdated, is still relevant, for both men and women. This is the perspective that sees people as parts of the system in organizations, where they act like cogs in a machine and strive to climb up the ladder. However, many new forms of this concept have evolved, some of which even contradict organization man as the prevailing concept. Arthur et al. (1999) depicted the new type of careers in their book *The New Careers*. It seems that unaccustomed qualities are needed to sustain a post-modern career. There is less emphasis on stability, more on dynamism and openness. Career resilience is appreciated, and actually desired (Waterman et al., 1994) and required for career sustainability (Lengelle et al., 2017). People now look for 'employability' rather than lifelong commitment to one organization to sustain their careers, as the commitment has lost its original meaning of mutual relationship (Baruch, 1998a; Baruch & Rousseau, 2019). The next chapter will focus more on employability and its role in today's labour markets.

Career anchors: The development of a concept

The idea of career anchors was suggested by Schein (1978, 2012) and was further studied due to its prominence and relevance (e.g. Arnold et al., 2019; Gubler et al., 2015; Rodrigues et al., 2013). Career anchors are the perceived abilities, values, attitudes, and motives people have, which determine their career aspirations and direction. These self-perceived talents and qualities serve to guide, constrain, stabilize, reinforce, and develop people's careers.

The concept itself, and in particular its constituents – the anchors – have developed with time. Originally, Schein (1978) suggested five anchors, which are set out in Table 3.3. One problem with the initial set concerned the original sample from which the concept was developed: all were MBA graduates of a top US university (MIT). Schein increased the number of career anchors to eight by the 1980s, as presented in Table 3.3 (Schein, 1985). In my view, new anchors have emerged in the 21st century, and they should be added to the framework. Some may even replace some of the original anchors: among these new anchors I would include employability; work versus family balance and calling or spiritual purpose. Empirical studies generally support the idea of career anchors and their relevance for individual pursuit of careers. New studies, though, suggest to distinguish between entrepreneurship and creativity as two separate anchors, where empirical evidence support such separation as a better fit than that of the nine-construct model compared with the eight-construct model (Costigan et al., 2018; Danziger et al., 2008).

Table 3.3 Career anchors

	Schein 1978	Schein 1985	Early 21st Century, suggested by Baruch
Career anchors	Original five: Technical competencies Managerial competencies Security and stability Entrepreneurial/Creativity* Autonomy/independence	Additional three: Dedication to a cause (e.g. service) Pure challenge Lifestyle	Plus: Employability Work/family balance Calling/Spiritual purpose

Can be taken as two distinct anchors

Self-evaluation: Your career anchors

Can you identify your most prominent career anchor? Which of Schein's anchors does not really represent you or appeal to you? Can you list the eight anchors in descending order of importance for you?

Commitment and loyalty

The early work of Gouldner (1957) in the 1950s distinguished between 'cosmopolitans', people with a strong identification and with commitment to their profession, and 'locals', with strong identification with and commitment to their organizations. Gouldner went further to suggest that these commitments are orthogonal, that is, not necessarily associated or excluding each other. One person may be high 'cosmopolitan' and low 'local' (or vice versa), but people can also be high (or low) on both.

Multiple commitments

People need relationships, partnerships to rely upon, other parties to develop mutual commitment with. In the past, apart from the obvious spouse and family, the organization was the major entity people could identify with, feel part of, be loyal to, and in particular be committed to. The developments discussed in Chapter 1 show the destruction of people's ability to build on such relationships with organizations. From the individual's point of view, these developments may be associated with the rise of 'individual consciousness' mentioned earlier. Organizationally, they are associated with the competitiveness and financial orientation that changed secure relationships to bounded transactional relationships. So it is not surprising that there has been a clear decline in the level and importance of organizational commitment (Baruch, 1998a). What used to be a mutual bond between employees and employers has become more of a conditional attachment (Greenhalgh & Rosenblatt, 2010). Organizational commitment is lower in relation to new modes of work and new employment relationships, for example part-time employment, and has almost lost its meaning where multiple part-time work is involved. Albeit being perhaps less relevant, organizations still strive to improve level of organizational commitment amongst their employees for its role in improving employees' attitudes and performance (Kontoghiorghes, 2016; Riketta, 2002).

Nevertheless, people need a certain degree of commitment, and as a result we are witnessing the creation of multiple commitments to replace the traditional organizational commitment.

The multiple commitments people may have relate to the many domains of life that each person has, each comprising multiple constituencies.

1. *Work-related commitments*:
   a. Workplace commitments: to the organization; leader; team; department/unit; project (product); peers/colleagues; and so on.
   b. Commitments outside the workplace: to the union; profession, occupational association, and so on.
2. *Family-related commitments*: to spouse; children; parents (care of the elderly); others.
3. *Commitments in other life domains*: to country, friend, pet (and usually higher for a dog than a cat, and even less for a rabbit – according to the mutuality of the commitment), club, church (or any other religious institution), community, political involvement (e.g. political party), even to a house.
4. *Commitment to self*: time for self, hobbies/leisure activities.

In this book we focus on work-related commitments, but the reader should be aware of the limited perspective of this approach.

More than half a century after Gouldner's work, the focus of commitment and loyalty has moved from the organization to other constituencies. Such commitments may be to the work group, the leader, the business unit, the profession, the union, or generally the career (Klein et al., 2020). Further support for the idea that people have different sets of commitments was presented in a study of nurses' commitments. This identified four distinct commitments of nurses: commitment to the general NHS (the UK's National Health Service); to the organization (usually the specific hospital); to the work group; and occupational commitment (Baruch & Winkelmann-Gleed, 2002). Even career commitment is not necessarily a single construct. Another study, which constructed a measure for career commitment, identified a three-dimensional model of career commitment: career identity, career planning, and career resilience (Carson & Bedeian, 1994). A positive association was found between occupational prestige (or professional standing) and career commitment. Similarly, in examining the relationship between the construct of emotional intelligence and commitment constructs, a positive correlation ($r = 0.51$) was found with career commitment, but no correlation with organizational commitment (although a positive correlation of $r = 0.30$ was found between these two commitments) (Carson & Carson, 1998). The commitment systems may diverge or converge over time (Klein et al., 2020), when individual commitment 'portfolio' change in circumstances may cause commitment to split or converge across different commitment targets.

The theory behind multiple commitments emerges from the theory of social identity (Tajfel, 2010), which offers applicable insights into why individuals seek to identify with, and long to participate in, something meaningful, as partaking enhances their personal worth and self-belief. Members of an organization tend to apply the sociological categorization of the group or organization to define or transform the individual self. Thus, membership is linked to a deeper psychological process, and such processes end with feelings of commitment, loyalty, and trust (Ashforth & Mael, 1989).

For the professional, commitment may be to the profession: an academic scholar can move to another institution or university, but will stay within his or her scientific discipline; or a doctor can easily move to another hospital, but will remain a surgeon or an anaesthetist. For individuals, self-fulfilment can be achieved outside the organization or the realm of work, and within this realm, entrepreneurship may be more highly desired than being a good organizational citizen.

Box 3.2: Self-rating exercise: Where does your commitment lie?

Even as a student, you have several commitments, which it is hoped are developing. You can be committed to your university, to the school or department in which you are studying, to your lecturers, and of course to the discipline you have chosen. You will also have some commitment to the students' union, to your student societies, and so on. Are these all mutually exclusive? Can you identify a multiple commitments profile for yourself?

Constituency*	Commitment						
	Low						High
The university	1	2	3	4	5	6	7
The school/department	1	2	3	4	5	6	7
The lecturers	1	2	3	4	5	6	7
The discipline	1	2	3	4	5	6	7
The students' union	1	2	3	4	5	6	7
The society	1	2	3	4	5	6	7
Other:	1	2	3	4	5	6	7
Other:	1	2	3	4	5	6	7

Note: * These are all 'studying-related' constituencies, whereas your main commitment may lie with your family or partner

Where will your commitment lie in future?

This question is much harder to answer. As a graduate who will work in a particular profession, employed by one (or more) unique organizations, you will have many and varied commitments.

In the past, one of the strongest criticisms of MBA graduates was their tendency to leave organizations after a relatively short time, a tendency labelled 'job-hopping' (De Pasquale & Lange, 1971). Now that the nature of the employment relationship has changed significantly, a job-hopper may be perceived as a 'transitional developer', whereas it was previously regarded negatively. Today such moves are recognized as advantageous to both individuals and their employers, as wide experience can be gained and shared from such diversity (Direnzo & Greenhaus, 2011). Organizational mobility is associated with increased salary, in particular at early career stages (Lam et al., 2012).

At one time a person who had been made redundant would have carried the stigma of possibly being jobless for the rest of his or her working life. Today it is quite a common experience, and can be considered one of developmental and learning. However, long-term unemployment poses the risk of becoming permanently jobless (Amior & Manning, 2018). It is quite common for a person over 50 or 55 who has been made redundant to be unable to find an alternative, and never again enter the labour market.

The desert generation phenomenon

The discussion that follows is based on Baruch's (2003b) metaphorical depiction of transitional periods. One of the most amazing qualities of human beings is the ability to change, to develop, and to transform themselves. People learn – from their success, their failures, and even more importantly, from the experience of others. Such is the nature of individual development. However, we are also limited in our ability to adapt and respond to external changes, as much depends on the pace and depth of change. It is relatively easy to alter behaviour, more difficult to change beliefs, and almost impossible to swap values and mental frameworks. Some go so far as to claim that this limited ability is subject to the genetic make-up of human beings (Nicholson, 2000).

When their environment changes occur at a manageable pace, most people are able to adapt to the change or cope with it effectively. However, if what is needed is an all-encompassing change, requiring a totally new direction, with severe time restrictions, it is unlikely to be achieved without casualties. I will discuss here two examples of such a significant change in the nature of the 'rules of the game' in the management of people. These changes affected both individuals and organizations. The first shift has left many 'lost generation' employees behind and bewildered, in a situation analogous to that of the Israelites of the 'desert generation' in the Old Testament. The other one is taking place with the introduction of artificial intelligence (AI) and is sometimes labeled as the '4th industrial revolution' (Skilton & Hovsepian, 2017).

The first example is a story of a generation that experienced a breakdown of long-term employment expectations. To understand it, we can look at the story the Bible tells us about the members of the ancient Israelite tribe who were held in Egypt as slaves for about four hundred years. They were liberated under the leadership of Moses, by an act of God, and then left Egypt to return and conquer the Holy Land. Such a quest requires motivation, determination and the fighting spirit of sovereign, independent people. However, the behaviour of the Israelites, trapped in the mental attitudes of their former life, was very disappointing. They did not trust God and some even wanted to return to a life of slavery. God decided that they were to be left to perish in the desert while the next generation would be educated and raised as a free nation. Within 40 years, a totally different attitude, based on a changed set of values and beliefs, had developed. The people who perished were called the 'generation of the desert', or the 'desert generation'.

As organizations became 'lean and mean' (De Koeijer et al. 2014), new deals and different psychological contracts emerged (Rousseau, 1996). Subsequently, modern days' 'desert genera-tion' emerged (Baruch, 2003b) – people who were born, grew, and developed personally and professionally in a world where loyalty and commitment to the organization were the prevail-ing norm. Stable, long-term employment relationships with established career patterns were the rule. However, this old concept was fast disappearing, and for many, the new career con-cept was unimaginable.

The desert generation metaphor is limited; for example, the present generation has commit-ted no moral wrong. Change has emerged due to a combination of technological, economic, and political developments. Waiting for many years is not an option. The baby boomer genera-tion had the privilege of either managing those processes or have retired by now. Some remained in sectors, occupations, and professions that enable the 'good old days' framework to continue to function (mostly the public sector). The youngest, like generation X, Y and Z, those who grew into this situation, entered the labour market in a new era of industrial rela-tions. They do not expect too much commitment or loyalty from their employer. They are better equipped to cope with a labour market in a state of perpetual change, and with ongoing job insecurity. Since they have not experienced organizational and environmental stability, they will not wish to return to those 'good old days'. For current generations, the present realities of working life do not represent a new concept but just the way things are and always have been, in a similar way that the new generation of the Israelites experienced freedom. They were looking forward: born and educated as free people, with the clear goal of reaching the Promised Land, they would not long for the past or try to revive it. The special difficulties of young people are manifested in several studies on both sides of the Atlantic. Overall, different generations have different characteristics which require diverse approaches to their management (Kapoor & Solomon, 2011), as depicted in Figure 3.4.

The second example is that of the 4th industrial revolution (Schwab, 2017; Skilton & Hovsepian, 2017). This 4th revolution encompasses a range of technological developments, in particular robotics (for physical work) and AI (for cerebral work) that are anticipated to

Generation	Baby-boomers	Generation X	Generation Y	Generation Z
Typical position	Many have retired; others are either top managers or close to retirement	Established executives or late careers	Mid-career	Entry to the labor market
Stage	Phasing out	Struggling	New status quo	Volatility
Born in	1946–1965	1966–1980	1981–1994	1995+

Figure 3.4 Comparison of generations

fundamentally change society. One may expect some similarity with previous revolutions like the early Industrial Revolution, and more recently, the impact that electricity and digital technology had. AI may eliminate a significant share of the required workforce. It may create new generations of jobless people – consider, for example, those in transportation in a world when drivers are no longer needed.

Re-inventing one's career?

At a time of change there are many possible solutions to opt for. People are different and situations vary. A contingency approach is suggested here to identify different types of career orientations, and for each case a variety of solutions may be applied. Let us look at possible sub-groups of options for career change, distinguished by a two-dimensional framework: innovative versus traditional approach preference, and adaptive versus non-adaptive approach preference (Figure 3.5). For the desert generation there are four options:

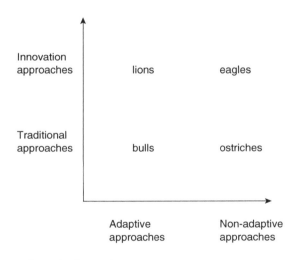

Figure 3.5   The desert generation – the four options

The ostriches: Those who cannot or are not willing to change mentally. They will perish, not necessarily literally, but as working people. They will cease to contribute to the society and the economy. Some of them will try to stick to old norms and paradigms ('It won't happen to me'), hiding their heads in the sand. People in this sub-group could become permanently unemployed, others may move around in a constant search for alternatives.

The lions: Those who can adapt and recuperate. They are the new breed of corporate middle managers, people with a real readiness and willingness for change, innovation, transformation. This sub-group is the source of the future generation of executives: as older age executives retire, they will form the new layer of leaders.

The bulls: Others will move into jobs and roles which retain some of the old norms, if not in competition in a different market, at least with the old-style career systems structure. Occupations such as teaching, even academia, some areas of the civil service, the army (a male-dominated environment), and nursing (traditionally a female-dominated environment) can still offer traditional career structures, although even some of the old ivory towers and fortresses have become competitive.

The eagles: At the other end of the spectrum, there are the entrepreneurs. They prefer to establish their own enterprises, to exploit new markets, through recognizing and grasping new opportunities. They will generally enjoy the rough and tumble of business life, and could encounter adventures as either entrepreneurs, creating new organizations, or as intrapreneurs, developing new ventures within their own organization.

Lessons

What is the proper approach for employers, how should organizations deal with the variety of sub-groups, in order to avoid losing the energy and motivation of a vast number of employees? How will organizations ensure that most will reach the productive and satisfactory work? And what may enable people to cope effectively with the changing environment, and the new era of employment relationships?

Implications for individuals

To borrow a Freudian concept, people can adopt several ways to deal with crises and threats. Withdrawal or denial may lead people to a track similar to that of the Biblical desert generation, though, in this era of the welfare state, not literally. Transference and sublimation can help people to 'fly high', to use the wings of their imagination and create their own promised land.

Those wishing to keep their present job should try to become indispensable to their organization, to build knowledge and skills, and excel in their performance. For example, they may make sure that they are occupied in more than one activity, so will always be engaged in one project or another. If, however, they are ready and willing to keep an eye on outside opportunities, they should develop networks, keep and nourish contacts with other organizations, suppliers, customers, and so on. These may turn out to be the next employer or contractor who hires their services.

For others the advice could be to develop a career portfolio, to be involved in a range of activities, perhaps to be part of a virtual organization. People should be prepared to act within a wider range of opportunities and boundaries and see the globe rather than their local environment as their field of operation. Of great importance is the ability to use technology, especially IT (by, e.g., developing their IT competence). Above all, the advice for the future careerist is: be brave and face reality.

A pause for reflection

What can and should organizations do to help and promote positive development, and at the same time to identify and prevent negative deterioration?

Implications for organizations

Turbulence and turmoil characterize many processes of organizational change.

Firms around the world try to reinvent their structures, processes, and strategies. Successful transformation is not guaranteed. Many firms failed in achieving success with these challenges. It is inappropriate to refer to all people whose skills are becoming redundant as a coherent group. The four sub-groups depicted above call for a strategic contingency approach that bears in mind the key factor too often neglected in such changes: the human aspect of attitudes, beliefs, and values, which are the building blocks of organizational culture. Revolutions have always resulted in casualties, and many have failed. What can be done then, on the organizational side? What advice may be offered?

Organizational HRM should be able to distinguish those more likely to perish and those who possess the qualities needed to survive. Different people have different career aspirations and 'motivational fit', and the use of the right approach may draw the line between anxiety and achievement when using both emotional and motivational control mechanisms (Kanfer & Heggestad, 1997). Proactive personality and self-control are predictors of career success (Converse et al., 2012).

Organizations should encourage learning and enable options for intrapreneurship (Parker, 2011). There are different ways to get the best out of people. Sometimes it may be necessary to outsource activities and operations, using 'out-of-the-box' strategies, for example, rehire former employees, which may prove worthy practice (Keller et al., 2020). If an organization has to make people redundant, it should apply best practice, to maintain good relations with both those who have to leave and the survivors. Above all, organizations must be fair and realistic with their people. Cliché or not, people are still the most important and valuable asset of any organization. There is further discussion of the organizational implications in the following chapters.

Boundaryless, intelligent, kaleidoscope, and post-corporate careers and career construction theory

The boundaryless career

The concept of the boundaryless career, as initially understood, is the lack of being bounded into a single work-related constellation, in particular to a single organization (DeFillippi & Arthur, 1994), and when multiple trajectories can be followed in pursuing a career (Baruch, 2004b). It has gained significant attention in the career literature (Arthur, 2014). The core idea is that careers can be viewed as boundaryless in a similar way that the borders between organizations and work environments become blurred (Ashkenas et al., 1995). Despite the broadness of its meaning (Arthur & Rousseau, 1996), it had been typically referred to quite narrowly (Briscoe et al., 2006; Sullivan & Arthur, 2006). Simply equating boundarylessness to moves across organizational boundaries is too simplistic and would not justify the attention the concept enjoyed. Even a geographical move does not always mean true boundary crossing because not all global careers are boundaryless, and certainly not all boundary crossings are global career moves (Baruch & Reis, 2016).

Further, the concept was challenged by Inkson et al. (2012), suggesting that in reality boundaries persist. Further, Rodrigues and Guest (2010) challenged the concept too, and later provided evidence to suggest that careers are even more restricted than in the past (Rodrigues et al., 2013). The meaning of the term has been recalibrated and refined over time. The nature of boundarylessness was considered in terms of mental preparedness of career actors to be resilient in their choices and expectations so they are able to adapt to environmental contingencies (Baruch, 2006a; Sullivan & Arthur, 2006). Preparedness to make a move even if not personally convenient is not the same as actual movement. Empirical work supported a two-dimensional structure of boundarylessness: mental preparedness and actual physical mobility (Briscoe et al., 2006). Therefore, boundaryless career encompasses both physical and psychological mobility (Lazarova & Taylor, 2009; Sullivan & Arthur, 2006), as well as other boundaries – sector, vocation, and so on. Career actors can be classified according to their position within these dimensions. Others prefer to focus on physical mobility (Greenhaus, Callanan & DiRenzo, 2008). Overall, boundaries are an inherent attribute of organizational and professional systems, and crossing boundaries is an integral part of contemporary careers.

Intelligent careers

DeFillippi and Arthur (1994) were the first to use the 'know why, know how, and know whom' classification as a set of career competencies, introducing these as the three elements of the intelligent career. Further studies indicate the relevance of the framework to understand careers and how to reach success in careers (Arthur et al., 1995; Arthur et al., 2016). Know why relates to aspirations and underpinning values, including ethical values (or lack of them). Knowing how is the skills, abilities and competencies (e.g. mathematical competencies) that enable people to perform well. Knowing whom relates to the contacts and relationship that people develop with others, in particular networking. On the relevance of 'know whom one can learn from the question:

Can one become president of the USA without the support of the Freemasonry network? (Rumour has it that Bill Clinton was a rare exception.) The ability to collaborate with a prominent leader, businessman, thinker, or politician can be crucial in making an impact. Mentoring offers another way of networking. (For more on mentoring see Chapter 7.)

The intelligent careers triad of competencies

- *Know why*: Values, attitudes, internal needs (motivation), identity; what motivates people to choose (and remain in) a certain career, job, and lifestyle.
- *Knowing how*: What comprises career competencies: skills, expertise, capabilities; tacit and explicit knowledge; and experience that enables high-quality performance.
- *Knowing whom*: Networking, connections, relationships.

The intelligent career framework was later elaborated by Jones and DeFillippi (1996), and this enlarged framework is presented in Table 3.4. Table 3.4 enhances Arthur and DeFillippi's original framework of know why, how, and whom by anchoring a person's career in its context. Why, how, and whom are primarily individual assets of motivation, skills, and relationships. Yet, individual careers evolve in specific contexts – which have spatial, temporal, and historical dimensions. Knowing where, when, and what are important in placing careers in their geographic, temporal, and historical contexts. As for 'knowing where', it is tough to succeed in the film world if one is not located in Hollywood, just as it is harder to succeed in high-technology if one is not collocated with a group of firms in Silicon Valley or Route 128 in the USA or in Slough in the UK. 'Knowing when' taps into industry life cycles that shape career moves – the dot.com bubble and its bursting had substantial effects on programming careers and career moves. 'Knowing what' defines the larger institutional rules by which careers are shaped. The rules of the game are more distinct in banking than they are in high-technology – from the dress code and a variety of interactional norms to the different criteria of success and how it should be measured.

Table 3.4 Intelligent career competencies, strategies, and challenges

Competencies	Strategies	Challenges
Knowing What: opportunities, threats, and requirements.	* Know the industry and its criteria for success * Cultivate your reputation: quick but quality work, excellent technical skills and good work attitude * Use industry savvy to win opportunities	* Remain "employed" and reduce variability in income * Adapt to bouts of frenetic activity and involuntary unemployment * Leverage your reputation to gain jobs
Knowing Why: meaning, motives, and values.	* Pursue your passion * Commit to your craft * Know what you value	* Maintain passion and commitment without burning out * Balance career and family

(Continued)

Table 3.4   (Continued)

Competencies	Strategies	Challenges
Knowing Where: entering, training and advancing.	* Enter, train and advance to the industry core	* Spot and cultivate opportunities that improve your skills and propel your career forward * Avoid "dead-end" projects
Knowing Whom: relationships based on social capital and attraction.	* Use social capital and personal charm	* Be both strategic and genuine in relationships
Knowing How: technical and collaborative skills.	* Hone your technical skills * Train cross-functionally * Develop and articulate your vision	* Evade commodity status by creating idiosyncratic value * Avoid obsolescence in a rapidly changing market
Knowing When: timing of choices and activities.	* Move on before you're trapped in a role or status * Break the other's frame of reference to move on * Get ready to get lucky	* Extend versus exploit skills * Synchronize projects and passion

Source: Adapted from Jones & DeFillippi, 1996, p. 91

Critical perspective on the intelligent career

The intelligent career concept assumes equity and honest transparency in career management decision making, a meritocracy in principle. In reality, political gaming and other considerations are influential in careers decisions such as promotion. To succeed in a hierarchical system, people should also be politically savvy. The role of personal values is important – and standing for your values might mean a risk of being victimized under corrupt systems, nepotism, and favouritism.

Finally, a related framework to the intelligent career is career signalling (Harris et al., 2015), which involves sending out messages about themselves in the context of careers. Individuals can indicate to their immediate and wider environments their career aspirations, intentions and directions. In making themselves visible in the wider community that may have an interest in them or in which they may have a possible impact, individuals develop their 'brand' via tools like LinkedIn, having a 'signature' to represent them when applying for a position. When on a job hunt, a CV and covering letter are the basic tools. They will be followed or supported by a selection interview, a meeting with relevant people, a conference, a performance review, and so on. The aim of the signals is to convey to others what the person has achieved in the past or is capable of achieving in the future, what they are doing now, and most importantly, their aspirations, what they wish and intend to do.

A pause for reflection

What if you have an opportunity to present yourself to a prospect future employer or recruiter, and you have one minute to tell them about yourself and why it would be great for them to hire you (not why it would be great for you to work for them!)? Did you prepare and rehearse a short speech for that purpose – or will you find yourself out of words? As we never know what chance will present us with, it could be a worthwhile idea to plan such a speech.

The kaleidoscope career

Mainiero and Sullivan's (2006) kaleidoscope career framework suggests that 'like a kaleidoscope that produces changing patterns when the tube is rotated and its glass chips fall into new arrangements, [individuals] shift the pattern of their careers by rotating different aspects of their lives to arrange roles and relationships in new ways' (2006, p. 106). The three kaleidoscope career mirrors are:

- *authenticity*, which refers to being true to oneself in the midst of the constant interplay between personal development and work and non-work issues
- *balance*, which refers to making decisions so that the different aspects of one's life, both of work and of non-work, form a coherent whole
- *challenge*, which refers to engaging in activities that allow the individual to demonstrate responsibility, control, and autonomy while learning and growing.

Empirical studies lend support for the relevance of this framework, in particular to understand gendered careers and generational differences (e.g. Sullivan et al., 2009; Mainiero & Gibson, 2018).

The kaleidoscope career was mostly addressing women opting out, yet women can also opt in, not just looking for balance but for authenticity, blending it with challenges continuing into mid-career. Authenticity was a powerful theme throughout women's careers (Elley-Brown et al., 2018). Changes came at a later stage, where women tend to have a stronger tendency to 'lean back' when their desire for authenticity became subjugated by their need for balance (Elley-Brown et al., 2018). It should be understood that the kaleidoscope career is not necessarily a chosen form or pattern, because the choices made may follow from an imposed and unpredictable turn of events. Organizations that wish to enable their members, men and women, to pursue their authenticity have to balance it bearing in mind that if each will follow their will, it might lead to chaotic, possibly dysfunctional human resource systems (Baruch & Vardi, 2016).

The post-corporate career

A general perception of the current labour market is that this is the era of the post-corporate career, with both the individual and the organization being in a time of transition. Peiperl and Baruch (1997) have considered past and current career models and set out a vision of future careers that differs from the past in one primary way: the existence of horizontal links that transcend geographic and organizational boundaries. As these links continue to grow, they will provide more opportunity and flexibility than were ever available under the previous systems – for those who have the knowledge and skills to take advantage of them. There is further discussion of the post-corporate career in Chapter 5.

Career construction theory

The career construction theory suggests that individuals construct themselves and their careers through the interpretive and interpersonal processes (Savickas, 2013). This influences, sometimes dictates, their vocational behaviour path, and helps them to make meaning of their careers. This theory views careers from a contextualist perspective, when progress and growth are driven by adaptation to the environment. Individuals plan and manage their careers through both personal and social constructionism. People make themselves into who they are through complex phases and multi-layered processes throughout life. This self-construction is done by three central perspectives: self as actor, self as agent, and self as author, when people are developed by life and work experiences.

How to reinvent and resurrect one's own career

Investment in the self, improving one's employability, acquiring updated competencies, and good networking are key for successful transition to a new career direction. Training and formal education are one clear route. Other life and job experiences will be essential to enable the transition.

Strategies

Which strategies can people use in order to gain career success, in particular external career success such as higher income and progress towards a better position?

Greenhaus, Callanan, and Godshalk (2019, p. 132) offered a framework for analysing individual career strategies, that is, the strategies people use to enhance their careers, to develop and make progress. They listed the following strategies:

1. Attaining competency in the current job
2. Putting in extended hours
3. Developing new skills
4. Developing new opportunities at work
5. Attaining a mentor
6. Building one's image and reputation
7. Engaging in organizational politics.

As will be demonstrated in Chapter 8, this framework is useful but US-biased. In other countries, different strategies will have different relevance or impact.

Let us examine each strategy in turn.

1. Attaining competency in the current job

This strategy emphasizes efficiency and effectiveness in job performance. A person who gets results will be successful, be promoted, and will gain more income. The practice of performance related payment is based on this concept.

It is clear that delivering results will be a prerequisite for promotion and success, but is not necessarily sufficient in all cases. Such a strategy will certainly help in the lower echelons of the organization, but later will have to be supported by further strategies.

2. Putting in extended hours

Investment in the job, such as energy, long working hours, and emotion shows commitment and loyalty to the organization or the project, and can improve performance. Extended work involvement may help also in getting better career results. Such a strategy, warned Greenhaus et al., may backfire as a person might lose their work–life balance.

3. Developing new skills

This strategy focuses on acquiring new skills, competences, and abilities, thus enhancing the know-how component of the intelligent career (Arthur et al., 1995). Again, this is an indirect way to improve job performance, as well as generating a portfolio that will enable the individual to gain further appointments (i.e. jobs that require certain knowledge, skills. and qualifications).

4. Developing new opportunities at work

A set of strategies designed to increase career options, mostly concerned with creating contact with organizational decision makers. Such strategies can be visibility and exposure. Visibility is being able to approach top management, therefore gaining an understanding of the require-ments for promotion; exposure is being seen by top management, therefore gaining recognition and sponsorship.

5. Attaining a mentor

Finding (or having the organization appoint for you) a mentor can be a great career move – as long as the mentor is indeed successful in both coaching and promoting the protégé. Such a relationship can be beneficial also to the mentor, but contains some risk for both individuals and organizations (see further in Chapter 7), if the relationship does not develop in the right direction. This strategy does not need to be restricted to a specific mentor, as other supportive alliances can be formed.

6. Building one's image and reputation

Conveying an image of and reputation for success, by external 'public relations' and appear-ance. This strategy resembles the idea of career signalling – see the discussion earlier in this chapter for elaboration.

7. Engaging in organizational politics

Being very positive towards bosses and organizational representatives. This can take the form of flattering, supporting organizational policy and practice, and backing organizational rules rather than complaining. Forming coalitions and cliques as part of opportunistic networking is also political. An example of the extreme opposite to such an approach is whistleblowing.

In choosing a strategy, one should bear in mind several points. First, the strategy should match one's own personality, for example, a very introverted person may be better to focus on competence in the job and skill development, whereas an extrovert may be better off working on image building. Also, it is rarely efficient to apply a single strategy – a combination should be sought.

Seibert et al. (2001) added a proactive behaviour aspect to the Greenhaus et al. (2019) framework while Crant (2000) provided an integrated review of the research on proactive behaviour in organizations. Crant defined proactive behaviour as 'taking [the] initiative in improving current circumstances or creating new ones; it involves challenging the status quo rather than passively adapting to present conditions' (p. 436). Seibert et al. also provided a further detailed classification of career proactive behaviour, identifying four career-related proactive behaviours: voice, innovation, political initiative, and career initiative. Therefore there is a certain overlap with the Greenhaus et al. framework. In fact, all seven strategies are concerned with individual proactivity. Organizations need to make sure that the right people, not necessarily the outspoken people, are given the right opportunities.

Education

Associated with the second strategy is wider skills development, that is, not merely a short training course to acquire specific competencies, but the wider context of education. Education is perhaps the single most important factor in determining whether a person will obtain a managerial position. In some countries (see Chapter 8), the degree obtained and, even more, the type of university attended, will have an overwhelming impact on a person's future career. A first degree is a common requirement for any substantial position, in particular as the percentage of university graduates is constantly growing. Furthermore, to gain access to the higher echelons of organizations, a degree in management, in particular an MBA, is increasingly becoming the norm. A master's level degree can also help graduates in changing direction (see Box 3.3 for the impact of an MBA). It is not just the MBA which yields positive career outcomes for graduates. Many now choose to study for a specialized management degree, such as an MSc or MA in marketing, accountancy, HRM, and so on.

People with no formal education may undertake professional training or even as a 'mature student' may enroll on a first-degree course. Other options are apprenticeship programmes (quite often used in Germany), on-the-job training, and government programmes to provide vocational qualifications.

Box 3.3: Education and career: To MBA or not to MBA?

Good question.

What does an MBA degree contribute to the career prospects of a graduate? Studying for an MBA requires a huge investment in terms of time, money, and dedication (an MBA in the USA can easily cost some $30,000–50,000, and in top places like Harvard it would be over $100,000 a year). The question is: is it worth it? What are the possible benefits of an MBA in terms of career development? Should employers encourage their managers to embark on this route? Should they look to recruit from the pool of MBA graduates? An MBA helps individuals to gain better competencies and greater self-efficacy from their studies (Baruch & Peiperl, 2000b), and self-efficacy is commonly perceived to lead to higher performance.

An MBA is directed at improving managerial competencies. In part, an MBA is becoming almost a prerequisite for managerial roles in certain industries. However, the costs are substantial, in time and money invested, in additional stress levels, and loss in terms of work (either because one leaves the labour market for a full-time study programme, or because one has to divide one's time and show marked dedication by combining work with a part-time MBA). For managerial roles in some professional sectors an MBA would not be an advantage, and the same is true for those who have already studied for a management first degree. In some organizations, an MBA graduate might become a job-hopper (De Pasquale & Lange, 1971), although later evidence indicates that this is not necessarily the case (Baruch, 2009; Dougherty, Dreher, & Whitely, 1993).

When considering whether or not to undertake an MBA, people should consider the cost as well as the prospective benefits for their career (Baruch, 2009). Evidence suggests there are positive outcomes, but there are also possible pitfalls like being over-qualified, and the investment required of individuals and organizations must be evaluated (Baruch & Peiperl, 2000b).

Career inspiration and aspiration

The banal question usually addressed to children, 'What do you want to be when you grow up?', is replaced in the job interview with, 'What are your long-terms plans?'. As depicted in Figure 3.6, without a clear direction we will not reach our aim. Of course, having a clear aim and direction does not mean people will manage to reach them. These are conditional, but not sufficient.

A key question in job interviews is, 'What would you wish to be known for ten years from now?'. The answer could make or break the prospects of a candidate hoping to embark on a promising career in a top institution, even if the other signals indicate the existence of other essential ingredients (e.g. competencies). Perhaps signalling demonstrates both the level and the direction of motivation. If the organization needs these, all that is left to see is the person's prospects of fulfilling the promise. The next stage in the selection process is to see whether the person is capable of fulfilling this via personal qualities and competencies (see the parallel with know why and know how). Finally, the political issues of whom you know and what can you bring in will prove to be decisive.

SELF-ANALYSIS EXERCISE

When you prepare for a job interview, can you demonstrate your level on the three 'knows' in the intelligent career?

   Remember that the organization will look at all of these, as well as at you fit with their culture.

- Alice: Would you tell me, please, which way I ought to go from here?
- The cat: That depends a good deal on where you want to go.
- Alice: I don't much care where...
- The cat: Then it does not matter which way you go...

Carroll, Lewis. *Alice's Adventures in Wonderland*. London: Macmillan, 1865

Figure 3.6   A sense of direction

Summary

This chapter summarized the concept of individual careers and career models. It covered models of individual career development, such as the protean career, and innovative career concepts (such as intelligent, kaleidoscope, post-corporate, and boundaryless careers). The chapter critically analyses the notion of career success and introduced the metaphoric model of the desert generation phenomenon. The chapter ended with advice on reinventing and resurrecting one's own career.

KEY TERMS

Boundaryless careers

Career success

Intelligent careers

Kaleidoscope careers

Post-corporate career

The desert generation

DISCUSSION QUESTIONS

LESSONS AND FOOD FOR THOUGHT

1. *For the working student*: Is there a career system in your organization? Does this career system match the individual needs presented in this chapter?

    Does this career system recognize the variety of contingencies, the variety within the labour market? Does it permit flexibility in the management of people?

2. *If you aim to become an HR consultant*: What career advice could you, a consultant, offer organizations or individual people, managers, and executives?

    How prepared are you to provide advice to people seeking career counselling?

    Which career models do you use to realize people's needs?

    What would be your advice for individuals wishing to embark on a new career (a second career, a career break, a career change)?

    How do you identify people's career anchors, how do you point out a fruitful direction in life for bewildered people going astray in the modern work environment?

3. *For the student*: What were your career aspirations at the age of ... 5 ... 15 ... now? Are you proactive or reactive in reaching your career goals? Where would you place yourself in terms of Schein's career anchors? What kind of career would best fit your needs, aspirations and competencies?

Employability, Sustainability, and Entrepreneurship

4

LEARNING OBJECTIVES

After reading this chapter you should be able to:

- Identify the meaning of employability and its role in contemporary careers
- Understand how employability can be developed and help career sustainability
- Recognize employability as a future commodity in the global labour market
- Explore entrepreneurship as a viable and promising career path

Chapter outline

Introduction

In this chapter we focus on employability and sustainable careers. We will also cover entrepreneurial careers as viable career paths, and how to deal with internal and external inputs to careers, as well as how to benefit or positively exploit life events to lead a successful career. Last, we will introduce the process of phasing out of the labour market – retirement or other options. Students may be less interested in this career stage, being themselves at the earlier stage, but gaining a comprehensive view of the full work–life cycle is important in gaining a full perspective of individual careers.

Employability

As labour markets become dynamic and fluid, careers are less stable, and many career transitions take place. When there is lack of stable and secured employment in the corporate world, people cannot depend upon their current employer to unconditionally provide them with employment. They have to take responsibility for achieving their own sustainable career. The new currency in the labour market, then, is employability: the ability to independently find a job as and when necessary, whether being forced to leave a job or because one chooses to leave a job. Employability is determined by two factors: individual perception of the self; and the status of the labour market, where from an economic perspective, employability depends on labour supply versus labour demand.

The concept of employability continues to attract attention from both academics and practitioners. There is growing literature that focuses on the way people interpret their positioning in the labour market in terms of how reliable their employment condition is (Artess et al., 2017). Within the study of careers, employability is typically used as the perception of an individual's capability of finding a job (Rothwell & Arnold, 2007). Significant work has been devoted to the study of graduates' employability and the role of employability within national and global labour markets.

Employability means more than simply an ability to gain employment when needed. Just because a person studies (e.g. for a university degree), this does not mean automatic employability. Some qualifications may not guarantee future jobs. Graduates might become over-qualified and unable to find a suitable job. Nevertheless, without learning and developing, no one will find a job, and qualifications are required in line with the prestige of specific careers. Continuous learning is critical for having a sustainable career (Heslin, Keating, & Ashford, 2020), and this should last throughout the full period of working life. A combination of motivation, knowledge, experience, attitude towards work and life (e.g. resilience), and in particular the ability and will to learn and develop, can generate employability. Employability starts with getting a job, and continues with progress throughout the individual's career.

For individuals, employability is a frame of mind – employability is a perception of the individual, the belief that they can find new job, post, career, if needed (Fugate & Kinicki, 2008). It is also what other people may think of you – do they think that you will be able to be employed? But this is not a hard fact. Employability depends on circumstances. The COVID-19 pandemic is a unique example how people who thought they were very much employable found themselves out of the labour market for long periods.

Employability is a psychosocial construct and 'a constellation of individual differences that predispose employees to (pro)actively adapt to their work and career environments' (Fugate & Kinicki, 2008, p. 504). Fugate and Kinicki proposed a five-factor dimension of dispositional employability: openness to change at work; work and career resilience; work and career pro-activity; career motivation; and work identity. Those who have developed themselves along these dimensions have the best prospects of a sustained career, backed by a strong sense of employability.

Other definitions of employability can be more precise, like Rothwell and Arnold (2007) who consider employability as 'the ability to keep the job one has or to get the job one desires'. Alternatively, Hillage and Pollard's (1998, p. 12) definition is: 'Employability is about the capability to move self-sufficiently within the labour market to realise potential through sustainable employment.' The UK's Higher Education Academy (Pegg et al., 2012) suggested that employability is 'a set of achievements, skills, understandings and personal attributes that make graduates more likely to gain employment and be successful in their chosen occupations, which benefits themselves, the workforce, the community and the economy'. This last definition includes both competence and attitudes, and refers to the role of employability beyond the individual perspective.

The perception of employability depends to a large extent on what people may or may not attribute to themselves. In particular, factors like competence, knowledge and skills, capacity, and will for learning and development, and the understanding of the labour market (e.g. how to conduct effective job searches) are critical. Further, the general ability to plan and manage one's career, having career resilience, and strong self-efficacy, at both personal and professional level, help improve employability. The labour market can be internal within an organization, external at the level of country or region, or global. Employability in terms of relationship to the labour market also includes the contacts and networks that can be critical for learning where opportunities exist and eventually attaining a job. Often jobs that need to be filled are not advertised at all, or are communicated to very few. In the case of high-level positions in organizations, many if not most of the vacant jobs are filtered through the services of headhunters.

When promoting employability, there can be certain advantages for employers too: investing in employees, as the 'most important asset of the organization', will be worthwhile in the long term, as this will enhance employees' capacity and satisfaction. It may help in time of need for functional and numerical flexibility (Valverde et al., 2000), and it can be part of general strategic plan for future management (Ghoshal et al., 1999). Yet, the firm and the employees do not need to be fighting each other; rather, they may share the vision for a better future, where employable employees may leave if they wish so – but why would they wish so if their employer invested in them and considered them as a highly praised asset? There is also a paradox in expecting employers to invest in the employability of their employees. Why would they prepare them for a move to a competitor? Exploring employers' attitudes about employability, this view was confirmed by Baruch (2001a), when HR managers questioned the need for investment in generic skills and competence (compared with firm-specific skills).

Employability is not a guarantee for employment. Having a perception of employability does not necessarily result in an actual employment, which Thijssen et al. (2008) call *work transition*. They refer to two required transition conditions: individual conditions related to career competencies, such as career planning and job-efficient search methods; and contextual conditions, such as the labour-market demand, regulations, and company support.

Apart from the above, it might be that the perception individuals have about their employability is wrong or unfounded. How valid the perception of employability is depends on reality: people may over-estimate the value of their skills and competence, or misunderstand the actual level of demand for their work in the labour market. Further, being employable refers to a desired position, whereas in certain sectors, in particular the gig-economy, jobs can be found but do not necessarily allow for self-development and autonomy (Kost, Fieseler, & Wong, 2020).

How to develop employability?

To develop employability it is important to realize that it is a multidimensional construct, and is influenced by myriad factors (Van der Heijde & Van der Heijden, 2006). Employability may be best considered from a competence-based approach, which was developed under the principles of the resource-based view of the firm (Barney, 1991, 2001).

Employability career aspects include physical suitability, cognitive suitability, career development, learning, de-specialization, flexibility, adaptation to (fast) changes, and mobility. This was suggested by Van der Heijde and Van der Heijden (2006), who listed four key issues that would allow for the understanding of employability and its role in contemporary labour markets. First, they suggest that employability is advantageous for both career outcomes and firm outcomes, thereby connecting two levels of analysis – individual and organizational. They did not refer to a national level of analysis, which would mean a lower level of vulnerability to unemployment in countries where the population benefits from high employability. Indeed, employability is important for national competitiveness (Wilton, 2008). Second, at the employee level, employ-ability is advantageous for both present performance on the job as well as career outcomes (long-term performance, implying the process of adaptation and learning). Third, besides adap-tive behaviour, employability may contain personal elements such as personality, attitudes, motivation, and ability. As an example, motivation might mean readiness to comply with a culture of 24/7 and blurred boundaries between work and home (Huws et al., 2018). The fourth issue highlights the nature of employability in its representation of a combination or blend of specific and more generic competence.

Van der Heijde and Van der Heijden (2006) further developed their framework by identify-ing five dimensions of employability:

1. Occupational expertise, which constitutes a substantial element of employability.
2. Adaptation mode of anticipation and optimization, a proactive aspect.
3. Personal flexibility, a more reactive aspect.
4. Corporate sense, being engaged as members of the team, having a certain identification with their organization – its goals and values.
5. Balance – between own interests and employers' interests. This is when both parties, the employee and the employer, balance their investments and profits.

While 1 is the basic foundation for the ability to acquire new job, others are important and complementary. For example, both 2 and 3 relate to adapting to changes and developments at a job-content level and at higher levels – like whole career. The 4 and 5 reflect on the need to position employability also at the corporate level, at least at the relationship between the employee and the employer. This relates to the psychological contract, as discussed in earlier chapters.

How to test your employability?

Some measures for employability are general whereas others were specifically designed for students (Rothwell et al., 2009). Students can use such measures for self-evaluation of their employability (see Box 4.1), based on the framework that encompasses three dimensions. The measure by Rothwell et al. (2009) suggest that employability covers all these subcategories of employability. The student may use the items listed in Box 4.1 for a self-test of overall perceived employability. The ultimate test for actual employability is conducting a job search, even when not looking for a new job. To estimate the more commonly referred to thinking of employability, the employability perception can be measured too. Rothwell and Arnold (2007) offer a succinct way for evaluation of self-perceived employability. In Box 4.1 you can see a general measure and a measure that fits well for students too. These are measures for the perception of individuals about their employability prospects. For the full set of items and how they were validated, see Rothwell and Arnold (2007), Rothwell et al. (2008), and Rothwell et al. (2009).

Box 4.1: Test your perceived employability

How will you check whether or not you gained employability, working for your present employer? The practical answer should be of concern to HR managers who believe in employability as a share of the deal the organization has to provide: the ultimate way to check one's own employability is to apply for a different job! This way the person will know whether they can indeed be easily employed. The peril of this exercise, for the present organization, is that the 'test' can be so successful that the employee will decide to accept a job offer. One example is revealing the risks and opportunities in career systems: in a workshop conducted in a leading business school for bank executives, about half (all mid- or senior-level managers) admitted that during the last year they had applied for different jobs elsewhere, not intending to accept the offer but just to see if they would be successful in being offered the job. Of course, the executives participating in the training were still employed by the bank. We cannot know how many others had tried and succeeded in the test, and had already left.

Can you quantify the level of your perceived employability?

The following items fit for the wider population for such an evaluation:

- I have good prospects in this organization because my employer values my personal contribution.
- I can use my professional networks and business contacts to develop my career.
- People who do the same job as me who work in this organization are valued highly.
- People who do a job like mine in organizations similar to the one I presently work for are in high demand by other organizations.
- People with my kind of job-related experience are very highly valued in their organization as well as outside the type of organization they have previously worked in.

To measure their five dimensions of employability, Van der Heijde and Van der Heijden (2006) developed a scale made up of 47 items, which they have validated in an empirical study. The full set of items can be found in their 2006 paper. Later, a short-form set of fewer items for those employability sub-scales was developed by Van der Heijden et al. (2018). Note that this inventory scale is of a better fit for working people and less so for students. The sets of items are available in Van der Heijde and Van der Heijden (2006) for the full set, and Van der Heijden et al. (2018) for a shorter version.

Examples of representative items for each dimension are presented in Box 4.2. Note that this inventory scale is of a better fit for people in full employment, less so for students.

Box 4.2: Measuring the five dimensions of employability

Occupational Expertise

During the past year, I was, in general, competent to perform my work accurately and with few mistakes.

I consider myself competent to weigh up and reason out the 'pros' and 'cons' of particular decisions on working methods, materials, and techniques in my job domain.

Anticipation and optimization

I consciously devote attention to applying my newly acquired knowledge and skills.

During the past year, I associated myself with the latest developments in my job domain.

Personal flexibility

How easily would you say you can adapt to changes in your workplace?

How quickly do you generally anticipate and take advantage of changes in your working environment?

Corporate sense

I support the operational processes within my organization.

I share my experience and knowledge with others.

Balance

My work and private life are evenly balanced.

I achieve a balance in alternating between reaching my own work goals and supporting my colleagues.

These sample items would give you an indication about how you may estimate how employable you are – beyond your general feeling, which might be biased. Some people may over self-estimate whereas others under-estimate their qualities.

How to improve employability?

Be competent, in general and in your own specific knowledge area. This is important, but fairly basic, and insufficient on its own. To be truly employable one must have the capacity for continuous learning, being agile and resilient. These qualities are essential for keeping a sustainable career (Heslin et al., 2020). From the employers' perspective, they have the obligation to invest in their employees, which may follow from the psychological contract they have, national regulations (such as minimum training per employee per year), and the practical need to have employees who can perform their jobs in an effective and efficient manner. A proactive employee will be on alert to learn about available training and other developmental activities the company or institution has to offer. They can also look out for external training on offer, and ask their employers to help. Some employers will do so, for example, by paying for courses, including university qualifications like an MBA, or releasing work time to enable the employee to study and train.

Finally, an additional element essential to employability is using networks of all kinds, both virtual and non-virtual, which can help in securing employment (Wanberg et al., 2020).

Employability – when and for whom?

Employability is needed for everyone, at any career stage. Within contemporary careers people may count on their employability rather than the fallacy of assumed job security (Baruch, 2004a; Clarke & Patrickson, 2007). When no job can be secured, the ability to gain employment is the factor that helps people cope with uncertainty. This applies to all employees, though in some sectors there is relative job security (e.g. public sector); no one is immune from losing their job. Being able to move to a different employer gives bargaining power when a salary increase or promotion is at stake. It does not mean the need for an actual move, just that the current employer will believe that the employee can move, which gives the employee this bargaining power.

As for 'who is in charge' of employability, the answer is complex and multi-layered. Certainly individuals should have the highest interest in their employability, invest in it and make sure it is sustainable in the long term. Employers need capable and competent employees, therefore although their interest may not be the individual, their investment in employees will contribute to the employability of their workforce. Universities have an interest in the employability of their graduates, both out of care for their students and because the level of graduates' employability is widely used as a measure for institutional success. Nations look for competitive advantage (and sometime, within a single country, there would be competition at a regional level). The practices of national engagement and involvement with universities vary. For example, a study that compared two countries – the USA and the UK – found significant differences between their national approach. Government policies were a focal point in the UK, and the discourse on employability for university graduates targeted preparation for employment. In the USA the emphasis was centred upon the institutional vision and social inclusion agenda (Chadha & Toner, 2017).

The next section will look at graduates' employability.

Graduates' employability

For students approaching the end of their studies, finding a job is a top priority. Universities and other higher education institutions understand the new rule of the game. Part of their role now goes beyond simply educating and disseminate knowledge. It is their role also to prepare graduates for the world of work (Suleman, 2018). Further, in many countries, employment performance records of graduates is linked to public funding (Silva et al., 2018). Therefore, universities can and should help. Universities care for the success of their graduates – they are also measured and assessed on students' success. One clear and widely used measure is employability, and as a result, universities prepare their students for finding and keeping jobs. Indeed, developing employability is of particular importance for graduates, in the critical stage of career, looking for their first (serious) job (Baruch et al., 2020).

The matrix of student's self-perception of employability uses two dimensions: self-belief versus general field of study; and the state of the university versus state of the external labour market. Box 4.3 presents the two dimensions and nine 'cells', where each one represents one element or input to the level of employability.

Box 4.3: A framework of graduates' employability (adapted from Rothwell et al., 2009)

The university standing

	Academic performance and engagement	General strength of university brand and reputation	Strength of university brand and reputation in specific field	
Individual self-belief	Confidence in one's competencies	Level of ambition	Status and credibility of the specific field	Field of study
	Awareness of opportunities for employment	Economic condition of the external labour market	Labour market demand for people in the field	

Perception of the labour market

How can each cell in this matrix be assessed? Rothwell et al. (2009) developed a scale for self-evaluation, which is relevant for some of these. External sources can provide answers to some of the others. A valid and reliable evaluation is key, and to understand the position in each cell would require knowledge – about self and about the business environment.

Success in studies is quite simple to check – what level are the grades, or grade point average (GPA). It is not just the grade but how one compares with their class (e.g. being top or in the top 10% of the class). The grade scale in the USA is on 1–100, where top students may reach GPA of 95+; conversely, in the UK, a first class degree, which is typically the top 10%, is gained when the grade average is 70+, and it is very rare to have GPA above 80.

Another question refers to the university: how well is it considered by employers? Do employers participate in their career fairs? The answer can be gathered also from various 'league tables' of universities' reputation. Typically, research-led universities are more prestigious than teaching-focused ones. For private institutions, the level of fees are an indicator too. It is important not to look at a single table – most are biased for many reasons, some of them political. Yet, there is a certain consensus that some universities are top, or at least top within the country. A good sign is if employers specifically target certain universities in order to recruit individuals, either in general or for particular subject area(s).

It should be remembered that there is no direct correlation or association between the reputation and strength of the university and the specific area of study. Some universities might have a moderate overall reputation, but have a very highly regarded reputation in a particular field of study.

Moving to the middle row in Box 4.3, confidence is very subjective. Self-efficacy (Bandura, 2010) is a factor in employability. It is a pre-condition to being able to perform and deliver, and the self-belief the person has that he or she can produce desired effects by their own actions (Bandura, 1997). Perceived self-efficacy is concerned with people's beliefs in their ability to influence events that affect their lives. Those who lack the confidence in their competencies will not perform well. Showing a lack of confidence at an assessment centre or during a job interview will likely put the applicant at a distinct disadvantage of being shortlisted.

When applying for a job it is essential to be motivated to succeed, and present well at interview. Other influencing factors will help; for example, if one wants to live in the same city as their partner, that is a motivational factor in getting the job compared with, say, if the new job requires a geographical move or adds significant commuting time.

Also, motivation to gain employment with a specific employer depends on the reputation of that organization as an employer (e.g. 'Best employer' recognition), as suggested by Bowman and Bastedo (2009).

The discipline is an external factor. The status associated with different vocations vary. While some national variation exists, certain hierarchy is typical; for example, being a judge is highly prestigious, a road cleaner much less so. Different career choices would have different currency in the labour market. Some professions tend to be in high demand and high status (medicine, law), while others offer fewer career opportunities (archaeology, history).

Last but not least, awareness of opportunities for employment can be gained from personal and wider networks. It is important for students to be engaged with the constant search for opportunities. Sometimes just listening to news will offer insight into the local or national economic conditions that influence the labour market, as well as the specific need for the qualities and competencies gained by the student.

Timing is an issue too with regard to demand for graduates: the dot.com bubble in 2000 made a significant number of IT experts redundant. The 2008 financial crisis left many financial expert out of a job, whereas usually these professions are in high demand. For non-degree professions, the future of driving as a job, for example, could be at risk if autonomous vehicles replace all drivers.

The role of universities in enhancing graduates' employability

Universities are expected to prepare students to think for themselves and consider who they might want to become. Universities are measured for their success in many ways, and one prominent factor is the level of employment amongst their graduates. No matter if they are state-funded universities, where they are expected to help in national competitiveness, or private, the ability of all graduates to find appropriate employment is important. Some league tables even list the average earnings of graduates following graduation.

Box 4.4: How much can graduates from top universities earn?

Look at: http://rankings.ft.com/businessschoolrankings/global-mba-ranking-2020

In 2020, MBA graduates from most top global 100 business schools could expect to earn, on average, between $100,000–$200,000 a year (only two earned a bit less and four a bit more).

These figures are extreme, of course, and not representative of expected earning for undergraduate students, or even for MBA students from the vast majority of global universities.

What can and should universities do?

Universities need to be attentive to the changing patterns of employer demand for particular knowledge, skills, and competencies, whether generic or specific. Although this is a well-known and agreed goal, for decades employers have questioned graduates' work readiness. Reaching an agreement on graduates' preparation for the labour market should take into account the changes of labour force patterns, technology developments, and the way the economy develops. The changes in technology mean that universities must prepare their students for jobs, industries, and technologies that are currently only in their infancy or do not even exist yet. Most students have an idea about their preferred future (hence their choice of field of study). Others may not be sure, and the role of universities is to work on prompting and preparing them to consider what they might want to do.

Amongst the practices and support mechanisms universities may employ are activities that are usually managed by career services, but can be done at school or faculty/college level.

Incorporating employability in the curriculum of studies

Universities can include employability in many ways, one of which is devoting a full module to careers and employability. Another option is to make sure that employability and ways to improve it are part of skills development. Yet another activity is arranging expert talks and presentations/seminars about careers. Employability can and should be part of studies' curriculum (Ehiyazaryan & Barraclough, 2009). An example of a complementary process is using consultancy projects as a form of enterprise. Exploring such activity, O'Leary (2015) identified how an institution can apply an initiative using live projects as an alternative to the more traditional dissertation of the final year. In this activity, the final semester postgraduate students have managed to enhance their understanding of client needs, as these projects were conducted in real enterprises. They also improve self-confidence and team-working abilities.

Career services

The purpose of career centres in universities is to support students in their quest to find the right career. For most this means help in finding their first job, though for others it may be help in starting self-employment or a business venture (see later in this chapter on entrepreneurial careers), or for yet others, finding the right path for higher education (Master or Doctorate degrees).

Universities' career centres typically offer advice and consultation about writing a CV, covering letters and personal statements, offering feedback on CVs and applications, and preparing for interviews (e.g. conducting mock interviews). They may help in looking for options, provide careers guidance, advise on how to do well at online tests, and so on. They will arrange career fairs, which may be general or specific for certain degrees (e.g. for engineers; for social sciences). The university or specific schools can be in contact with prospective employers, with alumni who may be in a position to offer support, for example, by setting a 'Buddy' system with volunteering alumni.

For those who are still unsure of what they want to do by the end of their studies, career services will help to identify possible directions. They may have the capacity to run psychometric tests and have practical workshops about self-realization and being mindful about future aspirations and how these may be fulfilled.

For those who consider or wish to continue studying, they would help finding the right postgraduate course, how to apply, and where to look for stipends or funding. Career centres will have material like books, leaflets, audio/video recordings that will help in the process. For example, *What Color is your Parachute* (Bolles, 2011) or *Brilliant Graduate Career Handbook* (Done and Mulvey, 2016) and other career-focused books (including this book, hopefully).

The university, sometimes schools or faculties within the university, may offer full employability-related modules/courses. These can be a course or module on its own, or combined with other HR-related issues that are important but might not be enough for a full module (e.g. diversity management).

Placements and internships

Universities and other higher education institutions see it as part of their role to support the insertion of graduates into the labour market. One of the institutional mechanisms applied to facilitate students' transition to work is placements or internships. The career centre or specific schools can offer support with looking for internships and part-time jobs. Universities can help their students' prospects by offering these practices either as an option or as a mandatory requirement. Evidence for the effectiveness of these mechanisms is scant, but some data demonstrate that including internships as part of degree studies significantly enhances graduate employment (Silva et al., 2018). They also found that expanding and undertaking several internships enhances the prospects of being selected for a job. The role of placements and internships in employability is important as it is a time when the student is working but not formally employed, thereby gaining work experience.

The purpose of placement or internship is to offer temporary posting of a student in a workplace – typically for one year, for example, between the second and the third year of the university course. It may be paid or unpaid work, but not defined as a 'proper' employment. This will enable them to gain work experience and apply the knowledge gained through their studies. It will also help them to realize the nature and meaning of the work they do, so could be instrumental for their choice of employment upon completion of the degree. It enables the employer to benefit from enthusiastic temporary employees, who may become future employees following graduation.

In many cases, the student will be offered a permanent position after finishing the degree studies because of the positive mutual impression the organization and the student had on each other during the placement. Another advantage for internships is that they typically facilitate learning and development – in particular back at university following the internship (Clark & Zukas, 2016).

Risks and their management

Not being sure of one's future career when going to university is typical for many. A significant proportion of young people, at age of about 18, are not sure about their future or what they want from it. One way to learn and delay the decision is to take a gap year for reflection and further thinking. Others can try temporary work before opting for a permanent job or attending university. One way to reduce the risk for those who feel they should attend university is to choose a degree that is more versatile and may offer various options for the future. Business management or law are typical examples of degrees with multiple opportunities at the end of studies.

On being overqualified

Employers tend to refrain from employing over-qualified people for the logical view that they will not remain long in a position that does not fully use their competence. Studying for a university degree and trying jobs that do not require such qualification might prove a wrong decision. Similarly, continuing for Master level or Doctorate studies without a specific plan might mean being over-qualified for many jobs.

Can employability be taught?

Employability reflects the ability to navigate within an increasingly complex and dynamic labour market, where boundaries are blurred, structures are in constant flux, rules and regulations change, and external factors may help or hinder success. Understanding the meaning of it and how to acquire it are first steps in realizing individual potential for a sustainable career in times of change (De Vos and Van der Heijden, 2015).

This book is not about how to learn; there is a wide literature about learning, such as the framework of experiential learning in Kolb (2014). Here it is sufficient to point out the need for continuous investment in self-development via learning. The following quotes reflect on the value of learning from failure.

A pause for reflection

'I've missed more than 9,000 shots in my career. I've lost almost 300 games. 26 times I've been trusted to take the game winning shot and missed. I've failed over and over and over again in my life and that is why I succeed.'

Michael Jordan, NBA Legendary Basketball MVP

An intriguing view suggested by Winston Churchill is that 'Success is stumbling from failure to failure with no loss of enthusiasm'.

Organizational perspective of employability

Under the new psychological contract there are no long-term expectations of mutual loyalty and commitment from either the individual or the organization (Baruch & Rousseau, 2019; Herriot & Pemberton, 1995). It is the role of the employee to make sure that they have the needed competence to perform in the job and if the worst come to worst, to use their competences, skills, and capabilities to gain a new job. That is the essence of employability. While organizations still have to invest in their employees, providing them with 'employability' is not taken as a primary role but as a conundrum (Baruch, 2001a). Why should employers prepare their employees to move? It is in the interest of the individual to maintain their employability. Nevertheless, as explained above, organizations that do not have the capacity to deliver will fail, and this capacity is highly dependent on the competence and motivation of their employees.

These will not be maintained without investment in employees. For the organization, the logic in investing in its employees' employability shows trust. Improving the competence of your talent will attract better employees. Therefore, training employees and creating a learning environment at the workplace is beneficial to organizations (Bui & Baruch, 2012; Trede & McEwen, 2015). Individual factors can also be relevant for understanding the value of learning, particularly the availability of training and development for younger employees (van der Heijden et al., 2016).

Employability tools

The ultimate way to check your employability is to test the labour market by applying for jobs, even if you are not really looking for one. Will you be selected for an interview? Yes – you are probably employable. Such an exercise, though, is quite stressful and puts strain on individuals. The ethics of such conduct is doubtful. Yet, based on anecdotal evidence, some people do it – and on occasion would even accept an offer, albeit without true initial intent. So, the 'risk' is that sometimes success in finding a job through this test may lead to an actual, unintended move. A more subtle test would be to check the skills, competences, and requirements detailed in job ads or job descriptions (often found on the company website). Compare also your level and your salary to the required level and potential salary. This is not easy to find, but you may gain ideas by looking at web pages like https://www.bbc.com/worklife/article/20200928-should-you-get-paid-based-on-where-you-live.

CASE STUDY 4.1: COVID-19 IMPACT

The COVID-19 pandemic provided a painful reminder that employability can be vulnerable to external threats. People in certain professions simply could not work. Workplaces were closed down, restrictions imposed, leaving people jobless for long periods, to the level that many need to rely on benefits, sadly even on food-banks.

People who perceived themselves to have strong employability realized that in the context of lockdown and other restrictions, this perception was spurious. In particular, many entrepreneurs in the retail sector, and most of those in the hospitality sector, had experienced lost of employability.

The events of the 2020 COVID-19 pandemic inflicted sobering realities at a global scale. Interestingly, certain jobs were more immune from the impact of COVID-19, such as those which could be performed from home and did not require physical contact with others. Conversely, many jobs and occupations were not feasible, such as in the retail industry, leaving many in a much more vulnerable state. For example, during the period of March to May 2020, the level of claiming universal credit (social support benefit) in the UK was 10 times the usual level.

First job – first income

The first job is the first chance to perform in the labour market, to be noticed, and to set the opening step in a long career journey. This first job may function as either a 'stepping stone' or as a 'trap' (Scherer, 2004). Some modern jobs in the gig economy could be such traps, and this can be in the lower end or the higher end of the job market: for example, Uber driving at the lower end (Cramer & Krueger, 2016); adjunct academic at the other (Feldman & Turnley, 2004; Yakoboski, 2016). The initial salary has long-term implications for future earnings, as it sets a base benchmark for both the employee and the employer. To optimize it, one should be prepared: knowing one's own worth and the likely income for suitable jobs.

Know thyself

The first advice would be: know your worth – and adjust your expectations, which means studying the labour market. How strong are you on competences required for the type of jobs you wish to be employed in? Your worth in terms of your income will reflect a number of factors. Competencies (abilities, skills, knowledge) are paramount, but does the job require all those competencies or more? Competence is not enough – reputation is a major factor. Which university (and other educational history) did you graduate from? What area? How flexible are you in terms of geo-location for the future? Consider also the profession, sector, location.

In earlier chapters we had the opportunity to self-evaluate some of your characteristics and competencies. Be prepared: which also means check what kind of work and tasks are performed in a job, the working conditions, and, yes, how much money is paid. Here it is important to look at the whole package – it may be better to have a slightly lower salary if the side-benefits (e.g. pension) are higher than in other positions. Check with others (alumni, career services, and so on) how much a role is worth, and adjust (e.g. cost of living will be a factor in any country). Sometime you may earn less but be left with more free income; for example, housing costs in rural areas compensate for a lower salary than could be achieved in cities where the cost of living is higher. Knowing all that will enable you to use your bargaining power effectively. Indeed, beware of your bargaining power: do you have unique specific knowledge? Unique specific network to bring resources? Are you free to travel? Anywhere? Are you restricted to one place? To certain work arrangements? Do you have other obligations like caring for young children or elderly parents, which might limit your ability to contribute?

Career sustainability

A sustainable career is one in which individuals enjoy at least a moderate degree of productivity, health, and happiness across their lifespan (Heslin et al., 2020). It is a career that would enable the person to be at least reasonably healthy, happy, and productive, and this should last a lifetime (De Vos et al., 2020). Some can achieve this, but in todays' economy, in particular the gig economy, jobs are more precarious and far from being sustainable or offer opportunities for sustainable careers. Another definition suggests that sustainable careers would be 'sequences of career experiences reflected through a variety of patterns of continuity over time, thereby crossing several social spaces, characterized by individual agency, herewith providing meaning to the individual' (Van der Heijden & De Vos, 2015, p. 7). The concept of career sustainability incorporates the evolution of careers across several dimensions, in particular time, space, agency, and meaning, to recognise the complexity of careers and their management, which call for a comprehensive, overarching view. Such a theory, the career ecosystem theory (Baruch, 2015; Baruch & Rousseau, 2019), will be presented in the following chapters.

To sustain one's own career, the following three steps are important.

1. Develop realistic expectations

It is not how much you would like to get, but how much your future employer may be ready to pay – and like you, they have options. It is important to understand the nature of the labour market because when people take on a first job they might be over-qualified or under-qualified, and this can influence their future career. The nature of the market is influential too: when working in a flexible model there are higher chances of making up for initial disadvantages, but in tightly regulated and segmented markets a poor start might lead to stronger entrapment in lower-status positions (Scherer, 2004).

2. Be proactive

Being proactive is critical for career success, at any stage (Seibert et al., 2001). Think where you want your career to be, and apply accordingly. You do not have to wait for a job post – if you really want to work for a specific employer, it is fine to 'knock on the door' and ask if they have any vacancies.

Start your career planning early during your time at university, and submit as many applications as possible – do not give up or wait for an application to be processed as you could lose valuable time and other opportunities. Be confident, but not over-confident. If your university offers placements, have a go at it. Your work placement may become your future permanent employer.

In a report bearing the intriguing title Mind the (Graduate Gender Pay) Gap, Cornell et al. (2020) presented data regarding graduate salaries in the UK, exploring also the gender pay gap among university graduates. They identified a persistent, even widening, pay gap between the genders post-graduation. This is not new, but their analysis points out that the gap cannot be fully accounted for merely by factors such as subject choice, prior attainment, ethnicity, institution of study, or social background. Partially, the gap may be attributable to tendencies towards different values in employment: men are more likely to prioritize high salaries whereas women would value ethics and personal fulfilment. Yet, on average, males tend to expect higher salaries than women – and this level of expectation sets the benchmark. Further, men are more likely to network with possible employers, reflecting differences on the job-seeker side. On the other side of the equation, employers' bias exists too. Cornell et al. recommended that careers services make graduates aware of these gender pay gaps and the apparent reasons for them, to inform students' career strategies. To employers they suggest taking steps to address biases, even to specifically target women, for example, by offering them opportunities such as internships.

3. Be positive

This last piece of advice is less a management issue and more about individual psychology. A positive approach to life and work tends to lead to positive personal outcomes (Hart, 2021). The field of positive psychology is concerned with valued subjective experience (Seligman & Csikszentmihalyi, 2014). The focus is on wellbeing, satisfaction, happiness (for the present), hope, and optimism (for the future). Interestingly, the pursuit of happiness, along with life and liberty, was granted in the US Declaration of Independence as a constitutional right, one that the government is committed to protect, even in 1776.

Happier people are more inclined to apply to more positions when looking for jobs, have a higher rate of being invited to job interviews, and secure jobs that are better paid and more prestigious than unhappy job seekers. Happier employees are well performing, engaged, and productive, demonstrating creativity and flexibility (Walsh et al., 2018). Therefore, it is much better, of course, to be happy. This book cannot teach you how to be happy, but it is important to keep in mind the role and importance of happiness in life and at work.

A pause for reflection

What does happiness mean to you – in general and in working life?

How can you boost your happiness?

Entrepreneurship as a promising, viable career path

Why work for others when you can work for yourself? Would you rather have your own small business? If you feel so, entrepreneurship may be the best career for you.

In pursuing an entrepreneurial career, there is an important role for individual passions, coupled with the will and ability to run a business. Those who have the right family heritage and resources are at a distinct advantage. The cases in Box 4.5 are testimony to that.

Entrepreneurship as a field of study was defined as a field that 'seeks to understand how opportunities to bring into existence "future" goods and services are discovered, created and exploited, by whom, and with what consequences' (Venkataraman, 2019, p. 120). The role of entrepreneurship is important for individuals who wish to pursue this path, but also for nations – entrepreneurial activity is a major factor in job creation and the establishment of new wealth.

Not all is rosy; risks for entrepreneurs are substantial, uncertain, and dependent on limited knowledge of the business and the business environment. A very high percentage of all start-ups fail within a few years, many within the first year (Hogarth & Karelaia, 2012). Failure of venture capital firms may be mitigated by employing robust investment strategies (Dimov & De Clercq, 2006). The reasons for failure vary, and can be due to reasons concerning the individual (the entrepreneur), the firm, and the business environment (e.g. sector, region, external events), or a combination of these. With so much at stake, stress levels of entrepreneurs might be more severe compared with employees who work for an organization. Yet, the owner is in control, and being in control mitigates against stress.

One of the primary goals of developing students towards entrepreneurship (e.g. by supporting an entrepreneurial mindset) is so that they will recognize entrepreneurship as a highly positive, beneficial career path that opens new options. This mindset relates to calling, which, for the entrepreneur, can be expressed as 'occupational calling' (specific passion for a particular occupation), and also as 'entrepreneurial calling' – a passion for wealth creation and for doing business (Tran et al., 2019). Further, even if not opening their own business, someone with an entrepreneurial mindset would offer valuable benefits as an employee of an organization, in particular a large one. Therefore we will discuss here both intrapreneurship as well as entrepreneurship.

Individual traits have significant impact on the success or failure of new ventures, because human capital is critical for success of new ventures (Unger et al., 2011). Some traits are relevant to any career success, like the 'need for achievement'; others are more relevant for entrepreneurial success including the 'need for autonomy'. Holding a contemporary career orientation like the protean career is a factor too: self-employed people with higher self-directeded career management and a boundaryless mindset had more engagement with employability activities and had higher professional commitment (Lo Presti et al., 2018).

Focusing on psychological characteristics, Chatterjee and Das (2015) studied the entrepreneurial literature and identified several factors that are important to entrepreneurial success. Some of them are critical to any managerial activity while others may be more relevant to entrepreneurship; these unique entrepreneurial needs are presented in Table 4.1.

Table 4.1 Entrepreneurship needs

Needed for success in most managerial roles	Needs of special relevance for entrepreneurs
Need for achievement	Tolerance of ambiguity
Locus of control	Risk-taking propensity
Self-efficacy	Innovativeness
Optimism	Independence and autonomy

The list in Table 4.1 is not all-encompassing; many individual characteristics can be relevant for a successful entrepreneurial success. Self-awareness is an example. The representation of self at work in the future reflects the hopes and aspirations individuals have in relation to their career (Strauss, Griffin, & Parker, 2012). They found that the clearer and more accessible this representation, the more salient the future work self. Future work self-salience was positively related to individuals' proactive career behaviour, which is a critical ingredient for success for any career, certainly for entrepreneurs (Seibert, Kraimer, & Crant, 2001).

Circumstances matter too. A push to an entrepreneurial career may be due to job loss and lack of options to acquire traditional employment. It does not have to reach the level of job loss – people can become disillusioned with their organizational career, feel unhappy at work, or have poor work relationships with their managers or co-workers.

Building a business requires an understanding of the self and of the market. When entrepreneurs decide on what type of business they want to create, they have many options: nature of the business and type of activities or operations required, the sector, the prospects for growth, and so on. For entrepreneurs, keeping their career sustainable is more challenging, but when they succeed, the benefits, both intrinsic and extrinsic, may be highly fulfilling.

Box 4.5: Building one's own business: High-tech and traditional sectors

Jack – Entrepreneurship in music business: Traditional retail	Ed & Yip – Entrepreneurship in high-tech forecasting industry
Since childhood, Jack was surrounded by pianos. His grandparents had a business in the piano trade, and Jack studied piano performance. He enjoyed music and its studies, but decided not to make a professional career as a musician, a profession that is highly competitive and demanding (Dobrow Riza & Heller, 2015). At the same time, working for the family piano business, he learnt all about sourcing high-quality pianos and marketing them to customers. He decided to combine his love of music and pianos with the work–life balance of a small business owner, trading since 1999, and later in 2015 opened his piano shop near London, UK. Now a few year later, the shop, called Chiltern Piano Gallery, is doing well enough to provide him with both a satisfying career and an income. He envisages a growth in the business, and aims to expand within the same field.	Upon finishing his PhD studies, Ed joined forces with his former supervisor Yip to create a new start-up firm called Previsico (https://previsico.com/) as a spin-out of Loughborough University. Previsico commercialized a flood forecasting technology developed at the university. This provides property level flood warnings to people and organizations globally. After securing grant funding, they partnered with tech giant IBM to scale up their offering, which primarily targets the insurance market, helping insurers support their customers with pre-event support. The firm was established in 2019 with a mission of preventing avoidable flood impacts globally. True to their values, they rapidly grew to a team of 20 within two years, supporting both businesses and humanitarian organizations with their new technology.

Entrepreneurs may have different aims – some are in it for the money or for fame or for the pursuit of their quest. Successful entrepreneurs can become global celebrities, like some restaurateurs (see Box 4.6), though the vast majority of successful restaurant owners remain small, and typically struggle financially.

Box 4.6: Small business entrepreneurship: Having a very special restaurant

Ben Shewry, Grant Achatz, Vladimir Mukhin and Corrado Assenza are examples of chefs and owners of restaurants that became recognized as top global restaurants. All of them had a humble start, working in their family business from a very early stage of their life, moving on to open their own restaurant and each becoming a celebrity chef. It does not mean that a family experience is a prerequisit for success in small businesses – and in fact, the majority of top chefs did not start with a family business (Elbasha & Baruch, 2019) – but they fell in love with their vocation.

The example in Box 4.6 suggests that following an inner calling, which may develop with time, can be a decisive factor in attaining career success (Hall & Chandler, 2005; Praskova et al., 2015). Yet, having a calling is not enough on its own. It should be coupled with investment at work, self-management, and applying career strategies, so that career satisfaction and highly perceived employability will follow (Praskova et al., 2015).

A pause for reflection

Becoming an entrepreneur may be your first (and possibly only) career; yet, you may decide to start with working for a large firm to gain experience before starting your own business. Consider the pros and cons of each path. When would one be a better choice compared with the alternative?

See Box 4.7 for some ideas.

Box 4.7: Straight to your own business or gain experience first

Why straight to the business?	Why experience first?
The idea is 'burning' in you, the urge to fulfil your dream is strong. You do not wish to waste time working for others.	In some types of professions (e.g. being a consultant), theoretical knowledge is not enough. A graduate with no experience will not be attractive to firms looking for advice.

(Continued)

Why straight to the business?	Why experience first?
You are afraid that you might be lured into the safety of working for others and will never be brave enough to make the move.	Working for a well-known consultancy firm will be instrumental for success as a self-employed consultant.
The Labour market – you may not be in a position to get into an established firm due to fierce job competition.	Financial issues – you may need to earn some money (and, of course, experience) to enable you to make the investment required for the new business.

A note: I started the entrepreneurship section with a discussion about entrepreneurial failures. Yet, much can be learnt from failures, in particular for entrepreneurs who go on to have a second try. Indeed, some people become serial entrepreneurs, moving from business to business, and if they learn from experience, they are in a much stronger position for their future (Fang He et al., 2018).

Before embarking on an entrepreneurial career

There are several factors that would make or break the prospects of success. Probably the first is the type and viability of the business. Opening a travel agency would have been be a very solid option in the late 20th century; today, the need for such service is in continuous decline. Conversely, web page design was not on the cards on that time, and today is a fine option. Becoming a taxi driver is still an option, but with the Uberization of this profession, it is not easy to enter the market as a freelance driver, and with the scope of autonomous cars it might also be a vocation in decline. Opting for a totally new idea can be risky but would create chances for a high-added value. The challenge is to forecast if the business idea is strong. How would it fare with the type of investors found on Dragons' Den? Would banks be interested in offering a loan? This is the type of test to run before going ahead, from the business point of view: demand for the product or service, by whom? How much would it be worth for potential buyers?

The personal issue is no less critical. How important is autonomy compared with security? Risk-seeking versus risk aversion is a decisive factor, amongst other personality traits, like tolerance for ambiguity. Family status is a related factor: a single person with no significant financial worries is in a much better state to become an entrepreneur or self-employed compared with a person with a family and mortgage to pay on a monthly basis. What do I want in life; what do I want to be remembered for; how important is it for me to be rich compared with being relaxed? All these relate to individual personality and circumstances, and would be critical when deciding on entrepreneurship or self-employment versus looking for employment.

Phasing out – the ending of working life

Every story has a beginning, a middle, and an end. Most research studies on working life focus on the first two. Yet, the last stage, ending working life, is important on its own. It can be gradual, it can be abrupt – either way, it should be planned ahead. Retirement is the stage where individuals withdraw, physically and psychologically, from working life. In the past, it was legally enforced upon reaching the statutory age. These days, it can be subject to individual decision, as many countries abolished the legal retirement age, or extended it. Many factors allowed for this change, in particular the improvement in life expectancy and general health, at least in developed countries (Alcover et al., 2012). People are living well for longer while working for shorter time periods: in the past, most young people started working at the age of 14, then 16, and then 18 (see Chapter 2). Now, in the OECD countries, it is typically the age of 18, and for close to half of the population, university studies delay the age of starting to work to the early 20s. At the other end of working life, many find themselves opting for early retirement, either because they want it or because they were made redundant and cannot find alternative work. In contrast, because apart from work that requires significant physical input, in most professions people can continue to work beyond the arbitrary age of 65, many people do not wish to retire, and sometimes they do not have an option to do so if they want to keep their quality of life in terms of earnings (Baruch et al., 2014).

Historically, there were two periods of ending working life. Until the end of the 19th century, people worked their whole lives. Then came the Chancellor Otto von Bismarck of Germany. His convention of setting a statutory pension age of 70 was initiated in 1883. In 1916 the age was lowered to 65 because, amongst other reasons, during that era, by that age, the vast majority of the population would perish. That threshold placed minor financial constrain on the state. Further, at the time, most jobs required physical ability and stamina. The situation has since altered significantly on both accounts: living many years after retirement means a major financial burden on the state and pension funds. The typical requirements of work are more cerebral and the ability to provide services and office work are not influenced by age as are physically-related tasks. This means that formal retirement age will need to be reconsidered, changed, or abolished (Baruch et al., 2014).

For most readers, it would be too early to contemplate, but when reaching retirement stage, they will be faced with several options:

* Retire at the conventional, sometime legal, age of retirement.
* Reduce work commitment (possibly gradually).
* Continue working full-time.
* Start a second/new career (paid-for or voluntary; as an employee or self-employed).

Similarly to these, Boveda and Metz (2016) suggested four options: non-retirement, retirement, bridge-employment, and encore-career (change of career after retirement). They reported the results of a survey of working adults in the USA by Merrill Lynch (2006), which found that 50% of the participants intended to retire by age 61, though at the same time they planned to continue working in some capacity for an average of nine years into retirement. As for the perceived ideal work arrangements in retirement, most of the participants said they would like to cycle between periods of work and leisure (42%), followed by working part time (16%), starting their own business (13%), and working full time (6%). Two-thirds of those who expected to work after retirement said that they would like to change their line of work.

Many would end working or reduce their working commitment to focus on other facets of life. People may wish to start the 'golden age' of leisure, enjoy a hobby, cruise the world, or just relax. This is particularly relevant for the baby-boomer generation (Boveda & Metz, 2016). Yet, continuous family obligations such as support with care for grandchildren and elderly parents at the time of retirement means that many will be engaged with these activities.

Others would prefer to work as long as they can and as long as their work is still contributing. With the abolition of retirement age, more can opt for a healthy continuation of working life. For others, continuation of work is essential financially, for example, those with no pension (some firms which collapsed did not keep enough slack for their pension funds to be sustainable).

Last, others can decide to start a new chapter in their career, starting new ideas, as either employees, volunteering roles, or entrepreneurs. With no strains of regular work and with unfulfilled dreams, this is their last opportunity to embark a new adventure. Many want to be artists (Cheung & Shih, 2018) or teachers (Castro & Bauml, 2009) to fulfil a different inner calling. For them, this is the last chance, and with full life experience under their belt, they would be in the best position to fulfil their dreams.

Summary

This chapter summarized the concept of employability and its relevance for individuals, employers and for national decision makers. Specific attention was devoted to graduate employability and the role of universities in helping students develop a sustainable career. We also explored the role of entrepreneurship as a viable career option, and identified for whom it may best fit. The pros and cons of this path were highlighted. Last, we touched on the important issue of how to draw working life to a close.

KEY TERMS

Employability

Entrepreneurial careers

Entrepreneurship

Graduates' development programmes

Placements and internships

Retirement – phasing out

DISCUSSION QUESTIONS

LESSONS AND FOOD FOR THOUGHT

Are you employable? How will you test it? When?

Is your employability sustainable? What will you need to make it sustainable in the near and long term future?

As an employee – even when you think that all is well, organizational change, new leadership, or external events may mean redundancies, job losses and unexpected surprises. Be prepared, any time, for 'what if'. Keep your networks alive; be sure to undertake training and being considered indispensable (as far as can be) for your current employer, and attractive to alternative employers.

As a student – timing is important. During your first years of studies, there is no need to worry and be concerned about finding a job or deciding on your future career. It is best to focus on acquiring the competencies and qualifications that will allow for your employability. During the second part of your final year is the time to be proactive, start making inquiries, attend career fairs, submit your CV, and so on.

Consider the pros and cons of entrepreneurship. Is it for you? When would be best to start?

What age would you believe best for you to retire? Or maybe it would be best not to retire at all?

The Dynamic Nature of Career Management

5

LEARNING OBJECTIVES

After reading this chapter you should be able to:

- Understand the nature of career dynamics
- Be acquainted with the career as metaphor
- Critically analyse labour markets

Chapter outline

Transitions

This chapter deals with the implications of environmental and organizational changes on career systems. Peiperl and Baruch (1997) and Baruch and Bozionelos (2011) considered past and current career models and set out a vision of future careers that differ from past careers. Individual agency is a major factor in this dynamic (Hall et al., 2018), but one primary attribute of the change in the nature of contemporary careers is the existence of horizontal links that transcend organizational and systems boundaries (Arthur, 2014), including geographical ones (Dickmann, Suutari, & Wurtz, 2018). As these links continue to develop, there would be more opportunity and flexibility than was ever available under previous systems. The new rules of the game best fit those who have the competencies – mostly knowledge and skills – to take advantage of them, and those who will be proactive (Spurk, Hirschi, & Dries, 2019). The way forward in understanding the future of careers and how they can be sustainable (Van der Heijden et al., 2020) is to explore the balance between individual and organizational perspectives (Baruch, 2006a).

Organizations have always been subject to change and cutbacks, and individuals within them were subject to competition and, occasionally, lay-offs. The difference now relates to the scope and pace of the phenomenon – the number of organizations whose career systems have been thrown into disarray, and the number of people affected, seems to have reached a turning point.

Exploring careers among US workers, Bidwell (2013) used a longitudinal research design to identify a decline in the mean length of time spent with each employer (tenure). This reduction was attributed to the changing nature of employment relationships and industrial relations (Baccaro & Howell, 2017) and the decrease in levels of unionization – in line with the 'new careers' (Sullivan & Baruch, 2009).

It is now the norm, rather than the exception, for organizations to have no fixed career paths and for individuals within them to see no further than a few years ahead, if that, in their own careers. We can no longer depend upon career tracks (themselves subject to stable organizational structures) to ensure that we progress merely because we are competent and hardworking. And many people who joined their organizations with an expectation of such career progress are learning this lesson the hard way.

Organizations simply can no longer offer a commitment and loyalty-based relationship, thus the need to move towards a transactional relationship or to generate relational relationships. This shift is based on transformational leadership and employment relationship of a renewed psychological contract (Baruch & Rousseau, 2019).

	Career ecosystem and changing psychological contracts		
	Influencing factors	Strategies, policies and practices	Outcomes
Individual level	Needs, goals, attitudes and predispositions as well as personality. Human and social capital, future time perspective and demographics: Age, gender, health, etc.	Pre-employment education/ training Socialization Career trajectories Risk management Insecurity – employment, income, retirement Engagement with family	Career success Career resilience Cognitive performance Well-being at all levels (health, economic)
Organizational level	Business environment and strategy, market position, stakeholders' focus, plus corporate social responsibility	HRM strategy Incentives Industrial relations Talent management	Attractiveness and reputation Talent flow Performance outcomes
Society/national level	Education system; legal system, in particular labor laws; government involvement in labor contracting; economic dynamism and rate of business formation	Wider employment stakeholders Entrepreneurship Welfare practices Labor force quality – capital Education and social services	Brain-gain/brain-drain Labor productivity Competitive advantage National well-being
Global level	Economic zones, political stability, societal prosperity	Global mobility	Convergence vs. divergence of people management
	Influencing factors: Push- and pull- forces; individualization of society; talent management; entrepreneurship		

Figure 5.1 Career ecosystem and changing psychological contracts (adapted from Baruch & Rousseau, 2019)

One way to develop a transactional relationship is by employability, as discussed in Chapter 4, which will benefit individuals, but can hardly serve as a substitute for loyalty on the organizational side of the equation. Employability offers people a different kind of psychological contract so that they will feel a fair deal exists rather than feeling betrayed. Organizations can no longer afford to offer (or to promise) people a stable workplace and a long-term commitment to employment. In the information age this should be understandable. To replace this traditional notion, employees will receive 'employability'. The organization makes a fresh promise: we will invest in you, make you attractive for other employers so that if you have to leave (i.e. when we will fire you), you will be able to find a new job easily. To put it bluntly, this is the essence of employability, according to many who have written about the concept (e.g. De Vos et al., 2020; Gazier, 2017; Ghoshal et al., 1999; Waterman et al., 1994). Others see it from a more positive point of view, that investing in the employability of the employees is a worthy investment for organizations. The context of labour markets has changed, in particular due to the global competitive market, when it is not feasible to stick to traditional relationships. However, an increasingly large share of the general workforce consists of sophisticated, highly-educated people, and for them, employability can also be read as 'in the future we will prepare you for the next round of restructuring, when you will be made redundant'. This fits well with the cynicism that may exist with HR managers, but explains some of the dynamics of careers.

Figures 5.2 to 5.4 show the dynamic nature of HRM and career systems.

Figure 5.2 implies that a major change in the career landscape has been taking place since the end of the 20th century. It necessitates revised organizational career systems, in particular in the planning element. Many unpredictable elements enter the equation. Careers were assumed to be in transition to a state of VUCA (volatility, uncertainty, complexity, and ambiguity), reflecting on these factors for the wider business environment (Bennett & Lemoine, 2014). The diversity of inputs and options requires the HR manager to be open to both internal and external work environments. They should develop excellent networks not merely within the organization but also in the relevant labour market environment, to anticipate both possible departures and either likely or imaginable options for replacement and alternative resourcing. In a complementary way, even with the end of conventional thinking about career ladders, a hierarchy still exists in medium and large organizations. Exploring new options does not mean fully abandoning the traditional system that is still applicable for a vast number of people.

Figure 5.3 emerges as a direct consequence of the implications of Figure 5.2. The traditional recruitment flow for most organizations was into the entry level, for both rank-and-file and managerial posts. Occasionally a few managerial openings would occur at higher levels, a few in particular at the top executive level. The Sonnenfeld and Peiperl (1988) model depicts it as a 'supply flow', that is, a source of new employees. The flow can be internal (only or mostly from the lower grades), or external (at all hierarchy levels). The transformational model depicted in Figure 5.3 indicates that the trend is towards an external supply flow, due not necessarily to choice but to necessity, as the dynamics of careers enforce the need to refill positions at all levels when necessary. Individuals taking control of their own careers do not have the traditional barriers that force them to stay within the organization, so may leave at any time.

From: Traditional career systems, organzational focused

To: Contemporary career, individual focused

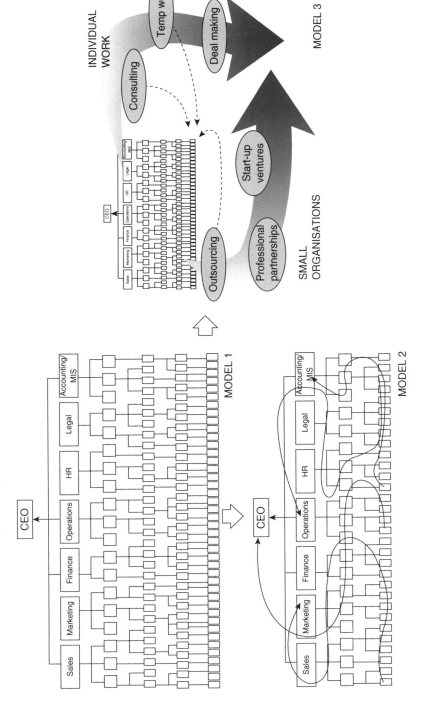

Figure 5.2   The transformation of career planning (based on Peiperl & Baruch, 1997)

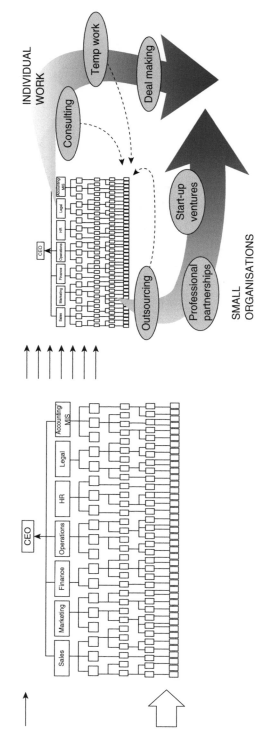

Figure 5.3 The transformation of recruitment (based on Peiperl & Baruch, 1997)

From:
The Dunlop (1959) model of IR:
Trade Union-led collective bargaining

To:
- New psychological contract
- Individual negotiation shared by the individual and the organization

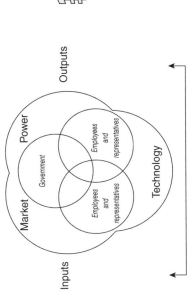

IR system
Dunlop model

Power

Government

Employees and representatives

Employees and representatives

Market

Technology

Inputs

Outputs

Feedback

Figure 5.4 The transformation of the industrial relations system (based on Peiperl & Baruch, 1997)

While Ghoshal et al. (1999), Hammer and Champy (1993) and their followers (e.g. Grant, 2016) argued for the need to cut the number of managerial levels, in practice organizational control mechanisms still rely heavily on hierarchy and lines of authority. In addition, people depend on hierarchies and structures to re-establish their own identities and achievement levels. In any case, career entry points are now spread fairly evenly throughout the managerial levels. As a result there is a growing need to acquire managers at all levels of management in organizations.

Figure 5.4 posits a stimulating perspective for US, European, and other national boundaries. The transition of employment relations is apparent, although the change in the legal and industrial relations system is conventionally slow to respond to fast environmental, sociological, and organizational developments. From the traditional Dunlop model (1959) of simplicity and a structured relationship of identifiable players at the three representative levels (employees' representation, organizations, and governments), there is a transition to the ambiguous and multivariate level of analysis depicted in Figure 5.4 as the 'fluid' model. The new model clearly distinguishes negotiation between the organization and the individual and the distance between core and peripheral employees. The new deal model is obviously distinct from the traditional one.

Negotiation now takes place between several constituencies of the organization: management (and HR representing the organization) and individuals on both 'hard' issues of payment and conditions as well as 'soft' elements of employability, commitment, and investment in people (e.g. competencies). There is a difference between core and peripheral employees, and some negotiations are conducted with external agencies and sub-contractors responsible for outsourced work. In most cases, unions have lost their wide powers (Bryson et al., 2011). However, there is an interesting aspect of the change in labour markets. Traditionally, trade unions had a strong hold in manufacturing and public service industries (e.g. government bodies). As the share of public services rises, paradoxically union membership also grows. Nevertheless, the bargaining power that derives from the ability to strike has become less of a threat to employers. In the early 2000s, Fiat, the Italian car manufacturer, announced that it would lay off one-fifth of its 40,000-strong workforce due to overcapacity (the demand for Fiat cars is about two million a year, while the firm can produce well over three million cars a year). By 2020 the situation was not much different: The Volkswagen Group announced in March 2019 that the VW brand would cut up to 7,000 jobs as part of an initiative to boost productivity and deliver annual savings of €5.9bn (US$6.7bn) by 2023. Similarly, Audi said that it will cut 9,500 existing jobs by 2025 (Kahl, 2020). The car workers' union power to object to such realities of the market has diminished, and in most cases they are only able to try to negotiate a better deal for those leaving. Cheap labour on a global scale elsewhere has posed a dilemma for trade unions: if they play too hard they might lose the whole employment deal. The trend towards individualism also means that the legal aspects of industrial relations are dealt with more often via individual contracting than via collective bargaining.

Psychological theory would suggest that individuals affected might feel bitter towards organizations for changing the comfortable and uncomplicated structure of the conventional hierarchy. They might lament the loss of the recognition and appreciation of loyalty and commitment which this hierarchy provided.

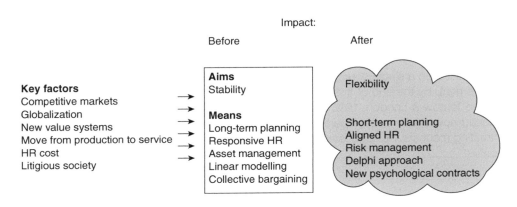

Figure 5.5 The transformation of strategic HR planning (based on Peiperl & Baruch, 1997)

Figure 5.5 depicts the influence of several factors on strategic HRM planning and consequently on a long-term career system development. Strategic HRM is critical for organizational performance, as found in several studies, including meta-analytical works (Jiang et al., 2012: Tzabbar et al., 2017). The role of strategic HRM is important in times of stability, but even more so in turbulent times. The dynamic nature of current labour markets means moving from familiar and approachable systems characterized by stability and enabling long-term planning, to ambiguity, resulting in short-term planning.

Career dynamism

Beginning to reason is like stepping onto an escalator that leads upwards and out of sight. Once we take the first step, the distance to be travelled is independent of our will and we cannot know in advance where we shall end (Singer, 1982).

We live in exciting times. The realities of the workplace can be harsh, but can bring thrills and enthusiasm to people and organizations. Change makes life interesting, as the old Chinese proverb says. Cascio (2000) listed six key business trends that inflict changes in the world of work, following the major change in the way people are managed (Ulrich, 1998). These are globalization, technological change, intellectual capital, speed of market change, and cost control. To these we can add continuing socioeconomic developments and individual consciousness, discussed earlier.

Box 5.1: 360 degrees – an indication of the dynamism in career system practices

360-degree feedback will be discussed in Chapter 6, but it serves as a good example of the dynamism of developments in both the theory and practice of HR, with implications for career systems.

Performance appraisal (PA) grew out of organizations' need for a more objective measure than informal managerial networking for managing people (e.g. for promotion, training needs, etc.). PA provided feedback on employees' input and contributions, as well as their needs. But PA was based on a single source of information, and suffered from poor reliability and invalid measurement. By the end of the 20th century, 360-degree feedback was strongly advocated (e.g. see Tornow & London, 1998). By the end of the 1990s, some misgivings were raised as HR faced new challenges, in particular when cultural differentiations viewed this practice in contrasting manners, as suggested by Bracken and Rose (2011).

A philosophical perspective on the basis for change may focus on the shift from a collectivist to an individualistic society (reflected, in the career context, in Hall's protean career). Post-modern values reflected this shift. People developed high individual consciousness, with a pre-eminent focus on individualism and concern with self (Singer, 1997; Wolfe, 1998), the care for their wellbeing, and balance between work and life (Jones et al., 2013).

A pause for reflection

What can and should organizations do to manage careers in a positive manner, and at the same time identify and prevent negative factors that would lead to deterioration (e.g. massive departure of key employees)?

How, then, would you advise line managers and HR executives about how to approach the new realities of organizational career systems? In what way did the understanding of the individual perspective (presented earlier in the book) help you in reaching your conclusions?

Implications for organizations

In managing careers, organizations should not rely on traditional models which build on stable and clear hierarchies. They need to realize that one should no longer act as if the old notion of organizational commitment and loyalty is valid and applicable. Greater awareness of the multiple commitments employees have is necessary, and especially the decreasing importance of organizational commitment within these multiple commitments. This requires the development of a different new psychological contract (Baruch & Rousseau, 2019), like idiosyncratic deals tailored for individual employees (Rousseau, 2015), as well as new forms of legal contracts. Such is the zero-hours contract, which is now widely applied to non-core positions in order to enable flexibility for both parties (Datta et al., 2019; Koumenta & Williams, 2019). It is a contentious form of employment that concentrated in a small number of occupations and sectors, typically applied for non-standard employment features like temporary or part-time work. Employees under these zero-hours contracts are paid less than others, and perceive inferior job quality and underemployment (Koumenta & Williams, 2019). Adjustment of expectations are required from both individuals and organizations when considering both psychological and legal contracts.

Lewin's field theory (1951) was useful for describing and analysing changes in a relatively stable period. He suggested that there are three basic stages for any change. Change should be perceived as occurring in a field of forces, in which 'push' and 'pull' forces operate in different directions. In terms of work, these forces can push towards a decision of starting a second career, for example. For a change to occur there needs to be a 'de-freezing' stage, then change develops, and this is followed by a final stage of 're-freezing', leading back to stability, until a further need arises, which will trigger the next change. The model works well (i.e. has strong explanatory power) within a timeframe that allows the three stages, ending with re-freezing. However, today it seems that organizations are subject to constant changes that do not permit any re-freezing. Fluidity rules, as suggested by the VUCA of contemporary labour markets. Some fifty years ago, in his book *Future Shock*, Toffler (1970) warned that there was a feeling that the rate of change was accelerating, and that 'change was out of control'. The events and development in the employment landscape of the 21st century confirm his prediction.

Peiperl and Baruch (1997) describe how career systems develop, under which career sustainability can be achieved by adjustment and change of frame-of-mind (Van der Heijden et al., 2020). In humanity's earliest days, all men had similar roles, that of the hunter–gatherer. Nicholson (1998, 2010) claims that the ways of thinking and feelings developed in those days are still deeply rooted in our cognitive map. Later, even when civilization started to flourish, there was no career system for most of the population: the vast majority of people worked on the land, in workshops, or primitive industries, and generally did so near their homes. Careers and their management is a relatively modern phenomenon. Peiperl and Baruch show how models of careers have evolved, with an interesting return to 'square zero', but not literally – perhaps it has been more of a spiral than a circular development.

Box 5.2: Hidden work

Hidden work is work that takes place outside the legal system, and is a wide-range, global issue (Schneider & Buehn, 2018). It is usually undertaken by individuals (but is sometimes arranged in syndicates). Hidden work is prominent in some Eastern Europe countries, following the collapse of communism. In Western societies much money moves through illegal drug trading, a

(Continued)

relatively new sector among the many 'traditional' sectors of hidden employment. Hidden work is under-studied for obvious reasons, in particular accessibility, but deserves more attention (Noon & Blyton, 1997). The majority of people, however, are engaged in conventional employment, where paradigms are changing.

Hochschild (2016) expand the view of 'hidden work' to those workers who are invisible to customers, be they in developing countries or outside the framework that people can relate to.

VUCA – perpetual motion

Events in life influence careers, and these events can take place simultaneously in various levels. At the individual level, people can be influenced by a chance event or other career shocks, as discussed earlier in the book. Moving on to the institutional level, an organization may win a lucrative contract, or expand to new markets and geographies, meaning new opportunities. This generates more demand for employees, more opportunities to progress, or options for expatriation. Conversely, organizations can lose customers by continuing to produce dated products and failing to move with the times. This was the case of Kodak, for example, which refused to accept new technology, which led to its demise as a global leading enterprise (Lucas & Goh, 2009). As Lucas and Goh observed, Kodak's management could not contemplate the need for a transition to think digitally. The results were devastating: Kodak has experienced a nearly 80% decline in its workforce. This was inevitable due to major loss of market share and a tumbling stock price.

At the wider society, national level and beyond, global events can change the career structure and landscape. For example, the end of the communist regime in the post-Soviet Eastern Europe had led to a profound shift in business environment, and therefore career systems. The financial crisis of 2008 influenced the finance sector in many countries, and was felt more significantly in countries which depend on this sector, like the UK. The aftermath of the crisis showed how people with different identities may be engaged with their career in different ways. For example, individuals without a strong professional identity or profession-consistent learning goals were more likely to anticipate and engage in career activities unrelated to their professions, whereas those with a strong career identity and profession-focused learning were more likely to anticipate and engage in career activities tied to their profession (Simosi et al., 2015). Another global event influencing careers at a vast scale was the COVID-19 pandemic. It influenced certain sectors more than others, for example, the hospitality sector (Alonso et al., 2020), crushing many businesses, yet creating new jobs and opportunities for firms like Amazon and Zoom.

The survivor syndrome

The above cases remind us that job loss is a typical and reoccurring event in life. What could replace the old paradigms and how do organizations manage the processes of motivating people and maintaining their commitment when job security is no longer a valid concept? With the old paradigms and concepts of stability and job security being no longer relevant, the challenge is to get the best out of people in a new framework.

Downsizing, namely shrinking the size of the workforce, is designed to reduce expenses or enhance competitiveness. Redundancy means a career shock to individuals who have lost their jobs. Yet, the impact is far-reaching, as redundancies also influence those who remain after redundancies have been made. The term 'survivor syndrome' has been coined to refer to and describe the reaction of people who remain in employment after an organization has undergone a redundancy or downsizing programme. It has been argued that those who stay in an organization often experience the adverse effects of change as profoundly as those who have left (Brockner, 1992; Travaglione & Cross, 2006). Scholars have suggested multitude negative consequences of survivor syndrome: for example, O'Neil and Lenn (1995) argued that inappropriate redundancy would end in anger, anxiety, cynicism, resentment, resignation, and retribution. Job insecurity and fear of further restructuring add to stress in the workplace (Shoss, 2017). To these negative effects, Downs (1995) added low morale, overworking, and the possibility of sabotage. The impact on survivors can be destructive, leading to a dysfunctional impact on commitment, loyalty, and performance (Baruch, 1998a; Brockner et al., 1992a; Bui et al., 2019). Another prominent writer on downsizing, Cameron (2015), has cited overload, burnout, inefficiency, conflict, and low morale as possible negative consequences of survivor syndrome. Businesses that understand these attitudinal and motivational issues will be able to manage the process in order to enhance the performance of these survivors and thus of the organization (Doherty & Horsted, 1995).

As Baruch and Hind (1999, 2000) state, organizations must overcome the psychological transition from 'It won't happen here' to 'When is it going to happen?'. Individuals need a similar change of frame of mind, from 'It won't happen to me' to 'What do I do if or when it does?'.

How to manage the survivor syndrome

When an organization is considering specific factors to focus on in order to preserve employee morale during downsizing, Mishra et al. (1998) suggest the following:

1. *Deciding*: use downsizing as a last resort; construct a credible vision, based on the business case; and ensure downsizing is not seen as a short-term fix.
2. *Planning*: form a cross-functional team, who are unified on the reasons for downsizing; identify all constituents and address their concerns; use experts such as outplacement counsellors to smooth the transition; provide training to managers and supply adequate information on the state of the business.
3. *Making the announcement*: explain the business rationale; announce the decision, notify employees in advance where possible; be specific, time the announcement appropriately; offer employees the day off.
4. *Implementing the decisions*: tell the truth and even over-communicate, provide job search assistance for leavers; announce subsequent separations as planned; be fair in implementing

separations; be generous to leavers; allow for voluntary separation; involve employees in implementation; provide career counselling; and train the survivors where necessary.

Baruch and Hind (1999) argue that, although detailed, the above list is lacking in two respects. First, it consists of a set of separate, dissociated issues, and does not provide a coherent, comprehensive framework (which they produce – see Figure 5.6). Second, several key elements are missing. Mishra et al. (1998) ignore the trade union issue, perhaps because they refer mostly to the US private sector. For this reason their advice may be of little help in organizations with unionized and protected labour. This may be a critical factor, as many employees and their representatives view the new psychological contract as a threat. Another factor omitted, again perhaps of crucial importance, is the provision of counselling to survivors as well as to leavers. Often, counselling is offered only to those exiting the organization. One of the most important elements in a downsizing programme is the perception of the process used to select those to be made redundant (Klehe et al., 2011). The selection needs to be based on clear, performance- and operational-related criteria, with obvious links to the business case and rationale. 'Best practice' should be implemented in managing downsizing (Gunnigle et al., 2013). It is also important to implement decisions swiftly.

Figure 5.6 presents a flow-chart diagram for the process of downsizing and redundancy, representing the options and their determinants. The figure suggests a sequence that organizations should anticipate in managing the survivor syndrome effect. What is to be expected, then, and what should be done?

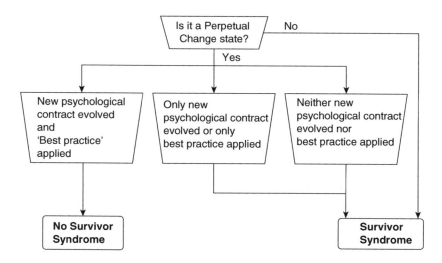

Figure 5.6 Downsizing and the survivor syndrome effect

The first stage is characterized by relative stability and traditional psychological contracts. Such conditions represent utopia in the industrial world, but may still exist in certain sectors or some developing countries. If an organization has managed to maintain a feeling of stability and the 'old deal', any deviation will cause survivor syndrome, argue Baruch and Hind (1999). However, in most business environments, 'perpetual change' is already the new way of life. For example, most large organizations, and the vast majority of Fortune 500 companies, have had constant rounds of redundancy cycles since the 1980s (Cameron, 2015).

If a state of perpetual change is not recognized, organizations must first create awareness of the concept of a 'fast-changing environment'. Generating an atmosphere of urgency enables people to go through a transformation process, which will permit them to operate and perform while realizing that they are doing so in a 'perpetual change' mode.

In the following stage (characterized by perpetual change, which is recognized by both employees and management), the organization should develop a new psychological contract. This in itself is necessary, but not sufficient. The next stage is using 'best practice'. Only when all three pre-conditions are met may the organization hope to avoid the survivor syndrome.

Best practice indeed? Are there do's and don'ts for downsizing?

What is best practice? Is there one general 'best practice' or are there many possibilities? Several scholars, practitioners as well as academics, have suggested various concepts to use in developing best practice. These are recommended in order to improve people management and subsequent organizational performance (Tzabbar et al., 2017). Given the existence of so many sets of conditions, environments, and other antecedents, more than one contingency should be considered to achieve a smooth process and to minimize the survivor syndrome effect. Chapter 7 provides a general framework for 'best practice' for CPM practices. Regarding downsizing, the advice for organizations is to use redundancy only as a last resort. It is advisable to prove to or show employees that it was indeed the last resort, only after all feasible options have been tried. Such options or alternative practices include:

- early retirement
- reducing or halting recruitment for a limited period (but not for too long, otherwise organizations will have a 'missing generation' in the future)
- selling part of the company (e.g. via a buy-out)
- promoting entrepreneurial activity like spin-out initiatives
- job-sharing
- secondments (temporary work for other firms or organizations).

Of course, upon implementation the organization should be supportive towards leavers, help in their job search, provide training and career counselling (see Chapter 7), and so on.

The Peter Principle and organizational career systems

The art of ensuring that people are effective is the principal role of career systems. In the past, one of the most problematic obstacles to the effective management of people and consequently to organizational effectiveness was the Peter Principle. It was seen as a valid concept in the traditional hierarchy-based organizational structure. The Peter Principle is simple: in a bureaucracy, employees progress up the hierarchy until they reach their level of incompetence, that is, where their performance is unsatisfactory, and at that level they will stay. This paradoxical idea is found in many organizations where people progress 'up the ladder', where tenure is the most significant factor in decisions on promotion and where redundancies are rare. The Peter Principle reflects a wastage in the system, known as the 'dead-wood phenomenon', where individuals end their productive phase but still retain their position, with no prospects of career progress (Veiga, 1981).

Where the Peter Principle applies, organizational effectiveness deteriorates. This was particularly true in many rigid organizations, and was an unfortunate phenomenon while job security was the rule. The change in industrial relations systems and the loss of job security have meant that the Peter Principle has become less of a threat to organizations. People who cannot function according to their level of responsibility and authority have to leave. In this case, the firm segregates their labour-force into the following segments: a fast stream, a slower stream, the 'right level' group (for lateral movement), and the Peter Principle group, the latter destined to look for employment elsewhere.

The meaning of organizations becoming 'lean and mean' (Thirkell & Ashman, 2014) is: no more room for 'fat' or reserves; no options left for people who are not performing to their best. The luxury of maintaining slack means less competitiveness, and organizations cannot afford this.

Like Parkinson's Law (see box below), and stripped of its humorous elements, the concept is disturbing due to its valid reflection of real-life situations. The lack of an option to get rid of 'dead wood' made the Peter Principle a fact of life during the industrial era of the 20th century. However, the changing nature of HRM and career management created a different climate. Those incapable of performing, unfit to perform well in a position, can no longer maintain that position. Lateral and even downward movement became feasible, and redundancies became the norm.

Box 5.3: Parkinson's Law

Parkinson's Law is a classical management concept (Gough, 2011), which denotes that every bureaucracy tends to grow in number of employees and in hierarchy structure because work expands to fill the time allocated to it, the available time (Hasija et al., 2010).

Rothwell (1995) associates HR planning with careful career planning, and even more important, with corporate policy towards career-matched policies and approach. HRM planning is a critical activity in retaining talent and ensuring that organizations can fulfil their goals (Chakraborty & Biswas, 2019). An example of corporate policy can be the decision to have a balance between promoting from within and introducing new employees and managers. This may be a decision to implement an 80:20 insider:outsider ratio of managers, even when the firm has a preference for employing internal labour (Beattie & Tampoe, 1990).

CASE STUDY 5.1: ABANDONING THE SYSTEM – THE CASE OF OTICON

Oticon is a Danish high-tech firm in the hearing aid industry (the third largest in the world), which employs some 5,000 people (the majority of whom are located globally). It went through radical changes that came via a new leadership vision, which followed budget and operational crises (Larsen, 1996). They abandoned the traditional hierarchy, cut out the entire managerial structure, and established a project-based firm, a fluid organizational structure (DeFillippi & Arthur, 1998; Wikström et al., 2010). The implications for the career management system were overwhelming (Larsen, 2002). In the new career development system there was no rigid, and hardly any structure at all. Each staff member could become a project leader, and at the same time retain a position as project member in other projects. There was only one layer of top management, with no intermediate level. A few former experienced managers have become 'centres of professional expertise'. This led at first to certain feelings of a lack of HRM input, therefore a new type of role was introduced, that of 'coaches' to serve as mentors and holding HR responsibility. This framework requires people to match their career expectations to a totally different system. While many in Oticon felt they could not go through such a change and left, the rest, continued to make Oticon a success story with long-term sustainability (Foss et al., 2015).

Student question

Would you like to work for an employer that practices such a different view of an organizational career?

Qualities dynamism

In the past what mattered was having formal qualifications. Competencies, and even more importantly, the ability to learn, have become critical, no less than the formal qualifications – which are, of course, essential to gain a job with prospects for future progress. Self-efficacy, self-esteem, and resilience are the basis of the successful career path for the new careerist.

One of the most crucial core competencies of an organization is the knowledge of its employees. People strive and build their success on knowledge and other individual competencies. These can be professional/vocational related, or managerial. Tables 5.1a and 5.1b list a set of competencies that individuals may gain from managerial education, all of which are sought by MBA graduates (Baruch, 2009; Baruch & Peiperl, 2000b). The table also shows differences between MBA graduates and non-MBA managers on these competencies.

Table 5.1a Competencies and managerial education

	Perceived competence		
	MBAs	**Others**	**Sig**
1. Effective reading	5.32 (5.22)	4.93	**
2. Oral presentations	5.21 (5.18)	4.83	**
3. Written presentations	5.54 (5.52)	5.04	***
4. Time management	5.05 (4.83)	4.4	***
5. Interviewing	4.75 (4.69)	4.56	ns
6. Financial skills	4.89	4.35	***
7. Managing change	5.25	4.89	**
8. Stress management	4.54 (4.72)	4.36	ns
9. Career management	4.52 (4.72)	4.03	**
10. Research skills	5.07 (4.94)	4.49	***
11. Accountancy skills	4.02	3.27	***
12. Working in teams	5.40	5.14	ns
13. Negotiating skills	4.75 (4.71)	4.55	ns
14. Self-confidence	5.33	5.01	*
15. Decision making	5.51	5.28	**
16. Interpersonal skills	5.18	5.09	ns
17. Abstract thinking	4.91	4.58	ns
18. Managing others	5.12	5.02	ns
Mean all (CMPT)	5.03	4.66	***

ns: non-significant difference, * α<.1, ** α<.05, *** α<.001.

Source: Based on Baruch & Peiperl, 2000a; Baruch & Leeming, 2001.

Table 5.1b   Competencies of learning skills

Competencies of learning skills; based on questionnaire	Specific abilities; based on critical incident analysis
Leadership	Efficiency orientation
Relationship	Planning
Helping	Initiative
Sense-making	Attention to details
Information-gathering	Self-control
Information analysis	Flexibility
Theory building	Self-confidence
Quantitative	Empathy
Technology	Social objectivity
Goal-setting	Persuasiveness
Action	Networking
Initiative	Negotiating
Total: Self confidence	Group management
	Developing others
	System-thinking
	Pattern recognition

Source: Boyatzis, et al., 2002

To these lists, cross-cultural competencies was added by Mendenhall et al. (2013).

The diversity of competencies possessed by individuals enables them to flourish in their jobs and to survive in a tough labour market. At the organizational level, employing a diversity of employees will be of benefit. It is a managerial responsibility to keep up to date with labour market trends.

At the practical level, companies wishing to ensure a diversity of qualities should widen their talent pool. Here, demographic diversity can help (for which see Chapter 9). Effective management of diversity requires the harnessing of the special needs and different characteristics of different people, which may be associated with their different life and career stages. Chapter 7 presents, among other practices, some that are specifically directed towards particular groups, for example, dual-career couples, the pre-retirement population, or high-flyers. Career plans need to incorporate the singular qualities of all individual members of the organization.

Succession planning (see Chapter 7) provides an example: in a well-planned scheme each person would have several options for career moves, whereas for each position there would be several candidates to fill it.

Career communities

Parker and Arthur (2000) associated the intelligent career's 'three ways of knowing' (know why, know how, and know whom) with a diversity of career communities. The idea of people having multiple sets of commitment is not new: each individual can have commitments in more than one realm of their life (Baruch & Rousseau, 2019). Multiple commitments refer to several levels of meaning: identification, association, and relationship (as discussed in Chapter 3). These relationships can also depend on the career stage that a person has reached (Cohen, 1991). In the careers context, Parker and Arthur offered a basic list, which is elaborated below: industry (sector); occupation and professional association; region (from local to national); ideology; religion; alumni (of school, university, military or reserve forces service where applicable); support groups; family; virtual; and organization.

Within the organization, commitment need not be general to the organization, but is usually shared among different constituencies: the organization, the leader and/or mentor; the team; the department/unit; the project (or product); and peers/colleagues. Commitment to a union can be classified as work-related, but its boundaries lie across organizational borders. For the organization this means that individuals manage a very complex network of commitments within multi-level communities, and the organization cannot and should not see itself as the core base for employees' self-identity and the focal point of their life.

A pause for reflection

What are the major communities from which you gather your strength and hope for the future? What role would the ideal organization play for you as one of these communities?

The dark side of careers

While a career community is just one of many positive frameworks that were developed to explain the meaning of careers and their management (see Baruch et al., 2015; Lee et al., 2014), the less positive features of careers and their management are typically under-studied or suffer from lack of scholarly attention. Yet, contemporary carers have a dark side strongly attached to them (Baruch & Vardi, 2016). They offer a balanced career perspective that consists of opportunities versus threats, truth versus untruth, and positive versus negative aspects, all of which are inevitably embedded in careers. Whereas the dark side of personality may have some influence on career success perception (Paleczek et al., 2018), it is the dark side of organizations and their leaders that can cause harm to the careers of others (Cohen, 2018).

When considering the ideas behind contemporary career concepts and theories, the literature can be misleading. For example, while for some the boundarylessness of careers may be a refreshing and challenging source of optimism, for others it is bound to create confusion, anxiety, and career despair. Uncertainty of opportunities could enhance stress rather than increase motivation (Baruch & Vardi, 2016). Similarly, the post-corporate career is typically imposed on individuals rather than being a choice, with the consequences of increased stress, anxiety, and loss of perceived stability. As for the protean career model, they argue that it mostly fits a minor segment of the labour market, and less answers the needs of change-adverse individuals – for them it is a risky approach, or even a career-destructive one due to the stress and ambiguity it is associated with. Some prefer the organization to plan and manage their working life. With regard to the kaleidoscope career – again, not necessarily a chosen path but inflicted due to circumstances and unpredictable turn of events, keeping the career actor on her or his toes. At the organizational level, employers who wish their employees to achieve a balanced and authentic career might realize that it is a luxury they cannot afford. For the employer, it could interfere with planning and generate chaotic and dysfunctional human resource systems.

Overall, the dark side of careers can be the result of dark side personalities (Furnham et al., 2014), and the hidden elements of career systems (Baruch & Vardi, 2016).

A pause for reflection

How will you avoid the dark side of careers?

In general, try to opt for a career system that fits your personality and aspirations. If you hold a protean career orientation, enjoy the dynamics of the private sector, perhaps give entrepreneurial activities a try. If you prefer stability and security, look for sectors that still offer it, like public services.

More specifically, aim to choose an employer that does not have a toxic work environment. Easy to say – how can this be achieved? Rigorous investigation before accepting a job offer. If possible, using your networks (see below) to identify pros and cons of your future prospective employer.

Career networking

Much of the success of individuals' careers and the organizational career system depends on the ability to develop and use effective networks for communication and learning. For individuals, these help to identify and initiate the best next career move. For organizations, it is essential in the practice of talent management (Claussen et al., 2014), where network size is a significant factor in predicting the chances of benefiting from promotion at mid-level management.

What is the position of a person who has no network, if they have worked for years for a company that encouraged internal networking and practically barred external career networking? When such a person is made redundant they face a severe problem of re-entering the labour market. If that is the case, the company may show a degree of responsibility and support by offering outplacement services, either internally or via the use of external agencies (see Box 5.2)

CASE STUDY 5.2: OUTPLACEMENT SERVICES: DOUBTING THOMAS

Tom arrived at our offices depressed and angry. He had been informed by his employer on the previous Friday afternoon that his style did not fit the new organization culture. He was 'Too aggressive, too uncomfortable to have around and his job no longer existed.' He was offered outplacement counselling as part of his severance package.

Tom was convinced that outplacement was conscience money from his employers.

That first meeting had Tom primarily living in the past – going over meetings and conversations to try to understand how things had come to this. We dealt with his feelings and his focus, which was entirely internal. It took some time to get him to even consider the future and how we could help. We convinced him that he was our client and that we were here to help him irrespective of who paid for our service.

He reluctantly agreed to do some homework before our next meeting. This work consisted of Tom identifying the things that he had found of value both in his career and his personal life, and also to write a description of himself and his life to date.

At our second meeting a few days later Tom had started to realize that his life to date had been pretty successful. He had married and raised two lovely children. He was a home-owner and well regarded within the community. His career had been successful up until this point. Tom hadn't changed – the environment had. The skills and attributes which had made him successful would be valued in many companies.

This self-analysis proved a powerful reinforcement of Tom's self-esteem. It provided the basis for examining and identifying his life and career goals. At 42, Tom wanted to use the skills he had developed in his previous two companies to continue his career trajectory. We discussed other options such as consultancy or running his own business. Tom was concerned about the risks these options may place on his family.

Having completed a comprehensive analysis we were ready to prepare a marketing plan. This included CV development, targeting sectors, companies, and relevant consultancies. Approach letters and advert analysis also featured.

Tom's depression receded and returned on a number of occasions, usually associated with rejection letters. We kept him doing positive things and maintained a high level of momentum. His interview skills were developed using video feedback to help him modify his behaviour and present himself in a positive manner. Our extensive access to job and company databases helped keep his activity level high.

He also accessed our web facilities regularly. He then started to get first interviews followed by rejections which lowered his morale. We analysed each interview in detail and discovered that some residual bitterness was coming through.

We convinced him to put the past behind and look at his current situation as an opportunity. Eventually after three months Tom found a vacancy on our database. It was in his discipline but outside his previous sectors. His first and second interviews went well and the company made him an offer. He was unsure if he should accept so we did a positive/negative analysis which showed that the positives far outweighed the negatives.

We helped with his negotiation tactics and secured the best offer possible.

Tom started his job with our jointly developed integration plan to help make an impact and maximize his early effectiveness. He is doing well and has taken to his new sector, bringing added value by his cross-sector expertise. We talk regularly and he knows we are here for him if it does not work out. His Christmas card read 'Thanks for listening, thanks for the guidance, the outplacement experience has affected me in a way I would not have thought possible.'

This case was kindly provided by The Quo Group Ltd.

Student question

Under what circumstances would you wish to use outplacement services?

Careers as metaphors

The use of metaphors can be helpful for understanding career concepts, and they are widely used to clarify meanings of careers-related concepts and theories (Baruch et al., 2015; Inkson et al., 2016). There are many ways to describe careers in a metaphorical way (Inkson, 2004).

Box 5.4: Metaphors – food for thought*

Metaphors are 'the application of a name or a descriptive term or phrase to an object or action to which it is imaginatively but not literally applicable, e.g. a glaring error' (*The Concise Oxford Dictionary*, 2014). The use of metaphors for understanding organizations has been advocated by, among others, Morgan (1997) and Hatch and Yanow (2008), and it is a well-established practice in depicting organizational features (e.g. Cornelissen et al., 2008; Smircich, 1983). Applying metaphors in the study of organizations has contributed to the development of organizational as well as many other types of theory. The advantage of using metaphors for understanding organizations has been well demonstrated by Morgan in his conceptual framework, and is widely applied in organizational studies (cf. Czarniawska, 1997). Metaphors transposed from more established sciences, for use within the science of management, can be advantageous in the sense that the analogy can enhance the understanding of relevant phenomena. 'Metaphor facilitates change by making the strange familiar, but in that very process it deepens the meaning or values of the organization by giving them expression in novel situations' (Pondy, 1983, p. 164). In addition, Avelsson (1995, p. 45) claims that certain phenomena are always regarded from a certain point of view. This means that all knowledge is metaphoric, since knowledge is perspective dependent.

*Note that the label of the above box is also a metaphor.

Box 5.5: Inkson's nine images of careers

In his 2004 paper, Inkson suggested nine metaphors to depict careers. These were explicated later by Inkson et al. (2015) and are presented below.

1. Legacy metaphor: Career as inheritance

This metaphor refers to the background that each person brings to their career, inherited from earlier generations. Starting with the basic individual characteristics such as gender, ethnicity, and no less important, sometime relates factors of social status and the socio-economic background of the family.

2. Seasons metaphor: Career as cycle

A metaphor used to associate the progress of careers with the time element, like seasons of the years. Most career stage concepts are focused around this metaphor.

3. Craft metaphor: Career as action

Here the focus is on personal agency, on acting towards ones own goals (and sometimes the inaction and its consequences). Building on theories like social learning and career construction, it helps to explain career decisions.

4. Matching metaphor: Career as fit

Looking at the fit between the individual and the career: the job, organization, occupation, sector. The metaphor elucidates the need for a match between the individual characteristics, in particular personality, and their chosen path.

5. Path metaphor: Career as journey

Perhaps the most clear metaphor to illuminate the view of careers as a progress of discovery, a trajectory of moves across working life.

6. Theatre metaphor: Career as role

Here we learn that in different situation we put on different 'masks' to act according to need. Our experience and identity form the way we develop our career and act accordingly.

7. Network metaphor: Career as encounters and relationships

Relating to the 'know whom' of the intelligent career, life put us in constant encounters with others in social contexts. These end with both short- and long-term relationships, which are essential to the continuation and direction of careers.

8. Economic metaphor: Career as resource

Career is not just about what we put into work, but what work gives us. In terms of tangible resources, we gain income (salary, benefits, remuneration, earnings, profits). The intangible resources gained from our careers shape our identity and meaning of life.

9. Narrative metaphor: Career as story

Each person's career is a story, and it could be told from various perspectives. It starts with the past, and can help lead through to the future. Usually the person narrates their career stories to reflect reality or to enact coming into terms with the way their has career evolved.

Perhaps the most current prominent use of metaphors in career theory are the boundaryless career, the protean career, and the kaleidoscope career. At the more nuance level, an example of a metaphorical use to capture the meaning of the interim manager's career was presented by Inkson et al. (2001). They suggested a series of complementary metaphors, including: displaced person, spare part, dating agency/marriage bureau client, hired gun, and bee. Together, these series of vivid images encapsulate the transience, alienation, mobility, ambiguity, and temporary fragile nature of the interim manager's career.

The use of linguistic metaphors can become more complex: 'paleonymics' means retaining old names while grafting new meaning upon them (Culler, 1982, p. 140). Boje et al. (1997) use the term 're-engineering' to demonstrate paleonymics; the 're' in re-engineering is an example of paleonymic grafting. It marks a difference or a gap in the word 'engineering' that is being supplemented. The 're' in re-engineering is a supplement, a little something extra added to complete engineering. The 're' also signifies adding a little something extra to bureaucracy. In the context of redundancy, Downs (1995) went so far as to use the context of capital punishment in his book title. In similar vein is the desert generation metaphor, and we can also identify the new meaning of resilience in Waterman et al.'s 'Toward a career-resilient workforce' (1994). Both are mentioned earlier in this book.

A more positive orientation is to look at career management via the gardening metaphor. It can be used as a strong analogy for career practice management in organizations. Bearing in mind the constant need for nourishment and support, developing people and nurturing plants share much in common. In his book *Being There*, Kosinski (1970) depicted a gardener who was assumed to be able to care for people, and even more.

Box 5.6: The garden metaphor

Kosinski (1970, p. 45) writes: 'It's not easy sir,' he said, 'to obtain a suitable place, a garden in which one can work without interference and row with the seasons ...' 'Very well put Mr. Gardiner, isn't that the perfect way to describe what a real business man is?'

The garden metaphor (as well as the will of people to hear what they want to hear) is quite convincing: Rand invites the president to meet Chance; the president was already told that Chance is a very intelligent business man. When Chance repeats the statement about the garden the president doesn't doubt for one second that Chance is being metaphorical. 'I must admit, Mr. Gardiner,' the president said, 'That what you have just said is the most refreshing and optimistic statement I have heard in a very, very long time.'

Let us look at caring for people via the metaphorical analogy of gardening (Table 5.2).

Table 5.2 Nourishing careers: a gardening metaphor

Gardening, for plants	Career management, for people
No two plants are alike – different soil, sun and watering conditions will get the best out of different plants.	No two people are alike – different conditions will get the best out of different people. The person-environment fit concept is applied here.
Have a variety of species to make the garden alive.	Encourage diversity of the workforce.
Don't let them all ripen at the same time.	We don't want all managers to be ready for further progress at the same time.
Start with seeds and small plants.	Use the internal labor market when possible: in developing people it is important to get them early – so that they will acquire the organizational values, attitudes and culture.
Don't let the tall ones block the light and take the space of the growing one.	Allow development for a new generation of managerial layers, don't let existing managers hinder the development of new talent.
Use only best quality seeds – ensure they fit the soil and conditions.	Make sure your recruitment and selection get you the best people for your needs.
Give the better plants enough space and good conditions. Thin out the poor one and the weeds.	Don't hesitate to make non-performers redundant.
Provide quality water and compost.	Remunerate your employees properly. Otherwise they will leave – after all, they are not plants.*

*Any metaphor is limited, and, yes, there are also differences between gardening and people management.

The garden metaphor is not the only one to be used. The role of the organization in career management can be understood via other metaphors, revealing several layers. Some of the more popular metaphors are outlined below.

Career as a journey, travelling the roads

This metaphor is perhaps the one most commonly used to tell stories of life and career. A career is a journey, which you may plan, but you never know where or even when it will end. The organization paves the roads, develops new paths, and holds the map. However, people can take different roads, outside the plan set by the organization. Career decisions, according to this metaphor, occur whenever people reach a road junction. Robert Frost, in his poem 'The Road Not Taken' said:

Two roads diverged in a wood, and I –

I took the one less travelled by

And that has made all the difference.

Several variations of this metaphor are:

- *Career as rowing down a river*: starting from the spring, merging with flows from new directions; no way back; and the pattern of the river may change in the future, so will be different for those that come later.
- *Career as climbing up a mountain*: almost the opposite to the former, but a strong metaphorical image is the climbing – and in today's career landscape it need not be a single mountain, but a group of hills, a chain of summits, each calling for climbers, posing a challenge. Starting from the plains, focusing on reaching the top, but with many alternative routes, people look on it as an adventure.
- *Career as navigating at sea*: no path, the way is navigated via tacit knowledge, one does not always know the destination, how long it will take to get there, or what obstacles there may be on the way (under water?).
- *Career as wandering in space*: no road map, random progress and development, lost in space (actually cyberspace).

The metaphor most frequently used, the career as a journey, implies that we use maps to navigate. In most of these metaphorical models, career structures are constructed around maps, and the organization holds the key, while the level of transparency varies. The options for mobility, the boundaries, and the landscape are becoming more transparent so that individuals can take a more active role in navigating their career in this uncertain world.

In contrast to the innovative, contemporary metaphors, the old-fashioned one sees the organization as a ladder or steps to climb.

Career as moving up in a building or ladder

The organization constructed the building or set up the ladder and gives you the best ways to move about. The walls are rigid, the steps are fixed and determined. Some places you will never see (i.e. if your career is in marketing you will never experience operations or finance).

More than the others, the following career metaphor can help us in understanding and confronting the role of the individual vis-à-vis that of the organization. It is the metaphor of the career as a play in the theatre of the world.

Career as a play in the theatre of the world

The management of careers is divided between the two players:

- Individual career management: which mask do we put on in each episode?
- The organization: stage management, setting the scene, ensuring continuity.

This is a metaphor that sees employment as a theatre. Career development is a part of a play, and in the play we perform different roles according to the mask we are wearing at the time.

People can put on a 'Manager' mask, a 'Big boss' mask, but also a 'Caring' mask, as well as many others. In different circumstances people play several parts and roles in the theatre of organizational life. A manager may need to wear the mask of 'Mentor' for supporting a protégé, five minutes later wear the 'Tough guy' mask for dealing with the union representative, and then swap to the 'Visionary' mask when seeking to inspire shareholders. This mask/theatre metaphor reflects the general behaviour of people at work, not just career management, but has strong implications for career systems. The organization can teach, educate, and train managers to use different 'masks' for their different career-related roles. Different qualities are needed in mentoring and in disciplining.

Organizational career systems resemble, for this metaphor, setting the stage, while the HR manager takes the role of director or producer of the play. However, life is never as structured and rigid as this implies, and theatrical improvisation may represent a more suitable metaphor in this case. What is clear and fits well with this metaphor is the way we are all expected to put on a 'mask' to fit the specific role or circumstances we face. What makes the theatre of life more complicated for many people is the discrepancy between their own inner qualities and the requirements of the role, especially when they have to perform a variety of roles. This happens in differences between work and home, for example, when the tough policeman returns home and becomes the loving father, but also in the work situation, when at one time you are appraising the performance of a subordinate, and the next you are facing your boss for your own appraisal.

Career as marriage

The metaphor that may best depict the relationship between employee and employer is that of marriage (with job separation resembling divorce, there being so much similarity in the feelings of people going through the process). Both relationships (marriage and employment) have suffered a severe blow in recent times. In both there has been a shift from an unconditional loyalty-based relationship to conditional attachment.

Companies may now see themselves as 'teams' rather than 'families'. A cynical interpretation for this new metaphor might be partly because you cannot fire a member of a family, but you can fire a member of a team.

From marriage to conditional attachment

One may see a strong association, correlational rather than just metaphorical, between the nature of marriage and employment relationships. In the past both marriage and employment were considered to be lifelong relationships, at least at the intentional level. In the latter part of the 20th century both establishments were cracking. Marriage has ceased to be the only form of cohabitation. Many people live together on a trial basis, and only if this works do they get married. Similarly, there are many temporary workers or people on short-term contracts, which can be converted to full employment if all goes well. Many marriage terminations occur because divorce is possible. Similarly, many employees, perhaps the majority, enter employment relationships with no intention of maintaining them for life. And the typical termination of an employment relationship does not occur at the time of retirement from a single employer. Employment relationships most frequently end as a result of redundancy or voluntary exit.

Career as a tournament

Despite all the changes to career systems, one metaphor that is still valid is that of the tournament. With fewer managerial layers, and people's strong need for visible progress, the tournament element of careers can become fierce. This perspective of career progress was initially offered by Rosenbaum (1979) to describe career mobility in large corporations. It has strong explanatory power, especially in a male-dominated workplace. A more recent review indicated how the career patterns of managerial progress are diversified (Vinkenburg & Weber, 2012).

Changes in specific occupations and the emergence of new vocations and business sectors

While some occupations are relatively stable, new occupational systems have emerged and evolved. Among these are some that existed in the past as a hobby-related activity, and others which are totally new.

One area that has expanded is sport as a career. If you were a football player in the 1960s–1970s, this was a spare-time activity. You had to have a job to earn your living. Hanging up your shoes at the end of a sporting career at the age of 30–35 usually meant going back to low-level jobs. If you were particularly successful (e.g. a leading player in the premier league), you might open a pub or sports shop and hope that your former fans will form a base of loyal customers. Times have changed, and the sums people earn in the top leagues in Europe have made a career in football a lucrative one. A retired footballer may move directly to the stock exchange to play with the money he has amassed or invest in a whole retail network. The same implies to other branches of sport too, most notably tennis and golf.

Another area of growth is that of emotional work. This includes not just psychology and psychiatry, both of which started as professions in the 20th century, but a wide range of consultancy and conciliatory work. Noon and Blyton (1997) have long ago argued that the need for this work is on the increase, as reiterated by Zapf et al. (2020).

Changes in the labour force and operational sectors

There have been gradual changes over the centuries in the labour market, first from the hunter-gatherers of prehistory to the introduction of agriculture, then the development of trading and the growth of a service sector and small-scale industry. The Industrial Revolution led to the development of large-scale manufacturing, the growth of cities, and a reduction in the numbers employed in agriculture. In the 20th century, improvements in technology led to further changes in the balance of employment in Western economies, with service-sector employment exceeding that in manufacturing. It is estimated that some 80% of the US workforce is in the service industry (Hochschild, 2016). In other countries, the composition of the labour force is changing due to other factors, such as mass migration from developing countries, mostly from Africa and Asia to Europe (Crowley-Henry et al., 2018), and from Mexico to the USA (Pries, 2019). Inner moves are within country – most notably the mass migration from the rural country to cities in China (Guo & Baruch, 2020). Unemployment in both old and new sectors has continued to rise as the pace of production and efficiency have improved. To this general trend, the impact of COVID-19 has generated further unemployment at an unprecedented level. The future, unfortunately, is not too promising; a question for the future is what will happen to the people who are no longer needed in agriculture, production, or services? Most want to work but we do not know where, in what or how they will keep their jobs. The last chapter of this book offers some insights into this issue. With digitization and the growing acceptance of AI to replace human beings, unemployment might become a permanent feature, with many having to consider a 'career' with no employment, relying on the new social initiative of universal basic income (Koistinen & Perkiö, 2014).

Digitalization of careers is extremely important. Working in a digital era means abundant use of IT, to begin with, and more increasing in importance and relevance, use of AI as part of understanding the future of careers. The difference in digitization and digitalization is clarified below as these words are sometimes confused (Bloomberg, 2018): *digitization* is the process of converting data into a digital format, whereas *digitalization* is the transformation of business processes.

Digitization is the technical process by which analogue materials are converted into digital bits (Brennen & Kreiss, 2016). This means automating business process, in line with the expectations and direction of the so-called new age businesses are looking for – disrupting the market (Markovitch & Willmott, 2014). Digitization can reinvent or redesign business processes, for example, minimizes required steps, documents, and automating decision making thereby delivering digital services and products with full access to information.

Digitalization is the integration of digitizable technologies into our daily and working lives. In terms of careers, it is a new landscape, where humans and AI interact and complement each other.

The pace of the sweeping changes described above was by no means uniform. The first took millions of years, the second, a couple of thousand years, the third, a few hundred years, and the last, only a few dozen years. At the present time there are many career options for those thrown out of the labour market, ejected from conventional jobs. One of the most amazing qualities of human beings is the ability to adapt, to develop, to transform. This ability, however, is limited, and depends on the pace and depth of change. It is relatively easy to alter behaviour. It is more difficult and demanding to change beliefs. And it is almost impossible to swap values and mental frameworks. As the widely-held value of work is instilled in the mindset of most of the population, expecting people to accept life without work, relying in universal basic income, could be a far too out-of-reach expectation. When the environment changes slowly, or when time is not a scarce resource, most people can adapt to change or cope with it effectively. However, if what is needed is an all-encompassing change, leading in a totally new direction, and with severe time restrictions, it is unlikely to be achieved without severe adjustment problems.

Another associated development in the pace of change is the spread of practices and labour market divisions from Western societies to the rest of the world. The great advances in transportation and telecommunication have made geographical boundaries less significant (although cultural and legal boundaries remain intact). They have accelerated the spread of changes from the leading economies to the rest of the world. With a significant share of economic activity conducted virtually via the Internet, challenges will even increase.

A significant general trend reiterated in this book is that of transferring responsibility for the management of careers from organizations to individuals. One aspect that individuals need to consider is how to promote themselves in a world in which the patronage of the organization is lacking or entirely missing, how to stand out from the crowd. One way of 'self-promotion' is impression management and career signalling (see Chapter 2).

Change versus stability: Implications for career systems

Table 5.3 compares change and continuity and looks at the implications for careers (building on Noon & Blyton, 1997, p. 204 and Baruch & Rousseau, 2019).

Table 5.3   Change and continuity: Implications for careers

Change	Continuity	Career implications
New patterns for service, production, consumption	Persistence of work ethic, but what is ethical vary across cultures	New ways of work, work is still needed for most, but may not be required from all in the near future
Rise of service sector and impact of AI on the service	Continual existence of routine, mundane and sometimes boring jobs	Innovative career patterns alongside traditional ones; division of work and AI to replace people
Technological development, need for high-skills	New types of low-skills jobs (e.g. delivery drivers)	Career frustration for educated new generation
Increase of emotional labor	Under-evaluating of social competence	Discrepancy between inner job satisfaction and remuneration
Wider diversity in the labor market	Gender division of work, discrimination	Inclusion as a managerial intervention
New forms of work with time and space flexibility	Traditional work still dominates	Alternative work arrangements, work from home, 24/7, stratified labor markets
Work intensification	Control over workforce	Empowerment and delegation, trust, and applying Idiosyncratic deals
Emergence of post-corporate organizations	Taylorism/Fordism still exists	Multiple approaches in career management

Summary

In this chapter we explored career dynamism by seeking to understand the phenomenon of employability and its implications for individuals and organizations. We looked at redundancies and the prospect of the survivor syndrome, trying to identify best practice. We explored new career perspectives via career communities and networking, and by examination of a set of career metaphors. The chapter concluded by placing the discussion in historical perspective and analysing past and future changes.

KEY TERMS

Best practice

Career communities

Career cynicism

Career metaphors

Career networking

Digitization of careers

Employability

Survivor syndrome

The dark side of careers

The Peter Principle

DISCUSSION QUESTIONS

LESSONS AND FOOD FOR THOUGHT

1. *For the HR manager:* What kind of changes can you detect in your immediate business environment that will have a profound effect on the way you manage careers in your organization?
2. *For the HR consultant*: What kind of changes can you detect in your immediate business environment that will have different effects for different organizations?

   What will the different effects be and how would you recommend organizations to adapt their career systems to such a change?

3. *For the HR teacher*: To what extent should you incorporate into your HRM teaching elements from history, sociology, geography, and technology to clarify trends and dimensions in career systems, but not to distract your students from the main subject?

EXERCISES

Exercise 1

The suggested exercises for the student in the above case studies can be developed into an interesting class comparative session, using the 12-level ranking system and comparing responses for the different attributes.

Exercise 2

Consider the anticipated impact on the labour market if, within a very short period, all careers will be autonomously driven.

Exercise 3

The list of attributes people may look for in their career is part of the psychological contract exercise. First, complete this for yourself (placing the attributes in order of importance for you from 1 to 12). Then, ask people from the generation above to fill in the same form; and if possible, do the same for people from two generations above. Can you see a trend? Does it fit with what you have learned by now from the book?

What do (did) you expect from your employer?	Order of importance
Professional challenge	_____
Financial provider	_____
Source of inspiration	_____
Social status	_____
Job security	_____
Professional development	_____
Good working conditions	_____
Source of motivation	_____
Life structure	_____
Work–life balance	_____
Safe working environment	_____
Feeling needed and valued	_____
Increased employability	_____

Organizational Career Systems – The Career Active System Triad (CAST)

6

LEARNING OBJECTIVES

After reading this chapter you should be able to:

- Understand organizational careers
- Be acquainted with the CAST concept
- Critically analyse organizational career models
- Understand how organizational characteristics influence career systems
- Recognize future directions of organizational career management from a three-levels perspective – strategy, policy, and operative

Chapter outline

Food for thought

Think of two identical twins, who grew up together, studied at the same university, the same degree (say business and management), and upon finishing (with quite similar grades), explored the labour market. They had two different job offers. One was accepted by a large, established corporation, whereas the other joined a new venture, a business start-up.

Although they shared the same background, their careers will inevitably take quite different trajectories. Why?

The major reason would be that different organizations provide different career systems, leading to different career path options. Even if such identical twins were to work for organizations of similar size, in the same industrial sector, they would face different career systems, and this is due to the variety of ways by which organizations choose to manage careers.

From an individual focus to an organizational perspective

The core asset for the vast majority of existing organizations is not the building, the equipment, or the money pertaining to it, but the people who comprise it. And there are several similarities at the conceptual and the metaphorical level between people and organizations. Both possess identity and 'personality' (see below), both plan ahead and manage their future according to explicit and implicit goals. Individuals and organizations are interconnected actors in a wider career and labour market ecosystem that is in a continuous evolving state (Baruch, 2015).

However, when dealing with an individual career perspective, our discussion, analysis and understanding derive from the behavioural sciences – psychology and sociology in particular. While much of the understanding of individual careers stem from psychology and other behavioural sciences, the study of the organizational career perspective focuses on managerial issues, in particular the HRM aspect. Whereas each individual 'owns' his or her unique career, organizations, as a collective, plan, direct, and manage systems wherein careers develop.

An organization is a combination of brains, bodies, and behaviours. That is the source for the parallelism between individuals and organizations: organizations have identity (Gioia et al., 2013; Hatch & Schultz, 2002; He & Brown, 2013), which bond the organizational members (Elsbach & Kramer, 1996), they hold values and culture (Ravasi & Schultz, 2006), and even possess 'personality' (Stapley, 1995). This 'personality' will influence the type of people who will want to develop their career in these organizations (Zhu et al., 2021). The identity and values of the organizations are influenced by its leadership, and can influence organizational performance (Voss et al., 2006). These, of course, are developed by the collective community and, more particularly, by the leaders who founded the organization, who manage, inspire, control, and direct it. Dutton and Dukerich (1991) argued that any organization has an image and an identity, which may guide and activate individuals' interpretations of certain issues and generate motivations on. The management of organizational image is important for its reputation (Schuler, 2004), and much of it is done via the media and the Internet (Gilpin, 2010). Such interpretations and motivations affect patterns of organizational action over time.

The metaphorical humanization of organizations and its relevance to their being the landscape of careers does not end here. Lipman-Blumen and Leavitt (1999) speak of an organizational 'state of mind', for example, doing good and not so good (Vesa et al., 2019). In extreme cases, the dark side of organizations can be depicted as organizational miasma (Gabriel, 2012). When this is the culture of the organization, talent management will be needed to make a real change, otherwise best employees will leave. Another humanization of organization is the attribution of memory to organization (Roth & Kleiner, 1998), where organizational memory is a major factor in the context of the 'learning organization'. Indeed, when people leave, part of the collective memory departs from the organization. Organizations have life cycles that can resemble the seasons of life of individuals (Levinson, 1978). Like a person's life, organizations might die (Sutton, 1987), but unlike human beings, organizations can re-invent themselves and re-emerge for a new life (Zell, 2003). All in all, there are quite a few similarities (and, of course, many differences) between the individual and the organization.

To maintain these life cycles, to survive and strive, organizations need not only to recruit the right people, but also to retain them. *Organizational career management* is the comprehensive system that organizations apply to manage people's careers. This chapter will provide a systematic view of the underlying basics of such a system, following the discussion of the dynamic nature of business environment, where careers take place. In the next chapter we will focus on the activities undertaken by organizations that comprise the building blocks of such a system. This chapter introduces the career active system triad (CAST), a multi-level conceptual framework developed to help in understanding the human side of career management.

The career active system triad (CAST)

The components forming the CAST perspective that I offer here can be set at three levels of analysis (see Table 6.1): values, approaches, and behaviours. The basic underlying level of values – the principles, morals, and culture – forms the roots from which the other levels emerge. The second level is that of transformation – approaches and assumptions – which translates those values into the third level – action, behaviour, and practice. The values convey the aspirations (for individuals) and strategy (for organizations) into the attitudes (for individuals) and policies (for organizations) to direct them, so that in the final observed outcome, people will act and apply at the practical level of behaviour or operation, and organizations will use managerial practices. By its nature (and as implied from its title), this is an active system, always in perpetual motion, since it needs to respond to both external requirements (the environment) and internal requirements (both the organization and the people). These requirements alter on a continuous base (think about yourself – have your future plans stayed similar to those you had while in school? When you started university? Now?).

The CAST perspective encompasses three levels of analysis for the understanding of careers management. It covers both individual and organizational perspectives, and associates them together. Following Chapters 2 and 3, which focused on individual careers, the CAST concept helps to facilitate a further step of integrating the needs and provisions of the two principal participants in the system: the individual and the organization. The third major participant, which lies more in the background, is general society – the local community, area, state, region, and humanity in general.

Table 6.1 The career active system triad (CAST)

Level	Individual	Organization
Values	Aspirations	Philosophy (strategy)
Approaches	Attitudes	Policies
Behaviours	Actions	Practices

The CAST as a metaphor

We noticed in the earlier chapter the role and importance of metaphors to understanding various phenomena, in particular in the field of careers. The word 'cast' is taken from the theatre and movies industry: appointing certain roles to certain people, which is indeed what is being done when appointing people to jobs. *Note*: The interested reader may find a fascinating and useful application of this metaphor in the real-life entertainment industry in an article by DeFillippi and Arthur (1998).

Box 6.1: The CAST metaphor

Using the concept of metaphors, we try to envisage how a theatre metaphor may be applied to explain the CAST. As in casting a play (theatre) or movie (the film industry), the management need to decide which person will take each role, to plan ahead to find the right people, to train them for their specific roles, and make sure that a replacement can step in if a member of the cast leaves (voluntarily or involuntarily).

In life, certainly at work, we often find ourselves in a need to 'wear a mask' and act in a way that is expected from the player in the role, even if sometimes it does not fit for us. Disciplining employees is not nice, but when you do it you could consider acting like a policeman. Public talking, including teaching in class, is another example of various masks we put on to match the needs of the specific circumstances (Baruch, 2006b).

Let us explore how the CAST corresponds with the individual A's and organizational P's.

The individual three A's

Individuals have career *aspirations* about what they want to achieve in their wider life and in their working career. Their career aspirations are reflected in their goals and aims. Of course, it is not enough to have an aspiration, since competence is required to reach career goals. If a person has no ability, skills, or talent with which to fulfil his or her aims, the aspiration will become irrelevant or, worse, misleading and frustrating. A realistic approach will help the individual in setting career targets that relate well to their aspirations (hence their interests) as well as to the ability to gain them. These career aspirations will influence people's attitudes towards work, career, and life in general. With their aspirations in their minds, and with cultural, educational, and family influence, and the surrounding community, people develop *attitudes* – towards their work, their organization and, subsequently, their career. At the practical level, the individuals will move on to *actions* and behaviour. They will apply career activities to plan and manage their careers. Taking part in specific training, workshops, finding the right mentor, focusing on specific roles, and many other activities, will enable a person to improve their chances of success in their career. The three levels are associated with each other – actions are subject to attitudes, and both are derived from aspirations.

The organizational three P's

Organizations have a certain *philosophy* and strategy that guides them in their development, growth and maintenance. This philosophy provides a direction to the organization. To manage well, organizations should aim to apply best practice at the operational level and target it to fulfil their strategic goals. Such strategic decisions will focus on career issues too (e.g. see Chapter 8 for strategic choice in managing expatriation, or Chapter 9 on diversity strategies). To translate the strategic goals into operational activities, the organization develops a wide variety of *policies*, many of which are concerned with people issues. These serve to direct actions, that is, at the operational level the HRM unit will apply a wide range of career *practices* (see elaboration in Chapter 7) that maintain the continuity of the human resource part of the organization.

Put together, the CAST helps to comprehend and interpret the relationship between individual and organizational CPM.

Box 6.2: The CAST

Your CAST

- What are your career aspirations?
- How do they evolve from your approach to life? To work?
- What actions do you take to fulfil your aspirations?

Your organization CAST

You may be working now, you may be a full-time student. Still, you probably have in mind certain dreams about the organization which you most wish to work for.

So . . . the questions are:

- In a perfect world, what type of philosophy would you like your organization to hold?
- How should the organization translate this philosophy into a set of clear, directive policies?
- What type of practices will enable your 'dream employer' to facilitate your career to fulfil your own aspirations?

Organizational career systems

Contemporary organizational career systems need to be based around several remits. First, the organization is no longer the only, or maybe not even the main, focal point for career management. Sociological, economic, and technological trends summarized in Chapter 1 contribute to an increased involvement and responsibility on the individual side. These are mirrored, for example, by the protean career concept (Hall, 1976, 2004, presented in Chapter 3) that means more emphasis is placed on individuals' responsibility for taking their destiny into their own hands. The world of work and employment experience presents a significant transition in psychological relationships between employers and employees (Baruch & Rousseau, 2019), and in the growing number of new or alternative work arrangements. Already in the 20th century, practices like remote work (teleworking/telecommuting), virtual teams, international assignments, small and medium enterprises, and small project-based forms of organizations (Sparrow, 2000). The benefits of flexibility are also accompanied with challenges, like loss of attention, consideration, and even respect to those under non-traditional arrangements (Bartel et al., 2012). To these we can add new forms of work arrangements such as contingent work, multiple part-time employment, and cyberspace employment. At the extreme case, AI may reduce the need of employing many people, creating long-term or even a lifetime with no employment (Susskind, 2020). Spreitzer et al. (2017) have identified three dimensions of flexibility that undergird alternative work arrangements: flexibility in the employment relationship; flexibility in the scheduling of work; and flexibility in where work is accomplished. These – nature of relationships, time, and space – are critical factors

Several trends require the upgrading of the traditional methods of career planning and managing, as conducted by the organization. Among these trends are the competitive markets and business environments that, together with other forces, initiated the globalization of business, redundancy, and delayering and the boundaryless career. In addition there are conflicting trends, which produce a set of different contingencies for career systems.

One of the most dramatic processes that emphasize such a chaotic environment is the contradictory trends in organization size. On the one hand, we find the rise of large organizations such as huge conglomerates (many due to mergers and acquisitions), and on the other hand, the flourishing of small businesses and start-up enterprises. The growth in mergers and acquisitions (M&As) is partially responsible for the creation of mega-corporations (Cartwright and Cooper, 2012). A few well-documented examples are the Exxon-Mobil amalgamation in 1999, the Swiss Bank takeover of Warburgs and later merger with UBS in 1998, and the PriceWaterhouseCoopers creation (see below). The latter has shrunk the number of global accountancy giants. The merger of pharmaceutical giants Glaxo-Wellcome and Smithkline-Beecham, to form the world's largest drugs developer and producer, is another prominent example from a different business sector. Cultural clashes are typical in M&As (Ulijn et al., 2010; Weber & Tarba, 2012), like the case of Volvo and Samsung represented in Case study 6.1 (Lee et al., 2015). Legal issues have arisen in relation to the HP merger with Compact in 2002. Such mergers create major challenges to the companies' career systems, and hinder their ability to retain all the talented people from both firms. Many failures of M&A are linked to people management-related issues (Avetisyan et al., 2020).

CASE STUDY 6.1: CAREER IMPLICATIONS OF M&A

Sweden's Volvo and South Korea's Samsung

Following the merger, Volvo's managers did not understand the local culture; for example, one said: 'I cannot understand why [Samsung] employees stayed at the office although they finished their job for today. Isn't it better to go home earlier?' On the other side, Korean employees felt that 'Foreign executive and staff members were aware that cultural differences might cause some serious problems ... it seems that their understanding of our culture is superficial. Quite often, they make decisions that cannot be easily accepted in the context of Korean culture.' They criticized Volvo's hesitation in investing in human capital (e.g. career development programmes).

(Based on Lee, 2015)

UBS acquiring PaineWebber

The acquisition of PaineWebber by UBS is just one example of the continuity of this trend and the consequences for individual careers. The primary impetus for the merger came from UBS, which wished to widen their retail network by acquiring PaineWebber, renowned for their strong position in the US market. However, in other countries PaineWebber's operations were minor.

This acquisition caused many employees who lost the status they had held in the small operation to re-think their positions. Although they now had open to them career opportunities in the larger UBS, for example, in the City of London headquarters, many did not wish to become just a cog in the machine. Some of them would rather have the broader responsibility they enjoyed in the small operation.

Exxon-Mobil

The merger of Mobil and Exxon created a giant company. It was presented as a merger, but many former Mobil employees saw it as a takeover. Most senior positions are held by former Exxon personnel. The headquarters of the new conglomerate is located in Texas, and many Mobile executives who refused to leave Virginia have left the amalgamated company. Yet, the firm remained a top-Fortune 500 firm, ranked second in 2018.

A different area, involving acquisitions rather than mergers, has developed with the globalization of businesses. This trend has also meant the penetration of foreign manufacturing operators through the purchasing of local plants in different countries to exploit gaps in labour markets. Such an approach has wide implications for career opportunities and the developmental options for companies choosing this method. The operators of the Japanese companies Toyota and Honda in the USA and Nissan in the UK, and the German company Volkswagen in Brazil come to mind in the car sector.

While M&As can create successful giant corporations, many do fail. As the cases above indicate, failures are usually due more to cultural mismatch than to the strength of, or the lack of, financial attractiveness of the deal. Human factors can make or break a newly formed company. Different career paths, contrasting approaches to the management of people, lack of sensitivity, all contribute to the failure of some M&As.

In 2021, the world's largest consulting firms, labelled as the 'Big Four', account for nearly 40% of the industry's US$150 billion global market. These are PwC, Deloitte, EY, and KPMG. Alongside these global major consultancy firms, many small consulting companies strive, while the large ones maintain different career paths. For example, before the Enron affair, Andersen Consulting employed more than 65,000 people in 48 countries. Andersen Consulting emphasized their dominant global status and their commitment to transforming the e-commerce marketplace. They then had to change their name to Accenture but managed to overcome the crisis, employing in 2020 some 150,000 employees in India, 48,000 in the USA, and 50,000 in the Philippines. Such global consultancy firms work with highly dynamic, new, and agile e-commerce businesses through consulting, developing new dot.com and business ventures. Many of the consultants in the Big Four are working with start-ups and spin-offs. The case of Andersen Consulting sadly shows that even the best most highly regarded career is subject to luck, in that case, the bad luck of working for a company which apparently bowed to greed rather than to professionalism.

Many people choose to be consultants but not necessarily for large accounting firms. Some may be redundant engineers, marketing, operations, and other executives, who decide to create their own business. Often, their starting point and first customer is their former employer.

Another Big Four global consultancy firm is PriceWaterhouseCoopers, which employs some 276,000 people and has a presence in over 150 countries and territories. The history of today's PricewaterhouseCoopers is paved with a sequence of M&As. The major one was the merger of two firms – Price Waterhouse and Coopers & Lybrand – each with historical roots going back some 150 years. Set out in Box 6.3 are some of the key milestones in the history of both firms (taken from the company's website).

Box 6.3: PWC history

1849 Samuel Lowell Price set up a business in London

1854 William Cooper established his own practice in London, which seven years
    later became Cooper Brothers

(Continued)

1865 Price, Holyland and Waterhouse joined forces in partnership

1874 Name changed to Price, Waterhouse & Co.

1898 Robert H. Montgomery, William M. Lybrand, Adam A. Ross Jr. and his
      brother T. Edward Ross formed Lybrand, Ross Brothers and Montgomery

1957 Cooper Brothers & Co. (UK), McDonald, Currie and Co. (Canada) and
      Lybrand, Ross Bros & Montgomery (US) merged to form Coopers & Lybrand

1982 Price Waterhouse World Firm formed

1990 Coopers & Lybrand merged with Deloitte Haskins & Sells in a number of
      countries around the world

1998 Worldwide merger of Price Waterhouse and Coopers & Lybrand created
      PricewaterhouseCoopers

2002 entered the Chinese market via merger with local Arthur Andersen

2009–2012 rebuilding of their consulting practice via a series of M&As

2017 PwC accepted bitcoin as payment – the first of the Big Four accounting firms
      to accept virtual currency as payment

2019 the 900 equity partners in the firm received average pay of over $1,000,000

2020 PwC employed over 250,000 people worldwide

Being a partner in a Big Four firm is the ultimate career success dream of many accountants and MBA graduates. This position brings power and influence as well as immensely high earnings. The career path in a consultancy firm offers a clear goal to each apprentice – to become a partner, and in larger firms there is an even higher level – that of senior partner. A contrasting trend is the increasing growth of start-up firms and small businesses, a trend largely supported by governments. The cliché that each large corporation started as a small business is true, and serves as a source of inspiration to many entrepreneurs. The small-business sector produces increasing numbers of new job openings, and many are taken by people who have left their former large employers (voluntarily or not). The individualistic aspirations of many of the X/Y/Z generations combined with new opportunities, many of which are provided on the Web or via its use, all contribute to the emergence of a multitude of small enterprises. These generations may feel much safer in virtual organizations, another fast-developing sector with innovative career options.

Merging organizations, merging career systems

One great challenge that faces organizations, following a merger, is the creation of a single coherent and sustainable career system, from two different, usually distinct, career systems.

The differences are due to different structures, hierarchies, compensation systems, performance appraisal systems, and different systems succession planning, where these exist.

In a large merger of two leading global consultancy firms, the two merging companies had compensation systems that were similar in terms of cost to the organizations, but different from the employees' viewpoint: salaries were higher in one organization than in the other, but training was minimal, and people were expected to invest in their own development. In the other partner, which paid lower salaries, there was widespread investment in training and development. The difference in salaries in the range of $120,000 (typical in these companies) was about $20,000 per annum. The HR challenge was to merge the two different compensation systems in a cost-effective manner.

Management buy-out: business innovation, career novelty

To be an entrepreneur one does not have to start a firm. Individuals, but mostly teams, can purchase an existing firm, usually where they are already working. The purchase of a substantial shareholding in a company by its managers – the management buy-out (MBO) – was pioneered in the USA in the early 1970s. Since then MBOs have become an everyday global feature of corporate life and an established stage in the corporate cycle (Wright & Coyne, 2018; Wright et al., 1991). In any private enterprise society, where the ownership of productive businesses may change hands, there will be opportunities for suitably motivated managers to run such organizations more efficiently than their current owners.

The MBO offers the leading managers the status of ownership. It has also created a niche labour market. This comprises venture capital companies, investing banks, solicitors, and dealmakers, all of whom are engaged in providing financial and managerial support for the managing team. The strength of the managers both as individuals and as a team is widely accepted as the most important success factor of MBOs (Baruch & Gebbie, 1998). The buy-out process is a time of great opportunity and high risk, but the end results can be tremendous in terms of financial and personal career gains.

The impetus for many MBOs may come from the managers themselves. They are capable of realizing that the parent company is not able or willing to invest sufficiently in their subsidiary or that the constraints imposed by head office are preventing the growth of their business. MBOs, like greatness, are nevertheless often thrust upon people. Taking over one's own workplace is very different from being employed by it.

Organizational frames and career dynamism

While the previous discussion depicts a wide range of novel organizational frames and career dynamism, there are still many traditional and conventional organizations, in both production and services, with traditional career systems characterized by a relatively clear hierarchy, career paths, and central control systems. Among them there are organizations with bureaucracy based structures with conventional career ladders. Sometimes these are associated with particular occupations. In teaching, the civil service, and certainly in the armed forces, the police, and the health sector, career systems still offer a relatively clear hierarchy and alternative paths. In certain systems, the vocation dictates a flat career structure (such as teaching), whereas in others there are clear routes for managerial development up multiple ladders.

Organizations, whether they are a small, a medium, or a large conglomerate, a traditional bureaucracy or a novel organizational framework, play a significant role in the management of careers. Line managers and HR units share the role of running the operational part of HRM (McGuire et al., 2008), including career systems. In small enterprises this role is carried out by general managers, in addition to their broad operational roles. The larger the organization, the more can (and should) be done in the specific area of career systems. At the micro level, HR should aim to help individuals to gain a balance between work and other facets of life, in particular the family (Kelliher et al., 2019). This involves a shift from the 'telling' role of the paternalistic approach, to consultation and mutually shared planning. In the emerging career systems, organizations are taking on a supportive, consulting role. At the macro level, the HR manager, director, or vice president will deal with strategic issues of HRM and with the strategic alignment between HRM and the operation of the organization, including career-related aspects.

Strategic HRM, strategic career systems

The strategic HRM approach was introduced in the early 1980s by Devanna et al. (1981), Fombrun et al. (1984), and Beer et al. (1984), and continued to be a research topic of high relevance (Bamberger et al., 2014; Beer, 2015). According to strategic HRM, the HR strategy should be developed alongside the general strategy of the organization, to acquire a cultural fit within the organization and with the outside environment. Such strategic alignment should lead to high organizational effectiveness and performance (Holbeche, 2009). Strategic alignment or business integration focuses on aligning the people, processes, and technology with the organization's evolving strategy. It enables organizations to make the most of their capabilities by implementing their strategic vision through a systematic approach.

For individuals, strategic alignment offers increasingly significant learning opportunities, especially in today's environment where the parameters of business are rapidly changing. It provides versatile options for developing various different career paths in which employees can enrich their competencies and skills, develop new ones, and generate future career options.

Taking a strategic view of the management of people, and seeing human resources as the most essential ingredient for organizational success, the resource-based view (RBV) can serve as a useful framework (Kraaijenbrink et al., 2010). Wernerfelt (1984) and Prahalad and Hamel (1990) built the resource-based theory around the internal competencies of the firm (Russo & Foults, 1997). Grant (1991) classified organizational resources as tangible, intangible, and personal based. The RBV puts the emphasis on the internal resources of the organization (Hoskisson et al., 1999). It is critical for bottom-line outcomes, as has been widely suggested by management theory and practice, as well as for the social dimension (Tate & Bals, 2018). For the organization, a resource could be both tangible and intangible assets which bring a high return on investment over extended periods of time (Wernerfelt, 1984).

Applying the RBV of the firm, HRM scholars argue that a high-commitment human resource strategy leads to firm competitive advantage, namely better performance (Collins, 2020). This is in line with a wide range of studies confirming such relationships (e.g. Jiang et al., 2012; Tzabbar et al., 2017) which follows from creating greater firm-level employee-based resources.

The predominant property of the human asset is that it is an intangible asset. People are one of the organizational assets, perhaps the most crucial, that enhance firm performance, and HRM is the system designed to obtain output, measurable in terms of company performance compared with investment in HRM (Delaney & Huselid, 1996; Harel & Tzafrir, 1999). Competitive advantage is based on the internal resources of the firm, and in particular the human capital, though evaluating the intangible human assets is not simple, yet possible (Hajrullina & Romadanova, 2014). While optimizing the human asset is cited as the most important for increasing competitiveness, managing it becomes a crucial element in gaining competitive advantage (cf. Pfeffer, 1998). Part of the work is acquiring these resources (recruitment and selection), which takes a very short time. The other part is maintaining the people, developing, growing, and improving this resource, or in other words, managing their career. That part is spread over a much wider timeframe – the duration of employment of the people, which can last for their entire working life (a common phenomenon in the past, now quite rare).

A crucial consideration when developing HR strategy (hence career management and system strategy) is the need to match HR strategy and organizational strategy. Such a need for congruency was most notably depicted by Meshoulam and Baird (1987) in their seminal discussion of the association between the organizational and HR stages of development. They argue that while it is important to develop an HR strategy, it would be disadvantageous for the organization to have its HR strategy lagging behind its overall organizational strategy, and similarly there would be problems in having a highly developed HR strategy while the organizational strategy is in its infancy. In their framework they provide five-scale level of strategy development: initiation, functional growth, controlled growth, functional integration and, strategic integration. Efficiency will be best achieved when the levels of HR strategy and organizational strategy match, they claim.

Hand in hand with the emergence of the strategic HRM conceptual framework, came theoretical works relating to careers as a system within the organization (Garavan, 2007; Von Glinow et al., 1983), and relating them to strategy and HR practice. However, Gill and Meyer (2011) have identified a wide gap between corporate policies and their applications in practice, in line with both the Meshoulam and Baird (1987) framework and the CAST concept. In addition, there has been little examination of the actual process of career management within organizations. Bagdadli and Gianecchini (2019) and Baruch and Peiperl (2000a) emphasized the importance of career practices and activities and the increasing efforts exerted by top management in many organizations. These career practices will be elaborated upon in Chapter 7. Organizations have assumed more responsibility within this area, even if not always by means of traditional, long-term approaches, and the career management practices that they employ need to be better understood.

However, the practices employed derive from the strategy. In fact, this is what principles of good management dictate, but of course, many organizations apply 'off-the-shelf' practices without strategic consideration (Yarnall, 2008). How strategy guides practice (the framework of Sonnenfeld and Peiperl, 1988; see Box 6.4) provides a general answer.

Box 6.4: Strategic career systems – the Sonnenfeld and Peiperl model

Sonnenfeld and Peiperl have integrated several streams of research to create a contingent framework for understanding organizational career systems as a strategic approach. They posited that, rather than there being one best model for organizational careers, the particular type of career system used should be appropriate to the strategy of the firm, linking the typology with the four strategic types – prospectors, defenders, analysers, and reactors – proposed by Miles and Snow (1978).

The typology (shown in Figure 6.1) contains two dimensions: *supply flow*, which ranges from completely internal supply to largely external supply of managerial labour; and *assignment flow*, which indicates the degree to which assignment and promotion decisions are based on individual performance on the one hand as against overall contribution to the group or organization on the other. According to the model, organizations vary in terms of these dimensions, which generate four career system 'types' (one for each quadrant): academies, clubs, baseball teams and fortresses.

The Academy is represented in the quadrant having internal supply flow and individual-based assignment flow. Firms of this type are characterized as being committed to early career hiring and long-term professional growth. Firm-specific skills, lateral or dual career paths, and the tracking and retention of talent typify this group.

The Club is the name applied to organizations in the internal supply flow/group-based assignment flow quadrant. Here 'security and membership are the essence of commitment', and there is strong concern for status in a fixed hierarchy. Clubs typically have some kind of monopoly protection from markets, often combined with a public interest kind of mission (such as might be found in a utility, military, or religious organization).

The Baseball Team designates the external supply flow/individual assignment flow quadrant. Such organizations would not offer employment security and are most concerned with innovation and star performance. Commitment to the organization is low, but energy and ambition are high, as everyone perceives a chance to become a star. When such expectations are dashed or when the firm is perceived to be in trouble, people quickly move to new organizations, often in similar businesses.

The Fortress has both external supply flow and group-based assignment flow. These are firms fighting for survival, because of either economic conditions in their industry or crises specific to their business.

This model focuses on the need to associate HRM theory and practice with the general organizational operation and strategy. The model was supported by case material and was used successfully to illustrate the movement of individuals in the managerial labour market.

Source: Based on Sonnenfeld and Peiperl, 1988 and Sonnenfeld et al., 1988

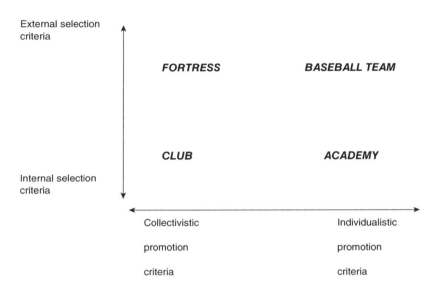

Figure 6.1 The Sonnenfeld-Peiperl model of career systems(adapted from Sonnenfeld & Peiperl, 1988)

A pause for reflection

If you had a choice, which type of career system would best fit your own career aspirations and attitudes?

This is the easy question. The more difficult and practical question is:

How can you learn in advance about the type of career strategy adopted by an organization that has advertised a job you may wish to apply for?

Flexibility and competitive advantage

Flexibility means the ability to meet a variety of needs in a dynamic environment (Sanchez, 1995). This environment is both internal and external to the organization. Sanchez distinguished between resource flexibility (the extent to which a resource can be applied to a wide range of alternative uses), and coordination flexibility (the extent to which the organization can rethink and redeploy resources). In terms of the human factor, the resources reside with the people, their competencies and skills, knowledge and abilities, and in their commitment and loyalty. Such flexibility needs to be manifested via the application of a variety of career management practices (see further in the next chapter). Wright and Snell (1998) applied the Sanchez framework to encompass the HRM perspective, as presented in Table 6.2.

Table 6.2   Strategic HRM indicators of resources and coordination flexibility

Strategic HRM component	Resource flexibility	Coordination flexibility
Practices	Applicability of practices across jobs, etc. Rigidity of application across jobs, etc.	Malleability of practices Speed of feedback on impact of practices
Employee skills	Individual skill breadth Ability to acquire new skills	Variety of skills in the workforce Ability to acquire diverse skills from contingent workers
Employee behaviour	Rigidity of script application	Complementarity/conflict between scripts of different groups

Source: Adapted from Wright & Snell, 1998

Flexibility as a strategic response

Organizations embrace flexibility as a strategic option to gain competitiveness (Birkinshaw, 2000; Rabenu, 2021). In terms of HRM, flexibility has several meanings. There is functional flexibility, numerical flexibility, time and space flexibility, and, above all, mind flexibility. Functional flexibility means the ability of the organization to use people's competencies in more than one role. This should not be restricted to job enhancement/enrichment, but also to a multiple choice of needed competencies, developing the missing or needed qualities. Numerical flexibility is manifested via different level of anticipated commitment and formal legal contractual ties. The company may define a 'core' group of employees, those responsible for the company's competitive advantage, and distinguish them from peripheral employees. The latter would have different contracts, sometimes short term, sometimes on an hourly or a daily basis. Time and space flexibility are all about where and when jobs are done. Working from 9 to 5 at the office no longer needs to be the standard convention, not even the rule for the majority of the employees. The COVID-19 pandemic showed that work could be done from home for some half of the working population in OECD countries. Later in this chapter these aspects will be elaborated upon.

A pause for reflection

Are you flexible (i.e. can your organization rely on your flexibility in order to maintain the flexible management of people)?

Can you offer functional flexibility (i.e. how many roles can you fulfil within the realm of your organization's operations)? What competencies would you need to develop that will enable you to fill possible further roles?

Do you see yourself as a 'core' employee, or are you able and ready to work in different organizations if needs change?

Are you flexible in terms of time and space – would you consider working from home? During non-conventional working hours? Sharing a job?

What other qualities of flexibility can you offer your employer?

These types of flexibility help both the individual and organizations, and are now quite established (Christensen & Schneider, 2011; Kossek et al., 2015). However, what enabled these practices to emerge and succeed is what I call the 'mind flexibility' of the managers who accepted such non-traditional principles at the time. With the increasing embedment of the X/Y/Z generation to the workforce, further attention is given to issues like work–life balance (Riyanto et al., 2019; Sánchez-Hernández et al., 2019). Mind flexibility, therefore, is the most important for the management of people and for career management, as mind flexibility will enable and develop future types of flexibility in management. It is up to executives on both the HR and operations side to realize that there is no one best way to deliver, and that although enabling a variety of options might look (and indeed is) complex, such an approach will enable better output via creativity and innovation. In this sense, creativity refers to the generation of novel ideas, innovation to their successful implementation.

Kossek et al. (2015) warn against three types of work–life balance related traps they present, arguing that these can emerge when implementing workplace flexibility. These are altered work–life dynamics, reduced fairness perceptions, and weakened organizational culture. They suggest to avoid applying flexibility for politically correctness reasons, and rather make it part of organizational change that empowers individuals and teams. The three traps are:

Altered work–life dynamics: This could mean several issues, starting with reduced contact between flexibility users and other organizational stakeholders (flexibility users, non-users, and the organization). The transition period may be tainted by difficulties and challenges. One may also expect difficulties in managing careers and performance for both flexibility users and their managers. The interaction between the job and family issues may influence the success of flexibility application.

Reduced fairness perceptions: This refers to inequality and stigmatization. The gains made by the employee who applies or benefits from flexibility might be seen as unfair by other colleagues. For example, if the majority work from 9.00 a.m., the occasional late arrival does not make much of an impact, but if the majority arrive later, those who arrive on time would have had to cover for them. Another fairness issue is how the gatekeepers of flexibility are seen. They might be taken as being arbitrary or unfair in awarding flexibility to employees. This can arise when there is lack of clarity on how non-users should work with flexibility users. Flexibility users might also suffer from negative stigma.

Weakened organizational culture: Inappropriate implementation of flexibility will be perceived as less supportive and less useful, leading to negative rather than positive outcomes. There are two possible extremes: the exploitation of workers or the creation of an entitlement culture.

The first strategic decision an organization needs to make is which type of career system will be applied. The two basic options are the traditional system or a system embodying a certain kind of flexibility in the employment relationship. Of course, an organization may decide to apply a hybrid employment relationship arrangement. It will become apparent, through reading this book, that most organizations will have to adopt a flexible system that will take into account both the nature of the individual inclinations of the X/Y/Z generations and the turbulent nature of the economic market. For most it will be impossible or illogical to try to adhere to old-style bureaucracy when hierarchical ladders lose their meaning and relevance in most systems. Still some organizations (e.g. the Army, the Church) will not be able to move fast, and for them it might be better to stick to the traditional ways.

The concept of flexibility is not free from academic criticism: initially there were suggestions that went so far as to claim that there is no real meaning to the concept of the flexible workforce (Pollert, 1991). Pollert highlighted conflicting evidence for the reality beyond the rhetoric of flexibility (see also Legge, 2005, on rhetoric versus reality in the HRM area). Furthermore, in different countries, flexibility could mean different things. For example, in France and the UK 'flexibility' means 'fixed short-term contracts' whereas in Sweden and Germany it means multi-skilling, qualifications, and training (Pollert, 1991). Much depends what the impetus for flexibility derives from – whether it is the need for cost control or a genuine interest in developing employees.

Competitive advantage and redundancy programmes

The concept of 'competitive advantage' is often associated closely with redundancies, layoffs, and job cuts (Cascio, 2010). Being competitive is concerned with the ratio between organizational inputs and outputs. Outputs mean products or services. Inputs are organizational assets – capital, which may be land, buildings, machinery, money, knowledge, and, above all, people. The inputs form the major difference for each of the outputs. A competitive organization produces more or better products or provides better services with the same level of assets, or uses fewer assets to achieve the same outcome. Labour and labour costs play a central role most of the time.

For individuals, having higher wage and employee benefits is a very positive factor in their financial and general wellbeing, but for firms it means higher labour costs and can directly reduce companies' profits, and indirectly reduce the number of employees, and working hours. National policies and industrial legislation set factors like minimum wage, overtime pay, and payroll taxes, which also affect labour costs. As a result, the level of labour costs can substantially affect both employment and working hours, for both specific firms and for the overall economy (Hamermesh, 2021). Realizing that numerical flexibility is an 'easy choice', many executives opt for job cuts as a first resort. Another firms' policy about the reduction of overall labour costs can be moving production overseas (more on that option in the global careers chapter).

Even when labour costs are not relatively high they are more open to manipulation than other fixed organizational costs (Noon et al., 2013). An example of labour costs' role is the airline industry, where labour costs represent only 25–35% of total operational costs (Doganis, 1994; Tsoukalas et al., 2008). Nevertheless, the costs of aircraft and fuel are highly rigid, whereas labour costs are subject to both numerical and pay-level flexibility, therefore people on the payroll are one of the few available variable elements of costs, at least in the short term. Regarding the human component of the organization as a cost centre rather than an investment base is the foundation of this approach. In addition, using the metaphor of 'cutting fat', there may be some justification for certain cases of reducing workforce size.

However, when this becomes the first resort in operational restructuring, redundancies might be reduced to a vicious cycle, ending with poor organizational outcomes. There is intriguing evidence that might surprise some chief executive officers. In contrast to the widely held belief that 'cutting fat' is an effective strategic response, De Meuse et al. (1994) analysed all 52 relevant cases of Fortune 100 companies to come up with surprising findings. Contrary to expectations, financial analysis indicated worsening financial performance over a long time-frame (five years), which followed substantial cuts in the labour force. When this is added to the destructive harm it causes firms' reputation (Flanagan & O'Shaughnessy, 2005) and the traumatic impact of the 'survivor syndrome' (Brockner et al., 1992a; Datta et al., 2010), it requires organizations to have second thoughts before making redundancies. These negative outcomes tend to end with reduced organizational performance (Gatzert, 2015).

Incidentally, empirical evidence indicates how the survivor syndrome and other negative impacts following massive redundancies can be avoided or minimized (Baruch & Hind, 1999, 2000; Datta et al., 2010). Such evidence re-emphasizes the crucial role of 'best practice' in career management, in particular if the organization has no alternative but to make people redundant.

A pause for reflection

If you were working for a large company facing financial difficulties, how would you wish to be treated in terms of decision making, communication, fairness, and justice?

The blurring of boundaries

In their book *The Boundaryless Organization*, Ashkenas et al. (1995, 2015) wrote about the diminishing traditional boundaries within organizations, and mentioned the following four aspects to demonstrate the breaking of the chains of organizational structure:

- vertical
- horizontal
- external
- geographic.

By 'vertical' they were referring to the breaking down of rigid hierarchies, which this book discusses widely. Diminishing horizontal boundaries means merging the different departments and units within an organization. The traditional structure divided the organization into various departments according to their specific function (e.g. marketing, logistics, production, HR, etc.). Today's organization needs to react to environmental changes and be proactive at the same time, therefore, such separation is not healthy for the functioning of the organization. Of course, this implies that career paths for future managers will include non-traditional options. By 'external', Ashkenas et al. meant that the distinction between the organization as such and the environment is now not as clear-cut as it was. In HR, for example, performance appraisal can build on customers, suppliers, and others that deal with the organization's members. People may be seconded to other organizations (see Chapter 7 for further details), external personnel can act as consultants, and employees can be working for temporary agencies. The last aspect is geography: many organizations now do not have a specific location. The virtual organization is an extreme case, but many organizations work part or fully virtually, in particular following the experience from the COVID-19 pandemic. Virtual organizations operate alongside the physical and complement each other (Lee et al., 2020), offering new career patterns to people who prefer a virtual work environment or are restricted to it due to personal circumstances. Other types of operation are not restricted to a specific place. The physical building is no longer the essence and representation of the organization.

In addition to these boundaries, we can identify others that represent further disintegration of the traditional separation between the organization and its environment. Clear boundaries once existed between the domain of work and other facets of life, but these are fading away now. There are several dimensions where such distinction between work and non-work boundaries is diminishing. Time, space, and commitment are mingled in the current fluid organizational systems. The first two are quantifiable and measurable, whereas the latter is involved with inner thinking and feelings. As was pointed out earlier, 'mind interaction' means that individuals think and have emotions about work-related issues during their time away from work, and about home/family issues while working (Ten Brummelhuis & Bakker, 2012). This phenomenon occurs in conventional settings to a certain extent, but where boundaries are blurred the distinction between work and non-work is harder to maintain.

One framework where mind interaction can be managed effectively is that of remote work (discussed later in this chapter). For this mode of work to be effective, people need to be judged by results rather than by their physical presence at a place of work. Remote work reduced work-related stress but increased home- and family-related stress, although the overall impact was stress reduction (Baruch & Nicholson, 1997). A more recent literature review summarized findings of many papers (Tavares, 2017), concluding that telework would yield more good than bad outcomes in terms of health for the individuals who work from home. More important for the organization, the extant literature suggests that teleworking enables better performance (Torten et al., 2016) and positive wellbeing (Nijp et al., 2016). Such indications encourage both individuals and organizations to see remote work as offering new career opportunities. In some cases, social isolation and detachment from face-to-face networking is thought to have detrimental effects on future career prospects.

A pause for reflection

In the past, this was more of a hypothetical question. Few occupations could allow teleworking, and most importantly, organizational culture prevented it (Baruch, 2001b). Later, more organizations, almost two-thirds of US employers, for example, allowed at least part-time working from home (Kossek et al., 2015). The COVID-19 pandemic forced about 50% of the workforce to operate from home, making this question less hypothetical.

Would you prefer working from the office, working from home, or a combination?

What would you gain, what may you lose?

Did the experience of the COVID-19 influence your preference?

Outsourcing

Another totally different way to gain flexibility is concerned with outsourcing HR activities, including career management practices. The advantages are clear – outsourced activities can be conducted by professional external vendors as needed. Costing will be clearer (though not necessarily cheaper), and such activities will be performed within the available budget.

Much has been written on outsourcing HR (cf. Greer et al., 1999; Sheehan & Cooper, 2011) but very few have tried to clarify what they mean by the term 'HR outsourcing'. The convention relates to outsourcing HR activities rather than the determination of HR strategy. In the career area there are certainly many practices that can be easily outsourced, while outsourcing others would give rise to grave doubts about the organizational commitment of decision makers.

Activities such as developing a performance appraisal system, and even analysis of the outcome of the process, can be done by external agencies. Of course, eventually line managers have to make their own evaluations, and the HR department has to make the relevant decision based on that analysis. Similarly, job analysis can be conducted by professional agencies, and pre-retirement and other career workshops can be outsourced. Cultural training (preparing expatriates for the new culture to which they are to be exposed) is better done by external people who are fully acquainted with those cultures. Recruitment and selection, in particular for top jobs, has, of course, for a long time been carried out by HR agencies and headhunters.

However, some decisions can only be taken by the organization itself. An external agency may prepare the salary accounts, but the organization needs to decide who receives what level of income (and external tools such as the Hay Group system can be useful in that task). Other tasks cannot be outsourced – mentoring (a positive facet), discipline (a negative one), industrial relations, career planning, so these activities should stay under organizational control and management.

In addition to the nature of the activities feasible for outsourcing, one needs to be able to assess the benefits of having top-quality services from vendors, compared to what can be provided from within the organization. Moreover, once an activity is outsourced and the internal capability of performing it is dismantled, it would be very difficult and costly to gain it back.

To sum up, outsourcing career practices is a way to gain flexibility, which can be cost-effective, and is low risk in the short term, but in the long run makes the organization dependent on external agencies.

Question: Outsourcing career advice?

Who would you like to provide you with career advice – your line manager, HR department, or external agency? Who would be your preferred mentor – a different manager from your organization? Perhaps an external private consultant?

Work stress and control over time

Stress at work has become of great concern for organizational managers as well as for political leaders. Stress is having an enormous negative impact. At the practical level, it is a major cause of work-related illness and absenteeism. At the wider context of concern for this book is the major long-term outcome of people totally abandoning employment, or moving to lower-level work, producing less added-value output in their jobs, as a result of high stress levels. The cumulative effects of stress have a highly detrimental impact upon individual wellbeing and health, as well as on organizational processes (Cartwright & Cooper, 2012). Ever-increasing stress causes many to focus on work and neglect other domains of life. The TINS syndrome (two incomes, no sex) is an extreme manifestation of the way work might take over our life (Baruch, 2004a). Much of people's feelings depend on their perception of time sovereignty, that is, who is in charge.

As regards working hours, there are two contrasting trends in the industrial world. First, due to social legislation, and the influence of trade unions (which still have a certain level of power in Europe and other countries), the permitted number of weekly hours worked is being reduced overall, mostly in the manufacturing and some service industries. This reduction helps to preserve jobs that might otherwise be made redundant. The second factor is derived from two major issues that have the opposite effect: the market demand for a 24-hour, 365-days-a-year response, and global competitiveness, which implies a demand for long working hours and in particular for managers to work overtime (which is coupled with the compensation practice that pays no overtime to employees in managerial positions).

Other factors exist too: geography has an impact. In many economies, organizations need to operate across several time zones, even within the same country (e.g. USA, the EU, or Russia). The generational differences add to the complexity: the X/Y/Z generation tend to give higher priority to work–life balance compared with the baby boomers (Twenge, 2010).

Another distinction exists between different 'classes' of employees, in particular between managerial staff and professionals as opposed to rank-and-file employees. In Spain, for example, the number of hours worked by employees is similar to that in many other European countries, but the daily pattern is different. Most workers go home in the middle of the day for *la comida*, the lunch break, and later return to their place of work. In contrast, their managers take no break, and work more than 50 hours a week on average. Similarly, the relatively long working week of British employees (averaging 42 hours a week) includes many less-skilled workers working shorter hours, and managers and professionals working 60 or even 70 hours a week.

These conflicting trends in the pattern of working hours create a distinction between the 'haves' and the 'have-nots', in terms of time (and subsequently in terms of quality of life). Those covered by the legislative protection of the EU's working time regulations have a reasonable workload while those not so covered, mostly managers and professionals, work overtime without direct compensation. In France and the USA, most managers are in the exempt category. In other parts of the world working hours are longer. Both managers and workers in manufacturing in South Korea work long hours. In Samsung, for example, a day shift of 11 hours for 27 days a month was the routine in the 20th century (Hillriegel et al., 1992). With so much time devoted to work, both life and careers will focus around the workplace, and work-related stress might become an influential factor in people's lives. Reviews of the literature point out possible detrimental effects of long working hours on health (Virtanen & Kivimäki, 2018; Wong et al., 2019) and on wellbeing (Ganster et al., 2018).

Murphy (1988) offers a three-level analysis of stress prevention: primary, of stress reduction; secondary, of stress management; and tertiary, of organizational support mechanisms. All levels should be implemented by the organization, and the career system can take a leading role, in particular at the last level, in providing organizational support, beginning with alternative work arrangements and ending with employee assistance programmes (Cooper et al., 1996). Cartwright and Cooper (2012) include job security and job performance (or its evaluation) as two career development issues in stress management that need to be dealt with by the organization. While job security is difficult to achieve, self-efficacy, resilience, the development of competencies and improved employability can serve as relevant factors in reducing work- and career-related stress. For individuals, there are ways to tackle work-related stress. An example of study into coping behaviours of students by Fares et al. (2016) advise helping to reduce the incidence of stress and burnout. These include promoting strategies that focus on personal engagement, performing extracurricular activities (physical exercise is a common advice in this context). In terms of mindfulness and self-awareness, it is important to develop positive reinterpretation and expression of emotion. Specifically for students, there are student-led mentorship programmes, evaluation systems, career counselling, that can be found in most established universities, and in some cases, life coaching can be looked for.

Stress and time management

Control over one's career gives one greater control over one's time and life. A wide range of options are now recognized as pertinent by organizations and individuals. These include remote work, multiple part-time jobs, job sharing, and myriad time management options. However, in many cases competitiveness and retaining a managerial job means endless working hours, as for example when Dilbert's boss tells him he must work 18 hours a day to compete in the industry. Dilbert suggests in reply that they just *say* they work such long hours, and that then perhaps their competitors will die trying to match them. The sarcastic boss asks, 'Would it work?', to which the equally sarcastic Dilbert answers, 'It almost worked on us'. As pointed out above, working culture of 'nine-to-nine' or 24/7 can be detrimental to both work and life (Presser, 2005).

Box 6.5: Timing

How much time, ideally, would you like to devote to work? Would you be ready to work long hours? What may cause you to agree to work 45 hours a week? 50? 60? 70?

If an important project deadline is approaching, would you be willing to work during the weekend? If yes, what if such project deadlines arrive as frequently as once a month? Once a week? What would your spouse say about it? What would you do if you had young children?

Moreover:

As an executive, what moral right do you have to ask a manager reporting to you to stay till late at night?

However:

Doesn't organizational commitment require a readiness to exert effort and sacrifice something for the success of the organization? It should be reasonable for the organization to expect people who accept responsibility to do whatever is necessary to make sure their job is done properly. And for 'impression management' purposes, working long hours will mark you as someone who is ready to invest in his or her job and career.

Assignment:

Assume that you are a consultant to an organization. Individually or in a small group, prepare a draft of an organizational policy on overtime work for managerial and professional workers. Remember that this draft policy should be derived from and reflect your organizational culture and values. Further, it must be capable of being translated into operational practices.

Alternative work arrangements

Alternative work arrangements or flexible work arrangements include a variety of practices. Kelly and Kalev (2006) list different flextime (where workers can set their own starting and stopping times), compressed-work-weeks (where workers work, for example, four long days and have one weekday off), place of work – remote work, and voluntary part-time work, particularly job sharing (splitting a job with another person). Similarly Gottlieb et al. (1998) refer to an array of flexible work arrangements that characterize practices, all of which have implications for career management. At the core of these practices is the need of organizations to recognize and be proactive in dealing with the interface between home, family, and work. Various flexible ways of managing people and people's careers have been developed to enable the most effective utilization of human resources.

To benefit from using a diversity of human resources, organizations need to find ways to maximize their use of, first, their own people who otherwise would be left on the outside (e.g. via remote work), and second, the external labour market, to ensure the best fit between resources and expected outputs. A curious aspect of the employment situation in recent years is that there was high unemployment at a time of full employment (in the 1970s and early 1980s), and yet unemployment reached new low levels in the West (in particular in the USA) following the large-scale redundancies of the 1990s and early 2000s. Part of the explanation may be the growth of part-time employment, and another part perhaps the disillusionment of many unemployed people, especially the older generation, that have given up altogether any hope of future employment. Events like the 2008 financial crisis and the COVID-19 pandemic generate such cycles of unemployment and later recovery.

One of the most effective and successful methods of alternative work arrangements is remote work (also called home working, telecommuting, or teleworking). It is enabled by technological improvements and an increase in the use of IT, on the one hand, and on the other hand, by an unconventional managerial approach, which posits that work is what you do, not a place where you go to. Toffler (1980) suggested that the information age 'could shift literally millions of jobs out of the factories and offices into which the Industrial Revolution swept them right back to where they came from originally: the home.' Telecommuting was expected to be the 'next workplace revolution' in the 1980s (Kelly, 1985), whereas we only recently started to witness the 4th industrial revolution (Schwab, 2017).

Figures 6.2 and 6.3 present the factors that influence remote working, and the two ways by which remote work can become a blessing or a curse for organizational outcomes. Table 6.3 presents the possible benefits and shortcomings of remote work.

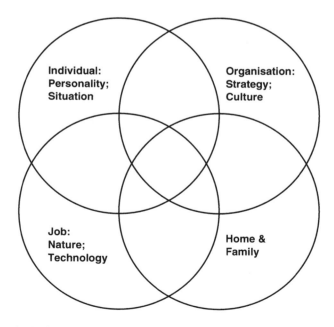

Figure 6.2 Remote work: the four aspects and their overlap (adapted from Baruch & Nicholson, 1997)

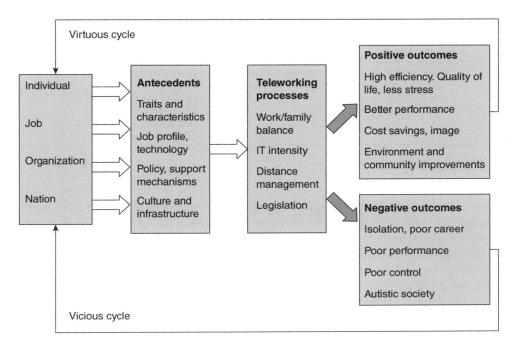

Figure 6.3   The virtuous versus the vicious cycle of remote work (Baruch, 2001b)

Table 6.3   Possible benefits and shortcomings of remote work

Level	Possible Benefits	Possible Shortcomings and Challenges
Individual	*improved performance / higher productivity *less time spent on commuting *satisfying need for autonomy *improved quality of working life (e.g. working environment) *less work related stress *more time with the family *could be the only way to work at all (mothers of infants, children with special needs etc.) *Avoid office politics *Privacy *Saving costs of travel + food *Feeling of being trusted	*less opportunities for affiliation, detachment from social interactions *less influence over people and events at workplace *questionable job security and status *fewer career development options *lower 'visibility' / promotability *work-related use of private space and resources *more home related stress *management of work–home interface without time/space buffers *more time with the family
Organization	*higher productivity *wider labour market to draw upon *space and overheads savings *less absenteeism *image of a flexible workplace *legal requirements	*control over teleworkers' activities and monitoring performance *control over health & safety *need of alternative motivation mechanisms *less committed employees *loss of team-working benefits

(Continued)

Table 6.3   (Continued)

Level	Possible Benefits	Possible Shortcomings and Challenges
Society	*less commuting, less pollution, congestion, accidents *support for local, in particular rural, communities *more people can work *less discrimination	*the creation of a society where individuals are atomised and isolated from social institutions *need to adapt legal system *could lead to weight gain

Source: Adapted from Baruch, 2001b

From the career point of view it seems that, overall, telecommuters need to exert more effort than conventional office-located employees to ensure that their career opportunities match those of the office workers. In the early days of teleworking, it was considered that, for some, working from home might have created new career opportunities (Evans, 1993), whereas for others it may be a dead end: out of sight (of headquarters) may be out of mind (when promotion decisions are being taken). This was the case until recently (Sewell & Taskin, 2015). The global COVID-19 pandemic changed the view of teleworking because it meant everyone was 'out of sight', making it irrelevant. The readers of this book in the years to follow will know how lasting the impact was. Writing this book during the pandemic year, I assume that while not all remote working due to having no choice will continue, but many who benefitted from this option will continue to practice it, and many managers who opposed it before will accept it. If before the pandemic, just some 6–7% of the workforce applied teleworking; during the pandemic it came up to some 50% of the workforce. My prediction is that the future percentage of the workforce will be somewhere in between. Early evidence suggest that, at least, this is the intention predicted by teleworkers during the lockdown in the UK (Parry et al., 2021). Their evidence from the lockdown periods of 2020 suggest that employees were keen to balance the accumulated gains of working from home with the social aspects of the office. Three-quarters of their participants expressed a future preference for hybrid working (Parry et al., 2021). From the organizational perspective, employers now have an opportunity to utilize job design to curate more flexible working patterns that maximize both productivity gains around working from home and opportunities for collaboration and innovation around colleagues' co-presence.

Part-time work

At another level of work flexibility and the employment relationship we find the new phenomenon of the multiple part-time (MPT) work pattern. MPT is a new alternative work arrangement, forming part of the emerging 'new deal' in employment. MPT represents a shift away from paternalistic and benevolent secure employment, to an emphasis on continuous responsibility for self-development and employability on the part of the employee.

Part-time work (indeed, single part-time work) grew very quickly, and this evolution has been linked mainly to four factors: (i) high rate of unemployment in many developed countries.;

(ii) increased participation of women in the labour force; (iii) the need of business firms to cut costs, to enhance operational flexibility, or to increase access to scarce human capital and to enlarge the pool of talent upon which the organization can build; and (iv) state incentives, in particular in Europe, aiming to increase employment rates have actually increased the use of part-time jobs as a win-win case, for both employers and employees.

Working part time is not always a choice. Involuntary temporary and part-time work have a negative impact on the perception of job quality and wellbeing at work (Kauhanen & Nätti, 2015).

The percentage of part-time working is steadily growing, with clear gender differences. Some 40% of the women compared with just below 10% of men work part time (and for women with young children it can be 56–57%), as a UK survey shows (Warren & Lyonette, 2018). Multiple jobholders typically combine a full-time job with a part-time job (sometimes termed 'moonlighting'). MPT is implemented by a significant minority of the workforce, and its popularity is growing steadily. Organizations that opt to hire part-time employees may realize that their part-time workers have another part-time job, which means a divided commitment, but also is a possible valuable source of knowledge and experience to be shared.

Flexi-time

'Flexi-time' means the flexibility to change the time of work from the conventional 9 a.m.–5 p.m. schedule. Arrangements vary from starting and ending work earlier or later than the 'standard' to working according to pressure when work is subject to different demands. Such demands can be on a weekly, monthly, or annual basis. For example, in the accounting profession there is greater pressure of work at the end of the month, and on a yearly base, in April and December. It would make sense to enable employees to work fewer hours during the year, and work for longer hours when financial reports have to be completed. The extent to which management accepts such an option would be a clear sign of their mind flexibility (mentioned earlier).

Job sharing

Job sharing is yet another alternative work arrangement, which enables more than one person to share a certain role. It came mostly as a response to the needs of working women who were mothers, but might mean a loss of opportunities for advancement for those working under such arrangements (Gottlieb et al., 1998).

The CAST and career ecosystem to alternative work arrangements

Applying the CAST framework to alternative work arrangements means that individuals will act according to their aspirations. For example, people who put an emphasis on work–life balance or have the ideal of 'family first' may be more likely to be attracted to alternative work arrangements. Many aspects of attitudes to work, for example commitment, are associated with people's career aspirations. Their behaviour or their action of opting, for example, for remote work is subject to their attitudes to work. People may have a high need for autonomy (which would pull people to remote work), a high need for affiliation (which would push people back to office), and a high need for control (which will prevent managers from allowing remote work). People who wish to explore a multitude of experiences may prefer working on a temporary basis, moving from one workplace to another continually. For organizations, the CAST framework implies that if their philosophy puts a high value on a culture of flexibility in management, this will be translated into having policies reflecting all types of flexible work arrangements. The interplay between individuals and organizations reflect the changing nature of 'deal making', such as increasing use of idiosyncratic deals (Bal & Rousseau, 2015; Rousseau et al., 2006) as part of a wider reassessment of the psychological contract with multiple players and multiple relationships (Baruch & Rousseau, 2019).

The use of alternative work arrangements is increasing (Spreitzer et al., 2017). A further evidence for both the increase in use and the nature of alternative work arrangements in the USA was presented by Katz and Krueger (2019). The percentage of workers engaged in alternative work arrangements – defined as temporary help agency workers, on-call workers, contract workers, and independent contractors or freelancers – rose from 11% in 2005 to as high as 16% in 2015. They widen the practices to include:

- general alternative work arrangements, and then
- independent contractors
- on-call workers
- temporary help agency workers
- workers provided by contract firms (which can be single or multiple jobholders).

While only 0.5% of the workforce, Katz and Krueger point out that the fastest growing segment of alternative work comprises those working for an online platform or intermediary web-related function such as Uber or MTurk.

Table 6.4 presents the expected positive impact and challenges on HR presented by each of these alternative work arrangements.

Table 6.4 The pros and cons of alternative work arrangements

Alternative work arrangement	Expected positive impact	Challenges
Flexitime	Enabling the employee to schedule their working hours in a way that will not clash with their personal activities and commitments	(a) The flexibility of certain policies is limited (b) Eventually work is expected to take place on employer's premises
Compressed hours	Enabling employees to benefit from chunks of time off work when they need it	(a) It might be difficult to find time for 'paying back' those chunks (b) Such arrangements imply that on certain days people will work extremely long hours, which could lead to fatigue and stress

Alternative work arrangement	Expected positive impact	Challenges
Remote work	(a) Self-management of time and operation (b) Reducing travel – saving time (discussed later in this chapter)	(a) Reduced teamwork (b) Reduced visibility (c) Social isolation (discussed later in this chapter)
Part-time	(a) Enables people who would otherwise have to quit work to participate in the workforce (b) Can provide variety if combined with another part-time job	(a) Part-timers might be regarded as 'second-class' citizens; they may have lower levels of compensation and other benefits (b) Part-timers tend to have low job security
Job-sharing	High-potential employees that otherwise would drop from the labor market can perform tasks that usually require a full-time employee	There might be an issue of equity and comparability of inputs from different people

Organizational developments and career systems

The development of career theory follows naturally from the development of organizational theory. Changes in organizations and society alter the structure and the culture in which careers develop, as well as the basic assumptions of the nature of career progress. Schein (1978) introduced the career cone model. This represented a mould-breaking approach to career modelling, from functional, hierarchical progress within a single sector to a multidisciplinary approach that enables sideways development. The cone model allows for spiral progress that integrates knowledge and practice from a variety of functional sections in the organization.

The Sonnenfeld and Peiperl model (1988), as partially validated by empirical evidence (Baruch & Peiperl, 2003), is presented in Figure 6.4 and is one of the more analytical models of organizational career systems. Their typology posited that, rather than there being one best model for organizational careers, the particular type of career system used should be appropriate to and derived from the strategy of the firm.

The core of this model is the requirement to match individual and organizational needs/ wants and provisions. Added to this are the concepts of procedural and distributive justice, as well as the development of relationships (or 'psychological contract', to use another term) as an end output. Procedural justice may be defined as the degree to which the rules and procedures specified by policies are properly followed whenever they are applied. In the organizational career context, procedural justice concerns the means (rather than the ends) of social justice decisions (Folger & Cropanzano, 1998; Greenberg & Cropanzano, 2001), that is, the basis on which career decisions are made. For example, procedural justice is an important mediator in the relationship between career calling and career outcomes (Chen et al., 2018). Employees will be willing to accept organizational policies and practices if these are based on fair procedures. They value not just being treated with dignity and respect, but also being provided with adequate information about these procedures (Cropanzano & Greenberg, 1997).

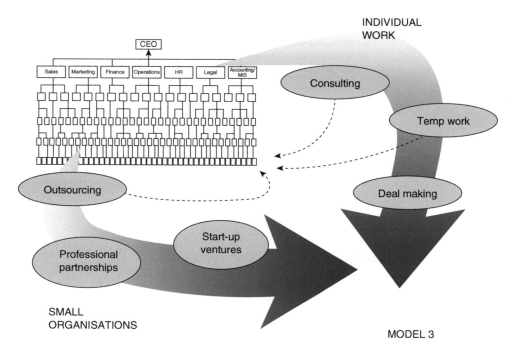

Figure 6.4   Contemporary careers: leaving the organization behind (Peiperl & Baruch, 1997)

Recruitment, selection and, career systems

Recruitment and selection are usually not perceived as integral parts of the organizational career system. Their role is to make sure that there is a match between the individual and the nature and demands of the role within the specific organizational context. Two issues, however, make the distinction between the recruitment process and the career system artificial. First, it is still desirable to recruit a person for a career, rather than for a job. Second, to make sure the right match is found, the organization needs to have as clear an idea as possible about the requirements for each position. If these issues are borne in mind, the process of selection will be part of the strategic management of the human resources (e.g. applying the competencies framework – see Iles, 1999), or looking for wider talent pool – see Zikic, 2015). Let us look at these two issues in Box 6.6.

Recruitment for a job or for a career?

Once having a career was performing the same job throughout life. For a few this is true even today. Teachers, for example, can start and end their career in the same position. For most professions and vocations, the nature of the job includes systematic development,

---

Box 6.6: Selection and recruitment

Iles (1999) suggested a framework for understanding selection and recruitment based on four distinct theoretical perspectives:

- the strategic management approach
- the psychometric approach
- the social process approach
- the critical discourse perspective on assessment.

Each is concerned with selection and recruitment as part of the overall career.

---

sometimes associated with a higher status level and further progression within the hierarchy. Again, in the past it was common to find people developing along certain vocational career paths in a single organization. However, for most, changes in the world of careers have altered that situation. The average time people spend in one organization had been reduced to a few years by the end of the 20th century, therefore career horizons within a single organization are limited. In fact, Hall (1996: 5) cited the CEO of General Electric describing contemporary psychological contracts as 'one-day contracts'. Nevertheless it is the core people, those who would stay for longer and develop within the organization, that are the real target of the organizational career system. Moreover, many people would still like to experience a long-term relationship with their employing organization, if not as a promise, at least as a possible option.

There is a difference in the perspectives on matching for different hierarchy levels, in particular for managerial levels (cf. Forbes & Piercy, 1991). At the lower managerial level the focus is on performance, efficiency, qualifications, and needed competencies (know-how), whereas at the executive level the focus is on a match with the business strategy and culture, and a fit with the other members of top management. Moreover, for top roles and CEO posts, evidence of strong networking is of particular relevance – what the individual can bring to the organization in terms of external resources and contacts (know-whom) (Koyuncu, Hamori, & Baruch, 2017). As for rank-and-file positions, qualifications and work experience play a significant role.

As highlighted earlier in the book, people's need for advancement and promotions within the organizational ranks are the most visible way of achieving this aim. From the organizational viewpoint, promotion is a process comprising decision making, political interventions, and setting future directions for organizational performance and effectiveness. It aims to maintain the continuity and survival of the system in relation to jobholders. The interplay between the many actors in the career system generate an equilibrium of flow – people transitions within and outside organizations (Baruch, 2015; Hall, 2002).

'New deals'

The so-called 'new careers' idea emerged towards the end of the 20th century (Arthur et al., 1999), but received also criticism for its limited relevance (Inkson et al., 2012). The radical restructuring of many organizations has changed the traditional concept of the career and subsequently the way they manage their career systems. A prominent change was the developing and maintaining of a psychological contract between employers and employees. Appendix 6.1 at the end of this chapter will help to unfold the features of the changing nature of psychological contracts (see also Baruch & Rousseau, 2019). The table is based on several complementary works and reviews, most notably the seminal work of Herriot and Pemberton (1995), as well as Sullivan and Baruch (2009) and Cascio (2000). The idea of the 'psychological contract' was presented earlier in the book, and here we can see how it is reflected in a wide variety of innovative approaches to careers, which organizations must recognize. The roots of such contracts are probably deeper than those of formal legal contracts, and we can examine Rousseau's *The social Contract or Principles of Political Right* (1762/1974) as a framework of social order where people have agreed upon certain 'rules of the game' with society. Similarly, the psychological contract focuses on the tacit dialogue between the individual and the organization. This is in the 'unspoken promise, not present in the small print of the employment contract, of what the employer gives, and what employees give in return' (Baruch & Hind, 1999).

Psychological contracts differ from formal, legal employment contracts in their context and expected impact (Spindler, 1994). They have been described by Hall and Moss (1998) as a learning and development contract with the self rather than with the paternalistic and protective organization. Most of the new psychological contracts deal with situations where there are no long-term contracts but a commitment on the part of the organization to provide the employees with training and development, in order to develop a 'portable portfolio' of skills. With this they will be able to find alternative employment if the company no longer needs their services (Handy, 2012).

The new contracts are based on an interactive (relational) process and an exchange (transactional) model (Shore & Terick, 1994). When the expectations are not met, there is a perception of psychological contract breach (Bankins, 2015; Parzefall & Jacqueline, 2011; Robinson & Morrison, 1995) where emotions and mutual actions are intertwined in the process of attributing responsibility and finding reasons for the breach or explaining it. Employees, as the more vulnerable side, do not always welcome the transformation. The new contracts do not offer lifelong employment (or a promise of such), nor the necessity of mutual commitment and loyalty. The typical old, traditional deal was that employees offered loyalty, conformity, and commitment whilst the employers offered security of employment, career prospects, training and development within the company, and care in time of trouble. Both sides based the relationship on 'trust', which can mediate the adverse impact of breaking the psychological contract.

Under the new deal, employees offer long hours, assume added responsibility, provide broader skills, and tolerate change and ambiguity, whereas employers offer high pay, reward for performance, flexibility, and, ideally, the opportunity for lifelong learning and development (Herriot & Pemberton, 1995). Under such conditions, when there is readiness for change and adjusted expectations, there will not be a process of disillusionment and a feeling of betrayal on the part of employees, as suggested by Brockner et al. (1992b).

New terminology has sprung up around the contemporary psychological contract, which was presented in Chapter 3; DeFillippi and Arthur (1994) and Arthur (1994) were perhaps the first to use the term 'boundaryless career', while Ashkenas et al. (1995) wrote about the boundaryless organization. Later, Arthur et al. (1995) suggested the phrase 'intelligent careers', Waterman et al. (1994) with 'career resilient workforce', Mainiero and Sullivan (2006) with the 'kaleidoscope careers', and Peiperl and Baruch (1997) with the 'post-corporate career' used different terms, but all reflect a change from what we had known in the past. Managers and HR professionals need to re-create commitment and maintain confidence and performance using different expectations and incentives based on the new contract. Instead of a sequence of promotions and pay rises within an organization, individuals have suffered a loss of security of employment and prospects of promotion. The consequences for employees' morale and organizational innovation are beginning to be felt, and organizations are at a loss as to how to manage careers in the future. Individuals, likewise, are trying to maintain their employability in the labour market by developing marketable skills (Herriot & Stickland, 1999).

A pause for reflection

What is your preferred psychological contract? Can you identify dimensions of your expectations that differ from those of your employer? Can you identify what would be fair for your employer to expect from you? Appendix 6.1 at the end of this chapter is provided to help you identify your ideal psychological contract.

Empowerment

'Empowerment' is not a new buzzword introduced merely to inspire current trends in management science (Zimmerman, 2000). It is an attempt at formalizing and quantifying degrees of freedom or options people may have (Salge et al., 2014), and comprises an innovative approach to working with people and a shift from the top-down management styles which have dominated control mechanisms and managerial concepts in both theory and practice since the Industrial Revolution (Baruch, 1998a). According to the new deal and the new psychological contract, organizations now empower people not only in operational terms, but also in managing their career, their development, their progress. Weick (2001, p. 207) argues that traditional career management by the organization is replaced by more self-reliance. This implies empowerment in terms of a self-managed rather than an organization-led career.

Within work environment, empowerment means 'finding new ways to concentrate power in the hands of the people who need it most to get the job done – putting authority, responsibility, resources and rights at the most appropriate level for the task. It also means the controlled transfer of power from management to employees in the long-term interest of the business as a whole' (Clutterbuck, 1994, p. 12).

Empowerment is part of a set of motivational techniques designed to improve employee performance through increased levels of employee participation and self-determination (Vecchio, 1995). To lead to desired results, there should be trust in management as a condition (Kim et al., 2012). Traditional paradigms were based predominantly on strong managerial control, a concept originating from the Greek philosopher Plato some 2,400 years ago (Clemense & Mayer, 1987). The modern concept of empowerment relates primarily to the delegation of decision-making power to people at lower organizational levels, but empowerment means more than merely delegation (Malone, 1997). It is concerned with trust, motivation, decision making, and basically, breaking the inner boundaries between management and employees as 'them' versus 'us'. The impact of empowerment can cross levels, for example, individuals and teams (Chen et al., 2019). However, there is a difference between the meaning of empowerment and the rhetoric of its implementation, and the latter is not always in line with the good intentions of its originators (Hales, 2000).

Conger and Kanungo (1988) viewed empowerment in the organizational context as a set of conditions necessary for intrinsic task motivation. Thomas and Velthouse (1990) define four components of empowerment:

- Choice: Not only providing employees with genuine job enrichment and opportunities to have their voice heard, but also giving them real power to control and influence work processes.
- Competence: Enabling people to be confident of their capacity to make these choices; enhancing their self-efficacy as a pre-condition to making decisions and standing by them.
- Meaningfulness: Valuing the work done by the empowered people.
- Impact: Letting people have influence over what is going on in the organization, ensuring that their decisions make a difference.

All of these components apply to the transformed organizational career system. Many of the roles traditionally held by the organization have been passed to individual employees. This transfer is not always, however, the best course, as some transferred responsibilities should remain with the organization. Baruch's (1998a) model of empowerment offers four ways of classifying organizational approaches to empowerment. The model proposes that the perceptions, attitudes, beliefs, and values of senior management can be described by constraints that can be grouped into two domains, labelled *belief* and *fairness*. Subsequently a 2 x 2 model emerges for analysis of empowerment in organizations, which may be relevant to career systems as well as in general empowerment.

The two dimensions of the model are:

Belief: The extent to which top management genuinely believe in the underlying ideas of empowerment and its potential benefits. This will depend on the values the people at the top hold. The bona fide notion of empowerment implies the transfer of actual and rectified delegation of power and decision making to the lower echelons of the organization. In terms of career management, it means passing responsibility to both line managers and the employees themselves.

Fairness: The extent to which the approach of senior management to employees is fair and just/honest. Here we have a clear problem, for justice and fairness are loaded terms, not easily measured. In terms of career fairness, this relates to the support the organization is prepared to give to help people in their career.

Combined, these dimensions project four prototypes of the organizational approach to and the interpretation of empowerment. The first dimension, belief, determines whether career empowerment will be applied in the organization; the second, fairness, implies the support and investment of the organization for the empowered people. These are portrayed below.

If the organization and its representatives do not believe in the concept, and apply a 'fair' approach, they will take 'career empowerment' off the agenda. If they do believe in the concept, and apply a 'fair' approach, they will delegate decision making to individuals and will support them accordingly.

If the organization and its representatives do not believe in the concept, but for reasons to do with political correctness, compliance with fashionable theories, and image building, prefer to be seen as applying best practice, they may try to apply simulated career empowerment. If they believe in the concept, but do not wish to play a 'fair' game, they may just off-load the burden of career management onto employees.

These four dimensions have been labelled respectively as the Dissociated, the Enlightened, the Fraudulent and the Miser (or mean-spirited) (see Figure 6.5).

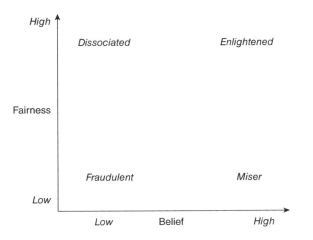

Figure 6.5   The four dimensions of the empowerment model (Baruch, 2004a)

Career management and the litigious society

The surge in general trend of litigations, including employment-related litigation, is apparent in Western society. While some suggest that it is more of a myth (Engel, 2016), the perception leads to the phenomenon being taken seriously by employers and employees alike. In the UK, with a labour market of 26 million, the central agency for Advisory, Conciliation and Arbitration Service (ACAS) witnessed significant level of legal inquiries, culminating in a surge of individual actions against employers (Sisson & Taylor, 2006). Many other private individual cases reach court via other channels. This trend can be attributed to several elements: a decrease in the level of unionism; improved employment rights; an increase in the sophistication of people with multiple competencies and wider knowledge; a proactive approach by individuals; and fewer bonds between employers and their workforces because of the increasing flexibility and individualization of work.

The implications of such actions on the management of employment relationships with a large workforce are destructive. Taking a matter to court means ending a trust-based relationship, and long-term career development is based on such relationships. A large proportion of employment-related cases concern career issues, in particular on the issue of promotion and equal employment opportunities. One issue which may possibly lead to litigation is the management of diversity and equal employment opportunities. More on this will be presented in Chapter 9.

A specific emphasis in this book is on how to determine best practice in various HR-related decisions, if there is any 'best practice'. It should be remembered that there is an argument regarding the existence or relevance of apparent best practice. Cappelli and Crocker-Hefter (1996) claimed that no such 'solution' is feasible, yet several meta-analyses cited earlier (e.g. Tzabbar et al., 2017) indicate the relevance and impact of best practice. Baruch (1998b) advised HR managers how to walk the tightrope of people management by trying to find the golden route, a balanced way between extremes, in both strategy and practice. In terms of career management, the balance between individual and organizational perspective is long accepted (Baruch, 2006a; Lips-Wiersma & Hall, 2007). Acute problems concern the ambiguity and complexity of the issue of managing people. And people are not only the most important asset of organizations, they are also the most difficult asset to manage – they are unpredictable (at least to some extent), they have their own will and plans (which do not necessarily fit with those of the organization), and they are affected by the external and internal organizational environments. These issues affect how career management can be dealt with, and limit what executives can expect from organizational career management systems.

To put it at its most basic level, the role of HR is to acquire and maintain the right talent (Noe et al., 2017) or, as traditionally stated, 'to obtain and retain employees' (Cuming, 1986). 'Retaining' is basically the role of career management. To find the right people, HR managers have to engage in an explicit search to identify the implicit qualities needed for effective management in the organization.

Maintaining motivation requires the investment of even greater effort. It requires a continuous role of developing people, responding to individual and organizational needs and being proactive in inspiring as well as in directing people (Baruch, 1998b). Applying best practice and fairness is the best answer to the prospect of litigation on the part of both individuals and external agencies (such as government, unions, etc.).

Organizational learning mechanisms concerning career practices

One important question about practices is how far they are applied. Chapter 7 reviews a wide portfolio of career practices. It is feasible to evaluate, for each practice, how far employees (as well as senior managers) are aware of its existence, to what level they implement these practices, and how they feel about the outcomes of these practices.

Perhaps the most important question to be asked is, 'Does this make a difference?' What are the consequences for the individual and for the organization? As shown by Huselid (1995), good HRM practice leads to better financial performance of firms, and this was verified by many studies (Jiang et al., 2012; Tzabbar et al., 2017). The role and importance of implementing CPM was reinforced by the work of Bagdadli and Gianecchini (2019) and Baruch and Peiperl (2000a).

Employees have little knowledge of career-related HRM practices, considerably below the expectations of HRM theorists and practitioners (Baruch, 1996b). Probably the most interesting question to be examined is why some practices are used more than others. The answer could be connected to fear on the part of organizations of creating career expectations in their employees. These concerns increase both in times of recession and in response to changes and instability in business life. Long-term planning becomes more difficult, sometimes irrelevant, and organizations tend to plan career developments mainly in the short term. Even if planning long-term developments, organizations will present and discuss them in vague terms rather than as a commitment.

There is also disagreement, both among senior managers and among employees, about whether the practices were in use. This disagreement may be due to two main reasons: either the ambiguity of the nature as well as the definition of the different techniques; or a genuine lack of knowledge that can be caused by distortions in organizational communication.

HRM is about the management of people in order to achieve desired results (Armstrong & Taylor, 2020). Similarly, Storey's (1995: 5) definition of HRM includes the wording: 'HRM is a distinctive approach to employment management which seeks to obtain competitive advantage through the strategic deployment of a highly committed and skilled workforce, using an array of cultural, structural and personnel practices.' How can HR and career managers in organizations gain a true picture of employees' perceptions of career systems? A simple way is to use internal employee, surveys. These may be used for comparative analysis, but their validity is questionable. Additional sources include sessions with mentors, managers, sample employees, and some recommend using exit interviews.

Evaluating career systems

In a similar way to performance appraisal at the individual employee level, organizations should evaluate their business unit performance and effectiveness. Management should be able to evaluate the operational and performance quality of its units, departments, and subdivisions for two major reasons: the need to be well acquainted with what is happening in the organization; and in order to identify and isolate possible problems and difficulties which might be due to poor performance (Baruch, 1997). However, it is never simple to evaluate the 'soft' management issues covered by HRM. Moreover, different clients or constituencies have various expectations of HRM, as defined by Tsui (1987, 1990).

One way to conduct such an evaluation is to look at 'customer satisfaction' – and one major customer is the employees as a whole. Attitude surveys have several advantages and are widely used (Leonardi et al., 2014). However, they are limited to employees' perceptions, and their shortcomings include accuracy problems and questionable reliability and validity, and the fact that it is not only employees who are the clients of HRM. Furthermore, employees may not be familiar with some of HRM practices, such as succession planning.

Another means of evaluation is to measure the extent to which the unit has achieved its goals, which in career system management may be manifested by employees' career satisfaction, and by a proper flow of appointments at the organizational level (e.g. there is no need for crisis head-hunting when people leave the organization). Nevertheless, 'goal attainment' requires criteria to be defined in terms of clear, measurable objectives, and in people-related issues it is difficult to reach agreement about the meaning and importance of such objectives. Also the timescale that is needed to assess goal attainment in the area of HRM is fairly long.

A different evaluation method will focus on analysing organizational career practices. This builds on Townley (1994), who referred to HRM as a set of practices and techniques. Such evaluation should relate to both *what* is being done and *how* it is being done.

Each of these three methods can be implemented to evaluate organizational career systems. Goal attainment can be assessed by comparisons with either specific organizational goals or wider goals (e.g. set by national professional bodies). Employee surveys can include employees' perceptions of career management. Chapter 7 provides a comprehensive set of career practices that can serve as a basis for conducting an evaluation.

There are several methods of obtaining feedback on organizational career systems (and other HR systems). Certain unique knowledge may derive from exit interviews, which may take the form of a survey, or interview via phone, video, or face-to-face sessions. They offer a validated manner by which to explore the complexities of reasons for leaving one's workplace (Kulik et al., 2012). Most argue for conducting exit interviews at the time of leaving, or on the last day or in the last week. This is not always the best option (see Case Study 6.2).

CASE STUDY 6.2: EXIT INTERVIEWS

John Sullivan of San Francisco State University argues that exit interviews should be conducted 3–6 months after the departure date since there is a significant difference between the answers given then and those given on leaving. There are several reasons for this. First, leaving may be traumatic and such an interview can provide an opportunity for people to air their frustrations. Second, it is only after some time that people can compare the new employer to the former one. Another aspect is that in an interview at the time of leaving the employee must be polite, bearing in mind that the former employer will be providing a reference (recommendation letter) for future employers.

Therefore, it is not surprising to find problems with exit interviews and surveys. AT&T Mobility's experience with post-exit questionnaires, posted to the home of former employees, was poor also. There being no real incentive to return the survey, most responses were from very disgruntled employees who frequently ranted about how

bad the company was while offering little in the way of substantive, useful information.

In view of such disappointing outcomes, HR can opt for pre-exit interviews, sometimes called 'Why do you stay?' interviews as opposed to 'Why are you leaving?' interviews. An organization being strategic and proactive will ask its key people why they stay and what the barriers to their productivity are. By identifying symptoms before they get out of hand, an organization may be able to circumvent the cause.

Question: As a future manager, will you want to hear why people leave your organization (and you)?

The practicality of evaluating career systems

Baruch and Peiperl (2000a) suggested a descriptive model for understanding contemporary career systems and practice along two dimensions: 'Sophistication of the career management practices' and 'Involvement necessary on the part of the organization' to apply them appropriately. Baruch (2003a) advanced this framework by adding four dimensions to enable deeper and better understanding of career systems, and their evaluation. These are: strategic orientation, developmental focus, organizational decision-making relevance, and innovative approach.

Strategic orientation is based on the strategic HRM approach (Fombrun et al., 1984), which implies that HRM should not be seen as a set of distinct practices but as part of organizational strategic management as a whole (Bailey et al., 2018).

Developmental focus questions the relevance of career management practice to the personal development of employees, as compared to the simple acquisition of specific organizational needs. With human resources being seen as the core asset and as the source of competitive advantage for the firm, it is in the interest of companies to develop this resource (Swart et al., 2012). This means, of course, investment in developing people's competencies, but will be reflected in the bottom-line outcomes of the firm (Pfeffer, 1998).

Organizational decision-making issues is the degree to which the practice is relevant, such as the selection of top executives (cf. Nutt, 1999; Ones & Dilchert, 2009).

Innovative approach (in contrast to conventional and orthodox approaches) concerns the extent to which specific practice reflects novel ideas and concepts. Among the academic contributions of the last decade of the 20th century are several innovative concepts that require a non-traditional career approach.

All in all, the six-dimension model offered by Baruch aims to further develop career theory by offering and critically examining a normative model for integrating the available portfolio of organizational career practices. Such a model also assists an understanding of management practice in the area of careers. It can help to facilitate guidelines for evaluating organizational career systems along these six dimensions:

Involvement: From a very low to a very high level of organizational involvement needed when dealing with the specific career practice.

Sophistication and complexity: From very simple to highly sophisticated and complex.

Strategic orientation: From very practical, or 'tactical', to very strategic.

Developmental focus: From low to high relevance for developing individuals.

Organizational decision-making focus: From low to high relevance for organizational decision-making processes.

Innovative: From very traditional or conventional to innovative and unorthodox.

Summary

In this chapter we moved from the individual to an organizational perspective, from a focus on psychology to a focus on management theory. The CAST framework was introduced and discussed in detail, representing the basis of organizational career systems. Further, we dealt with career dynamism and how contemporary careers are significantly different from traditional style careers, in terms of both the practice and the strategy. A dominant theme was the need for flexibility, both as a strategic response and as a tool for gaining competitive advantage. Dealing with new trends in managing organizations and people we discovered the blurring of boundaries, the advantages and possible perils (such as increased stress). Alternative work arrangements, 'new deals', and empowerment were presented as part of the new career system construct. Last, we looked at a method for evaluating career systems.

KEY TERMS

Alternative work arrangements

Empowerment

Exit interviews

Flexibility

Litigious society

Management buy-outs

Mergers

Moonlighting

Multiple part-time work

New deals

Opinion surveys

Organizational career systems

Remote work

Strategic career management

The CAST concept

Working hours

DISCUSSION QUESTIONS

LESSONS AND FOOD FOR THOUGHT

1. *For HR managers*: Using the CAST concept, how would you distinguish between practices, policies (e.g. do you have a set of established policies?), and strategies (if they exist). Do you have an organizational strategy? Is there a match between this strategy and the HR strategy? Were they developed simultaneously?
2. *For the HR consultant*: What would be your advice to HR managers in developing a comprehensive approach to an organizational career system?
3. *For the HR teacher*: How would you integrate new forms of organizations (M&As, MBOs, new ventures, the virtual organization) in the traditional teaching of career systems?

4.   *For the student*: What is the timespan of your career plan, and how far would you genuinely involve your organization in your career plan? How would you obtain involvement and commitment from your organization towards the development of your competencies and skills to ensure further advances in your career?

REVIEW QUESTIONS

1.   What is the role of the psychological contract concept in the CAST framework?
2.   What type of alternative work arrangements will you wish to have? What type of alternative work arrangements will you be ready to offer your future subordinates?
3.   With relation to your role as a student, in what ways would your university learn about how to improve its operations if it were to listen carefully to an exit interview which might be conducted with you after your studies? When will you be in the best position to provide fair and useful feedback – as soon as you finish? A couple of months later? Or further on in your career?

CRITICAL THINKING

1.   If you are a student now looking for your first job, what are you looking for – simply a job, a career, an experience?
2.   Which type of alternative work arrangements would you be ready and willing to adopt?
3.   What would be a realistic career expectation, from your viewpoint, from: (a) your organization; (b) your direct manager?
4.   What would empowerment mean for you in your job? What type of empowerment will you delegate to your subordinates?

EXERCISE

Are you aware of your career aspirations? Can you formulate them in writing? List two or three of your more important career aspirations.

Now try to consider what action you may take in the near future to help you reach your career aspirations.

Appendix 6.1

Psychological contract exercise*

The short questionnaire below is intended to help you in formulating your 'most preferred new deal' in employment. It is hoped that filling it in will lead you to a better understanding of the ways in which individuals and their employing organizations can develop mutually rewarding relationships in the future. Should you expect your future organization to fulfil *all* your needs?

Certainly not! Yet, we hope that our organization will meet some of our most important needs. The table below asks you to compare a list of possible expectations that you wish your future organization to fulfil with what you actually expect in practice. Perhaps only a few of the options are important to you, and you will try to build your relationship with the organization around them.

Please circle the number that best represents your answer (1 being the lowest, 7 the highest).

Expectations: What I want, or what I am reasonably expecting

1 2 3 4 5 6 7	professional challenge	1 2 3 4 5 6 7
1 2 3 4 5 6 7	filling in my time	1 2 3 4 5 6 7
1 2 3 4 5 6 7	shelter from family/spouse demands	1 2 3 4 5 6 7
1 2 3 4 5 6 7	learning environment	1 2 3 4 5 6 7
1 2 3 4 5 6 7	emotional support	1 2 3 4 5 6 7
1 2 3 4 5 6 7	social companionship	1 2 3 4 5 6 7
1 2 3 4 5 6 7	skill development	1 2 3 4 5 6 7
1 2 3 4 5 6 7	opportunity to manage others	1 2 3 4 5 6 7
1 2 3 4 5 6 7	opportunity to be managed	1 2 3 4 5 6 7
1 2 3 4 5 6 7	financial provider	1 2 3 4 5 6 7
1 2 3 4 5 6 7	source of inspiration	1 2 3 4 5 6 7
1 2 3 4 5 6 7	social status	1 2 3 4 5 6 7
1 2 3 4 5 6 7	career aspiration	1 2 3 4 5 6 7
1 2 3 4 5 6 7	job security	1 2 3 4 5 6 7
1 2 3 4 5 6 7	open communication	1 2 3 4 5 6 7
1 2 3 4 5 6 7	professional development	1 2 3 4 5 6 7
1 2 3 4 5 6 7	personal guidance	1 2 3 4 5 6 7
1 2 3 4 5 6 7	good working conditions	1 2 3 4 5 6 7
1 2 3 4 5 6 7	source of motivation	1 2 3 4 5 6 7
1 2 3 4 5 6 7	life structure	1 2 3 4 5 6 7
1 2 3 4 5 6 7	safe working environment	1 2 3 4 5 6 7
1 2 3 4 5 6 7	feeling needed and valued	1 2 3 4 5 6 7
1 2 3 4 5 6 7	fair treatment	1 2 3 4 5 6 7
1 2 3 4 5 6 7	increased employability	1 2 3 4 5 6 7
1 2 3 4 5 6 7	honesty in dealing with me	1 2 3 4 5 6 7

* The questionnaire was developed by Baruch and Hind

You may add here any other expectations you have, not mentioned above:

....

Similarly, should you expect yourself to fulfil *all* your organization's requirements?

Again, certainly not. This table asks you to compare what the organization may expect from you and what you are actually planning to give in return. As before, do not expect yourself to meet all the expectations in the relationship.

Organizational expectations: What will be expected from me to actually give

1 2 3 4 5 6 7	high-quality performance	1 2 3 4 5 6 7
1 2 3 4 5 6 7	long hours	1 2 3 4 5 6 7
1 2 3 4 5 6 7	commitment	1 2 3 4 5 6 7
1 2 3 4 5 6 7	desire and ability to learn	1 2 3 4 5 6 7
1 2 3 4 5 6 7	emotional support to others	1 2 3 4 5 6 7
1 2 3 4 5 6 7	punctuality	1 2 3 4 5 6 7
1 2 3 4 5 6 7	be a source of motivation to others	1 2 3 4 5 6 7
1 2 3 4 5 6 7	maintain a safe working environment	1 2 3 4 5 6 7
1 2 3 4 5 6 7	being managed	1 2 3 4 5 6 7
1 2 3 4 5 6 7	managing others	1 2 3 4 5 6 7
1 2 3 4 5 6 7	represent the organization positively	1 2 3 4 5 6 7
1 2 3 4 5 6 7	be flexible	1 2 3 4 5 6 7
1 2 3 4 5 6 7	develop the organization	1 2 3 4 5 6 7
1 2 3 4 5 6 7	open communication	1 2 3 4 5 6 7
1 2 3 4 5 6 7	be a good 'organizational citizen'	1 2 3 4 5 6 7
1 2 3 4 5 6 7	loyalty	1 2 3 4 5 6 7
1 2 3 4 5 6 7	honesty in dealing with them	1 2 3 4 5 6 7

You may add here any other expectations you have, not mentioned above:

....

Organizational Career Management Practices

7

LEARNING OBJECTIVES

After reading this chapter you should be able to:

- Define organizational career practices
- Identify the existing portfolio of career practices and how to benefit from them
- Understand how they are associated with each other as an integrated system
- Explain how organizations can develop a career practices system to match their needs

Chapter outline

Introduction: Career practices

This chapter takes on the more pragmatic task of focusing on career practices, a subsection of overall HR practices. The chapter outlines a comprehensive portfolio of HRM practices, which can be conducted by organizations to plan and manage employees' careers. It develops and expands upon earlier work of the author (Baruch, 1996b; Baruch & Peiperl, 2000a) and others (e.g. Bagdadli & Gianecchini, 2019). The chapter provides a systematic presentation and critical examination, rooted in both theory and practice, of a range of career management practices, techniques, activities, and programmes. For each career practice referred to, an explanation is given of how it may be implemented by contemporary organizations. The chapter also integrates these practices into a comprehensive organizational framework.

The importance and prominence of organizational career planning and management (CPM) as part of HRM has long been widely recognized (Gutteridge et al., 1993). From the early writing on modern career systems to recent inputs, academic scholars have emphasized that organizational career systems should ensure the fit between individual needs and aspirations and organizational requirements (Herriot & Pemberton, 1996; Schein, 1978). These organizational careers are changing with the wider changes in the economy and society (Best, 2020; Hassard et al., 2012). However, as pointed out earlier, much of the literature on careers has focused on the individual, whereas there is an acute lack of conceptual and theoretical formulation of organizational practices.

A good starting point for establishing a comprehensive updated organizational career system is to examine what practices were applied in the past and more currently. The chapter goes on to project which career practices will remain valid and relevant, which will need significant change and adaptation, which might become obsolete, and which new ones may emerge. The first part of the chapter critically examines a traditional portfolio for career practices.

There have been several attempts to establish what comprises a conventional set of organizational career practices. Several sources in the literature suggest specific lists of career practices, starting in the last decades of the 20th century (Baruch, 1999; London & Stumpf, 1982), when, for example, Walker and Gutteridge (1979) identified ten career activities, although some of these were closer to other constituencies of HRM than to career management. Perhaps the most comprehensive list was that provided by Gutteridge et al. (1993) in their study of careers in the USA. However, their study concentrated on large business organizations only (the top 1,000 US corporations), and might therefore have been non-representative of broader practice. More updated work manifests the proliferation of career practices undertaken by organizations, as well as their relevance and relationship with the HRM strategy (Baruch & Peiperl, 2000a; Bagdadli & Gianecchini, 2019).

A pause for reflection

Think what your organization can do for you, not (just) what you can do for your organization.

How well would you like to be treated by your organization? What kind of CPM activities would you expect? What may your organization plan for you without your knowing about it?

In this chapter we dwell on the third 'P', the practical level: the activities, actions and operations that form the practice of CPM.

CASE STUDY 7.1: ANALYSIS

In the USA, the 1,000th largest company (Carvana, in the Fortune 1000 list for 2020) employs some 1,500 people. Number 995, Align Technology, employs 10,660 people. Both have annual revenue close to US$2 billion. In the 25th place, Bank of America employs over 200,000 people. The number of employees does not always correspond to the firm location of the list. In the first place is Walmart with 2,200,000 people, but second in the list, ExxonMobil, employs only 77,000, whereas third is Apple with 132,000 employees.

Firm size in terms of employee numbers varies, with some companies employing more than 100,000 people. Such an amount of people requires clear attention to

(Continued)

the management of this workforce, including their careers.

However, the US labour market consisted of about 160 million people in early 2021, so the majority of people work in small or medium-sized companies. While all have a career, whether they all need a formal career system is another matter.

CASE STUDY 7.2: CREATING THE FUNCTION

Here is a question I used to give my HRM students in their final exam:

You have just been recruited by a company which employs some 1,000 employees, a company that previously did not have an HRM/Personnel department, for historic reasons and because the former CEO believed that HR issues should be dealt with directly by line managers. However, a new CEO is now in charge, and she believes that there should be a specific professional unit within the organization to deal with HRM/personnel issues. You have been recruited to create the new department and head it. The HR manager will be one of the board-level team (you would not have accepted the offer had this not been the case).

On your first day you set yourself the task of building a comprehensive system to include all the necessary HR practices. In particular, you need to decide which practices to apply and how these will be integrated.

Questions

If the situation in the company was satisfactory under the old system, and since we believe in delegation, why not continue letting the line managers be the HR managers?

What impact will the type of organization and its characteristics have on your answer?

The above scenario may vary, depending on such factors as: whether it is a production or service based firm; whether it is an established or new enterprise; which sector it is in – high or low technology; what form of control – centralized or decentralized; and others.

Questions

At what stage in terms of size of the organization should an HR function be introduced into an organization? At what stage in terms of size should a career management function be introduced into the HR unit? What characteristics will influence your answer?

As a consultant, the scenario depicted above may face you with a challenge: if you are ask to advise an HR director about how to rebuild their HR department from scratch, what would you be doing in terms of the constituencies of the department?

The use of career practices: empirical evidence

The list of practices presented and discussed in this chapter evolved from several earlier works on CPM practices. Most practices were covered in many sources, but some new ones were added to the list, including induction, special programmes for unique populations, and secondments (temporary assignments to another area/organization). Table 7.1 summarizes findings from studies which tested the use of career management and planning practices in organizations. The sources for the data in these studies are responses from HR managers, as they are considered most likely to be best acquainted with career practices, both as professionals and as representatives of the organization.

The rest of the chapter is devoted, first, to an elaboration of each practice, and second, brings them together in an integrated framework. The presentation of the practices relies on several studies that explored the use and application of such practices, and is in line with the classification offered by Baruch and Peiperl's (2000a) model, which comprises five clusters of career practices (see Figure 7.1). It is a descriptive model, that is, based on field-research data, gathered from almost 200 organizations, and was constructed using the statistical procedure of

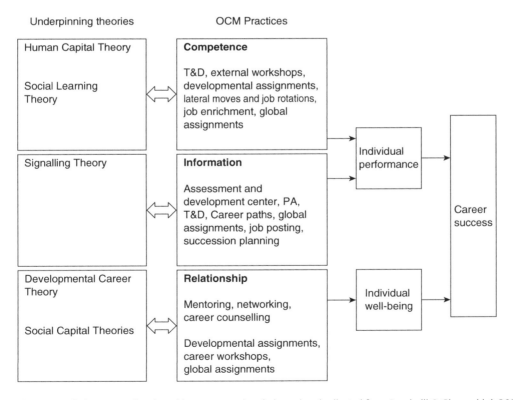

Figure 7.1   Associating career theories with career practices (adopted and adjusted from Bagdadli & Gianecchini, 2019)

factor analysis, a procedure utilized to measure interrelationships among variables. The classification is configured along two dimensions: degree of practice sophistication and level of organizational involvement.

It was Kurt Lewin who made the statement 'there is nothing as practical as good theory'. In a comprehensive literature review, Bagdadli and Gianecchini (2019) identify the relationships between career-related theories and organizational career practices.

Table 7.1 presents a summary of a set of papers which studied empirically organizational change management (OCM), as collected by Bagdadli and Gianecchini (2019). The studies

Table 7.1   Organizational career practices

Career practices that were covered by all those studies	Career practices that were covered by at least three of them	Career practices that were covered by one or two of these studies
Career counselling/discussion	Career pathing/common career paths	Promotability forecasts
Succession planning	Assessment (& development) centers	Psychological testing
Career planning workshops	Career workbooks/books and/or pamphlets on career issues.	Interview process
Individual counselling or career discussion with supervisor or line manager	Career resource centers	Job assignment
	Outplacement counselling	Other career information format
Individual counselling or career discussion with personnel (HR) staff	Skills inventory	Individual counselling or career discussion with senior career adviser or specialized counsellor
Replacement or succession	Pre-retirement workshops	
Planning	Career information handbooks	Informal canvassing
Career workshops	Career ladders or dual-career ladder	Staffing/appraisal committee
Individual counselling	Career resource center	Internal placement system
Formal career discussions with line manager	Job posting	Job enrichment or job design
	Skills inventories or skills audit	Job rotation
Workshops on career opportunities within the organization	In-house training and development programs	External seminars or workshops
	Mentoring system	Tuition reimbursement
	Performance appraisal as a basis for career planning	Supervisor training in career discussion
	Postings regarding internal job openings	Special programs for ethnic
	Formal education	minorities, women, people with disabilities, dual career couples
	Written personal career planning programs	Employee orientation program (induction)
	Training programs for	Quality circles
	Managers	Special programs for expatriates and re-patriates
	Outplacement	Special programs for high flyers (Talent management)
	Career resource systems	Building psychological contracts
		Secondments
		Other PA (like 360 degree)
		PA feedback

covered are by Gutteridge et al. (1993), Baruch (1996b), Baruch (1999), Baruch and Peiperl (2000a), Eby et al. (2005), and De Vos et al. (2009). The table identifies how common those practices are by distinguishing which career practices were covered by all those studies.

The table represents the wide range of career practices that are recognized and suggested by the extant literature for HRM.

Box 7.1: Normative versus descriptive models

A normative model is one that tries to establish what *should be* the right way to do something – to conduct a process, to develop a product, to form a relationship, and so on. In this case, it is to develop a comprehensive set of organizational career practices and to find out how they may be associated with each other.

A descriptive model is one based on factual reality, that is, how things are in real life. It is based on data collected and assembled, and is subjected to analysis that checks the relationships among constructs or variables.

The model depicted in Figure 7.2 is a descriptive model, based on empirical study conducted by Baruch and Peiperl (2000a), and applied also by De Vos et al. (2009).

While the majority of clusters as presented in the model appear to be logical, and are clearly based on factual evidence (i.e. a descriptive model, based on actual organizational cases), it is not necessarily the best model for developing a career system. Another way to look at clusters of career practices would be to develop a normative model – a model which tries to establish what career practices *should* be applied, and when establishing connections, to point to the right way to classify the clusters. In this sense, a normative model may add to our understanding and to the development of organizational career systems. The following set of dimensions may provide insights into the nature of each career practice (the first two were used in the Baruch–Peiperl (2000a) model, the rest were introduced by Baruch, 2003a).

Involvement: From a very low to a very high level of organizational involvement needed while dealing with the specific career practice.

Sophistication and complexity: From very simple to highly sophisticated and complex.

Strategic orientation: From very practical, 'tactical', to very strategic.

Developmental focused: From low to high relevance for developing individuals.

Organizational decision-making focused: From low to high relevance for organizational decision-making processes.

Innovative: From very traditional or conventional, to innovative and unorthodox.

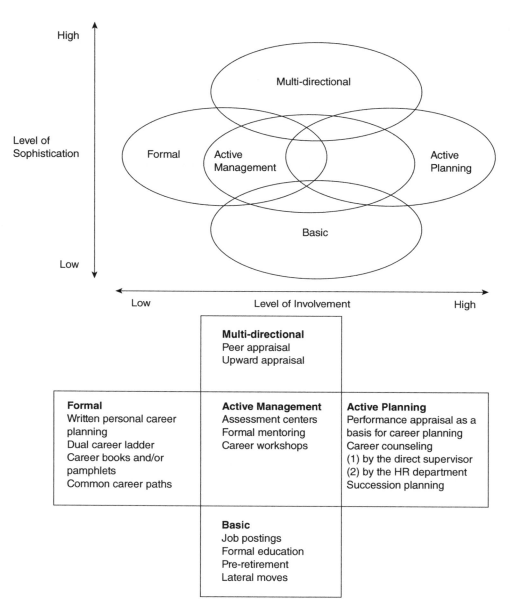

Figure 7.2   Two-dimensional model of career management practices (based on Baruch & Peiperl, 2000a and De Vos et al., 2009)

CPM practices: Clusters

Basic

The practices below were grouped under the title 'Basic' (low on sophistication, medium on involvement) by the Baruch–Peiperl (2000a) model:

- Postings regarding internal job openings.
- Formal education as part of career development.
- Lateral moves to create cross-functional experience.
- Retirement preparation programmes.

Formal

The practices below were grouped under the title 'Formal' (medium on sophistication, low on involvement) by the Baruch–Peiperl model:

- Booklets and/or pamphlets on career issues.
- Dual ladder (parallel hierarchy for professional staff).
- Written personal career planning.

Active management

The practices below were grouped under the title 'Active management' (medium on sophistication, medium on involvement) by the Baruch–Peiperl model:

- Induction
- Assessment centres
- Mentoring
- Career workshops.

Active planning

The practices below were grouped under the title 'Active planning' (medium on sophistication, high on involvement) by the Baruch–Peiperl model:

- Performance appraisal as a basis for career planning.
- Career counselling by direct supervisor.
- Career counselling by HR Department.
- Succession planning.

Multi-directional

The practices below were grouped under the title 'Multi-directional' (high on sophistication, medium on involvement) by the Baruch–Peiperl model:

- 360-degree performance appraisal systems.
- Common career paths.
- Special programmes for ethnic minorities, women, people with disabilities, dual career couples, and so on, expatriates and repatriates, high-flyers.

New CPM practices

The following additional practices listed by managers are not classified under any cluster in the Baruch–Peiperl model, but were suggested later:

- Building psychological contracts
- Secondments
- Intrapreneurship
- Mass career customization
- Tuition reimbursement.

Another general career practice is:

- Training programmes for managers to enable them to handle careers issues.

This practice is needed to provide managers with the skills required for handling their employees' careers. It is not one specific practice but combines several of the above-mentioned practices and activities, and is part of a training programme for managers.

A dilemma: as suggested by De Vos et al. (2009), the higher the level of career self-management, the higher the level of expectations towards organizational career management. This might put organizations off when developing career management practices. Yet, they also found that the higher the level of career management provided by the organization, the higher the level of employee commitment, which is a positive outcome for the organization. Overall, the challenge of developing a comprehensive career system is worth the investment when considering both high expectations and intangible outcomes.

Career practices for whom?

Each person, be they the porter or the CEO, has a career. Many develop their career outside the boundaries of large organizations. Among these are entrepreneurs, like the self-employed, people who run small businesses, freelancers, the unemployed. However, most working people are in organizations, usually as employees. Career practices are carried out by organizations to meet employees' needs. They exist to support employees at all organizational levels, but in particular those in the higher echelons. Managerial and professional careers are more complex than those of some of the rank-and-file personnel. Consequently, certain career practices are conducted only for managers. Throughout this chapter a distinction is made between practices directed mainly or exclusively at the managerial population and those aimed at employees at various hierarchy levels.

In considering career practices it may be advisable to review the above-mentioned practices to ascertain which are still valid and necessary, and which might be deemed unnecessary in the context of the 21st century. Even those expected to be essential in the future may need to be revised and adapted, for example, in the light of contemporary organizational and environment turbulence. The practices vary in their applicability and relevance to different kinds of organizations; small companies usually need fewer official bureaucratic and regulated systems, since informal procedures can be applied successfully. Organizations operating in different industrial sectors and countries may apply different sets of practices, or apply the same practice differently. A special case is large multinational companies operating in diverse cultures. For such companies, a variety of approaches in their different subsidiaries may be appropriate.

The final consideration is the impact that future innovations in IT systems are expected to have on how careers are managed. Most prominent are the AI systems that collaborate or interfere with humans – and in increasing cases, may replace humans (Malik et al., 2020). The implications of the ever-increasing use of the Internet is just one example where new labour markets emerge. However, the pace of technological breakthroughs in IT means that any attempt at forecasting long-term future practices may prove risky. The concept of the 4th industrial revolution was suggested just a few years ago (Schwab, 2017) and has already gained significant attention, including in the field of people management; for example, AI algorithms are used in selection (Jain & Jain, 2020).

Career practices: Detailed discussion

Advertising internal job openings

Whenever a vacancy occurs, the organization can look to fill it with either internal or external people. The choice depends on the level and type of position and the norms of the organization's career management practices. This should follow strategic orientation to the management of people and their careers (Sonnenfeld & Peiperl, 1988). Sonnenfeld and Peiperl's model identifies the typology of external versus internal recruitment.

For vacant rank-and-file positions, people may be hired from outside, even though there may be internal personnel who wish to apply for the new post, so creating another vacancy.

When the search focus is internal, the vacancy can be advertised within the organization. Many organizations have a policy that jobs are advertised internally before any external search is conducted. The growing importance of internal job advertising as part of a comprehensive organizational career system was demonstrated by Douglas Tim Hall and others. Extensive use of internal job advertising indicates to employees that the organization prefers internal promotion to recruiting managers from outside (i.e. a focus on the internal labour market).

Traditionally, jobs were advertised internally either on noticeboards or in the company newsletter. While the idea remains the same, almost all job posting is now done virtually. New positions or vacancies may be first offered only internally, though typically are also open to external applicants. If the post is first only offered within, for firms that focus on internal labour markets, only if not filled from within will these posts then made available to all on the firm's own web page, as well as on various Internet job search sites. For high-level positions, it is typical to pass the task to headhunters.

CASE STUDY 7.3: HOW DO LARGE FIRMS POST JOB ADVERTISEMENTS? WALMART EXAMPLE

On its recruitment web page (https://careers.walmart.com/), Walmart makes the following as a general statement: 'Don't just work harder. Career better'. This fits well with their credo 'Our people make the difference.'

As befitting for such a large and complex corporation, there are several options to apply for under the categories: stores and clubs; corporate; healthcare; technology; and distribution centres and drivers.

For each of these, there are a number of sub-job categories, for example, for 'stores and clubs' one can opt for Sam's Club Jobs, Sam's Club Management Jobs,

Support Services, Walmart Management Jobs and Walmart Store Jobs. For 'corporate', the number of sub categories is 19 (!), including, for example: accounting and finance; administrative and support services; business operations; data analytics and business intelligence; engineering; and others – even human resources. And, of specific interest to students – internship.

And within each of these there are different options, and many opportunities on offer, with a wide-ranging number of vacancies on offer; for some job types there are over 1,000 openings, others would have just a few dozen, like for example, within accounting and finance.

Formal education as part of career development

Organizations may select people of managerial or technical potential and send them on a formal training or study programme as part of their career development path. The formal education may be a first degree in engineering, an MBA, or other graduate or postgraduate studies for managerial personnel, or professional and vocational qualification courses for non-managerial employees. Education has always been associated with employability, as it provides both skills and competencies, as well as helping the self-esteem and self-efficacy of the graduate.

Once an organization has identified an immediate future appointment need, such education can provide a solution. Even if there is no acute need, the organization may identify people who are worth the investment and justify the trust associated with such investment. Alternatively, individuals can put themselves forward for such a programme. As the timespan for HR planning gets shorter, and with widespread redundancies, many organizations have been less prepared to offer such long-term investment in people. This is due not just to the short-term nature of modern job contracts, but also to the lower level of mutual commitment organizations might expect. This tendency is expected to continue, and organizations will prefer to acquire people who already possess the necessary qualifications rather than those who need to be sent on study programmes. As a consequence, short-term specific training may replace academic studies sponsored by organizations.

The qualification most frequently used to develop managerial competence is the Master of Business Administration (MBA) degree. Several studies have indicated the importance of the MBA, and the reputation of certain business schools (Alwi & Kitchen, 2014). An MBA degree from a leading business school can make a difference for its holder in terms of managerial competence, career progress, and remuneration (Baruch, 2009; Baruch & Peiperl, 2000b; Baruch & Leeming, 2001; Elliott & Soo, 2016; Ghasemaghaei et al., 2019), but the problem organizations face is the insecurity and instability of investment in people. Employees are not the property of the employer; they can move on to different jobs and organizations, with the new employer (who may be a competitor) benefiting from the former employer's investment. All in all, organizations need to be very careful in their long-term investment in training and development. If employees are promised that they will gain 'employability', investment in terms of training is the most visible manifestation of the commitment on the part of the organization to fulfil its role in this respect.

A related practice – tuition reimbursement

Under this practice, employers reimburse the costs of training and education taken by their employees outside the organization by providers of such training. It is a form of investment in employees, sometime subjected to formal obligation to remain with the employer, and one that improves commitment and relationships with the employer (Pattie et al., 2006). This practice not only improves the human capital of the employees, but also reduces their intention to quit (Manchester, 2012).

CASE STUDY 7.4: IS IT GOOD FOR YOUR COMPANY TO HAVE MANAGERS WITH AN MBA QUALIFICATION?

Here are two stories of leading global companies which place a high value on an MBA.

Verizon is an American multinational telecommunications conglomerate which employs more than 135,000 people in 2020. Some 10–15% of Verizon's managerial workforce has an MBA. For Verizon, an MBA is a valuable asset, and it expects the holder of an MBA to have a better strategic perspective and orientation, more sophisticated knowledge and awareness of its application, and a more balanced set of skills than a person without an MBA or one who is a specialist in a particular business discipline. However, in terms of who gains the most from an MBA, the perception is that the individual gets more tangible benefits. The benefits to the organization are harder to quantify and observe. When organizations are filling management positions, an MBA can be a tie-breaker and evidence of achievement, focus, skills, and commitment. Still, when one looks at what has happened in the past to Verizon employees who earned an MBA, they have not done particularly well: for a number of reasons, Verizon generally does not attract MBA graduates (perhaps because it is a mature business or because it has a 'sales culture').

Electronic Data Systems (EDS) was an American multinational IT equipment and services company, with just about the same number of employees (136,000 in 2020).

At EDS, with more than a few thousand MBA graduates amongst their managerial staff, the contribution of MBA studies stems from the knowledge and skills associated with an MBA curriculum which, according to EDS, benefits the company in all aspects of their business, but primarily in finance and accounting, strategic planning, and management development. However, since EDS does not impose a requirement to have an MBA for any particular job, there is no company policy on MBAs. Still, in terms of who gains the most from an MBA, the MBA graduate or EDS as their employing organization, the answer is clearly both. Therefore, in hiring for management positions, an MBA tends to generally be more of an advantage. In practice, the MBA tends to give a career advantage to the MBA graduate. All in all, while a benefit to start with, it is the knowledge and the performance that matters. MBAs from the 'top' schools do tend to produce very distinguished graduates. However, even among the graduates from a nearby state university evening programme, EDS finds good talent.

Lateral moves to create cross-functional experience

The traditional 'ideal type' of career move was 'up the ladder'. This has changed, and lateral or side moves are more typical today. They offer opportunities for further development before further progress, but can also be an indication of reaching a career plateau. Lateral moves to create cross-functional experience are increasing (Chudzikowski, 2012). When there are fewer hierarchy levels and horizontal communication is the key to success, people will no longer move up the ladder so fast.

Organizations need to indicate clearly that such a route reflects career success rather than failure, and this is a shift from the past practice, which perceived only 'climbing up' as evidence of career success. People should be advised that career advancement is not necessarily along the traditional upward path. Despite significant shifts in the nature of career, the diversity of career patterns has not altered significantly across generations, and millennials are not that different from earlier generations (Lyons et al., 2015).

Some of these lateral movements may take the form of developing new ventures, secondments, and cross-functional moves. Already in the 1970s, Schein (1978) presented the spiral cross-functional move, but that too was part of an upward progress (see Figure 7.3). Lateral moves continue to characterize the career path of managers (Lyons et al., 2015), while job rotations and role changes will be frequent for the rank-and-file workforce (Kraimer et al., 2011).

Retirement preparation (or pre-retirement) programmes

This practice is directed at the target population of employees – those approaching retirement and about to leave the organization. These programmes can be short, for example, a three-day workshop taking place a couple of months before retirement. In addition to the 'standard' programme, large corporations may have a diversity programme, such as pre-retirement planning for women or minorities. They can also be longer, in terms of both programme time and its spread over a wider timespan. An investment in this practice is evidence of high commitment on the part of the organization to its employees, an essential part of developing mutual trust and commitment (Eisenberger, Fasolo, & Davis-LaMastro, 1990). In these programmes the employee is prepared for retirement in several ways, for example, financial considerations and understanding pension conditions and tax regulations. The better programmes take into account also the psychological need to adjust to life without work, a transformation that, if not managed, might end in deterioration of the health and wellbeing of people used to full-time hard work. Information on leisure activities and other fulfilling tasks forms a significant part of the better programmes, and in some of them the spouse is invited to take part too.

A different shift in career thinking suggests that retirement may not be an essential, or not even desired, move. People may be ready and willing to continue working as long as they are productive. Abolition of retirement age was called for (Baruch, Sayce, & Gregoriou, 2014) and

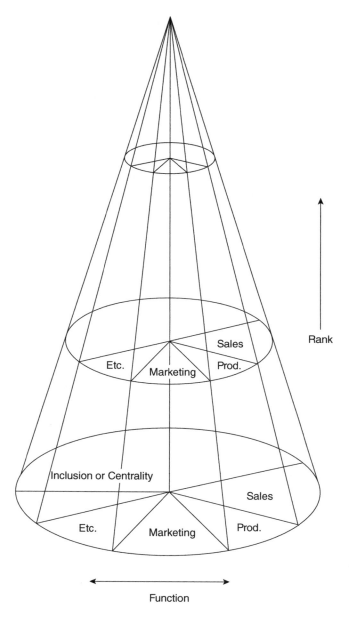

Figure 7.3 Schein's cone (1978)

adopted in many countries. This created some challenges for employers (Blackham, 2015), like the need of employers to discuss and agree on retirement on a case-by-case basis, negotiating I-deals with individual employee (see also Rousseau, 2015).

CASE STUDY 7.5: PRE-RETIREMENT PROGRAMMES

Companies may run their own programmes or acquire one from an external consultancy. Career Management Consultants (https://www.bizseek.co.uk/career-management-consultants-limited_2l-020-7776-4740) is one of many consultancies who offer companies to manage their retirement programmes to assist employees to plan for the transition to retirement. The preparation includes emotional adjustments and lifestyle preparation. Their specific programme takes into consideration:

- Financial realities
- Geographic preferences
- Physical and emotional services
- Planning for positive change
- Decision making
- Career change
- Volunteering
- Dealing with family reactions and adjustments

- Aiming towards happiness.

An internal programme is offered by the Wisconsin Department of Employee Trust Funds. Their motto is 'Retirement – A New Beginning'. The pre-retirement planning programme takes the form of a 12-hour course held in the evening for two hours a week for six weeks. The content of the course will typically include:

- Financial planning
  - o Social security
  - o Retirement benefits
- Insurance
  - o Life insurance
  - o Health insurance/Medicare
- Legal tips (e.g. taxes, wills and lawyers)
- Redefining life balance
- Consumerism, housing, employment and retirement, wellness in retirement, and leisure.

With changes in retirement age, traditional pre-retirement programmes might become quite rare in the future. The need for this practice obviously depends also on the age of the organization and the maturity of its employees. For organizations that have been in existence for about 20–30 years, with most founders being aged about 30 at the time of the start-up, there is no real need for formal institutionalized pre-retirement programmes. If there are only a very few due to retire each year, the issue may best be dealt with by a private consultancy.

As large-scale redundancy programmes are likely to prevail in the business environment, pre-retirement programme may be transformed into pre-redundancy programmes. In this revised kind of practice, the organization will first prepare the employees for the possibility that 'it could happen to you, too'. Subsequently, the focus will move to what can be done, how an employee whose career has reached a plateau stage can be trained to look successfully for a new job in declining industrial sectors. This means making older people employable – employability is not something that only early career needs. In a vibrant labour market the need for employability continues till the end of working life. Employability is critical for each career stage for a labour market with many career moves (Fugate et al., 2021; Thijssen et al., 2008). In addition to such a pre-redundancy programme, the organization that undergoes major redundancy will need a post-redundancy programme to deal with the 'survivor syndrome' which might affect those who have stayed. Professional use of best practice may successfully tackle the survivor syndrome phenomenon (Baruch & Hind, 1999; Brockner et al., 1992a).

Booklets and/or pamphlets on career issues

Booklets, pamphlets or leaflets (as well as any other career information format) are part of an organization's formal stock of career-related information. Today, they are rarely in the traditional format of printed material and are mostly available online. They introduce what career opportunities the organization offers and provide an introduction to all available CPM practices. Information that may be covered includes career paths, the competencies required for each position on the path, timescales (e.g. the minimum time to be spent in a certain position before promotion), and conditions for certain developments. The aim of such written material is to provide everyone in the organization with relevant information, releasing the direct manager from the job of presenting that information to subordinates.

Such information is directed at all employees, but is important especially for newcomers, either those recently recruited to the organization, or those recently promoted to the managerial ranks. In the age of the Internet, fewer of these booklets exist. With companies facing an increasing number of lawsuits due to a failure to satisfy employees' expectations, employers do not like to present what might later be seen as unfulfilled promises.

Dual ladder

The dual ladder is a parallel hierarchy, created for non-managerial staff, such as professional or technical employees. The major role of such a ladder is to provide 'upward mobility' and recognition for those who cannot or do not wish to hold a managerial role. The dual ladder emerged in response to the need to provide professionals in non-managerial roles a different promotion path. A typical case is that of the excellent, promising engineer who is promoted to a managerial role (because there is no alternative means of recognizing or remunerating them within the professional roles). Such promotions often end with an accomplished professional transformed into a poor manager.

The dual ladder is very important, but is suitable only for a particular group – professionals without managerial skills or with no aspiration to become managers. Many large firms and organizations use this practice, and its use is continually growing (Hölzle, 2010). A typical example is hospitals, where different progress ladders can be applied for medical doctors and for nurses (Kim et al., 2017). The reason for creating the dual ladder are valid in production and research and development firms, where engineers and technicians may have different promotion systems, and perhaps even more so where professionals are involved (experts, counsellors, etc.), not managers, but people working in crucial roles, with a responsibility and remuneration level similar to that of managers. The CPM system will need to identify the population eligible for this status, and ensure that only a small proportion of highly deserving individuals enter the stream of the alternative ladder. Otherwise, it will lose its power as an alternative system of recognition for those few who deserve it.

Induction

The process of introducing people to their new organization is the first CPM practice a new employee experiences (it will be entitled 'induction' or 'socialization'). This is a process whereby all newcomers learn the behaviours and attitudes necessary for assuming roles in an organization, and has long be recognized as a critical element for people's future in the organization (Antonacopoulou & Güttel, 2010). Part of it is formal, led by organizational officials, whereas other aspects are learned in an informal manner, not necessarily in line with organizational formal norms and policies (see, e.g. De Stobbeleir et al., 2011). Newcomers are not always passive in their search for information (Vandenberghe et al., 2021). It remains essential that employers should introduce newcomers to the varied aspects of their organizational life and their role within it. These can be related to ideology or philosophy, culture, policies, rules and regulations, norms, expected behaviours and performance, and any other information, including social, which will help them to master their jobs and become integrated into the new workplace.

One of the main changes witnessed in the contemporary labour markets is the much wider age-span of newcomers. Whereas in the old type of careers people joined organizations at an early age, and in many cases stayed for their whole working life in the same workplace, people now tend to have a multiple career path, and frequent changes of employers are common. An induction process for the experienced professional or manager is very different from that directed at young school leavers or new graduates, though follow the same principle.

Assessment and development centres

Assessment centres have attracted much interest in academia and from organizational practitioners. Assessment centres essentially serve two purposes: first, and most traditional, is selection and promotion; second, their use for developing managerial talent (Hermelin et al., 2007).

They have been found as a reliable and valid tool for selection to a job (Iles, 1999; Meiring et al., 2015), for evaluation prospects of success of managerial employees (Hermelin et al., 2007) and for the purpose of career development (Tansley et al., 2016). Due to their strong validity, the use of assessment centre is well established (Thornton & Byham, 2013).

In the recent past, assessment centres were used for two main purposes: as a selection tool for managerial recruitment and as an indicator of managerial potential; and for developmental purposes (Hermelin et al., 2007). Development centres evolved from assessment centres, and share many features with them, but are directed not necessarily towards selection but rather to general development and enhancement of the manager, preparing him or her for future roles. Large organizations may have their own assessment centres whereas small firms generally use external institutions. The use of assessment centres can also help to introduce and demonstrate fair selection practices and challenge the perpetuation of unfair discriminatory practices (Healy et al., 2010).

Mentoring

The principal aim of mentoring is to bring together a newcomer, usually a person with managerial potential, and an experienced manager, who is not necessarily that person's direct manager. The senior manager can provide advice, coaching and tutoring, serving as a kind of workplace coach. Therefore mentoring is directed mostly at managerial personnel, and is used frequently in graduate recruitment programmes. The potential of this practice has been suggested in many studies (e.g. Kram, 1985; Pan et al., 2011). Both mentors and protégés benefit from this practice, and the organization can shape the kind of mentoring relationships it wants. More recent work supported this notion, focusing on the benefits associated with mentoring not just for the protégé but also for mentors (Ghosh & Reio Jr., 2013). Such a win-win situation, when achievable, will be needed in the future too. Moreover, the organization is a clear beneficiary of having mentoring practice (Bozionelos et al., 2011; Scandura & Viator, 1994), in terms of protégés' attitudes and performance.

Mentoring also has pitfalls. Scandura (1998) analysed the main dysfunctions of mentoring, which she saw as negative relations, sabotage, difficulty, and spoiling. Another significant problem associated with mentoring is the possible clash of interests between the direct manager and the mentor. Mentoring can also give rise to questions of possible sexual harassment on the one side, and creating or encouraging unintended types of relationships on the other (Ramaswami, Dreher, Bretz, & Wiethoff, 2010). Problems of this sort may be mitigated by same-sex mentoring, which will be more feasible when more women enter managerial postions. The availability of mentors may also be a problem: with fewer hierarchical layers it will be more difficult to find enough people to serve as mentors – a factor which might reduce the present considerable use of this practice. To overcome these problems novel ideas are offered, for example, the introduction of peer mentoring, which was identified as an effective tool (Mayer et al., 2014). Mentoring may can be seen as a status symbol for mature and loyal managers, those who wish to contribute to the success of the organization and their protégés.

> ### A pause for reflection
>
> When you are entering a new organization, moving to a significantly high-level position, or moving for expatriation, ensure that you have a mentor. Many organizations will offer that in a formal manner, appointing a mentor to newcomers, though sometimes missing the point of the need for 'chemistry' between the mentor and the protégé. If they do not, you still have an option to look informally for a mentor that will help you early on in the role.

Career workshops

Career workshops are short-term workshops focusing on specific aspect(s) of career management, and aim to provide managers with relevant knowledge, skills, and experience. Participating in career workshops can contribute to the effectiveness of the employee (Lent & Brown, 2013; Sweeney et al., 1989) and are widely used in the industry (Kraimer et al., 2011). Career workshops usually focus on specific aspects, such as identifying future opportunities, rather than just general development (e.g. interviewing skills). They can be applied in higher education (Modise, 2016).

With frequent structural changes in organizations, people certainly need adaptation mechanisms, and workshops of this kind will help. Career workshops can improve the employability of the participants, enhancing their career resilience (Seibert, Kraimer, & Heslin, 2016; Waterman et al., 1994). The impetus for sending people to workshops can come from their manager or mentor or the HR counselling system. With an increasing number of organizations making redundancies or undergoing restructuring, future career workshops may concentrate on inter- and intra-organizational opportunities. Among the many ideas on which workshops can focus are: how to increase employability; how to create new satellite companies or joint ventures; the concept and practice of the management buy-out. Employability may be within the organization or looking externally to the labour market. These and other ideas can help participants to develop new insights into the future of their career – within the organization or elsewhere.

Performance appraisal as a basis for career planning

Numerous works emphasize the need for a close connection between the performance appraisal (PA) system and career development (e.g. Brown & Heywood, 2005; Murphy & Cleveland, 1995). PA systems provide critical knowledge for a number of purposes, including those related to career management (DeNisi & Murphy, 2017). Hall et al. (1989) demonstrated the gap between the theory behind PA systems and their implementation, suggesting the need to combine CPM with the PA system. PA systems were found to operate in most of the organizations studied. There is considerable empirical support for PA models as developed in the literature, manifesting its relevant to the wider field of people management (DeNisi & Murphy, 2017).

Of all the CPM practices, PA is perhaps the most fundamental. It can be implemented in HRM in a very similar way to that by which accountancy reports (such as the profit and loss account or the balance sheet) cater for the finance and accountancy systems. Valid and reliable PA would identify who should be promoted, who should be made redundant at a time of downsizing, and identify training and development needs. Nonetheless, any PA system may be subjected to biases and errors in the process, in the interpretation of the evaluation, and in its application (Javidmehr & Ebrahimpour, 2015). In terms of choosing people for future development (e.g. the selection of high-potential employees for assessment centres), this can be done on the basis of their PA results. A variety of CPM practices, such as appointing mentors or building succession planning, depend on the PA system. If the system is valid and reliable, it may serve as the foundation stone for an integrated CPM system.

Career counselling

Career counselling is a two-way communication with the employee and two main sources are available for conducting this. The first is the direct manager (or another higher manager) who has a good knowledge of the employee's attitudes, behaviours, skills, and so on; the second is an HRM manager. Depending on the complexity of an organization, and its financial resources, external counselling can also be provided. This practice can be closely associated with the core of the Herriot–Pemberton (1996) model, and the indication for a need to balance individual and organizational needs and aspirations (Baruch, 2006a; Farndale et al., 2014). The extant literature emphasizes the need to match organizational requirements and possibilities with individual career aspirations and abilities. Many agencies now provide career counselling services to both individuals and organizations (Kidd, 2006; McMahon, 2016).

Career counselling by direct manager and by the HRM unit

In many organizations the direct manager is in the best position to conduct career counselling, because they perhaps had the most accurate and up-to-date knowledge of the person. On the other hand, for such counselling to be fruitful, the person conducting it needs to have good standing in the organization, and to know the career options available and the direction of future organizational developments. In addition, serving as a counsellor can conflict with other roles of the manager, such as loyalty (i.e. whether his or her loyalty resides with the organization or with the subordinate). Career counselling can be conducted also by the HRM unit staff. The advantages of their doing the counselling include: knowledge of organizational goals and development; familiarity with HRM planning for the whole enterprise; and knowledge, skills and experience of counselling in general. The obstacle that frequently prevents HRM from carrying out this task is its detachment from the professional life of the organization.

Challenges can be that managers will consider this role as a bureaucratic burden, that they were not trained for counselling, and they may not be aware of upcoming changes in the organizational career structure. HR managers will be more aware of future plans, and consequently will be better equipped to deal with individual career counselling (Boxall & Purcell, 2016).

Multiple counselling, including external, may be useful. Sometimes counselling can touch on sensitive issues, and the individual employees may prefer the latter option. For personal matters which may require confidentiality, integration is not recommended (e.g. certain issues should not be reported to the formal PA system), but on the other hand, individual interest in secondments could be expressed and identified through counselling.

Box 7.2: External counselling

A worldwide downturn in the sales of machine tools caused an engineering company located in Birmingham to review its capacity, resulting in the loss of more than 100 jobs. The job losses included labourers, warehousing, operators, clerical, supervision, management, engineers, and apprentices.

They selected an outside consultancy (the Quo Group) due to their extensive knowledge and experience of the Midlands job market. They were able to provide counsellors with relevant sector expertise along with the empathy to work with the varying levels of skills and attributes in the company.

The programme consisted of a series of two-day workshops for all non-managerial staff* to attend. These workshops concentrated on identifying life and career goals, developing the appropriate action plan (including CV and interview preparation), mapping routes to the job market (including advertisement analysis, job and government agencies and networking), and dealing with offer negotiations.

Clients were seen on the consulting firm's premises and/or in individual sessions depending on their needs.

Major elements in the success of the programme were a mailshot to more than 500 companies within a 5-mile radius of the site, coupled with contacting local job agencies. These resulted in hundreds of enquiries. The Quo Group provided a job researcher, who matched enquiries to skills and arranged interviews for all concerned. In addition, a helpline was in place for those individuals who required support after the programme was completed.

Six weeks after the end of the programme, only 4% of those wanting jobs were still unemployed.

Note: *Managers were provided with the Quo Group's one-to-one executive programme.

Source: This case was kindly provided by the Quo Group Ltd.

Succession planning

Miner and Miner (1985) were apparently the first to suggest a framework of organizational planning in which the organization decides on the possible replacement of every manager within the organization, and evaluates the potential for promotion of each manager. Labelled 'succession planning', it became a clear best practice in people management (Groves, 2007;

Rothwell et al., 2015). By its nature, this practice is primarily directed towards the managerial workforce. Succession planning (also termed a 'management inventory') can be valuable in the context of long-term planning. It will be different, but not less important, in a flattened organization where lateral movements occur. In the latter, succession planning will be more complicated but will still show who should first be considered when a new vacancy arises or job rotation is planned. It should be noted that succession planning builds on the internal labour market, and looks mostly within the organizational boundary (Rothwell, 1994; Rothwell et al., 2015). With less loyalty and a higher turnover of employees, and managers in particular (Baruch, 1998a), succession planning may possess less predictive power in the future. The preparation of succession planning requires a clear structure, but could be challenging under the contemporary VUCA business environment (Mack et al., 2015). Figure 7.4 manifests how succession planning can be depicted for the higher echelons in an organization.

A different approach was advised by Leibman et al. (1996) and endorsed by Rothwell et al. (2015), who suggested the label 'succession management' be replaced by 'succession planning'. They emphasized the gap between the traditional and the contemporary approaches, the former prone to be rigid in form, based on skills and experience, whereas the latter is dynamic and flexible. The gap could be bridged if HR focuses on the competencies and leadership qualities of managers. Special attention is needed in responding to equal employment opportunities (EEO) or the equality, diversity and inclusion (EDI) agenda (see Chapter 9).

An example of a succession planning form is shown in Figure 7.4.

360-degree performance appraisal systems

The late 1990s saw a growth in unorthodox methods of PA, mainly 360-degree feedback (see the special issue of the journal *Human Resource Management* in 1993) with a variety of PA methods applied (Potočnik & Anderson, 2012; Tziner et al., 1997). 360-degree feedback can take the form of peer appraisal, upward appraisal, committee appraisal, or a combination of several sources in addition to appraisal by the direct manager (Baruch & Harel, 1993; Bernardin et al., 1995). Self and upward appraisal (Baruch, 1996a and Bernardin, 1986, respectively) are also valuable sources of PA, increasing the reliability and validity of the process. All signs indicate that this trend will continue, with PA being used more as a feedback tool and for development purposes rather than being used in gathering information for organizational decision making. The latter use will persist where individual performance-related PA is practiced (cf. Kessler and Purcell, 1992; Kessler, 1994). The application of 360-degree appraisals also leads to positive employees' perception of organizational justice and improves sustainability (El Haddad et al., 2018). While the literature supports the use of 360-degree feedback (cf. Tornow & London, 1998), it should be noted that this practice is very demanding in terms of time invested and analysis required, so it may not be easy to apply it routinely in organizations.

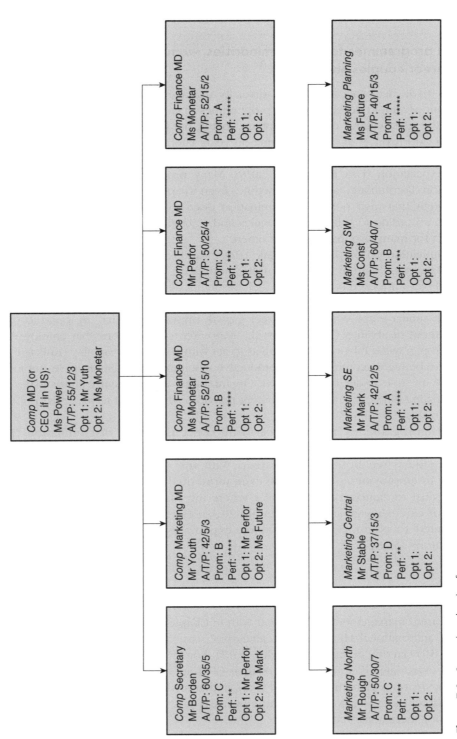

Figure 7.4 Succession planning form

Special programmes for ethnic minorities, women, people with disabilities, dual-career couples and so on

Chapter 9 will deal specifically with diversity management. Here it is sufficient to note that organizations should develop special programmes to tackle all possible kinds of discrimination, such as the 'glass ceiling' effect for women, that is, not being promoted above certain managerial level (Morrison et al., 1987b). Some 30 years later, the glass ceiling was broken and one can find women in many top positions, but their representation in leading positions is far below expectation (Fisk & Overton, 2019). Many programmes are intended to support the population discriminated against, sometimes even to apply 'positive discrimination'. It is important, though, that such 'positive discrimination' does not imply the abandonment of a policy of selection according to skills, competencies and suitability for the job. Problems of discrimination exist for many groups, not just women.

Discrimination on the basis of ethnic background, disability, age, and religion can prevent appropriate people from making a full contribution. For example, mass early retirements accepted by or imposed on people in their 50s might deprive organizations of a pool of talented and experienced people. The career prospects of people with disabilities (PWDs) suffer because they lack similar employment and career growth opportunities that are open to their counterparts without disabilities (Bonaccio et al., 2020). Yet, organizations that employ PWDs would benefit from a wider talent pool, as well as to act with social responsibility (Kulkarni et al., 2016). PWDs can be highly committed and productive when their disability is irrelevant to the requirements of the role under consideration. Organizations that recognize these issues will benefit from pursuing different career management practices with respect to particular populations with specific needs.

Special programmes are not necessarily concerned with discrimination. The case of dual-career couples raises another matter, that is, how to enable two people to develop side by side when both have a career. With the continuing growth in education and equality in employment, we will see even more dual-career couples in the future. The HR system must recognize this, especially where international relocations become necessary as part of career progress (Baruch et al., 2016a; Harvey, 1997). The trend of globalization is expected to continue, and managing expatriates is a crucial issue for multinational corporations (MNCs).

Special programmes for expatriates and repatriates

Global career management will be dealt with in Chapter 8. Here, I will note only that for some decades, international HRM is a fast-developing issue in the management of people (Cooke et al., 2019; Harzing & van Ruysseveldt, 2017). For MNCs or global enterprises, the management of expatriates is a crucial part of their CPM agenda (Black et al., 1992; Brewster et al., 2016; Dickmann & Baruch, 2011) and is applied according to their strategy (Baruch & Altman, 2002). Career paths in MNCs will include overseas posts as a crucial part of the developmental process for the managerial workforce.

Special programmes for high-flyers

All employees, as the prime asset of the organization, deserve investment in their career by their organization. However, the so-called high-flyers or talent are perceived as a special asset, with the potential to make a unique contribution to the future of the organization, and thus worthy of having greater attention and resources dedicated specifically to them. High-flyers are a scarce resource, and can be the source of future leadership for organizations, therefore sometimes labelled also as 'talent', which is developed via 'talent-management' programmes (see below).

Building psychological contracts

The concept that a psychological contract exists between the employee and the workplace was discussed earlier in this book, and is acknowledged as a crucial aspect of the relationship between both sides. Earlier works examined the results of breaking these contracts (cf. Rousseau, 1996; Morrison & Robinson, 1997). The beginning of the 1990s saw a significant change in the nature and notion of the psychological contract. Now employers need to clarify this concept – as a set of mutual expectations which need to be agreed upon, explicitly or implicitly – to their employees (Baruch & Rousseau, 2019). These expectations are, first, what the organization perceives as a fair contribution from the employee, and second, what the organization will provide in return. Employees will be persuaded and required then to 'sign' this unwritten contract. This is in line with Wanous' (1992) ideas of the realistic job preview, taking it in the broader sense of the realistic career. The cycle of career planning and development for each person joining the workforce will start with the establishment of a mutual agreement, a psychological contract, which sets the type and style of future relationships. Two different populations will be involved here: existing employees, for some of whom the old psychological contract will be altered; and the newly hired, for whom the essential part will be delivered during the induction period, with reinforcement to follow later.

Secondments

'Secondment' is the temporary assignment of a person to another area within the organization, or sometimes to another associated organization (such as a customer or supplier). Several of the respondents suggested secondments as an additional practice (Bagdadli & Gianecchini, 2019). Secondment is a period in which the manager acquires a different perspective within the company boundaries or from the outside; and a period of time spent in marketing, HRM, or finance can improve a production manager's knowledge of organizational processes, help build interrelations with colleagues, and increase communication thereafter. At a more advanced level, secondments can be taken outside the organization. Exchange programmes under which managers and executives serve a period of time in another company, sharing knowledge and gaining some insight in return, can provide a win-win situation for both companies involved.

As in the other practices described, the impetus to offer people secondments can come from their manager or mentor, or from HR counselling and PA systems. A possible problem with secondment programmes is the need for long-term HR planning and for mutuality, thus making it feasible mostly for large or well established corporations. There is a risk of losing successful managers to the company they are seconded to, and there is also the usual risk of benchmarking, where it might be that only one side benefits from the deal. If the practice of creating satellite firms develops in the West, as in Japan for example, the use of secondments will expand to a wider range of organizations.

Intrapreneurship

Different people have different approaches to their life and career. Employers should identify those who possess the qualities needed to generate new business within the organization. Organizations should encourage organizational learning, and provide employees with options for inner sources of growth via intrapreneurship. Instead of outsourcing activities and operations, organizations can use people from within who desire to develop something new, but still remain within the organization.

CASE STUDY 7.6: INTRAPRENEURSHIP AT THE TIMES OF INDIA GROUP

The Times of India Group is the largest media and entertainment company in India, with circulation of close to three million copies daily (as of December 2019). It employs some 7,000 people in the company directly, and about 1,000 on contractual appointment, a ratio typical in this business sector, and publishes a number of newspapers, magazines, has 12 radio stations, 10 retail stores and divisions in music (Times Music, the largest music company in India), the Internet, multimedia and a news syndication. A fast-growing group, with a heritage of 82 years, it is perceived as a highly vibrant and creative media company.

The Times of India Group has long recognized that the company can grow only when entrepreneurship thrives within the organization. Therefore, the Board of Directors have always encouraged employees to start new brands, sub-brands, and new ventures which augment the organization's mission to grow as the largest information and entertainment company in Asia. The company's 26 main brands and 116 sub-brands are largely accounted for by such encouragement of intrapreneurship.

In addition, the company has ventured onto the Internet (www.indiatimes.com), with some 800 million page views per month.

For most professionals, one of the most exciting reasons to work with the group has been the constant pace of growth of the company and the freedom offered to do one's job and to play with ideas and give birth to new ventures, and for those who have latent entrepreneurship talent, this has been a constant source of encouragement.

Many health surveys conducted in different companies show that most people at some stage in life want to do something new, fresh, relevant in a field that they are passionate about. Organizations like the Times Group of India offer this opportunity to harness the creative potential of each individual to benefit the company. In such a scenario, both the organization and the individual win.

Source: Thanks to Ashoke K. Maitra, HR Director of The Times of India Group, for providing this case.

Emerging practices

Talent Management

The term 'talent management' (TM) is widely used in both practitioners and scholarly literature, yet its meaning is not well defined. In a comprehensive literature review, Lewis and Heckman (2006) uncovered three distinct strains of thought regarding TM. The first defines TM as a collection of typical HR department practices, functions, activities, or specialist areas such as recruiting, selection, development, and career and succession management. According to this view, TM requires doing what HR has always done, but doing it faster or across the enterprise rather than within the specific HR unit.

The second perspective focuses primarily on the concept of talent pools, for example, following the practice of succession planning. TM, then, refers to a set of processes designed to ensure an adequate flow of employees into roles and positions throughout the organization.

The third perspective is more generalist. It considers TM without regard for organizational boundaries or specific positions. Organizations can view talent mostly as high-performing or high-potential employees being a resource to be managed primarily according to performance levels. Employees can be classified by performance level: the top, competent, and bottom performers (the latter category to be terminated). Alternatively, it can be argued that each employee has potential, and the role of a strong HR function is to manage everyone to reach high-performance levels.

The growing interest in TM was explained by the widening gap between job demands and the skills available in the labour market (Vaiman et al., 2021).

TM for global firms was defined by Collings, Mellahi, and Cascio (2019) as:

a. systematic identification of pivotal positions that differentially contribute to an organization's sustainable competitive advantage on a global scale

b. development of a talent pool of high-potential and high-performing incumbents who reflect the scope of the MNE to fill these roles, and

c. establishment of a differentiated HR architecture to fill these roles with the best available incumbents to ensure their continued commitment to the MNE.

Graduates programmes

Related to TM but designed for graduates, some organizations have their own graduate programmes to recruit and develop specifically those with university degree. They are considered a key talent pool for most large organizations. As a result, attracting, recruiting, developing, and retaining graduates en-mass (can be some 30–50 each year for a mid-size firm of a few thousand employees) is a key practice within a TM strategy, which is has drawn academic attention (McCracken et al., 2016). Firms and other organizations establish specific high-status, fast-track programmes for those graduates who are identified as future leaders (e.g. Bolander et al., 2017; Turner & Kalman, 2015). It should be borne in mind that such programmes present new challenges and uncertain outcomes. First, for those selected to participate, it is never simple to accurately spot leadership potential among graduates because most will have little or no work experience upon which to gauge their ability, a factor that exists for current employees (Kotlyar, 2018). Also, having such specific preference for the specific few means that other potential leaders, including graduates hired but not on the programme, will feel excluded.

Mass career customization

Mass career customization (MCC) takes the concept of career customization (Valcour et al., 2007) to the organizational level. It allows employees to adapt their career development along a multidirectional path to align it with their changing needs over the lifespan (Benko & Weisberg, 2007).

The organizations, via HRM, may offer employees the option or opportunity to specifically customize their careers through opting for their individualized choices in relation to the way they develop their careers within the organization (like the I-deals: Rousseau, 2005). When employees are able to make individualized career choices, for example, when dealing with diversity issues (Olsen & Martins, 2012), the advantages of workplace diversity can materialize. MCC goes beyond the temporary attention to flexibility needs in time and space, and early empirical studies indicated its usefulness for individuals and organizations, as well as possible pitfalls such as stigmatization (Bal et al., 2015; Straub et al., 2020). To be successful, MCC requires the support from the organizational executives for implementation (Bal et al., 2015).

Employees' wellbeing programmes

There is growing attention to employees' wellbeing at work, as well as helping employees to find the right work–life balance (Sonnentag, 2015). 'Wellbeing' is a general term, and Kruger

(2011) has identified five essential elements of it, which he listed as: 'career wellbeing, social wellbeing, financial wellbeing, physical wellbeing and community wellbeing'. This indicates the complexity of wellbeing, and the limited ability of the organization to have a full impact on the wellbeing of individuals. Yet, career wellbeing is strongly influenced by employment – what people do and how their employers treat them (Potgieter et al., 2019). The impact of wellbeing is expressed not only in individual happiness, but also in productivity, and studies confirmed the linkage between HRM practices, employee wellbeing at work, and performance (Baptiste, 2008). Having a high career wellbeing is associated with an inclination to be more generally happy and to prosper in life overall (Kruger, 2011). Looking at a specific population of immigrant employees, Shirmohammadi & Beigi (2019) found that under-employment negatively impacts subjective wellbeing. When supported by supervisors and colleagues, employees gain resources and improve their wellbeing.

For example, new technologies might influence wellbeing, partly due to the blurring boundaries between work and other realms of life, when remote work means expectations for 24/7 presence (Beigi & Otaye-Ebede, 2020). It is important for the management of a career to be shared with the employee, as career self-management (see Wilhelm & Hirschi, 2019).

HRM intervention can improve employees' wellbeing (Guest, 2017; Van De Voorde et al., 2012). For example, job crafting intervention can impact beyond the work performance relationship to employees' general wellbeing (Van Wingerden et al., 2017).

CASE STUDY 7.7: WELLBEING AT GOOGLE

Could being 'nice' really be the answer?

After years of searching for the perfect solution to workplace wellbeing, Google announces that it believes 'being nice' is the answer.

In 2013, Google began 'Project Aristotle', which was a project set to improve the productivity of its workforce by finding the right recipe for a good working environment and improved workplace wellbeing. … Google worked hard to keep employees motivated and happy within the workplace, offering perks such as massage rooms, free lunches, nap pods, haircuts, and even space within the company garden to grow their own vegetables! In true Google-style, the company measured and analysed the data they collected from these perks, and were at a loss when they found that the workforce were perhaps not as happy as expected. They found that teamwork is a critical factor, and to achieve effective and positive teamwork, the following were identified as the 'pillars' presented below in order of importance:

Psychological safety: Psychological safety refers to an individual's perception

(Continued)

of the consequences of taking an interpersonal risk or a belief that a team is safe for risk taking in the face of being seen as ignorant, incompetent, negative, or disruptive. In a team with high psychological safety, teammates feel safe to take risks around their team members. They feel confident that no one on the team will embarrass or punish anyone else for admitting a mistake, asking a question, or offering a new idea.

Dependability: On dependable teams, members reliably complete quality work on time (vs the opposite – shirking responsibilities).

Structure and clarity: An individual's understanding of job expectations, the process for fulfilling these expectations, and the consequences of one's performance are important for team effectiveness. Goals can be set at the individual or group level, and must be specific, challenging, and attainable. Google often uses Objectives and Key Results to help set and communicate short and long term goals.

Meaning: Finding a sense of purpose in either the work itself or the output is important for team effectiveness. The meaning of work is personal and can vary: financial security, supporting family, helping the team succeed, or self-expression for each individual, for example.

Impact: The results of one's work, the subjective judgement that your work is making a difference, is important for teams. Seeing that one's work is contributing to the organization's goals can help reveal impact.

Source: Wellbeing People (2017) https://rework.withgoogle.com/print/guides/5721312655835136/Wellbeing People, 2017

Phasing out practices

Common career paths

A career path is the most preferred and recommended route for the career advancement of a manager in an organization. Such career paths can lead people through various departments and units within the organization and, in multinational companies, in overseas subsidiaries. The use of career paths spread rapidly in the 1970s and 1980s in many organizations (Portwood & Granrose, 1987), and its significance was demonstrated by Carulli et al. (1989). The use of career paths was widespread in larger organizations, whereas one could find more informal paths or a complete lack of paths in smaller organizations. The base for the identification of and management of career path planning is stability and a wide range of layers and positions. With traditional hierarchical structures flattening and diminishing and with the creation of boundaryless and virtual organizations, it is likely that career paths will not develop much in future. In a VUCA business environment, where organizations are constantly restructuring, there is not much point in focusing on this practice. As Peiperl and Baruch (1997) have argued, it is now the norm, rather than the exception, for organizations to have no fixed career paths and for individuals in them to see no further than one or two years ahead.

Written personal career planning for employees

This practice was considered innovating and relevant in the late part of the 20th century, but most organizations have phased it out. Written documents generate commitment, at least on the organization's part. Long-term commitment (e.g. lifetime employment) became virtually extinct as a feature of organizational life in the 1990s and this trend continued in the 2000s. Written personal career plans are problematic also because they create expectations. Past experience of such plans provide examples of frustration, as where a plan suggests the same job for several people, only one can attain it. Few organizations use this technique (Baruch 1996b), and it could be that this practice will die out in the future, for reasons similar to those suggested for the common career path.

From a collection to a collective: Integrating practices into a system

Throughout this chapter, career practices have been discussed mostly in isolation, almost as if they are unrelated, albeit grouped in several clusters. However, careers in organizations are meant to be planned and managed in a joint manner. A system should be designed to answer the needs and requirements of both the individual and the organization. Professional, effective HR management will make sure that the career system operates in a well-integrated, comprehensive way.

Applying a two-fold level of integration is necessary to achieve a fit and to make the optimal use of career practices. These levels are the 'internal' (amongst the variety of practices) and the 'external' (integration between the career system and the organizational culture and strategy). Both internal and external integration should be strategy led: an HRM strategy that is part of and aligned with the whole organizational strategy, including the career area (Gunz & Jalland, 1996). Day-to-day management of career practices is derived from the strategy. Strategy, for example, will determine whether an organization should go international or stay within its national borders. The derived implementation of career practices following this strategy will deal with expatriation and repatriation policies and practices. HRM strategy will determine which is the preferred labour market (i.e. internal or external), and career practices will determine which type of job advertising will be implemented. Similarly, organizations will develop career practices according to the organization's wider HRM strategy.

Internal integration

Internal integration relates to the level of harmony between the various career practices; a fit for which there is a dire need. This has been demonstrated throughout the chapter in discussions of the relationships between specific practices: how the PA system is associated with other practices, how inputs from one practice (mentoring, for example) influence the use of others (e.g. workshops, secondments).

As indicated and presented above, career practices may appear in clusters, where groups of practices are interrelated. The wide range of career management practices may naturally be clustered in groups according to their common use and interrelations among them. Further, these clusters are associated with certain organizational characteristics such as size, age, or culture, and the clusters vary according to the sophistication and extent of involvement of the organization in the career management process (Bagdadli & Gianecchini, 2019; Baruch & Peiperl, 2000a). The future seems to promise more managerial complexity, resulting in a need for more sophisticated career systems. The involvement of the organization will vary too, according to the target population (e.g. characteristics such as employees' level of education, lifestyle, and so on.), the culture of the organization, and the business sector.

The integration may follow the 'cafeteria method'. Cafeteria-style career management programmes offer approaches to accommodate career pluralism in organizations (Brousseau et al., 1996). Fundamentally, cafeteria plans provide an array of career track options, training opportunities, performance evaluation schemes, and reward systems to enable employees to have career experiences that are most in line with their own career concepts and motives and with the strategy of the organization.

One of the most important ingredients of internal integration is the use of advanced IT systems, in particular AI and the 4th industrial revolution (Schwab, 2017). While there has been a wide attention to operational and technological use of AI in the future workplace (Huynh, Hille, & Nasir, 2020), less attention was devoted to the people management side of it. Internal e-mail systems are now often being used for the distribution of information not only on job vacancies but also on career workshops, booklets, training and development opportunities, and other features. Institutional websites have become the norm for organizations in attracting and developing the future workforce – to most levels within the organization. Part of the information available on organizations' websites relates to career options in the organization, the type of people who work there, and their roles (such data are available now for most universities or at least those of the industrial world). One may also find information on how to apply for jobs (see the examples presented earlier in this chapter), and more and more data will be accessible as organizational information continues to grow and expand. This is subject to the stability of the Internet, which is not guaranteed: the Internet might collapse as a result of misuse, terrorist action (including the spread of computer viruses), and other types of cyber-attacks.

Support systems, increasingly the IT-based ones, have an important role to play in the management of career systems. The results of PAs are likely to be processed by IT, particularly in view of the complexity of 360-degree PA systems. These systems require much integration and comparative analysis for the understanding and processing of the data. Similarly, creating reliable and valid succession planning depends on the use of IT systems to gather and analyse information from many sources. We are seeing an increase in the number of organizations utilizing performance related payment (PRP), with remuneration depending partially on individual and/or group performance. This seems to be the direction for the near future, in particular for knowledge workers. For complex PRP systems, IT may combine the career and payment systems to generate an integrated output, which will consider the variety of inputs into an accepted two-fold output. Internal integration will not be limited to the tangible element of payment. It will also enable flexibility and reflect the new type of psychological contracts between the employer (or employers, when individuals work in more than one workplace) and the employee.

External integration

As far as external integration is concerned, we observed that the career system that best fits the organization depends on the operational strategy of the whole enterprise. The Sonnenfeld and Peiperl (1988) career system model, presented earlier in this chapter, was based on Miles and Snow's (1978) seminal work of the organizational strategic model. This is in line with the theoretical works of Fombrun, Tichy, and Devanna (1984), who introduced the concept of strategic HRM. The career system should be developed in line with business objectives and needs (Boxall & Purcell, 2016; Holbeche, 2009). The types of practices carried out will depend on the culture of the organization. In a bureaucratic system, which is relatively stable (e.g. the civil service, traditional manufacturing), common career paths can still be applied for long-term career progress. In a dynamic, turbulent sector (e.g. IT companies), career paths will have to be revised every year or two. In this latter type of work environment career practices such as mentoring become even more important, although it becomes increasingly difficult to identify enough senior managers suitable and ready to serve as mentors. In terms of the continuum from individualism to collectivism, another recognized dimension in organizational culture studies, succession planning, or secondment will appeal to individualistic cultures), whereas group-oriented cultures will probably focus on developing induction programmes, workshops, and special practices for supposedly disadvantaged groups. The organizational culture will help in shaping the career practices and their use, but in a complementary way, career management can help in the reshaping of organizational culture.

Impact factors

Several factors are expected to influence the way career practices will be integrated. The most prominent are size, age, globalization, workforce diversity, and the chosen labour market. These factors will determine whether certain practices are applied and the importance of their implementation.

Size is crucial, as small organizations neither have nor need the resources required to implement practices such as succession planning or a dual ladder. In terms of age, new organizations will not need retirement-preparation programmes and will be less inclined to encourage secondments. The level of globalization of the company will determine the need for special expatriation programmes and the type of mentoring imperative for overseas appointments. Workforce diversity will influence not only special career programmes but also the tone of career counselling, booklets, workshops, and other practices, and focus on either the internal or the external labour market will have to be taken into consideration in any induction programme, mentoring, succession planning, and psychological contracts.

Sector and type of ownership can also influence the organizational approach for supporting employees career development. These may vary between the more stable public sector and the more dynamic private sector.

Implications for organizations

Organizations will find it increasingly difficult to rely upon textbook prescriptions.

Solutions developed to fit the latter part of the 20th century are not expected to match the needs of the 21st-century organization. As a general rule, more responsibility will lie with the individual. It will be very much up to the individual to look for information and to learn of opportunities inside and outside their present workplace. The role of the employer is changing similarly. As Peiperl and Baruch (1997) argued: 'The successful organizations of the next century will be those whose people have control of their own work and who make decisions to align that work with the goals of the organization.'

As suggested here and elsewhere (Baruch & Rousseau, 2019), a new type of psychological contract emerged in the 1990s and it may be the sort that we will have to live with in the coming decades. Employers will need to offer employees a psychological contract that they will appreciate and believe, and employers must ensure that they are able to fulfil their side of the new contracts. Sometimes the content of these contracts is demonstrated by the use of buzzwords such as 'empowerment', 'engagement', or 'employability'. Career management needs to create the right balance between empowering people to seek their own destiny and creating essential organizational support mechanisms to maintain and direct people's careers.

Outsourcing is another option – for non-core roles and activities. It should be used wisely, and not as a first resort. It seems better for an organization to use its own people when feasible, but outsourcing increases flexibility. Sometimes outsourcing works best with external providers of a temporary workforce. Whereas once such agencies mostly dealt with low-skilled workers, more professional roles and even managerial-level roles (i.e. the interim manager) can be filled by external agencies. To increase flexibility it may be useful for organizations not only to provide information on job opportunities within company boundaries, but to create a network of suppliers, customers, even competitors, which will generate a labour market of benefit not only to the organization's own staff but to all participants.

The general advice for organizations is: support your staff. Employees do not wish to be managed in an old-style paternalistic manner, but they need support mechanisms to enable them to fulfil their aims and ambitions. In a turbulent era people need more assistance. Organizations should ensure that their managers and HR people have both the capacities not only to make tough decisions and confront the consequences, but also to provide emotional support.

Some will be incapable of managing these seemingly two contradictory requirements, but the options should be made available anyway. Even those who appear tough may need support systems, not necessarily the same systems as for those who are made redundant, and for these, and especially for the survivors, individual counselling will be needed more then ever.

Summary

This chapter has outlined a comprehensive portfolio of HRM career-related practices, that is, practices which are used by organizations to plan and manage employees' careers. The practices have been discussed in no specific order of importance, but an attempt has been made to group them according to their role in a comprehensive organizational career system. Most of the career practices in use are expected to be developed and cultivated in the future, although some may disappear as there is no apparent managerial need for them. This will be mainly due to structural developments within organizations, re-defined business needs, and labour market culture, coupled with the new type of psychological contract. This characterizes a relationship between employees and employers which will be continued and developed in the organization of the future.

The portfolio has included a separate discussion of each practice, and an analysis of its fit for the future. The whole set of career practices have been combined into a broad integrated package which organizations may apply when implementing career systems. While I hope that the list is comprehensive and covers the whole area of organizational CPM, I make no pretensions to having provided a full or precise prescription, either for the present or for the future. First, with so many changes affecting individuals, organizations, and nations, it is very difficult to make forecasts. Second, there is huge variety within organizations, even within the boundaries of one nation or one sector of industry. Based on the outlines presented in this chapter, it is left to HR managers in each organization to determine and decide what practices are needed to answer their specific situation, using sense, sensibility, and professionalism.

KEY TERMS

Career planning and management (CPM)

Career practices

CPM portfolio

Integrated career system

Internal and external integration

DISCUSSION QUESTIONS

LESSONS AND FOOD FOR THOUGHT

Let us now reconsider the question given at the beginning of this chapter (see Case studies 7.1 and 7.2).

Imagine that you are the HR director of a company, and your CEO/Board are asking you to recreate the organizational career system (note: this is a reactive HR approach) or that you have decided that the organization needs an updated career system (a proactive HR approach). What would your plan look like? Which career practices would you apply, and in what order would they be introduced to the organizational setting?

Bear in mind:

- *Organizational characteristics*: Size, sector of operation, level of prosperity.*
- *The individual level*: Be aware of the different needs that may stem from the age distribution of employees, diversity within the workforce, professions.
- *The society/national level*: Labour markets, economic conditions, the environment. Comment: if you are not working in an organization, assume you work for a consultancy, and were asked to advise an HR manager of an organization of your choice.

Note: * What difference would it make if the organization has 10,000 employees rather than 1,000? What if there are only some 200? What difference would it make if the organization operates in the hotel or the software development industry? Give the logical and theoretical base to support your answer.

REVIEW QUESTIONS

1. How can one determine one's own organization's needs in terms of the matched career practices portfolio?
2. What can individuals manage?
3. If you are employed or can refer to an organization you know:
   - How will you develop such a system effectively?
   - The customers of the system – who are they and what are their needs?
4. In what way would the following factors influence the relative importance and relevance of the various career practices
   - Sector of activity.
   - Country of origin.
   - In case of a MNC – working in the home country or in a subsidiary.
   - Size of organization in terms of number of employees.
   - Geographic distribution of company location.
   - Level of education of most employees.

- Demography of workforce in terms of:
  - o Gender
  - o Age
  - o Ethnicity.

EXERCISE

In the continuous debate about organizational core versus peripheral operations, it was argued that certain operations, activities, and practices can be outsourced to gain better effectiveness and flexibility. Such operations include cleaning services, special marketing campaigns, IT maintenance, and so on.

There are arguments both for and against outsourcing the HR operation. Critically examine each of the career practices presented in this chapter, and classify them according to the following three categories:

- Practices that certainly can (or should) be outsourced.
- Practices that should not be outsourced under most circumstances.
- Practices for which you find conflicting arguments about the possible benefits and pitfalls of outsourcing them.

Compare and contrast your list with others in a small group discussion.

Global Career Management

8

LEARNING OBJECTIVES

After reading this chapter you should be able to:

- Distinguish between individual and organizational management of global careers
- Analyse organizational global positioning within several theoretical frameworks
- Identify the variety of strategic options for applying global career systems
- Understand the impact of individual background and organizational policies on global careers and global employability
- Understand how organizations can avoid losing their global workforce

Chapter outline

Introduction

Contemporary business is now more global than ever (Hamilton & Webster, 2018), and as a result, labour markets have also became global (Dickmann & Baruch, 2011). Technology makes the globalization even more complex and open, with high level of competitiveness (Manyika et al., 2015). Legal and regulatory issues add to the requirements that individuals and organizations need to comply with (Toffel et al., 2015). One characteristic of global management of a firm means the need to manage people across borders and culture. This is not a new phenomenon. Already in the 1960s, Hofstede (1980) conducted what is probably the largest comparative international study of work-related values. The results were published, using a false name (Hermes) for the company. However, it was very clear at the time, given that the company under discussion was a high-tech company, with operations in more than 40 countries, that it must be IBM. Today it would not be so easy to identify a company by the size of its multinational operations: most of the high-tech corporations (and others) in the Fortune 500 list have global operations in a considerable number of countries. Even today IBM is still typically used to demonstrate the archetype global corporation. Nevertheless, most companies over a certain size operate globally, and need to manage their human resources internationally. Even in businesses that were considered traditionally as local, like supermarkets, we find firms operating in different counties, with varying levels of business success: Walmart, US based; Lidl and Aldi, German based; Carrefour, French based; and Tesco, UK based, all have overseas subsidiaries.

Moreover, the IBM model is not necessarily the best strategy for them to follow, and different organizations may optimize their resources by employing different strategies and practices for managing people across borders.

In this chapter we will look at the globalization of careers at different levels. For individuals, we will study the meaning of being global, gaining global employability, and the benefits and possible pitfalls of becoming global. For organization, we will focus on how, when an organization moves from a country-based to a global-based operation, this process is reflected in career systems – in particular the management of expatriation, repatriation, and other forms of global mobility.

The internationalization of careers: Individual perspective

More than half a century ago, the world was first depicted as a 'global village' (MacLuhan, 1960). For many companies, indeed, the globe rather than their home country is the arena for their business, their sales market, and their labour market. Regularly operating across geographical borders has become the rule rather than the exception, in particular for large, blue-chip companies. From the career management perspective this means that people need to manage and to be managed beyond both geographical and cultural horizons. It poses two main challenges to HRM in these firms. First, the need to have consistent strategic and operational HRM system across all the operations in the many countries. This is hard, sometimes impossible to do because of the variety in legal, regulations, and cultural systems that apply in different countries. The other challenge is moving people within the operation – mostly as expatriation, but also a myriad of other alternatives to expatriation.

Few would contest what has by now become the 'bread and butter' of executive careers in multinational corporations (MNCs). Global managers are needed to provide answers for the challenges of global management (Bratton & Gold, 2017; Sparrow & Hiltrop, 1997). Truly 'global' managers are sought for, be they 'home-', 'host-' or 'third-' country nationals (see Box 8.1) as companies aim for global competitiveness (Drucker, 1999; Terpstra & Limpaphayom, 2012). Companies invest in the development of future global leaders (Conner, 2000) to ensure competitiveness in the international market. National boundaries are more permeable for crossing – though there is no full 'right to move' across countries (Reis & Baruch, 2013). Overall, the development of global careers answers the needs of many career actors (Dickmann & Andresen, 2018). Of course, not every manager is expected to be international, but 'a small core of international employees will be a key to successful globalization' (Shackleton & Newell, 1997). These employees, mostly serving as expatriates, are expected to make the firm global, and do so reaching strong returns on investment, which is hard to achieve, and also depends on the context (Doherty & Dickmann, 2012). This is in line with the principle of talent management (TM), as discussed in the last chapter, where specific attention to TM need to be allocated in multinational corporations (MNCs) (Collings, Mellahi, & Cascio, 2019).

Box 8.1: Which country? Some definitions

Home country: The country where the main operation was established, where the headquarters is situated, and most importantly, which defines strategy, retains control, and manages the operation of the organization. Most multinationals have a distinct culture determined by the home company (and national) culture. Employees from the home country will be sent as expatriates to the host countries.

Host country: The country where the home company ('mother company') operates. They will have mostly local, 'host-country' national employees, but also some expatriates, usually in managerial or professional technical positions.

Third-country: There may also be some employees who are 'third-country nationals' (TCN) – people who have moved from a different country altogether to work for the company. Some of them may have moved from an operation in one host country to one in another host country.

However, a clear definition of a global manager does not exist, since there may be several meanings to the title 'global manager'. According to more narrow definition, it can be: an expatriate manager (cf. Black & Gregersen, 1999); or more widely a manager who works across borders (cf. Bartlett & Ghoshal, 1992); or simply a manager in a company which operate across borders. While the last option is too all-encompassing, the first two are valid, and indicate the distinction between expatriates and other types of global managers, like the 'globetrotters' or 'travelling managers'.

A more detailed option to identify a variety of categories for global careers is offered by Baruch et al. (2013). They list a framework for the identification and differentiation across many types and dimensions of global careers.

Box 8.2: Classifying global careers

Global careers 'glossary'

Baruch et al. (2013) identified seven dimensions that help to classify types global careers:

1. Time of exposure.
2. Intensity of international contact through work.
3. Breadth of interaction.
4. Legal context.
5. International work instigator.

6. Extent of cultural gap between an individual's country of origin and the context in which the international work takes place.
7. Key cultural-related requirements of one's job/role.

The major modes of global careers

Traditional corporate expatriation

Self-initiated and non-organizational supported expatriation

Flexpatriates working in corporations

Expatriation from subsidiaries – inpatriates/impatriates

Secondments overseas

In-shoring

Short-term assignments

Globetrotting

Ex-host country nationals

Virtual global employees

Cross-border commuting

Immigration – legal/illegal/asylum

Temporary immigration

Government – diplomatic services

Government – armed forces

Governmental humanitarian and development organizations

International non-governmental organizations

International work experiences and voluntary overseas work

Students studying abroad

Sabbaticals

By far, the main mode of global work is expatriation. Expatriation comprises a period of time when an employee of the organization is posted to a subsidiary of the firm in a different country for a substantial time period. Expatriation can be corporate-initiated or self-initiated.

The expatriate is typically an employee who, as part of career path, is assigned to work in an overseas subsidiary of a company, and the initiation for this choice can come from the employer (e.g. via HR planning), it can be initiated by the employee, or it may be an employee that applies to work for the firm in an overseas destination. Expatriation is planned for a considerable period of time, three or four years being the norm or the convention (in the Far East, expatriation periods tend to be longer). The expatriate is usually accompanied by their immediate family (if they have one).

Expatriation adjustment and adaptation

To be successful the expatriate (and the family) need to adjust to the new situation. Poor adjustment might lead to a failure, most typically an early return (Aycan, 2001).

There are typical stages or phases of cultural adjustment. The following depiction of adjustment stages is based on several works, some focused on the expatriation (Feldman & Tompson, 1993; Lee, 2006) and others on the repatriation (Rodrigues, 2009):

First stage: Sometimes called the 'honeymoon stage', this takes place during the very first period following arrival. The expatriate (and family) feel like tourists, can be fascinated by the new experiences and the different culture. This stage can take just a few days (until the first 'disaster', or a few weeks at best).

Second stage: The 'cultural shocks' stage. Realization of difficulties, challenges, not understanding issues, and having a need to cope with real conditions on a daily basis. Above the regular issues of any start of a new position, for expatriates there is a need to get used to a new way of life, and the added factor of culture shock might lead to frustration and upset. In some cases even hostility towards the host nation and its people. This is the critical stage, which, if the situation get out of hand, can lead to an early departure, or to a long period of thwarting, which will influence performance.

Third stage: This is the actual 'adjustment stage'. The expatriate and the family gradually learn the ropes, adapt, sometimes endorse the local norms and values. Feedback from locals can accelerate the adjustment process. This can typically take few months.

Fourth stage: Normal performance, following acculturation. Can be called the 'mastery stage', when the expatriate can perform, interact with the locals, become part of the local operation, functioning well in the new culture. The stage that, if all goes well, would last for the rest of the assignment, normally about three years.

Fifth stage: Pre-repatriation preparation – 'time to say goodbye'. When it is time to return. The expatriate need to prepare for returning home (or to another country), with two major issues – preparing the ground for the successful integration of his or her replacement, and preparing the return to home.

Sixth stage: Re-adjustment to 'normal' – 'back to earth with a bump', which may not be the past normal (see at the end of the chapter for the 'reversed cultural shock' phenomenon).

These stages are typical for expatriation – either corporate expatriation, or self-initiated (the latter might end with naturalization, so will not go through the last two stages).

In contrast, different challenges are expected by other global movers. For example, the 'travelling manager' is a manager who routinely operates across borders, but has a base in one country, usually the country where the core operation is located. In their roles within MNCs, 'travelling managers' need to make frequent visits to different locations around the globe. There are others who operate similarly, for example, agents, merchants, solicitors, and so on who perceive the whole world as their operational field.

CASE STUDY 8.1: A GLOBETROTTING CAREER

Maarten is known to his friends as the 'Flying Dutchman'. He worked in the past for IBM, Unisys and Logica in The Netherlands, and as part of his career was expatriated to the UK and later to the USA. Now he works both as an interim manager for a large MNC, and at developing his own business, Quandar. His career motto is: 'They don't wait for you … so you have to take the initiative, create your own space.'

His present career has emerged from the earlier stages, but subject to his own inclinations. After more than twenty years in corporate life he has decided to embark on an entrepreneurial venture. Quandar Marketing, which he established, is a company specialising in marketing-on-demand services for businesses that want to outsource their marketing activities. In addition, since in the first stages of development such a company would not be needed on a full-time basis, he acts as an interim manager for an international communication consultancy firm. In this role, which requires some three working days a week, Maarten divides his working time between San Francisco, Amsterdam, and London. He has a six-months contract, where he has to spend most of his time at the Amsterdam operation, regularly visiting the headquarters, which is in San Francisco, and dealing with many customers located in London, where he lives.

Maarten is not concerned about the amount of travelling, especially as the flight time from London to Amsterdam is less than an hour. He is fluent in Dutch and English (and also in German and French), and knows the local cultures first hand. Living in London was his choice, and Maarten really sees himself as a citizen of the world.

Individual characteristics of global managers

Defining a global manager would never be simple, but some have tried. Borg and Harzing (1995) tried to 'profile' the international manager using both Tung's (1982) and Mendenhall and Oddou's (1985) criteria. Tung identified four groups of variables that determine the success of the global manager: technical knowledge and job skills; interpersonal relationships; ability to cope with environmental constraints; and family situation. Mendenhall and Oddou referred to a different set of dimensions: self-orientation (self-esteem, self-confidence, etc.); features that enhance capability to interact effectively with host nationals; the ability to perceive what the locals have in mind; and the ability to deal with cultures that are very different from one's own. Using the intelligent career framework, Cappellen and Janssens (2008) identified three sets of competencies: (i) the knowing-why competencies for global managers relate to their work–life balance, international exposure, professional identification, centre of decision making, career progression, and search for challenge; (ii) the knowing-how competencies that global managers develop relate to operational skills (e.g. strategic management) and general business understanding; (iii) the knowing-whom competencies, built on professional networks and personal networks that enabled global managers to obtain their position and recognition as global managers.

Baruch (2002) claims that these and other sets of criteria are all prerequisites for success in any managerial job, thus 'there is no such thing' as a global manager, although, to succeed in such a position one needs, perhaps, a 'global mind-set', a readiness and willingness to work within a global environment, to accept differences and to benefit from such diversity. The experiences of global managers are characterized and shaped by three types of tensions reflecting physical, organizational and personal issues. These are distance versus closeness, hierarchy versus culture, and work flexibility versus family equilibrium (Cappellen & Janssens, 2010). Put together, global management may call for certain qualities, of which the 'requirement' for a 'global mindset' for successful expatriation is a key factor. This view was reinforced by Goxe and Belhoste (2019). Baruch (2002) argues that while the concept of globalization reflects true business reality, the idea that there is a certain profile, which one should fit in order to be a successful global manager, seems flawed. Similarly, in terms of personality (e.g. the 'Big Five' – see Goldberg 1990; Judge & Zapata, 2015) it is difficult to identify specific attributes that will distinguish a person more likely than others to succeed in an international career. It seems that what makes an individual a 'global manager' is more a state of mind, an openness and willingness to cross borders – geographical and cultural – as part of the career. It is no surprise, then, to find that global assignments pose great challenges for managers and their families.

A pause for reflection

What do you believe are the qualities and specific circumstances that would make you a successful global manager? What do you believe are the qualities and specific circumstances that might prevent you from becoming a successful global manager?

Do these concern your inner qualities? Your job-related competence? Your family situation?

Global psychological contracts?

Guzzo et al. (1994) placed the issue of global HRM, in particular that of expatriation, within the current debate on the psychological contract. The psychological contract influences the adjustment process of expatriation, thereby enhancing the expatriate's opportunity to build career capital (Haslberger & Brewster, 2009). The firm benefits too, as expatriation of its employees offers opportunity to generate social and intellectual capital for the firm. Viewed from this theoretical perspective, expatriation is a specific case of the employment relationship. Guzzo et al. argue that these relationships will be relational rather than transactional. One indeed may have to make sacrifices when agreeing to expatriation, but on the other hand, one may gain in the long term. Nevertheless, many HR managers will challenge the contention of Guzzo et al., recognizing that in order to persuade employees to accept expatriation to a 'difficult' country, a higher remuneration package has to be offered. This is just one element of the building of a personal career, which needs to be taken from a dual-perspective – home and host country. The creation and the possible breach of psychological contract may arise from two sources: the home or parent firm, and the receiving host subsidiary (Kumarika Perera et al., 2017). Poor development of the expatriate's psychological contract could lead to a breach of the psychological contract, and ultimately to a failure (Kumarika Perera et al., 2017).

The psychological contract is established also for other forms of global careers, for example, flexpatriate, for whom a different psychological contract needs to be developed due to its distinctive employment relationship (Pate & Scullion, 2018). Flexpatriate assignments are composed of repeat visits to global locations, either single or multiple destinations and projects. Wickman and Vecchi (2009, p. 254) present a typology of variation in the nature of flexpatriates:

Commuters: Regular repetitive journeys to a specific set of destinations.

Explorers: A combination of regular and new destinations.

Nomads: A high number of destinations, thereby novelty in arrangements.

Missionaries: Travel to customers with the purpose of knowledge dissemination.

Visiting tradesmen: Those who work on customers' sites, such as project managers.

The development of a relationship between the firm and its global managers, in particular expatriates, is influenced also by individual characteristics. However, the effect of such characteristics is not straightforward. For example, age may have different implications: young people, especially those without children, may agree to expatriation quite willingly, as may older people whose children have left home and who have no responsibility for elderly relatives, while middle-aged people might find an international move problematic. Because age is quite closely associated with hierarchical level, and most expatriate positions are for middle-level personnel rather than very junior employees or senior executives, there are considerable challenges for HR managers in filling these positions.

Other individual issues include gender and marital status. Typically expatriates tend to be men, as women form merely 15% of expatriates' population (Berry & Bell, 2012). This is less relevant for self-initiated expatriation (Andresen et al., 2015). Organizations need to be realistic in assigning female managers to overseas posts, because although women make up a low proportion of corporate expatriates they can be very successful, and much is to do with organizational policies (Shortland, 2016). Challenges can also be external: in certain cultures female managers are not readily accepted or even face legal barriers. However, this is not necessarily so; for example, in Japan, US female managers were accepted primarily as professionals, as Americans, and as managers, and less as females (Taylor & Napier, 1996).

While some of the blame for the poor representation of female expatriation figures is due to managerial approach (both from HR and line managers), some of the reasons are self-inflicted by women (Fischlmayr, 2002). Amongst what Fischlmayr termed 'external barriers' are: HR managers reluctant to select female candidates (but this reluctance comes also from line managers); culturally tough locations or regions preclude female expatriates; and those selecting expatriates have stereotypes that negatively work against appointing women to expatriation roles. Yet, she also emphasize the self-established barriers, in particular: a limited willingness to relocate; being a member of a dual-career couple; and behaving according to gender-based role models.

Career systems must accommodate the marital status of employees. This is even more true in the case of expatriation. Dual-career couples, single parents, and people with caring responsibilities for elderly relatives or with teenage children pose challenges for the system. This means that when HR managers take career management decisions, they have to be very aware of the specific personal circumstances of their employees. Seeking such information might, of course, be perceived as intruding. This means that in managing expatriation, repatriation, and other types of global mobility, the organization needs to be engaged and involved also with family issues.

McNulty and Moeller (2018, p. 259) define dual-career expatriates as: 'Individuals with an unyielding psychological commitment to their professional careers which requires relocation abroad, in combination with a commitment to a personal relationship that may or may not involve the relocation of their partner abroad, and that the commitment to career and personal relationship is extended by both adult partners.' They identify the 'R' profile to represent different options or strategies taken, with associating each of them with a different propensity of success: ready, reborn, resentful, and resigned (see Figure 8.1).

Selecting dual-career couple employees for international assignments is another challenge, as a dual-career couple is far more typical in modern careers. Känsälä et al. (2015) reaffirm that readiness and willingness to accept expatriation can depend on family status and the differences in career strategies of men and women. In most cases, 'trailing spouses' that have their own career wish to sustain it while living abroad. Dual-career couples find it hard for one of them to leave their job or to serve as a house-wife/husband during an overseas assignment. It is difficult for spouses in professional and managerial positions to find suitable roles elsewhere. An innovative solution on the part of the company may be to offer either work or support in finding work for the spouse.

A complementary perspective of the impact of expatriation on the careers of the trailing spouse explored their career identity (Kanstrén, 2019). Suggesting that international assignments have a considerable impact on expatriate partners' career identity reconstruction, four perspectives were identified and labelled as: stable career identities, threatened career identities,

	Profile	Characteristics
High likelihood of success	Ready	Empowered, refuses to accept dual-career defeat, never accept trailing spouse file as the end result, and typically maintain the same career abroad as at home
	Re-born	Initially resentful, re-establishes new identity, and finds new career abroad after exhausting other options
	Resentful	Aggressive but defeated, angry and upset
Low likelihood of success	Resigned	Passive, defeated, depressed, ending with giving up and accepting spouse life

Figure 8.1   Ready, reborn, resentful, and resigned (McNulty & Moeller, 2018)

lost career identities, and emerging new career identities. The evidence, as well as simple logic, suggested that accepting an international assignment should be discussed beforehand and be part of the individual and organizational career planning.

Box 8.3: Wider perspective?

The framework of global management may be extended to include the issue of immigration and the way multicultural communities interact in a different cultural realm. Expatriation, especially self-initiated, may turn into immigration (Andresen et al., 2012; Latukha et al., 2019). Leong and Hartung (2000) discuss how career interventions such as counselling may be influenced by the target population (they focused on people of Chinese origin who grew up in Western cultures). They argue for the need to move from multiculturalism based on demographics to one that is based on mindsets.

Global employability

The majority of employability literature does not refer to the global context. As we noted in earlier chapters, employability is the new necessity to gain a job in the labour market. As the labour market became global, certain elements of employability would need to reflect this status. There is a skills shortage in most global economies (Sarfraz et al., 2018). Sarfraz et al. conducted a systematic research review to explore the key employability skills reported as important by employability stakeholders globally. They identified the top-10 most commonly reported employability skills as (in this order):

- Teamwork
- Problem solving
- Communication
- Computer skills
- Analytical skills
- Leadership
- Time management
- Creativity
- Interpersonal
- Organization

One specific set of skills was identified as global citizenship skills, such as: knowledge of another language, awareness of global issues, appreciation of diversity and multi-culturalism, and cross-cultural competence (the latter reflects earlier works on cultural intelligence) (Earley & Ang, 2003).

In principle, global employability extends the boundaries of employability from one country to the globe. People from OECD countries would have the advantage, for example, of an easier path to gain a work permit where necessary and recognition of qualifications. Immigrants from developing countries have to compromise their employability, for example, medical doctors having to work in low-skills jobs (Andresen et al., 2012), though some managed better than others (Al Ariss & Syed, 2011). Global employability can be higher in certain sectors, in particular technical jobs, for example programing computer software, whereas jobs like social work requires understanding of local nuances in terms of culture, values, and beliefs.

With a skills shortage in most locations, developed countries have advantage in their ability to attract graduates, many of whom may wish to remain in the country where they studied (Baruch, Budhwar, & Khatri, 2007). This is known as 'brain-drain' (Docquier & Rapoport, 2012). Yet, a different phenomenon is called 'brain circulation', where people move overseas, gain experience, and return to their home country, which then benefits from this experience. Such is the so-called Chinese 'sea turtles' (Guo, Porschitz, & Alves, 2013).

As graduates look for jobs, national borders pose less of an obstacle, in particular if those graduates adopt protean career orientation.

The push/pull model

A combination of individual values and needs, organizational approaches (see further discussion later in this chapter), and national culture is manifested in Baruch's push/pull model (Baruch, 1995; Baruch et al., 2016a). This model is based on Lewin's field theory (1951), and takes into account the economic, rights, and cultural realms (see Figure 8.2). Whenever a proposal to move across borders is put to any employee, there will be two forces operating in conflicting directions. One pulls the employee to move to the new place, the other pushes him or her back, that is, to reject the move. Each person will decide according to the strength of these forces, and these forces operate in all three realms. For example, the organization may increase the pull factor by offering high economic incentives. A push factor might be a strong dislike of the culture of the host country, or even of its physical climate. There are many legal constraints relating to the movement of people across borders, such as the need for a work permit, or which other-country nationals can work in specific countries. Cultural forces can pull people too; for those looking for adventure, some exotic places would have an appeal, whereas other people might resent being sent to those places. A difficult situation for the HR department in any MNC is dealing with a refusal to accept expatriation (Punnett, 1997; Baruch & Altman, 2002). Not only does a refusal leave a hole in the system to be filled, but it might have a snowball effect, in that people may refuse to step in once the post has been rejected by others. Therefore, organizations need to assess in advance how likely people are to accept or refuse global assignments.

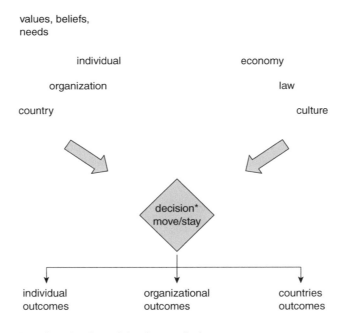

Figure 8.2   The push/pull model (Baruch, 1995)

Different national managerial cultures

Companies that operate across borders realize that even in Western cultures, there are different national cultures. A vivid example relevant to career management is the answer to the question: 'Which are the most important criteria for managerial success?' Scheneider and Barsoux (2003) compared and contrasted different answers.

In American culture the right answer is 'drive' and 'ability'. In France the criterion is whether or not the manager studied at one of the *grandes écoles*. The German model emphasizes technical and functional competence, whereas in the UK what matters is classical education and a generalist approach. The Japanese value a qualification from a top university, compliance, and loyalty.

Therefore, when MNCs operate in a country different from the headquarters country, the development of a career system will have to take into account such differences, and even so, the managers will face misunderstandings that stem from different managerial cultures.

CASE STUDY 8.2: THE HAMBURGER DISCIPLINE

I heard the following story from Dan, an American executive who worked for ExxonMobil as an expatriate in several countries, including Japan, Germany, the UK and, of course, the USA. This story manifests the different metaphorical hamburger you will encounter when you are disciplined in different cultures.

When you work in the USA and make a mistake, your manager will call you up to his or her office. At first you will be told something along the lines of: 'We know how good you are, valued by the company, and that usually your work is fine' (the lower bun). Then will come the 'meat': 'Yesterday you acted in such and such manner, which is not according to our policy,' and so on. So a warning or comment will be entered on your file. Then the manager will say, 'We do know that it was a one-off event, and we value your work, and wish to leave this behind,' and so on. That is the upper bun. You got your 'balanced' hamburger.

But if you work in Germany, most probably your manager will call you up to his or her office and will tell you exactly and to the point: 'Yesterday you acted in such and such manner, which is not according to our policy,' and so on. So a warning or comment will be entered on the file. That's it. Just 'meat'.

On the other hand, if this were to happen in Japan, your manager would call you up to his (probably not her) office, and tell you something along the lines of 'We know how good you are, valued by the company, and that usually your work is fine'. Then he will go on, praising your work, providing more nice positive comments, and will send you out (just the bun). Nevertheless, you will know, you will know indeed why you were called up.

This was the story. Now for implications.

First, in each country, people are easily able to recognize the method of disciplinary action, and how severe it is. Second, these methods are highly dependent on national culture. A problem will emerge, though, when people from different cultures mingle work together. For example, imagine that an employee with the German cultural orientation is placed in Japan, and is called in for a disciplinary procedure. He or she will probably never get the message. Or imagine a worse scenario, where a Japanese employee stationed in Germany is disciplined in 'the German way' by the local manager – it might lead to loss of face, immediate departure, or some other disastrous outcome.

No doubt people from each of the cultures feel that their way is the right one. But the question is not who is right. What matters is that the message must be delivered and understood, wherever the company operates. So now you get a feeling for the challenge.

Moving on from the metaphorical illustration of cultural differences, the typical progression into and out of organizations varies significantly across countries. As indicated in earlier chapters, in the UK and the USA people may enter the organization at the rank-and-file-level, and then develop within the organization, or may enter a managerial position (e.g. via graduate recruitment) and develop within that role, or they may be head-hunted to fill an executive position. Similarly, they may leave the organization from any position. In Germany and Japan, entry is almost exclusively to the lower echelons, and people will tend not to leave the organization. In Japan congruence, compliance, and obedience are crucial for promotion. In many Western cultures, being confrontational, playing the Devil's advocate, is a better way to introduce oneself to top management.

Culture is also about values, beliefs, and norms of behaviour. What may be considered as a bribe in one culture would be acceptable, even expected in another culture. Bringing a small present (e.g. a pen with inscription of your company name) may be OK; a 'present' such as gold pen or a Rolex watch is something totally different. How can one make the right judgment? What should the firm do in terms of policy, and what should the global sales-person do when a bribe is expected?

A pause for reflection

When serving your firm in different corners of the globe, you may find that certain practices that are considered unethical or unaccepted are actually the norm in the host country.

To what extent will you 'bend' your work moral when working for global firm?

Informal career networking

In studying management it is sometimes implied that organizational managerial processes are planned and managed in a systematic way, and that both individuals and organizations have a well-structured and formalized system for managing. This may be true for mechanistic aspects, operations, and regulations. However, in people management, informal relationships are no less crucial for the future career than formal relationships. Networking, reflecting the 'know whom' of the intelligent career (Arthur et al., 2016), will usually have a stronger impact on the future career. When people cross borders, they need to find out how to become a part of local networks. The way to enter the system, of course, is different in each country, and sometimes entry is almost impossible, but the first step is to identify the network. In the UK, networking is usually simple – it occurs in the pub, just after work is finished. In France, the best way to connect may be during long lunch sessions. In small countries it might prove difficult, as many networks develop from one's schooldays; and in countries where a period of armed service is compulsory many of the networks are formed during this service. From networks one gains informal advice, knowledge that cannot be delivered in formal meetings, the support of a key person for the next career move. The expatriate manager should figure out how the local informal system works, and do their best to get involved if they wish to become part of the system.

A final point to consider in the context of the global management of careers relates to the fact that the same company operates in a variety of cultures and career systems (Schneider & Barsoux, 2003). The MNC still needs to obtain and retain the right people, and to apply 'best practice' – across national borders. And clearly, what may be perceived as 'best practice' in one place may not be so perceived in another. Therefore, one major challenge for global career management is to find the right balance across the different operations, setting a policy that will take into account the strategy of the organization as well as local requirements.

A further major challenge concerned with career management is the management of expatriates and their expatriation and repatriation process. Both challenges are dealt with in the next section.

Global career systems: The organizational perspective

Organizational models of global management of people

The earlier part of this chapter dealt with the individual point of view. However, it was the combination of economic and social factors that caused the increase in global competition and global operations, and subsequently an acceleration of traffic in expatriation and repatriation (cf. Baruch et al., 2016a; Laurent, 1986; Porter, 2011; Porter & Tansky, 1999). Organizational-level analysis generates a different perspective on the management of international careers, or on the introduction of an international assignment to the organizational portfolio of career practices. Organizational models of the global management of people are those of Bartlett and Ghoshal (2003), Baruch and Altman (2002) and Perlmutter (1969).

There are two major aspects of global career management. One is the management of HRM across borders in a company that operates in more than one country. This means that there is a tension, sometime lack of compatibility between the need for applying the same HRM strategy, policy and practices in all the operations, and the need to accommodate local issues like legal and cultural differences. The other aspect concerns moving people across borders, in particular expatriation (followed later by repatriation), as well as other modes of global assignments.

HRM operating across borders: 'Glocalized' careers

How does an organization become 'glocal'? Operating in different countries poses a challenge to the management of career systems. First, there needs to be congruence and matching across the operation (i.e. being global), but then the operation is carried out in different countries, each with a different economy, legal system, and culture (i.e. being local). Even what may be perceived as simple for one person is not necessarily so. Very often, the secret of success lies in finding the right combination or level of compromise in reaching 'glocalization'. Let us look at the following issues: remuneration, performance appraisal, training and development, industrial relations, and health and safety.

Remuneration

The system of remuneration or compensation is problematic since one cannot use the same measure across borders. Decision about remuneration, compensation, wages, benefits, and so on for expatriates need to take into consideration many factors and be holistic (Suutari et al., 2012). The principal question is what should be the basis for payment, and the major two options are similarity of amount of money and similarity of buying power. Other questions will derive from this basic issue. For example, what should a company do with regard to variation in taxation levels?

Dowling et al. (1994) present five objectives a firm's remuneration system needs to satisfy, which are relevant to date. The policy should:

- be consistent and fair
- enable the firm to attract and retain the necessary employees
- facilitate the transfer of employees in a cost-effective manner
- be consistent with the firm's strategy, structure, and business needs
- ensure that employees are motivated.

What is not simple, for example, is the definition of 'fair'. What would you consider fair payment? Also the concept of 'consistency' loses its meaning when the system has to accommodate the requirements of different populations requiring separate systems (e.g. local managers and expatriates). The system can relate to both extrinsic and intrinsic components of payment (Logger, Vinke & Kluytmans, 1995).

The remuneration needs to be considered alongside the return on investment that was dedicated to the expatriate (Doherty & Dickmann, 2012).

Generally, a firm must decide whether the base for payment will be the country of the headquarters, the home country of the person involved, or the host country. If a company has a similar operation and hierarchy structure in two countries, the salaries of the local employees should relate to salaries in that country. For example, if a Swedish or American company has branches in Britain and Madagascar, the salary of the British branch manager should match the salary of a branch manager of a similar-sized operation in Britain, not that of the manager of Madagascar. Similarly, in determining the Madagascan branch manager's salary, the benchmark should be the remuneration of other branch managers in Madagascar, not the dollar salary of the USA, British or Yemeni managers in their own countries. Of course, the situation becomes more complex when expatriation is involved: for example, if an American IT firm sends two IT support technical managers, one to Japan and one to Brazil, or one to Switzerland and one to Portugal (both within Europe, it should be noted), should they have the same salary in dollar terms? The buying power of the dollar in the various economies is certainly different. The required quality of life may be a better measure. But then the company should realize that a portion of the family income is devoted to savings, or to paying a mortgage. This share can be kept at the level of the home country. Retirement is another issue, and the firm should make sure that individuals' retirement savings are not compromised. A policy of offering private pension schemes would pass the burden and the decision to the expatriates themselves. If the company has a policy of similar payments for similar positions, what needs to be done about tax differences? Even within the EU, the top rate of tax varies from some 40% to more than 70%. Again, a 'fair' but costly solution for the company is to pay the difference to compensate the employee.

In addition, the company should envisage the reaction of locals to marked disparity. Evidence from a Chinese study suggests that local workers might still feel that there is unfair disparity if expatriates earn much more than they do, but this feeling can be reduced if the expatriates receive salaries that are not too far above those of their local counterparts (Chen et al., 2002).

One thing companies are certainly expected to pay is relocation costs. These may also include yearly visits for the expatriate to the home operational base, to keep in touch with the home business, to meet with his or her mentor and career adviser, with colleagues and others. Policies will vary across companies, and according to the status of the expatriate and financial constraints and budgets. Among the issues to be decided are who will fly economy, business, or first class, and whether all family members are covered, what constitutes a reason for visiting the home country. What if, to deal with a family problem, the expatriate (or their spouse) must return home, and who defines what is a 'must' (a funeral for a deceased parent certainly is, but how about the birth of a niece, the marriage of a brother, etc.)? Companies should have a general policy and guidelines on these issues too.

When dealing with other types of global mobility, like flexpatriates, similar issues are even more relevant, as these are not one-off visits. Level of flight, accommodation, and other subsistence requirements should be determine at the company level.

An assignment of two or three years will be paid according to a certain scale of remuneration. This should be treated as a temporary appointment. However, if the expatriation becomes very long term or permanent (either in the same country or sequence of expatriate postings), the compensation should be reviewed and revised to keep pace with local levels of payments as compared with costs of living.

Figure 8.3 depicts the factors influencing expatriate remuneration.

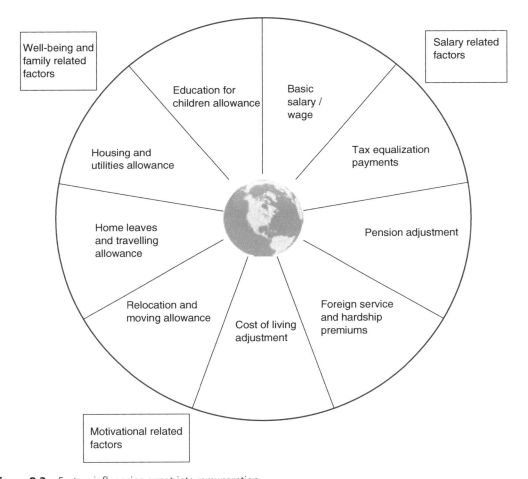

Figure 8.3   Factors influencing expatriate remuneration

To sum up, while the general guidelines should lead to a 'fair' and constructive system, situational factors will force companies to be inventive and flexible in setting and managing the remuneration system across borders. In addition, companies can rely on external systems that are designed to evaluate needed adjustments for spending power parity (such as the Hay Group system).

A pause for reflection

What do you feel would be the right combination that would be fair compensation for you if you were asked to move to a country in Europe? In South America?

Performance appraisal

When implementing a PA system the firm should decide which kind of system and what format (or forms) should be used. There is a variety of options for choosing relevant criteria, and in the global context these differ across countries. The system needs to be based on an appropriate measurement instrument or scale, for example, ranking, behavioural appraisals (graphic rating scales, anchored rating scales, observation scales, to name a few), the management by objective approach, and others. Some of these measurement scales would be suitable for individualist societies whereas others would suit the needs of collectivist societies. The MNC has three options: to apply the same system across the board; to apply different systems for different operations (either per country or per region); or to find a compromise or develop a hybrid model where PA in some countries share similar features but not identical.

To achieve coherence across functions, the system should be identical in different countries of operation. However, for many reasons, starting with legal but also cultural, a company may find that forms that are accepted and effective in one country cannot be used similarly in another country. This can be particularly relevant if the PA system is also used as a basis for performance-related pay (PRP). If this is the case, issues of remuneration discussed above are affected too (cf. Kessler & Purcell, 1992). It is used in business, in particular for those high on the hierarchy (Bender, 2004). Evidence suggests that PRP can be functional also in the public sector (Dahlström & Lapuente, 2010).

A clear example is the use of 360-degree feedback. In some countries this would be the best option for providing employees with rich feedback. The benefits of such a system in different cultures is that it can be valuable for increasing the reliability and validity of the process. In other cultures people might resent the use of this form of evaluation (Hofstede et al., 2005). Bernardin et al. (1995) argue that any PA system should apply: (i) legally defensible appraisal procedures; (ii) legally defensible appraisal content; (iii) legally defensible documentation of appraisal results; and (iv) legally defensible raters. Therefore, legal advice is important in adapting the global system to local considerations, and local legal systems vary considerably.

Another practical issue is that of mergers and acquisitions in international organizations. This means that when a MNC acquires a local company, the HR system is part of the purchase, and the mother company needs to decide if or how to apply the PA system to the new company. Doing this can be quite difficult if this is an overseas operation.

A pause for reflection

How would you feel about a 360-degree feedback PA system if you were appointed to work in a country in Europe? In South East Asia? Elsewhere?

Training and development

The wider the spread of a MNC, the more training is needed. The reasons for this include: reaching common ground within the company; encouraging an exchange of knowledge within the company; and preparing internal people for different operations across borders (mostly, but not only, for expatriates). The standard training programme of a one-nation company becomes complex when it needs to accommodate the different educational systems in various countries. What may be perceived as global knowledge in one country may be an exception in another. Also, unless the training and development is restricted to executive positions, it will have to be translated into many languages.

In addition to the general challenges of providing comprehensive training and development around the globe, there is the need for specific training programmes for expatriate managers. Such programmes should prepare them for the local culture, operation, and management practices. The training should include the legal system, the financial system, and most importantly the local culture. In addition, language training is essential – it is important that the expatriate achieves a conversational level of competence in the local language. Many programmes try to involve the family also in such training – both cultural and language.

Cultural training should include various aspects of local ways of behaviour, and in particular the approach to negotiation. Baumgarten (1995) provides an overview of available options for cross-cultural training, and offers the following:

- Simulations (such as role playing, case studies, instructional games)
- Programmed instruction (cultural assimilation)
- Expositive instruction (e.g. lectures, tutorials, reading, and audio-visual presentations)
- Sensitivity training (as in T-groups)
- Behaviour modification methods (such as modelling)
- Field experience (i.e. visits, assignments to micro-cultures, and meeting with experienced former expatriates or locals)
- On-the-job training.

Industrial relations

Local industrial relations vary considerably between nations. In some countries, unions, although not necessarily concerned with career systems, may have a say in decisions on promotion.

This may go against the culture, ethics, and ethos of many American executives (where the level of unionization is less than 15% of the workforce), but is practical and relevant where most employees are trade union members, including managers. The union can object to certain appointments, and it may be wise to consult the union in advance rather than have a dispute later on.

Health and safety

The COVID-19 pandemic brought to attention the interplay between caring for employees' health beyond the physical boundaries of work.

A pause for reflection

Sometimes external circumstances prompt companies to employ untraditional methods. During the height of the AIDS epidemic, some companies started to consider whether they should provide condoms, free of charge (and encourage their use), to all employees. While this was not necessary in many countries, the AIDS epidemic led some companies in Africa, South East Asia and parts of Eastern Europe to employ such methods. Studying large Tanzanian companies at this time, Baruch and Clancy (2000) (see Box 8.4) found a high number of staff had been affected by AIDS, in particular when transportation employees were involved. This was found to be the case across all levels of the hierarchy.

As with the issue of PA, legal considerations in relation to health and safety matters will vary across nations. In addition, environmental effects may be relevant, and in some countries bodies such as Greenpeace can cause companies publicity problems, which might affect a company's reputation and people management issues (as happened to Shell UK in relation to the demolition of the Brent Spar oil rig, and to BP in their Deepwater Horizon oil spill industrial disaster in 2010 in the Gulf of Mexico). The basic issue concerns which standard the company should adopt – that of the home base, or the local one. Adopting the home base standard may ensure better health and safety conditions, but may prove more costly than the local standard, and thus might make the operation less competitive than other local operations. The decision will inevitably include ethical questions relating to the value the company places on the health of its local workers. A different situation arises when, perhaps to its surprise, the MNC discovers that the local regulations and customs impose a higher level of safety than is standard in its home country. This may be for security reasons (e.g. areas subject to terrorist activities), a hazardous environment (e.g. a tough climate), or an epidemic.

Box 8.4: Managing careers in areas affected by AIDS

Africa tends not to be a focus for global HRM studies, but nevertheless many MNCs operate in Africa. The AIDS epidemic posed particular challenges for MNCs operating in Africa, with discrimination against those affected by HIV/AIDS being a particular issue of concern. The general findings of Baruch and Clancy (2002) at this time was that discrimination against HIV/AIDS would not be tolerated in the long term by governments and public opinion, and would eventually become illegal in most places. In their study, they suggested that flexible career planning be implemented, with regularly updated succession plans, as well as the following support mechanisms:

- Support groups
- Education and promotion of initiatives to support the prevention of AIDS
- Supply of medical advice and condoms
- Setting fair and reasonable policies for financial assistance in case of emerging
- cases and in cases of death
- Establishing organizational policies to cover:
  o recruitment and selection of new employees (without discrimination)
  o insurance
  o career management – succession planning
  o educational programmes, brochures, and other information available
  o training on appropriate sexual behaviour at work
  o supply of reactive prevention (condoms) and active treatment
  o financial cover for those affected by AIDS.

Some issues were specifically relevant to MNCs operating in Africa. These mostly concerned expatriation and repatriation to and from Africa. Having staff completing overseas assignments in countries with high levels of AIDS posed an issue for some companies. Some of these companies which encountered resistance from some employees had to consider how employees could be compensated for undertaking these assignments (compensation, planned career path, fit with personal attributes, and so on.). Fair treatment and a proactive approach can improve a company's image and reputation. In particular, the proper treatment and support of company employees suffering from AIDS could help to enhance the image of the company for the larger population.

Expatriation and repatriation career strategies

Expatriation is the clearest manifestation of globalization from an HR perspective (Brewster & Scullion, 1997; Porter & Tansky, 1999). For the global organization, career planning, starting right from the recruitment stage, through to the top, should involve international assignments (Theuerkauf, 1991).

One indication of the problem career systems face when dealing with international assignments relates to failure. The literature indicates that failure rates are high. Even if it is a myth (Harzing, 1995), the costs of expatriation failure are high for both the expatriate and the organization, more than local failure, for two reasons. The failure may be defined as early return, poor performance on assignment, and lack of learning from the international experience. Leaving the firm within two years of repatriation can be a wider definition of failure.

One seminal classification of strategic approaches to global management strategy was offered by Perlmutter (1969). His classification differentiates among global organizational configurations: ethnocentric (home-country oriented), polycentric (host-country oriented), and geocentric (worldwide oriented). Later, Heenan and Perlmutter (1979) added regiocentric (region oriented). This classification (ethnocentric, polycentric, geocentric, and regiocentric) fitted well with the American international outlook in the second half of the 20th century, and it is still appropriate for many MNCs in the 21st century.

In the *ethnocentric* model, most or all of the decision makers in the host operation will be people from the home country, sent as expatriates from headquarters. The reasons for opting for such a strategy include: a lack of trust in local people, a need for strong control by the mother company, being in the initial stage of operations (before moving on to other strategies), or simply a lack of technological or of a specific type of knowledge in the host country. While these may be valid reasons, applying this model frequently suffers from a misunderstanding of local culture and local ways of working, which might hinder the success of the home country managers. Another undesirable outcome is that host-country managerial personnel are prevented from progressing beyond a certain level in the organization and as a result they might lose their motivation and move elsewhere.

The *polycentric* model favours the appointment of local personnel to managerial positions. This leaves locals with ample development options, helps in reducing the costs of expatriation, and the length of time it takes an expatriate manager to adapt to local conditions. In particular circumstances this model helps to overcome local political hurdles and sensitivities. The major problem with use of this model concerns contact between the home and host companies, which might suffer possible detachment as compared with the position under the ethnocentric model. The latter, in many cases, aims to transfer the home culture to the host country operation. Also, the whole idea of multinational/international/global integration is inapplicable under this model, as a segregation remains in place.

The *geocentric* model shows a way to overcome the problems of the first two models. The basic premise of the geocentric model suggests that there should be no issue of nationality when making appointment decisions in a MNC. The person most suitable for the job will get it, no matter what his or her nationality. While in principle this sounds like a 'best practice' approach, this model is quite utopian or idealistic, in the sense that it may take many years for such a model to be fully developed across the globe. In fact, this model works quite well within the USA (across the states), and can work in many European nations. This model, though, will not help in transferring home country and company core values and culture in the way the ethnocentric model does. In practice, moving people around on a continual basis is quite costly in terms of training and remuneration.

The *regiocentric* model is an attempt to compromise and divide an operation into several regions, with the effect being that people move within, but not across, regions. This model allows host-country nationals to develop their careers further than in the polycentric model, but the barrier is not eliminated, just moved to the regional level. It can be a good intermediate strategy until the MNC can move on to becoming geocentric.

Another influential framework was that suggested by Bartlett and Ghoshal (1989). Their categorization of MNC strategic models classifies organizations according to a two-dimensional matrix comprising level of integration and level of responsiveness. This matrix forms a four-quadrant model with the following categories: international (low on integration and responsiveness); global (low on responsiveness, high on integration); multinational (high on responsiveness, low on integration); and transnational (high on both).

The classification offers an alternative and complementary approach to that often featured in the literature. For example, Bartlett and Ghoshal's concept suggests a stages-based model, where firms can develop up to the final *transnational* stage. This strategic model implies that the HRM strategy, in particular in managing expatriates, is aligned according to the four levels. The transnational model, which is similar to Perlmutter's geocentric model, is the ultimate goal. Both present a utopian model rather than actual working cases. One exception, perhaps, is Nestlé – the Swiss company with less than 5% of its workforce and operations located in Switzerland.

In contrast, a model suggested by Baruch and Altman (2002) focuses on expatriation and repatriation as part of global HRM strategies. The model proposes five distinct options, each with their relative advantages and disadvantages, and not necessarily on a graduated scale whereby each model is expected to be better than the former. The options are grounded in practice, and can match organizational strategies in globalization for both the business and the HR function. This concept supports the strategic alignment of HRM with business strategy (Holbeche, 2009), and provides benchmarking for the strategic choices companies have to make in developing their policies and practices. All in all, the set of options reflects the variety of cultural perspectives of a global economy at the start of the 21st century.

This theoretical framework focuses on the HR management of expatriation and repatriation as part of organizational career systems. A five-option classification expresses a variety of approaches organizations may take in managing expatriate careers. The main contribution of this approach is to break the mould of the model to which many well-known blue-chip MNCs aspire. Many MNCs desire to become 'transnational', that is, borderless company, but Hu (1992) claims that, in fact, there exist only national companies, which operate across borders. The fact remains that in most cases most of the employees and operations or the management and headquarters are located in the mother company's country (Nestlé, mentioned above, and Shell, located in both the UK and the Netherlands, are well-known, but rare exceptions).

Baruch and Altman's (2002) five options are different models or approaches for organizations to adopt in managing expatriation and repatriation. These are based on several dimensions: values, time, global as opposed to local focus, individual as opposed to company criteria, and nature of the psychological contract. Each option implies a different organizational approach to the management of careers and the meaning of international assignment as a part of people's career within the organization.

The five options are discussed in the following paragraphs.

1. *The Global (or Empire)*: This is the 'archetype' large global MNC, with an established reputation in expatriation management. The Empire corporate philosophy views expatriation as integral to organizational life. Both individual and organizational expectations accept it when planning careers, and period(s) of expatriation are an inevitable part of the career path for any executive. Some may not wish to be expatriated, but in this they will deviate from the norm, and thus they will be excluded from the mainstream career path. For the Empire organization, globalization is not a goal as such. It is an inherent property and part of the organizational ethos. The company will have a comprehensive set of procedures and practices in place. Moreover, people in the company as well as those joining would expect expatriation to be at the core of their professional and managerial career.

2. *The Emissary (or Colonial)*: The Colonial company has established overseas markets and a long-term view as to its international aspirations; however, it is firmly rooted in a particular culture and this serves as the basis of its ideology, its power base, and its source of expatriates. It is characterized by an organizational culture indoctrinated with an ingrained obligation – a sense of duty backed with high commitment and loyalty. Under the Colonial option some people may be asked to accept an expatriate role, and in line with the ethos 'for God, King and Country' are not expected to refuse.

3. *Peripheral*: This model fits companies operating in peripheral locations, where the experience of expatriation is highly desirable. Here expatriation is a means of benefiting employees. Globalization for the Peripheral company is an expansion strategy, as local markets are insufficient to offer growth. Or indeed the company may have chosen to target itself as export oriented. What is different in the Peripheral option is that people will be queuing up to get the chance of expatriation. It will be perceived as a perk by both the individuals and the employer.

4. *Professional*: The Professional strategic option is based on buying in knowledge and expertise. Its goal is to concentrate on home-country strengths and keep its people within specified geographical borders. Hence, the ideology drives the organization towards outsourcing cross-border activities, and delivery through people external to the company. These may be local people or TCN specialists. The company prefers to use external people, in effect outsourcing the expatriation process.

5. *Expedient*: This is the emergent approach for newcomers to the global scene, which characterizes most firms in the process of developing policies and practices. An ad hoc and pragmatic approach, the expedient option is quite a 'mixed bag'. It encompasses a wide range of companies that are entering globalized markets or wishing to become global players.

The principles that form the basis for distinguishing among the options are discussed in the following paragraphs.

Values as the strategic drivers: be they at the individual, organizational or national level, underpin attitudes and behaviours. Values are the bedrock of a company's philosophy and, consequently, strategy, on numerous issues. So, for example, the core philosophy of the Global company may be portrayed by the idea of 'organization man'; the manifest ideology of the Emissary organization is 'spreading the gospel'; hedonism encapsulates the Peripheral ideas of expatriation as a perk; while the Professional option is based on confined transactional relationships. The Expedient strategy, driven by pragmatism and immediacy, thrives on entrepreneurial values.

The time dimension (or assignment length): for the Global employee, though the career may be construed as a string of relocations, each one is short term (usually no more than three years' duration); an Emissary expatriate may have a somewhat longer-term posting; the Professional expatriate opts for an extended period of expatriation voluntarily; the Peripheral as well as the Expedient expatriate experiences more erratic expatriation assignments, but for different reasons. For the Peripheral expatriate, it is a perk to be shared with the many; for the Expedient expatriate, expatriation is ad hoc and therefore less predictable.

Where to look for expatriates (orientation): for the Global expatriate, as with the geocentric or transnational model, geography is of little consequence, while for the Professional organization, an international focus means sourcing from outside the home country. The Peripheral organization builds on the eagerness of its employees to experience the big world; the Emissary organization expects its people to give up the security and convenience of the home organization. The Expedient organization, with its ad hoc emphasis, is likely to be inconsistent in its sourcing.

Individual as opposed to company criterion: the core of the Peripheral and Professional organizations is the individuals – whether the professional expatriates in the Professional option or employees' expectations in the Peripheral company – and it is the individuals who drive expatriation. The reverse is true for both the Emissary and the Global company, since it is the company's requirements that drive the process. For the Expedient company, resolutions will be ad hoc and variable.

What psychological contract? In the Global case, the psychological contract is open-ended, with the employee and organization anticipating a long-term career. For the Emissary option, it is relational, underscoring the mutual commitment of employee and organization. The Professional option is transactional (market based), as is that for the Peripheral option (based on the lure of a lucrative position). As for the Expedient option, the psychological contract has to be developed for each case.

As a result of these differences, the strategy for each option is influenced by the firm philosophy and ideology, as well as the aims of the use of expatriation. These will determine their policies and practices, for example, use or avoidance of TNC.

The five options are posited as 'archetype' models, while in reality organizations have to respond pragmatically in managing expatriation processes. Therefore, one often encounters variations, that is, a hybrid of two or more options.

Overall, globalization will continue, and while much depends on political trends and legal requirements, international careers will prevail in the future. Evidence suggests that individuals as well as organizations should evaluate the prospective benefits of expatriation as against the possible pitfalls and the investment needed.

Will repatriation be needed?

Where will your people end up? Borg (1988) offered four categories for identifying where people sent on an international assignment ended up (see Table 8.1). He found that only 38% of managers had a single global assignment and simply returned home. The rest either stayed in the country to which they were sent (25%), or moved on to a global career with several consecutive global assignments, some remaining abroad (22%) whereas 15% returned home after a series of assignments.

What Borg does not tell us is what happened to people who did not stay with the company. Departure is an indication of the indirect failure of either the expatriation or the repatriation.

Table 8.1   Ending global assignment?

	Single global assignment	Multiple global assignments
Ending up abroad	Naturalized	Cosmopolitan orientation
Ending up at home	Local orientation	Unsettled

Source: Adapted from Borg, 1988

What is failure, how many fail?

Several studies have tried to analyse the failure rate of expatriation. One problem with these studies is the lack of clear acceptance of the meaning of failure. One indication is an early return, a pre-planned departure from the role. However, a more comprehensive approach should take into account the level of performance (or lack of it) while on assignment. A wider perspective would take into account also repatriation failure, for example, leaving the company after repatriation (Baruch et al., 2016b). Of course, it is not merely the company, but also the host country of the MNC that will influence the prevalence, the nature, and the success or failure of expatriation. A possible reason for the discrepancy in the literature on failure rates may be due to differences among cultures. There is empirical evidence that failure rates in Europe and Japan are lower than in the USA (Harzing & Ruysseveldt, 2017).

One thing is quite clear: the costs of failure of expatriation are considerably higher than those for failing in a conventional job. The real cost must take into account the loss of training, relocation costs, and the indirect costs of loss of reputation and further difficulties in finding a replacement.

Therefore, the actual cost of failure depends very much on the specific assignment – the destination, the training undertaken, the salary, and the two-way relocation costs wasted. What cannot be calculated is the loss of reputation and the damage caused to the future of expatriation in the relevant organization. An estimate of the average costs (Mendenhall & Oddou, 1985) is in the range of US$55,000–80,000 per expatriation for US companies. Other costs, claim Dowling et al. (1994), include loss of political contacts, morale, and productivity. As elaborated below, the one who may pay the highest cost is the individual involved. And this will also mean a loss for the company, if the individual's decision is to leave the firm as a consequence.

What are the reasons for failure? The answer depends not only on company practice, but also on the cultural origin of the expatriate. Tung (1982) found that for Europeans and Americans, the major constraint was the inability of their spouse to adjust. The Americans added other factors, the fifth on the list being the inability of the manager to cope with larger overseas responsibility. In contrast, this was the first and major reason for failure for the Japanese expatriates studied. The spouse's inability to adjust came only fifth in the list of factors for the Japanese expatriates. (It is quite likely that cultural values relating to the role of women were of significance in this ranking. At the time the study was undertaken, most of the Japanese expatriate population were male, and this is largely true today. Another factor is that many of the spouses opted to stay in Japan rather than accompany their husbands overseas.)

The contact with the home country is important. Line managers can be changed, HRM might not keep track of expatriates. 'Out of sight is out of mind' can be the case for many expatriates, 'forgotten' in the process. Having mentor at the home country, can help for keeping the connection and avoid such occurances.

Other factors include the level of hospitability of the people of the host country. Paris is notoriously unsympathetic to foreigners, as vividly presented by Dowling et al. (1994). The climate also has an impact. People from Spain may find northern Canada or Sweden too cold, whereas people from northern countries will metaphorically melt in the heat of the Middle East. Other countries pose even more challenges for strangers, ranging from religious differences to terrorist activities and danger from frequent kidnapping. Business visitors to Georgia are advised to hire a bodyguard to accompany them. Assignments in Afghanistan and Iraq have cost the lives of many expatriates. Even the simple fact that alcohol is banned in many of the Gulf states could deter expatriates from spending a significant amount of time there.

Repatriation and reverse culture shock

One of the most neglected aspects of expatriation is the repatriation process. In many cases HR managers, line managers, and colleagues assume that people will just happily return home, in the belief that there is no place like home. However, this has been proven only too often to be a totally wrong assumption. Some of the problems stem from managerial and direct career issues. Others concern reverse culture shock (RCS), the effect whereby people are surprised and shocked to encounter a new culture when they return home to what is apparently known territory.

RCS occurs as a result of several sets of changes. First, people change. In terms of their managerial role, the expatriate assignment gives people an invaluable experience. Many are given greater responsibility than they have held before, perhaps as head of an operation, having to make strategic decisions. Upon returning home, they find that even if they are at a similar level in the organizational hierarchy, they become a 'cog in the machine', and the vast experience they have gained is not appreciated – as found by Baruch et al. (2002) in a company that lost some 50% of its returning expatriates within a couple of years of repatriation.

Even more disturbing may be the changes that occur in the company while the expatriate is away. At one extreme there is the full collapse or disappearance of the company, with the result that the returning expatriate comes back to an entirely different company from that which they left (see Box 8.5). Even more subtle changes can also have a strong impact – restructuring, widespread downsizing, changing of market niche – and all these would change the career system to which an expatriate might have been hoping or preparing to return.

Box 8.5: Return home to find your firm went bankrupt or merged

The following examples are firms that were bankrupt in 2020.

A decade ago, Oklahoma City-based Chesapeake Energy helped turn the US into a global powerhouse by pioneering fracking, the technique of extracting oil and gas from rock formations by injecting high-powered water and chemicals. By the end of June 2020, buried under a mountain of debt, it was bankrupt and delisted from New York Stock Exchange.

Perhaps the most recent 'big name' firm to go bankrupt is Hertz, with liabilities of $24.3 billion. The firm made a statement: 'The impact of COVID-19 on travel demand was sudden and dramatic, causing an abrupt decline in the company's revenue and future bookings.' The company – which began in Chicago in 1918 by renting a dozen Model T Ford cars – filed for bankruptcy after it had already furloughed or laid off 20,000 employees, or about one-half of its global workforce.

This is not a new phenomenon. Two decades ago, the Enron collapse meant that their expatriates had a new employer to return to. At about the same time, employees of both Mobil and Exxon found new home restructuring taking place – the expatriates returning 'home' found a totally new home of ExxonMobil.

In terms of cultural differences, people learn how things can be done differently, sometimes better. They gain an understanding of others in another culture. If they believe they have seen better working practices overseas, they will have an extremely difficult time trying to persuade their colleagues to adopt such practices back home (and will almost certainly make themselves unpopular in the process).

Box 8.6: Alcohol

In the USA, one cannot legally drink alcohol before the age 21. In the UK, the age is 18. In the Arabian Gulf, alcohol is banned in most places. In some cities in the USA one cannot purchase alcohol.

A returning expatriate may be critical of some practices in their home country, comparing them unfavourably with those in the country where they have just spent some time. (The same may be true of their children also.)

Different countries applied different strategies to deal with the COVID-19 pandemic, with a major impact on the ability of expatriate moves, including returning home.

Another issue is that while an expatriate is overseas, unexpected changes may occur in their home country. For example, an expatriate who spent three to five years overseas might have been very surprised at the huge growth in the use of smart phones, and could have found the disturbance they caused to social interaction annoying. Moreover, being away means being away from local networking, missing out on important, and less important, events. It creates 'black holes' of knowledge about what has happened during their absence. People might become out of touch and feel disconnected from their former culture, yet not really part of the overseas culture that they have now left behind.

CASE STUDY 8.3: DETACHMENT

Willem and his wife suffered severely from RCS when they returned to the Netherlands after six years in the UK and the USA. They found that both the country and the company to which they returned remained the same, whereas they had moved forward. Personally, they were expected by everyone, family and old friends, to return and revert to what they had been in the past. In the company, the same people who managed it six years before were still in the same positions. Willem was not able to express and implement the rich experience and knowledge he had gained abroad. The 'black holes' in their knowledge of day-to-day life at home left the family detached. After a couple of years of trying to settle down in the Netherlands, they decided to return to the UK. This was their way of overcoming RCS, and they saw the UK as a reasonable compromise between the European culture they loved, and the American Anglo-Saxon approach in which they preferred to work.

What relevance does the cultural gap or distance between the home country and the host country have on the level of RCS? I offer here two contradicting hypotheses, which refer to the cultural difference between the home country and the host country.

The first hypothesis suggests that the 'closer' the cultural differences between the home country and the host country, the *less* RCS impact will be experienced. This simplistic hypothesis relies on the theory of person–environment fit, and suggests that it would be easier to return to a culture after serving time within a relatively similar culture.

An alternative hypothesis suggests, on the contrary, that the 'closer' the cultural differences between the home country and the host country, the *more* RCS impact will be found. The case for this hypothesis reflects the idea that when there are huge, significant differences between the cultures, in particular when the host country is seen as a 'less desired destination', people do not 'get used to it', will not blend in or try to adapt to local patterns of work and non-work life. They will always be waiting to return home, not making any attempt to change themselves. On the other hand, if a person (and their family) spends a considerable time in a culture that is relatively close (e.g. Americans spending time in the UK or Australia), they can easily adapt to the host country culture, which is nevertheless different from their own, and on their return will experience different behaviour patterns, lifestyle, and so on.

Which hypothesis is valid is not known yet, but even the presentation of the hypotheses serves to challenge HR managers in planning and preparing expatriates for their return.

How can a company anticipate RCS, and what can be done? Can a cultural gap be measured at all? Measurement of 'culture' is a sensitive matter, and the main measure, that developed by

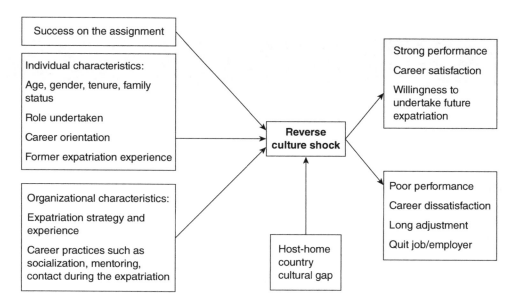

Figure 8.4 Factors affecting reverse culture shock

Hofstede (1980, 2011), is subject to debate. There are, however, other concepts for evaluating cultural differences, for example, the works of Ronen and Shenkar (1985, 2013) and Hampden-Turner and Trompenaars (2008) that can indicate the strength of the cultural gap. The model depicted in Figure 8.4 lists the factors that may influence the existence and level of RCS.

The implications for MNCs are very relevant. Identifying the problem is the first step in rectifying the outcomes. Recognition that repatriation requires attention will cause organizations to introduce repatriation programmes. Such programmes will be designed to prevent RCS, and will be tailored to each situation, and will depend on the cultures of both home and host country and the gap between them.

A pause for reflection

What will you do if, upon repatriation, you find that:

You have been forgotten by most of your former peers and superiors?

Most of your former peers and superiors have left while you were away?

Your place in the career development system has been taken by others?

The role formerly designated for you on your return has disappeared due to restructuring?

You (and your family) cannot easily re-adapt to cultural changes that have happened at home?

Your job is no longer involved with strategy making – you returned to become a cog in the operational machine?

During your expatriation, your mentor has quit, been transferred, lost status, and so on?

Now, what will you do, *while on expatriation*, to *prevent* the above or their consequences from occurring?

Virtual expatriation

Do we really need to expatriate people for them to operate for a company in a different country? Not always. Many call centres of UK companies are located far from the main premises of the organization. The first call centres were in Scotland, where unemployment was higher, and labour cheaper than in South East England, and companies turned later to India to gain even better cost effectiveness, using highly skilled employees in a low-paid area. Crabb (1995) tells us of how UK organizations employ people in India, benefiting from the wage gap, without moving people across borders: software engineers in India earn around £1,000 a year – a small fraction of the salary of their counterparts in the UK.

The employment of such people is very tempting for employers, and it does not require expatriation and repatriation, with all their difficulties and challenges. The application of new technology can save companies on the costs of their people management. Not all is bright, though: in practical terms there is a 5-hour gap in time zones between the UK and India, and this may cause operational problems (or cause Indian employees to work late at night). Politically, moving work overseas means fewer jobs at home, and this might cause political and image problems for companies, as happened in late 2002 to Prudential when they decided to close a UK operation and move the work to India.

The COVID-19 pandemic caused a very strange situation. The impact on different firms was subjected to sector differentiation. While hospitality (e.g. the cruise industry) was fully or almost fully halted, others flourished (e.g. Amazon). Many expatriates were 'locked' in their host countries. Travelling is not an option, so the globetrotters, expatriates and others succumbed to remote virtual 'visits'. As a result, it might well be that in the future there will be a significant reduction in business flights for travelling managers and experts.

Box 8.7: A case of timing

When planning a global meeting virtually, timing is of essence. The wrong setting will practically exclude participants who are located in specific time zones. For example, 9.00 a.m. in the USA is very convenient for Americans (both South and North America). It is also good for European countries, even falling within standard working hours if it is New York 9.00 a.m. as it is 3.00 p.m. in Paris, Berlin, and Rome. Less so if it is 9.00 a.m. in San Francisco, colliding with super time in Europe. As for the Far East, 9.00 a.m. in New York is 11.00 p.m. in Beijing and midnight in Tokyo.

Scheduling meetings with expatriates requires attention to this mundane element.

When I was the Editor of the academic journal *Group & Organization Management*, I had to communicate regularly with authors, reviewers, the publisher, and production staff. Only I lived in London, UK; the publisher, SAGE, is based in Los Angeles, 8 hours ahead, and the production took place in India, 3.5 hours behind. Stretching the daily working hours was a challenge, and expecting anyone to take it on a long-term basis is much to ask for.

Summary

The chapter focuses on the internationalization or globalization of careers and career systems. It starts with the individual perspective, trying to identify, if possible, the characteristics of global managers and whether a global psychological contract has developed. Global employability was presented as an expansion of employability. It proceeds to offer the general framework of the push/pull model to understand career movements, in light of different national and managerial cultures. Moving on from the individual to the organizational perspective, the chapter addresses two aspects of global career systems. The first is the implication for HRM and career management when HRM has to operate across borders (and the chapter discusses in depth the issues of remuneration, PA, training and development, industrial relations and health and safety). The second area is expatriation and repatriation, and the chapter presents three prominent models or frameworks for understanding expatriation and repatriation career strategies from the organizational perspective (at the three Ps levels: practice, policy and philosophy). The chapter ends with a discussion of the RCS phenomenon.

KEY TERMS

Bartlett and Ghoshal's classification (international, global, multinational and transnational)

Baruch and Altman's classification (global, emissary, professional, peripheral and expedient)

Expatriation

Global career

Global employability

Global manager

Glocalization

Perlmutter's classification (ethnocentric, polycentric, geocentric and regiocentric)

Repatriation

Reversed cultural shock

The push/pull model

DISCUSSION QUESTIONS

LESSONS AND FOOD FOR THOUGHT

1. *For the working student*: What will make you agree, or be willing to accept (or dissuade you from accepting) an international assignment as your next job? In five years? Are you proactive or reactive in reaching your career goals? What kind of company model best matches your own organization?
2. *For the student nearing the end of their studies*: What will you do to improve your global employability?

3. *If you aim to become an HR consultant*:

    a. How prepared are you to provide advice to people seeking a global career route? Which questions will you ask a manager before advising on a change to an international career? In what ways might your approach be different for female managers?

    b. Which organizational policies and practices will you suggest to an organization that wishes to embark on an international operation in the following countries: Germany, Sweden, Peru, Saudi Arabia? Can you analyse an organizational approach and place it within one of the models described in this chapter?

Equality, Diversity, and Inclusion: Careers Perspective

9

LEARNING OBJECTIVES

After reading this chapter you should be able to:

- Define equality, diversity, and inclusion
- Distinguish between a variety of diversities
- Identify the advantages and possible pitfalls in managing diversity and inclusion
- Understand the impact of diverse individual backgrounds on careers
- Distinguish between the legal and managerial arguments in managing diversity
- Understand the role of diversity in career systems management

Chapter outline

What is diversity?

No two people are the same. We all have unique qualities. Each person possesses a distinctive combination of internal and external characteristics that makes them different from any other person. Yet we share many characteristics with certain other people, forming collectives of groups with specific common characteristics (e.g. gender, skin colour, etc.).

Within the work-realm, organization and career context, 'diversity' relates to the existence of a variety of subgroups in the workforce. The dominant group in Western countries and many others are White men. In the past White men comprised most of the workforce, but this has changed, as they now form less than 50% of the workforce; for example, in the USA, only some 60% of the population are (non-Hispanic) White, and half of them only are males. Despite this, White males still hold the majority of managerial positions, and this disproportionate representation increases the higher up the organizational echelons one travels. White males' salaries are higher than those of women and other under-represented, most often disadvantaged groups. The substantial earnings gap between men and women varies in level, according to the country, the profession, and the sector. It is not unusual to find a 20%, 30%, or higher pay gap.

Under-represented groups include women (being the largest group that suffers discrimination) ethnic minority groups, people with a physical or mental disability, minority religion groups, older and younger people (although discrimination against older people is more prevalent in labour markets), LGBT+ people and people with different nationalities. And the list is not conclusive. Most of these sources of diversity are observable or easily detectable (e.g. an accent that reflects a national origin), whereas some are not clearly identifiable (e.g. sexual orientation, religion, some disabilities). Harrison et al. (1998) and Harrison et al. (2002) refer to 'surface-' versus 'deep-'level diversity. Surface-level diversity refers to demographic, mostly visible characteristics, whereas deep-level diversity refers to attitude or approach. They claim that the effect of time will mostly neutralize the effect of surface-level diversity, and will enhance the effects of deep-level diversity.

Box 9.1: Ethnicity, gender, and earning variations: The case in the USA

Among the major race and ethnicity groups, Hispanics and Black people continued to have considerably lower earnings than White and Asian people. The median usual weekly earnings of full-time wage and salary workers in 2019 were $706 for Hispanics, $735 for Black people, $945 for White people, and $1,174 for Asian people. The earnings for White men ($1,036), Black men ($769), and Hispanic men ($747) were 78%, 58%, and 56%, respectively, of the earnings of Asian men ($1,336). The median earnings of White women ($840), Black women ($704), and Hispanic women ($642) were 82%, 69%, and 63%, respectively, of the earnings of Asian women ($1,025).

Source: BLS Reports, 2020

What is inclusion?

The distinction between diversity and inclusion is that *diversity* refers to differences within a group, and *inclusion* is about how those different members are treated and how they feel (Puritty et al., 2017). When inclusion does not happen, people from less-represented groups may feel excluded, and opt out of the system, for example, quit or withdraw. A stream of the literature focused on the question whether women tend to 'opt out' or are 'pushed out' of leadership positions by the dominant male leadership (Kossek, Su, & Wu, 2017).

Inclusion may be considered as the extent to which specific employees are accepted and treated as an insider by others. This influences the degree to which individuals can access resources, gain information, be involved in work groups, and have the ability to influence decision-making processes. It is focused on the level to which individuals feel a part of critical organizational processes. The outcome of true inclusion is the ability of employees to contribute fully and effectively to an organization, no matter what their background is: 'There is a critical difference between merely having diversity in an organization's workforce and developing the organizational capacity to leverage diversity as a resource' (Roberson, 2006, p. 234).

Shore et al. (2011) studied inclusion and diversity at the work group level, and presented a typology based on the level of belongingness perception and the level of value in uniqueness (see Table 9.1).

Table 9.1   Levels of belongingness perception and value in uniqueness

	Low belongingness	High belongingness
Low value in uniqueness	Exclusion: The employee is not treated as an insider and not as offering unique value	Assimilation: The employee is treated as an insider when conforming to the dominant values, norms and culture
High value in uniqueness	Differentiation: The employee is not treated as an insider but as one offering unique value	Inclusion: The employee is treated as an insider and as one who is allowed or encouraged to be unique

What is discrimination?

Discrimination means treating people unfavourably because they belong (or are perceived to belong) to a certain subgroup. This discrimination will usually be illegal if it is not anticipated that their belonging to the subgroup will influence performance in the job. A typical example is of women being overlooked when a promotion becomes available, or having significantly lower salaries than men in equivalent roles. Discrimination can apply in many ways, even against White males. In practice, though, it is usually people from minority groups that suffer from discrimination, and when intersectionality – belonging to more than one minority – for example, non-White people with a disability (Crenshaw, 2017), then the discrimination can be even stronger (Baruch et al., 2016b).

Most discrimination on the basis of diversity is illegal, but not all of it. Discrimination on the grounds of nationality means that one cannot gain employment because of one's nationality – nationals of some countries may need to have a work permit, and gaining this requires substantial efforts. Within the EU, however, EU nationals can work in any country without the need for a work permit. For some employers, sexual orientation is a cause for legal discrimination (e.g. this was the case in many armed forces, though by now some have changed their recruitment procedures to allow for it). The legality of these kinds of discrimination is highly contentious and misaligned with many organizational cultures and human rights perspectives.

Discrimination does not need to be direct. Indirect discrimination occurs when one condition or requirement for a job or a position implies that the person belongs to a certain group which is then discriminated against. For example, a job advertisement may state that candidates with disabilities are encouraged to apply, but the office in which they are expected to work might not be fully accessible. A different case in the UK found that relying solely on referrals or recommendations for hiring in a plant where most of employees were White males constituted indirect discrimination against Black people.

Terminology counts too. It is important to use the right language to avoid causing offence. For example, in the USA, it is preferable to use the term 'African-American' to 'Black'. It is also more appropriate to refer to 'people with a disability' instead of the previously used term 'disabled people'.

The outcomes of discrimination can be in terms of poor representation of minority groups in the higher echelons (promotion), or in lower pay. The pay gap is a well-documented issue. For example, in the context of gender discrimination, there are four recurring themes related to the gender pay gap (Bishu & Alkadry, 2017). The first is about various estimations of the extent of the magnitude of the gender pay gap. The second investigates disparities in access to workplace authority as a driver of the pay gap. The third focuses on the HRM aspect of access to hiring and promotion practices as moderators of the pay gap. The fourth relates to the relationship between pay gap and gender representation (agency, occupation, and position segregation).

What is management of diversity?

'Management of diversity' means working systematically towards a workplace where the composition of the employees' diversity will reflect that of the general society. This involves taking proactive steps to promote a culture and atmosphere of equality and to ensure that there is no unjustified discrimination in the selection of people – both entering the organization and in promotional decisions. These can be the practice of recruitment and selection of new entrances, education and training of the existing workforce, career development initiatives (e.g. ensuring promotional opportunities for all), and specific practices such as mentoring – all with the aim of increasing and retaining workforce heterogeneity within the organization.

Inclusion would be the outcome of effective diversity management. By 'diversity' we refer to demographic differences among staff members. These can be observable, such as gender, race, age, or non-observable attributes such as culture, cognition, education, or a combination. Some can be hidden or open, for example, religion or sexual orientation. Diversity is considered a characteristic of a work group or organization. 'Inclusion', in contrast, refers to employee perceptions that their unique contribution to the organization is appreciated and their full participation is encouraged (Mor Barak, 2015). The relationship between these concepts indicates certain similarities but also distinctions (Roberson, 2006).

The issue of discrimination and diversity research is longstanding, and is covered by different streams of literature. Some are within the specific domain (e.g. gender studies, disability, etc.), and others are related to human resource management, for the context of people management and mismanagement (Triana et al., 2021).

Why manage diversity?

Aside from ethical and human rights perspectives, two of the key business reasons why organizations should manage diversity are: the legal aspect; and organizational performance, effectiveness, and outcomes. To be more explicit, Cox and Blake (1991) presented six managerial arguments to support the management of diversity in organizations:

1. *Cost*: the organization needs to be able to manage the full spectrum of the workforce, including segments that in the past were marginal, but are now becoming more dominant. Failing to do that will be costly and will prevent organizations from achieving full productivity.

2. *Resource acquisition*: Organizations with a favourable reputation for positive management of diversity (e.g. being in the Fortune 100 Best Employers list) will attract the most talented members of diverse groups.
3. *Marketing*: Organizations serve and produce for multicultural and diverse societies. A diverse workforce will have better insights and sensitivities to the needs of a diverse customer base.
4. *Creativity*: A diverse workforce should enhance the level of creativity and innovation.
5. *Problem solving*: A diverse workforce should produce high-quality decisions and solutions.
6. *System flexibility*: The better the management of diversity means more flexibility and faster and more efficient responsiveness to environmental changes.

Organizations are moving towards using the business case rather than the legal arguments in adopting alternative approaches to managing diversity. More specifically, the prospects of attracting ethical investors and government support are greater for organizations that practice positive management of diversity (Cassell & Kele, 2020). The ideas presented by Cox and Blake (1991) have been echoed by many. Organizations which apply practices to help tackle discrimination, for example flexibility practices (such as work–life balance or flexible work policies), are supporting diversity, but might be insufficient to enhance gender equity (Lewis & Humbert, 2010).

These arguments should help organizations, not just to note the issue of managing diversity through the eyes of the legal adviser, making sure they comply with the law, but to value diversity as a source of strength and competitiveness. Combining ethical and moral perspectives with cost-effectiveness and managerial best practice will result in recognition of the need to manage diversity for both strategic and pragmatic reasons.

Greenhaus et al. (2019) present two schools of thought on why organizations should manage diversity. One approach recognizes that the world and the workplace are becoming increasingly diverse. This trend is inevitable, therefore organizations must accept this new demographic reality, that is, hire and develop the most talented individuals from varying backgrounds in an effective and fair manner. Diversity is a fact of life and here to stay (and expand). The other approach goes further than seeing diversity as a necessity, and argues that diversity is inherently healthy and beneficial in its own right. This approach assumes that employees from different backgrounds will bring different strengths and perspectives, which, in turn, will enhance effectiveness.

In line with the first approach is the fact that certain changes in the composition of the workforce in Western societies are making the management of diversity even more acute and complex (Syed & Ozbilgin, 2019). Already in the last century it was noted that three groups have increased representation in the workforce: first, women; second, ethnic minorities (some of this increase was due to immigration and some to lack of parity in internal growth rates); and third; older workers, as we witness the phenomenon of the ageing of the working population (Syed & Ozbilgin, 2019). Other groups include people with disabilities and varied religious and cultural backgrounds. Following societal changes, the diversity of sexual orientation is becoming more prominent, as people today are less reluctant to hide their sexual orientation. It was found that within organizations, individuals who are actors for social movement can change organizational policies, though implementing such commitments or policies is challenging. LGBT+ advocates have developed resources to ensure that diversity policies were increasingly relevant for sexual minorities, as found for the case of France (Buchter, 2020). She found that LGBT+ rights activists increased their influence by developing implementation resources that corporations could readily use to introduce or revise their diversity policies and practices to promote the inclusion of LGBT+ employees.

Are the arguments presented in the second approach (the business case) valid? Studies on diversity in top management teams (Opstrup & Villadsen, 2015) indicated that diversity leads to more effective decision-making processes and better organizational performance. This may be due to the process of sharing and benefitting from a variety of perspectives and ideas. Promoting women and members of other under-represented groups into top managerial jobs is not always simple, but can be done with the right attitude and managerial support. In the end, the outcomes for the organization will be positive, as found by Harel et al. (2003) (see later in this chapter for elaboration of this point).

Whether one adopts the first approach, the second, or both, the consequences are that diversity should be managed.

A pause for reflection

How much of managing diversity is truly aimed at inclusion and how much is addressing political correctness?

Are there risks?

Is diversity inherently good? Should we expect only positive outcomes from diversity? It is argued that there can be some negative aspects of increasing diversity, and these are more severe if diversity is not introduced properly into the organizational culture. For example, sexual harassment is a serious misbehaviour (Fitzgerald & Cortina, 2018), yet, in a hypothetical single-gender workplace there would be no cases of men (or women) harassing women (or men). While earlier studies suggested negative outcomes of a lowered attachment of white people and males (Tsui et al., 1992), later work identified positive organizational outcomes (Gilbert & Ivancevich, 2001). As for decision making, evidence does not suggest that heterogeneous teams make better decisions (Martin-Alcazar et al., 2012).

Are the risks strong enough to discourage organizations from managing diversity? The answer is clearly negative. As indicated, diversity should be embraced. However, risk should be managed too, and awareness will help in prompting the setting of mechanisms to tackle any possible negative outcomes.

Awareness, toleration, and change

Lack of inclusion and respect is no longer tolerated by populations that have been oppressed and undermined in many ways throughout history. This is exemplified in Table 9.2 with the two cases of #MeToo and BlackLivesMatter. These are two influential movements; the focus of the former is more on work-related issues, whereas the latter is more about the basic element of life and resilience. Other forms of institutional fighting of discrimination exist at many national levels and globally, such as the Convention on the Elimination of All Forms of Discrimination against Women, which was adopted in December 1979 by the United Nations General Assembly. The Convention establishes not only an international bill of rights for women, but also an agenda for action by countries to guarantee the enjoyment of those rights. Whereas the principles and ideas are sound and accepted by many (though not all – see the case of Turkey), the reader should realize that over 40 years later, discrimination against women is far from being eliminated.

When it is not recognized, women suffer even more. In 2021, the Turkish President Erdogan issued a decree, annulling Turkey's ratification of the Istanbul Convention on violence against women. The protest that followed has not changed much at the time of publication.

Table 9.2   An overview of #MeToo and BlackLivesMatter

#MeToo	**Black Lives Matter**
#Me-Too is a social movement set against sexual abuse and sexual harassment. Under this movement, people publicize allegations of sex offences and crimes. It varies with context, for example local or international.	BlackLivesMatter was founded in 2013. It is a global organization in the US, UK, and Canada, whose mission is to eradicate white supremacy and build local power to intervene in violence inflicted on Black communities by the state and vigilantes.
It is a movement set to improve social justice and empower individuals to break silence (mostly but not just, women), doing so through empathy and solidarity and strength in numbers. The idea is that by making sexual abuse and harassment visible and showing how many women have survived sexual assault and harassment, especially in the workplace, the phenomenon will no longer be accepted as a reality.	The organization states: "By combating and countering acts of violence, creating space for Black imagination and innovation, and centering Black joy, we are winning immediate improvements in our lives."
	It is a movement striving for a world where Black lives are no longer systematically targeted for demise. It aims to contribute to society, and to resilience in the face of deadly oppression. The call for Black lives to matter is a rallying cry for ALL Black lives striving for liberation.
	Taken from: https://blacklivesmatter.com/about/

Managing diversity – releasing the hidden talent

Today, we live in a society that is, on the one hand, more conscious of diversity, but on the other hand, much more litigious (Baruch, 2001a). This means, amongst other things, that people have learned to safeguard their rights. The American phrase 'see you in court' means that an increasing emphasis is being put on being legally sound. Thus, one of the major impetuses for discussing the management of diversity is the possibility of discrimination and the means of preventing it in order to avoid litigation. The issue that should, however, take precedence, and was only recognized in the last few decades, is that of performance, as mentioned above. The effective use of the diverse competencies of a diverse workforce makes good business sense. Managing diversity should take the form of a holistic approach to creating a corporate environment that allows a variety of people to reach their full potential in pursuit of organizational goals and targets.

There are several interventions that organizations can adopt to tackle and manage diversity in an effective manner. These are strategic approaches, which are translated into practices for dealing with diversity, some positive, others negative (Kinicki & Kreitner, 2012). The most positive ones are inclusion, building relationships, and fostering mutual adaptation. Inclusion can follow AA programmes, when organizations may actively work to increase numbers of diverse employees at all levels. Fostering mutual adaptation happens when people recognize and embrace differences, and agree that everyone is free to be themselves and to grow, thereby allowing the greatest accommodation of diversity. Less positive interventions are trying to deny that differences exist, thus ignoring any possible impact of demography, trying merely to tolerate differences, or trying to assimilate minority groups so they learn to fit in and become like the dominant group. Worst are suppressing, discouraging differences to maintain the status quo, or isolating, maintaining the current way of doing things by pushing diverse people onto the sidelines.

Hybrid or multiple approaches can be applied simultaneously within any specific organization. Applying a positive response can be taken as a best-practice approach, leading to a general positive view of life and work thinking, such as positive psychology (Hart, 2021).

The first stage in managing diversity is recruiting a diverse workforce. Therefore, specific attention to diversity should be reflected in the selection process, for both the performance and legal arguments. Typically, employers focus on compliance with equal employment opportunity (EEO) and affirmative action (AA) legislation in the context of diversity – for both recruitment and promotion. In a complementary way, valuing, developing, and making use of diversity can lead to better performance. Diversity can be managed through effective HRM and specific career practices (Shen et al., 2009).

Diversity-oriented selection and recruitment practices in organizations can improve diversity, but needs to go beyond the formal application of HRM (Rivera, 2012). Organizations should ensure that their selection practices are non-discriminatory and continue their goals of increasing diversity. An analysis of such practices would include validating tests (e.g. use of CVs/resumes that show a person's age, gender, or photo) and performing job analyses to ensure that potential candidates were not unnecessarily and unjustifiably excluded. Interviewers would be diverse, including members of the population to which the pool of applicants belonged. Interviewers would be aware of potential biases that might exclude diverse workers or which might alienate diverse workers during recruitment and selection processes.

To reach a successful inclusion agenda, organizations should start with awareness, move to appreciation, and end up with an effective management of diversity. Valuing diversity is crucial (McMahan et al., 1998). It refers to the desire to include and use the assets of workers from various groups as potential employees, rather than excluding or limiting contributions of any potential employee because of any factor related to diversity.

Organizational approaches to tackling discrimination and improving inclusion

Many HR managers put an increasing emphasis on tackling all possible kinds of discrimination. EEO and AA legislation are high on the agenda, especially in relation to gender. Towards the end of the 20th century the phenomenon of the 'glass ceiling' effect was recognized. It means that women were often not promoted above a certain managerial level (Morrison et al., 1987a). According to Morrison et al., the glass ceiling is 'a transparent barrier, that kept women from rising above a certain level in corporations' (1987a, pp. 13 & 124). By the start of the 21st century, most of the glass ceilings were at least shattered, namely by women managed to reach top positions – yet, in many cases, those who made it were one-off cases or 'token' appointments, and the majority of top management teams, certainly CEOs, comprise men.

Many programmes are meant to support the population discriminated against, sometimes even to create 'positive discrimination'. It is important, though, that such 'positive discrimination' does not imply abandonment of selection according to skills, competencies, and suitability for the job. There is always a danger that positive discrimination could result in choosing someone with lower skills and qualifications, reducing future prospects of success for underrepresented populations. One well-documented phenomenon is the 'glass cliff' (Ryan et al., 2016), where women are disproportionately represented in leadership positions that have low chance of success.

Problems of discrimination exist for many groups, not just for women. Ethnic background, disability, age, and religious belief can prevent appropriate people from making their full contribution. For example, mass early retirements accepted by or imposed on people in their 50s might deprive organizations of a pool of talented and experienced people. People with disabilities can be disadvantaged where they are not supported with the right practical adjustments to enable them to fulfil their role. Organizations that recognize these issues will benefit from pursuing different career management practices for particular groups with specific needs.

Special programmes are not necessarily concerned with discrimination. The case of the single parent family brings up another issue that may require special attention, such as alternative work arrangements. The HR system must recognize this, especially where international relocations become necessary as part of career progress (Baruch et al., 2016a). The trend of globalization continues, and managing expatriates is still a crucial issue alongside other types of global mobility.

Beyond demographic factors

Diversity is not limited to demographic characteristics such as race, age, and gender, but has many not-so-obvious facets. First, there are the attitudes of employees, in line with the concept proposed by Harrison et al. (1998), of surface- as opposed to deep-level diversity; and second, the diversity may relate to variables such as work arrangements (contingent as opposed to the core workforce) in the organizational context and social status in the social-level context.

Research has shown that diversity affects group processes and performance (Chatman et al., 1998). While here, I will focus mostly on personal characteristics as a source of diversity; other types of diversity exist, and will be discussed too.

The most obvious negative outcome of diversity mismanagement is the possibility of people being discriminated against, not because of performance, attitudes, or other job-related factors, but because of an irrelevant personal background (Triana et al., 2021). It is important to realize that in both selection and career decisions the aim is to 'discriminate' – between the right people (who should be selected, promoted, etc.) and the wrong ones. The 'discrimination' that takes place should be undertaken according to fair, accepted, and relevant criteria, and should comply with the law and with principles of management (best practice). If the 'discrimination' is based on irrelevant factors (e.g. gender, race, etc.), this is a real discrimination.

What is a real and relevant difference, and what is a stereotype? A stereotype is 'a preconceived perception or image one has of another person based on that person's membership in a particular social group or category' (Greenhaus et al., 2019. Some stereotypes can be positive; others are quite negative. Nevertheless, organizational career decisions should not be based on stereotypes but on merit.

Procedural justice and distributive justice

Procedural justice refers to the process by which norms are implemented. *Distributive justice*, on the other hand, refers to the actual outcomes of such procedures. Procedural justice can be viewed as the degree to which the rules and procedures specified by policies are properly followed in all cases under which they are applied. In an organizational context, procedural justice concerns the means (rather than the ends) of social justice (Furnham, 2005). For example, 'pay procedures are more likely to be perceived as fair (1) if they are consistently applied to all employees, (2) if employee participation and/or representation is included, (3) if appeals procedures are available, and (4) if the data used are accurate' (Milkovich & Newman, 1996: 62). The underlying assumption is that employees will accept and comply with organizational policies and decisions if they are based on fair and just procedures.

Justice refers not just to being treated with dignity and respect, but also to being given adequate information regarding these procedures (Cropanzano & Greenberg, 1997; Vermunt & Törnblom, 2016). Therefore, organizational career systems should ensure that the process is transparent. HRM practices, and in particular career-related decision processes, are highly relevant to the evaluation and acceptance of procedural justice, which engenders a culture of trust.

Procedural justice as reflected in HRM-related decision making has a strong effect on employees' attitudes and behaviours (Gilliland, 1994; Konovsky & Folger, 1994). People need to know that a fair rule exists, and that it is applied to all. Then, of course, there is the issue of whether the rules and procedures are translated into actual fair distribution (distributive justice).

A pause for reflection

Question 1

Think of ways in which the traditional management system can pretend to apply rules justly, but refrain from doing so.

Question 2

Will people accept and believe such a system, or will they realize what is going on and resent the system or even quit because it fails to deliver?

The virtuous versus the vicious cycle of diversity

The starting point for the model presented in Figure 9.1 is the current labour market in most industrial societies. Many populations that once were not represented in the workforce (people of different ethnic origin) or in the managerial workforce (women and people from deprived social classes) now have the opportunity to become equal partners. The question remains whether this right, though legally valid, is only on paper, or whether it is a reality, and if the latter, the effect of this reality for organizations and individual employees.

The first question to be considered is how far the wide diversity in the workforce is reflected in any specific workplace. Can we expect a similar distribution of diversity? What should be the reference level? For example, sometimes national statistics should provide guidelines, whereas in specific regions regional statistics should do so. As another example, the representation of Roman Catholics in the management or organizations in Northern Ireland should be higher than that in Wales, as there are more Roman Catholics in Northern Ireland than in Wales. Similarly, the expected percentage of Hispanics in the managerial workforce in San Antonio, Texas, should be higher than that in Seattle, Washington, whereas in Seattle one may expect to find more managers of Far Eastern national origin due to the geographical proximity.

On the other hand, one can and should learn from industries where diversity has been proven to work effectively. Such is the case of women and ethnic minorities in the legal profession, though gaps still persist in representation (Aulack et al., 2017). Different people bring different qualities, different perspectives and different inputs. This is what makes variety so beneficial, on the one hand, but also so challenging, on the other.

Following Harrison et al. (1998), we can refer to visible as opposed to invisible diversity. Some types of diversity are clearly visible (e.g. colour of the skin, gender), others less so (e.g. religion, sexual orientation). In the latter cases, it is up to the person whether or not to reveal these aspects of their identity. In a study that empirically tested deep-level and surface diversity, Harrison et al. (2002) investigated the impact of time on both types of diversity. Their data supported the model presented in Figure 9.2, showing that, as time passes, integration reduces the impact of surface-level diversity (mostly demographic factors), but increases the relevance of deep-level diversity, as a factor that is considered in recruitment decisions (Casper, Wayne, & Manegold, 2013).

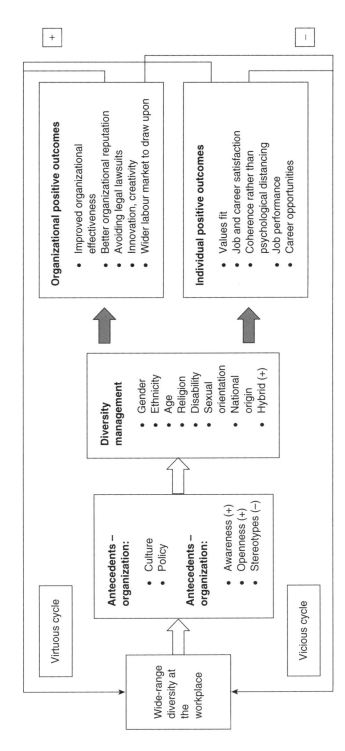

Figure 9.1 The virtuous versus the vicious cycle of diversity

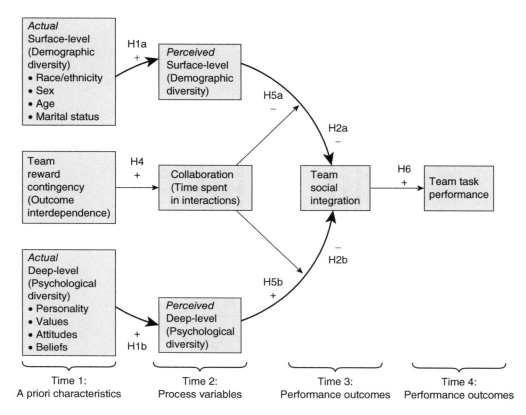

Figure 9.2 Intervening and interactive temporal mechanisms translating team surface- and deep-level diversity into social integration and performance (Harrison et al., 2002, p. 1030)

Clair et al. (2002) discuss the types of strategies people use to either reveal or 'pass' (i.e. hide) their invisible differences at work, the motives that lead people to reveal or pass, and the moderating effect of social and organizational context on the relationship between motives and strategies people use.

Building on social identity theory, Clair et al. (2002) identified several strategies for managing invisible, potentially stigmatized social identities at work. There are two basic strategic choices that individuals with potentially stigmatized social identities can make as they interact with someone at work: to hide (pass) or to reveal their invisible social identity. Within these two choices, there are a number of particular strategies that people may apply to pass or reveal their invisible difference during a workplace interaction. Passing is a category of identity management strategies, the outcome of which is to allow a person to be incorrectly classified by another person as someone without a discrediting or devalued social identity. Note that passing may also be unintentional. Individuals can rely on two different types of passing strategy: counterfeiting and evading. Counterfeiting is an active strategy of concealing part of the self to assume a false identity. An evading strategy results in passing because the individual evades all queries related to the invisible identity or social group membership in question.

Much has changed in society's attitude towards LGBT+ rights, and it is now much more frequent for individuals to be open about their sexual orientation, even in cultures where this was historically difficult (Papadaki & Giannou, 2021). This has implications, both positive and negative: the positive include improved psychological wellbeing and interpersonal relations, whereas the negatives are associated with social avoidance and disapproval as key costs by people holding homophobic views (Corrigan & Matthews, 2003). National and cultural differences play a crucial role in the actual outcomes of inclusion of LGBT+ people (Ozeren & Aydin, 2016).

While 'passing' is a category of strategies designed to conceal a potentially stigmatized identity or social identity group membership, revealing strategies are tactics designed to disclose to others an identity that would otherwise be invisible or unrecognizable. The three different revealing strategies Clair et al. (2002) propose are: signalling, normalizing, and differentiating. Individuals who signal are attempting to disclose their hidden identity, but rather than explicitly 'going public' and fully disclosing their difference, they send messages, drop hints, and give clues to those to whom they wish to disclose their full identity. Individuals employ a normalizing strategy by revealing their hidden, potentially stigmatized identity to others and then attempting to make their difference seem commonplace or ordinary, within the social norms of the organization, essentially denying that their identity matters. Differentiating means seeking to underscore difference, and this is sometimes done in an effort to change others' attitudes and behaviour.

The motives for choosing a strategy can be personal, instrumental, or both. For example, instrumental motives for revealing may be to obtain social support, to obtain accommodation, to create awareness, and to attempt creating social change. Of course, the organizational and cultural context will influence people's choice of a particular strategy.

A pause for reflection

What strategy would you adopt if you felt you were different? Why? How would you practice your strategy?

Specific groups and relevant issues

This section examines specific groups in terms of the following factors:

Demographic: gender, ethnic origin, age (young, old), disability, sexual orientation, religion.

Presence: deep-level diversity.

Intersectionality: existence of hybrid diversity (combining more than one possible source of diversity).

At its narrowest, the management of diversity refers to the propensity of an organization to have an appropriate EEO system of policies and practices to ensure that people are treated according to their abilities, competencies, contribution, and performance, rather than being judged by irrelevant factors. Therefore, gender discrimination and racial discrimination come into the so-called management of diversity. This is indeed a narrow approach. Unfair and unlawful discrimination can have a variety of grounds, as listed above. There is also a lawful discrimination when people of a different nationality face higher hurdles when applying for a job in a different country. With the rare exception of job searches within the European Union, countries actively discriminate against people of foreign nationality, refusing them employment unless they have a work permit (e.g. the US 'green card').

Box 9.2: Meet our first ...

The presence in senior management positions of members of groups that were previously the object of discrimination is often the result of the efforts of pioneering people. Many of the female executives studied by Morrison et al. (1987a) were the first women to reach that rank in their organizations. The same is true in relation to the first Black person in the job: Colin Powell was the first non-White Secretary of State in the USA, then came Barack Obama, the first non-White US President, and now Kamala Harris, the first female non-White Vice President. It can be about disability: the first blind person in a top political post was David Blunkett, a leading politician in the UK, an example that blindness does not prevent people from being able to lead, make tough decisions, and be part of the government. In many cases, the presence of these pioneers paves the way for the next generation of a diverse workforce.

It remains the case, however, that such appointments are sometimes made for reasons of image or publicity or to comply with legal requirements. 'Being there' as the first non-White male in a top role imposes a heavy burden on that person, who is put under strong scrutiny, knowing that if they are seen to fail, this will have a long-lasting impact for many future generations of non-White-males in the managerial ranks, in terms of public perception, rather than anything implicit. In other words, this could reinforce discriminatory views, rather than challenge them.

Gender variety

Women form some half of the population, but not half of the workforce. For two reasons it is difficult or impossible for women to make up exactly half of the labour force. First, in many countries women are forced or allowed to retire at an earlier age than men. Second, for biological reasons, many women do leave the workforce for a period to give birth and to care for their infants. Nevertheless, and to some extent affected by the greater involvement in recent years of fathers in caring for children, the trend is towards near-equality in terms of male and female participation in the labour force.

The negative aspect of this trend is that, in terms of the pay gap between men and women and promotion to top positions, the movement towards equality is much slower. Women still earn significantly less than men. The unadjusted gender wage gap varied from around 2% to 32% among OECD countries in 2018 (OECD, 2018), and the World Economic Forum (2020) reports a 31.4% gap globally – albeit women represent half of the world's population and human capital.

Representation at the top is even less equal, but, again, there are some improvements. When Morrison et al. published their seminal book, *Breaking the Glass Ceiling* (1987b), only 1.7% of corporate officers of Fortune 500 companies were women, and only one woman was a CEO. Among the 'very big names' in the early 2000s, Carly Fiorina was a pioneer female CEO when leading the merged HP/Compaq company. Now, 20 year later, many top leaders are women: Marissa Mayer as the CEO of Yahoo!, Susan Wojcicki of YouTube, and Mary Barra leading General Motors are just some prominent examples.

According to the Global Gender Gap Report 2020 of the World Economic Forum (2020), the average global (population-weighted) pay gap completed to parity is at 68.6%, which although is an indication of continuous improvement on recent years, is a major gap. It means that there is still a 31.4% average gender gap that remains to be closed globally. Unfortunately, the same report states: 'Projecting current trends into the future, the overall global gender gap will close in 99.5 years, on average, across the 107 countries covered continuously since the first edition of the report.'

The Scandinavian countries led the way in introducing women as equal partners into the employment realm and are top of global league table for the lowest gender pay gap (World Economic Forum, 2020). The origin for these achievements are rooted in developing new social models of gender equality at the end of the 1960s and in the 1970s (Moen, 1989). Much of the trend towards gender equality was supported by legislation (Enquist, 1984), and there is still considerable legal action to enable and encourage EEO in Western societies. Hull and Nelson (2000), for example, explore three different theoretical models of gender differences in professional careers. They discovered, in line with other scholarly findings (cf. Hall-Taylor, 1997), that differences in career path and achievements cannot be fully explained by career choice, and that there are constraints affecting women's development. Conversely and controversially, Hakim (2000) suggested that part of the lack of equality is due to women's self-defeating approach to careers.

Although more women start professional careers now than in the past, they often begin in lower-prestige jobs than, and make slower career progress than, their male counterparts. A better picture is found where more diversity exists, such as in the civil service (Barnett et al., 2000; Riccucci, 2018). However, both the employment world (i.e. the labour market and employers' attitudes) and personal factors create and maintain the glass ceiling. Nevertheless, diversity is not restricted to the issue of gender, as will be discussed later in this chapter.

The stereotype of women is that they are more caring and better in teamwork and at creating relationships than men. Women can bring different and beneficial skills to leadership roles. In certain roles these qualities are more important than others. However, in the tough current business environment, such qualities are not necessarily advantageous. It could be said that this argument is based on a stereotypical view of women; more studies are needed to identify if this is indeed the case for women in management.

Box 9.3: The Formula One story

Imagine that you are about to participate in a car race, and that all participants have quite similar cars, but some, including yours, need to have a pit stop about half-way through the race. The other cars do not need to stop. What influence would that knowledge have on you?

You may decide that it is not worthwhile to race at all, with such different conditions. Alternatively, you may be highly motivated to be faster on the first leg, to reach the pit stop as soon as you can.

Now imagine that you have reached the pit stop, and have experienced the hardships, the dangers, the risks, and rough fights that characterize such a race. Now you have some time to think, and you are given a choice: to return to the race, or to take a different route. If you rejoin the race you return to the stress and competition, but your car is heavier with fuel and more difficult to steer, and you have lost much time in comparison with your competitors. The other route will give you a lot of satisfaction and you will earn appreciation from the crowd. Thus, although it is different from the route taken by Formula One winners, it does provide a good incentive. It is not hard to imagine that many will choose the alternative option.

The kaleidoscope career model calls it 'opting-out' (Mainiero & Sullivan, 2006).

Let us clarify the car race metaphor. The drivers that have to stop in the race are women who have had children and taken maternity leave. And during and following the break, when they experience motherhood, many realize that there are other incentives and different appreciations for people that are not in the 'fast lane' of the rat race of organizational life. If this metaphor reflects reality, studies will show that young women develop faster than men in their early career stages, but after a time leave the race.

While metaphors can clarify matters and provide clearer insights, they are not always perfect (Inkson et al., 2015). One clear difference between Formula One racing and the rat race of organizations is that when cars pull into the pit stop, they do so in order to receive (petrol, tyres), whereas women who have children stop in order to give birth and while men can now take paternity leave, the majority of cases of child-care are still taken by women. Some may raise a moral question about the role of society in general in ensuring equity and fair play for all. A similar metaphor was presented by Lyndon Johnson, the then American president, in 1965, when he compared the race between men and women to a 100-yard dash in which the legs of one of the participants are shackled together. In view of the fact that the other has a clear advantage, the race is then declared unfair. What is the appropriate course of action in such a situation – is removing the shackles enough? In a race the answer is clearly no. In the business world, positive discrimination might produce some other injustice.

Initially, it was felt that the way forward was to legislate to ensure equal terms of employment, with the hope that succeeding generations would overcome the old gap. However, thinking on equality issues progressed, and in the UK the Sex Discrimination Act 1975 helped to prevent gender-based discrimination (the Act was extended in 1986). Similarly, the Equal Pay Act 1970 was enacted to ensure equal pay for similar work. When it came into force many organizations tried to 'beat the system' by offering women only lower-level jobs (and more poorly paid). Heavy fines, however, make it not worthwhile for companies to try to avoid the law.

CASE STUDY 9.1: SUPPORTING WOMEN

The Center for Development and Population Activities (CEDPA) in Washington, DC aims to support women worldwide. In line with the idea that weaker groups deserve special support, the Center has been running the Women in Management (WIM) programme with the aim of preparing women to lead development efforts for several decades. The results are impressive. Among the thousands of alumnae in 138 countries there are parliamentarians, ministers, NGO presidents, and network coordinators. As women's roles in public life have expanded, these CEDPA alumnae have been at the forefront in identifying and addressing the critical issues that women face in the 21st century.

The programme helps women to develop personal and organizational strategies to bring about sustainable development in their countries. It covers the following topics:

- *Leadership*: How to cultivate a constituency and a committed team of staff members.
- *Visioning*: How to develop shared goals and garner support from the grassroots to policy makers.
- *Management*: Techniques for effective resource management (including human, financial, and other institutional resources).
- *Communication*: How to use strategic communication to educate, motivate, and energize the public and institutions.
- *Donor relations*: How to engage donors in a long-term partnership.
- *Participation*: Methods to involve the community and other stakeholders in programme design.

A variety of other support and developmental programmes to help women in management exist, leading to positive results in developing women leaders (Debebe et al., 2016).

Women and entrepreneurship

Women are active in the business community, accounting for a growing number of business start-ups. Yet, current discourse of entrepreneurship fundamentally disadvantages women (Marlow, 2019). Starting one's own business can be seen as 'an easy way to escape', although it only appears easy, as many entrepreneurs will testify.

CASE STUDY 9.2: START-UP AS A CAREER SOLUTION

Adriana was a broker in the City of London. After working for a number of years in a large multinational investment bank, she and her husband decided to raise a family. Less than two years after her first son was born, Adriana felt she needed the action of business life, but did not want to give up her family responsibilities.

Her husband remained employed in another job in the city, the type she would have had if she had continued her career. As a result, she decided to start her own small business, from home. She opened a business importing hair accessories and manages it all from the convenience of her home, close to London. After a shaky start she is beginning to see that the business should survive and grow while her family benefit from her being at home.

There is support for the effectiveness argument in a number of studies. Drawing on the literature of HRM, women in management and organizational effectiveness, Harel, Tzafrir and Baruch (2003) suggested a model (see Figure 9.3) bringing these perspectives together into a single framework. Their model, based on an empirical study of 102 Israeli organizations, indicates a significant and positive association between high-quality HRM and fairness in promotion of women in organizations. Fairness in the promotion of women into managerial ranks was also found to be associated with higher organizational effectiveness.

Davidson and Burke (2011) summarize prominent research findings about women in management:

- There has been progress in the number of women entering management, but the pace is slow, and attention to this issue is still needed.
- Managerial job segregation by gender persists (women are found in HR, public affairs, communication, and law, but less in line management). One problem with such segregation is that such jobs rarely lead to executive-level positions.

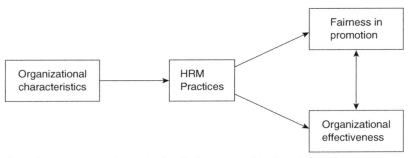

Figure 9.3   Fairness in promotion and organizational effectiveness (Harel et al., 2003)

- Intersectionality (hybrid diversity) (in their case, women of ethnic minorities) is even harder to overcome.
- Affirmative action is important for making progress towards closing the gap, although it might create problems such as tokenism and backlash.
- A new trend towards lean-and-mean business management may contrast with the (archetypal) qualities women bring to the workplace. Being mostly in mid-level management, they will be more dispensable than men.
- Flexible and alternative work arrangements might be superficial mechanisms that, in fact, limit women's career prospects.
- Women still carry higher responsibility than men in their 'second shift' work at home.
- Organizational culture tends to be mostly male culture, and this can work against women.
- The best argument for women in management should be the business case of implementation of resources.

Therefore, organizations should promote a culture where women and other minorities can succeed.

Gender identity

In the past, there were generally viewed to be two genders, male and female, but there is now greater recognition of other gender identities. There is still a long way to go on this front, and people who do not identify as exclusively male or female, who are non-binary or transgender, can face many forms of workplace discrimination; from not being able to access gender-neutral toilet facilities, to incorrect use of pronouns, or direct harassment. People may feel the need to 'pass' for fear of discrimination (Miller & Grollman, 2015).

Ethnicity

Race and ethnicity also produce a rich variety, and in many countries, the minorities comprise a combination of many different minorities. In the USA, the major groups of ethnic minorities are African-American, people of Asian origin (with Chinese, Indian and South-East Asian immigrants the source of this variety), Native Americans, and the fast-growing Hispanic people (mostly from Central and South America). It is estimated that by the mid-century, White people (non-Hispanic) will form less than 50% of the population (Craig & Richeson, 2018).

The racial issue goes beyond employment and careers. The Black Lives Matter movement has gained strong attention as it is concerned with the worth not only of the labour, but of the life of Black people (Szetela, 2020).

In the UK, many immigrants came from the former British Empire, including many from India and Pakistan, but other places too. In Germany, there is a growing community of Turkish-born immigrants. Other Western countries also have significant sub-populations of different ethnic origins. There have been continuous waves of migration from Africa to Europe, some for humanitarian motives, others are economic migration, which increases diversity minorities in Europe (Giménez-Gómez, Walle, & Zergawu, 2019), making countries like France and Sweden have significantly large sections of the population descended from Africa and the Middle East. Some of them arrived unauthorized, leading to further obstacles to enter the labour market (Carling & Hernández-Carretero, 2011).

In marketing and creative activities, ethnicity has to be taken into account. Some people may put greater trust in people of the same origin, when they encounter them in business situations, for example, representing companies in sales, negotiations, and deal making. Moreover, consumer companies that target the whole population should be aware of the specific needs and tastes of various groups within the population. Ensuring that the teams which make decisions about products and markets are representative and will make such targeting more effective. Such team members may also be a source of valuable (e.g. local) information.

Age

Age diversity in the workforce derives from the fact that those in work range in age from about 18 to 65, the formal retirement age in most countries. The two possible forms of age-related discrimination are that against young people and that against older people, with the latter gaining more attention from legislators and the media. The numbers of people of each age are easily identifiable, and trends are relatively simple to recognize.

There are several trends in relation to the age composition of people in the labour market. The age at entry has been rising as the proportion of school leavers who go on to university has increased, thus delaying their entry to the labour market (more than one-third of the current population in developed societies attend university, and the proportion will continue to grow). At the other end of the spectrum, we find people aged about 65 years are retiring from employment. So the main input for understanding age trends is the past birth rate. To take just one example, following the Second World War there was a large increase in births. People born in the late 1940s and the 1950s (termed 'baby boomers') entered the labour market in the 1960s, and these people are now approaching retirement. In contrast, in the following years the birth rate declined, so fewer people entered the labour market.

Developments in the age profile of workers have profound implications for the management of careers. Career structures that suited the traditional work attitudes of older generations do not suit the needs of more recent generations. Remuneration systems that reward seniority and tenure may prove too costly to maintain if there is a surplus of ageing employees in mid-level management, and might hamper a firm's competitiveness (Johnston, 1991). Another apparent problem is the tendency to perceive older people as reluctant to change, less creative, and with declining ability to undertake physical tasks. In many cases this is nothing more than a stereotype distortion. Some of these possible perceptions are invalid or irrelevant. Most older staff are not employed in manual labour, so the expected reduction in physical ability is irrelevant for them. For the few who are so employed, their wider experience may compensate for their declining physical power.

In managerial as well as clerical jobs, older employees are likely to possess wide knowledge and experience, and may prove to be more loyal and committed than younger personnel – qualities that will benefit their employees. On the other hand, as we saw in Chapter 2, these qualities are not always required in a world of redundancies, restructuring, and rightsizing.

Discrimination against young people may backfire too, as depicted in Case study 9.3. Such discrimination is problematic at the society level, as it might create a generation of people who will never enter the labour market.

CASE STUDY 9.3: TOO YOUNG, TOO INEXPERIENCED?

FinCorp is a large, established, and leading UK financial corporation. For generations they were known as a workplace that invested in their new talent, recruiting many graduates and training them as professionals in accounting, insurance, and so on. However, the firm realized that there was a consistent trend whereby young graduates who gained their first job with FinCorp tended to quit the company after some two to three years. They benefited from the investment and training provided, were able to put the name of FinCorp on their CVs, and were then happy to look elsewhere for jobs.

As a result, FinCorp decided to stop or reduce significantly their graduate recruitment and instead to hire people with a few years' experience. This way they would benefit from the investment that other companies put into their graduate recruits. But this also discriminated against young people entering the labour market.

The argument is clear, and to a certain extent the change in policy was effective. But are there flaws in the argument?

First, FinCorp should have checked *why* those graduates were leaving them. Maybe their compensation scheme was inappropriate? Even if it is an employer

(Continued)

who provides the training that makes an employee more valuable, the employer should recognize and reward that value. Maybe the roles offered to young managers were not challenging enough? Maybe they saw no future career prospects?

Second, by opting for this strategy, looking for people who are inclined to leave their employers, FinCorp would be able to recruit only people with a high tendency to quit their employers, that is, less committed staff. This may have been FinCorp's intention, but not necessarily. With their ethos of being an established firm, they need a core of able and committed people who are well integrated into their culture. By leaving it to other firms to provide professional training for those who may become FinCorp's future managers, FinCorp also has no control over the culture they may absorb – and it may be a culture that is not appreciated in FinCorp.

When formulating strategy and policies, organizations need to understand national-level trends. An ageing population, with falling participation rates amongst older workers, will adversely affect the labour market. The need to increase employment rates amongst older working-age women will become more and more important as employers face growing skill shortages.

The general ageing trend of the population in most developed countries is complicated due to increasing life expectancy, coupled with low birth rates. If older people will be excluded from the workforce, there will be fewer people to bear the burden of financing pensions for future generations. It is not merely for those over retirement age, but also many aged 50–65. This has led, amongst other factors, to the logical conclusion of abolishing retirement age or extending it (Baruch et al. 2014).

One challenge, which is a national rather than a company-level issue, is how to retain within the labour market the huge number of people forced to take early retirement, preventing them from becoming an unproductive, declining, and frustrated group. This trend is exacerbated by the 4th industrial revolution (Schwab, 2017), which may cause older generations to be in a position of lack of employment opportunities. Moreover, many of these people need to work in those final ten years or so of their working life in order to secure a reasonable level of pension income, otherwise they will become a burden on their close family and community. People forced to leave employment after a certain age will find it hard or practically impossible to rejoin the labour market. In some industries such as IT being over 40 means 'old'. Not employing these people is a waste to both organizations and society.

On the other side of the coin there are young people who feel that they cannot get proper job offers because they are too young, although they may be well qualified and trained for the jobs they apply for. One indirect impact of age on careers is that older workers may not hold the work attitudes and career perceptions an organization may expect its employees to hold. Attitudes are part of the 'deep' level of diversity discussed earlier in this chapter.

Disability

To benefit from a wider talent pool, as well as to act with social responsibility, organizations should employ people with disabilities (PWDs) (Kulkarni et al., 2016).

A significant share of the population has a mental or physical disability, and their employment levels are far below those with no disability. According to the US Bureau of Labour Statistics (2020), in 2019, 19.3% of PWDs were employed. For those without a disability, the figure was 66.3% employed in 2019 (US Bureau of Labour Statistics, 2021).

PWDs suffer lack of employment opportunities and career growth options available to their counterparts without disabilities (Bonaccio et al., 2020). They experience discrimination, stereotyping, and barriers to the employment (Mackelprang & Salsgiver, 2016). As a result, many tend to end with low employment, low-pay, job insecurity, and poor quality of life (Shantz, Wang & Malik 2018).

Due to past moral pressure, there are both legislative and government obligations on employers to recruit people with disabilities. The argument for doing so is not, however, merely ethical: PWDs prove to be highly loyal members of the workforce, with much lower turnover rates than others (e.g. Pogrund, 2018).

Physical disability

Physical disabilities are often visible. Managing diversity based on physical disability should in theory be simpler than managing other types of diversity. It is relatively easy to identify whether the physical problem would prevent, hinder, or interfere with the performance of the job. If the answer is negative, people should not be discriminated against on the grounds of that disability. In fact, organizations may benefit from the stronger level of commitment of such people, who have been accepted in spite of their disability. Further, the effects of physical disability are felt more in the realm of manual work than in managerial positions. The higher the level of managerial responsibility, the less the physical dimension matters.

Mental disability

There are plenty of jobs which people with learning difficulties are entirely capable of performing well. People with an intellectual disability are often extremely well motivated, loyal, and appreciative of their employers. Other learning difficulties may not prevent people from taking on managerial roles (e.g. dyslexia, a problem of reading/writing that is not concerned with intelligence or ability to communicate).

One additional challenge for an organization employing people with any disability or difficulty is to facilitate their induction so that appropriate adjustments and support systems are in place and their colleagues and managers feel equipped to discuss and support their requirements. As stated above, both on moral grounds and from the business case argument, employing people with disabilities may be best practice.

Religion

Religion can be a very highly emotionally charged issue. However, there are very few jobs or careers that require membership of a particular religion, and these are not found in business firms. In places like Northern Ireland, however, there is clear segregation between the communities, which is reflected also in the labour market and in the composition of the workforce in workplaces.

Sexual orientation

Sexual orientation can be an even more emotionally charged issue than religion, as some individuals object to people of non-conventional sexual orientation on moral grounds. No matter whether a person is an accountant or bricklayer, what they do in their private life remains their own business. Again, companies that will not recruit such people lose a wide pool of talent. The true number of non-heterosexual people is not clear, and can be anywhere between 2 to 13% (Day & Greene, 2008), as it is not easily disclosed.

When people feel that they are forced to keep their sexual orientation secret, their job satisfaction and commitment will deteriorate (Day & Schoenrade, 1995) because of the stress and negative feelings that accompany the need to hide something of such importance from close colleagues. On the other hand, companies may make changes to their policies so that benefits usually provided only for the spouses of employees will be made available also to same-sex partners. Otherwise they might find themselves in court, as was the case with El Al, the Israeli airline, which was forced to provide free flights to partners of stewardesses.

Deep-level diversity

Deep-level diversity mainly comprises attitudes and personalities. Different attitudes lead to different work behaviours, as discussed in Chapter 1 (the Fishbein–Ajzen model). Beliefs influence attitudes, and therefore organizations can and should train and educate people to value differences and to have beliefs based on facts rather than prejudice. When the various attitudes that exist in the community are reflected in the variety in an organization, the match between people and the organization, and between the organization and the environment, is greater.

People have different personality traits and factors. Cattell's 16PF model (discussed in Chapter 2), for example, shows 16 dimensions according to which people differ, and different roles require different personality profiles. For example, toughmindedness may be needed for a police officer, whereas tendermindedness is more required of a social worker. However, the best negotiation team may be one that comprises people who can lead tough discussions but can also be tender and who can understand the other side's point of view.

Attitudes to careers have changed in recent years, and as a result the new generation have different views about employment. People with a traditional, old-fashioned viewpoint may lament the death of *lifelong employment*. Others claim that this status never really existed, being merely a self-fulfilling illusion. The younger participants in today's labour markets (Generation X and those that have followed them) seem to be less interested in a lifelong job, and more interested in challenging and meaningful assignments for their self-development.

The Y and Z Generations (Generation Y born between around 1980–1995 and Generation Z between 1996–2010) are considered 'digital natives', and have high level of individualism. Like Generation X before them, they have high level of corporate skepticism, even cynicism. To attract them, companies should be perceived as ethical, green, and acting in the community interest as they did for Generation X (Tapscott, 1998), and in order to keep an individual orientation where work–life balance is more important than in the past to both men and women (Agarwal & Vaghela, 2018; Sánchez-Hernández et al., 2019). Should companies treat employees as capital, and if so, what would be the reaction of Generation X/Y/Z workers?

Belonging to a special type of family

Dual-career couples

Up until the late 20th century, the typical Western family comprised a father, a mother, and two or three children. The mother would have children in her 20s, and would not work outside the home thereafter. Many changes in society mean that people today tend to work, not merely for money, but for interest and challenge. Women may delay having children for many reasons, including the damaging effect of a career break on their progress. Many choose not to have children or to have one or two at most.

One of the most problematic issues in relation to dual-career couples is relocation. Whereas once this would have meant that the male would be moved to work in another place and the family would move too, now this requires that two people, with separate careers, have to move, or that one employer would have to accept an alternative working arrangement (e.g. telecommuting) for one of the partners, or to try to find a job for the partner in the new location, which may be in a different country (see Chapter 8). Career development now needs to take into consideration the whole family.

Single parents (mostly single mothers)

For social and political reasons, governments do not wish single parents to drop out of the labour market. In the UK, the government initiated programmes to help teenage mothers to return to education and enter the labour market (https://www.education-ni.gov.uk/articles/school-age-mothers-programme).

However, for such families, support mechanisms such as childcare facilities are essential. It has been found that married or cohabiting women are more likely than single women to be in employment. Employment rates are higher for women without children. For those with children, employment rates are much lower for lone mothers than for mothers who are married or cohabiting.

Intersectionality/hybrid diversity

Women may be discriminated against; Black people may be discriminated against. What happens to Black women? This is the case of intersectionality (Crenshaw, 2017). The glass ceiling becomes a concrete ceiling, according to some accounts (Bell & Nkomo, 2001), which is even more difficult to crack (Johns et al., 2019). Bell and Nkomo pointed out that it is not just ethnicity and gender, but social class that determines and hinders career development for people who are different in more than one way from the dominant group of White males. Legislation usually refers to a single factor, as is the case with the UK's Sex Discrimination Act 1975, Equality Act 2010 and the Race Relations Act 1965, but not to more than one. Recent evidence suggests that discrimination due to multiple factors is far stronger than that due to a single factor (Baruch et al., 2016b).

Organizational policies and their importance in managing diversity

The CAST model presented earlier in the book indicated that organizations should have clear policies for HRM and career issues. These policies translate the business philosophy and strategy into practice. When devising diversity policies, organizations must incorporate both the legal issue (stemming from the *compliance* strategy) of EEO and the business interest, which means getting the best out of the best people (stemming from the *valuing diversity* strategy). Such policies can include equal opportunity monitoring and fair procedures to ensure selection for recruitment into all levels of the organization (such as eliminating gender and age as selection criteria). A more proactive approach may be manifested, for example, in ensuring that there are no access problems for people with physical disabilities, setting recruitment targets for women, ethnic minorities, and so on. Once these people are in the organization, similar policies should regulate and monitor selection for training and development and nomination and selection for promotion. A different set of policy directives should relate to relationships and the prevention of harassment on various grounds. At a further stage of policy development, organizations can introduce steps to encourage – not just to enable – people of diverse backgrounds to apply and to work for the firm, and to promote wide mentoring programmes. Flexible work arrangements (teleworking, flexi-time, childcare facilities, job sharing, etc.) can be introduced. The COVID-19 pandemic gave a significant boost to the implementation of working from home (Dubey & Tripathi, 2020).

Nelson and Quick (2013) listed five main benefits organizations can reap from diversity:

- The ability to attract and retain the best available human talent.
- Enhancing marketing efforts.

- Promoting creativity and innovation.
- Improved problem solving.
- Enhanced organizational flexibility.

To balance the picture, Nelson and Quick also presented five main problems associated with diversity, factors that arise mostly because people are attracted to and feel comfortable with others like themselves:

- Resistance to change.
- Lack of cohesiveness.
- Communication problems.
- Conflicts.
- Decision making.

Summary

In this chapter we learned the nature of diversity, distinguished it from discrimination, and identified the meaning of the management of diversity. We explored the expected benefits as well as the possible pitfalls of managing diversity, focusing on a wide variety of organizational initiatives. We discovered that diversity does not end with demography, and explored the issue of organizational justice and fairness.

Specific sources of diversity analysed included gender, ethnicity, age, disability, sexual orientation, religion, deep-level diversity, belonging to a different type of family, and hybrid diversity (meaning more than a single diversity). The chapter concluded with some advice on organizational policies and their importance in managing diversity and inclusion.

KEY TERMS

Deep-level diversity

Discrimination

Distributive justice

Diversity

EEO (equal employment opportunity)

Inclusion

Organizational diversity policies

Organizational initiatives

Procedural justice

Surface diversity

Valuing diversity

DISCUSSION QUESTIONS

LESSONS AND FOOD FOR THOUGHT

1. *For HR managers*: Using the CAST concept, how would you develop practices, policies and strategies to tackle and manage diversity?
2. *For the HR consultant*: What would be your advice to HR managers in developing a comprehensive policy for managing diversity? How will your policy be influenced by the specific environment in which the organization operates?
3. *For the HR teacher*: In what way would you integrate new forms of diversity into existing career systems?
4. *For the student*: Do you belong to any of the above listed diverse sub-groups? Have you experienced discrimination in the past (see Exercise 1)?

REVIEW QUESTIONS

1. What are the major impetuses for organizations to manage diversity?
2. In what ways does your university encourage students from diverse backgrounds to apply for places? What practices does the university apply to support people of diverse backgrounds during their studies? If you had a disability (e.g. dyslexia or impaired hearing), how would your university help you?

EXERCISE

Did you encounter any discrimination *before* your present studies; for example, did you perceive different attitudes towards you as compared with your work colleagues of other backgrounds?

	Gender	Race/ethnicity	Disability	Religion	Age	Sexual orientation	Other
Not at all							
Very minor							
Minor							
Significant							
Very significant							

Please specify from whom (e.g. managers, peers, administrators, etc.) and in what connection:

Do you encounter any discrimination *as a student* (relate to your present studies)? For example, do you perceive different attitudes towards you as compared with your class colleagues of other backgrounds?

	Gender	Race/ethnicity	Disability	Religion	Age	Sexual orientation	Other
Not at all							
Very minor							
Minor							
Significant							
Very significant							

Please specify from whom (e.g. academics, peers, administrators, etc.) and in what connection:

Would you anticipate any discrimination *after* you finish your present studies? Will it be stronger or milder than that before your studies, that is, do you think that having a formal degree such as advanced degree in management can reduce or eliminate discrimination?

Source: This exercise is based on Cocchiara et al., 2010 and Baruch et al., 2016b.

Conclusion: The Future of Careers

10

LEARNING OBJECTIVES

After reading this chapter you should be able to:

- Reflect on the role career system management will play in the future

Epilogue

It is widely accepted that the careers of today are quite different from traditional careers. The stable and linear career systems of the past have developed into a transitional, fluid type of system. This is true from both the individual and the organizational perspective. The process of destabilization was caused by macroeconomic and social forces, as well as by workers themselves. On the one hand we have the boundaryless organization, indeed boundaryless society, with the breaking down of many traditional concepts, including many career barriers, and the building of new concepts that are innovative but challenging. On the other hand we see the trend towards individualism, which started some time ago, and is still accelerating. People are becoming masters of their own destiny; they see the world as their oyster. Much of the change is due to novel ways by which career actors interpret and pursue emergent labour markets. Economic forces and the competitive nature of commerce forced organizations to make dramatic changes to the way they treat employees, and forced them to look for different ways of managing careers within and outside the organizational boundaries. While 'boundary-less career' is a metaphor, not arguing that no boundaries exist, it is a new reality that there is a change in the attitude towards careers, not necessarily actual moves.

I hope that the book has provided an added value for students, as well as for practitioners and academic scholars interested in the subject area. The benefits stem from the book's broad scrutiny of the area of careers, as managed by organizations, including detailed analysis of practices and policies which must relate to the future rather than the past: in a time of change and confusion, managers need a relevant framework to guide them in managing people. People are most frequently cited as the most important asset of organizations, but managing this asset has never been clear, and new challenges continuously emerge. I believe that this book, as well as providing the student with general and specific academic knowledge, offers readers an opportunity to consider their careers: how to plan and manage it, how to ensure sustainability (e.g. via employability), how to interact with the many other stakeholders. People can re-think their own careers, perhaps to contemplate a career change or to re-shape their existing career plans.

Back to basics

Success in people management leads to business success (Jiang et al., 2012; Tzabbar et al., 2017). The basic roles of HRM are to obtain and retain employees. These two roles remain the primary goal for HRM, just as they were in the past. However, the nature of the activities that need to be undertaken in order to fulfil them has altered considerably. The 'obtain' element means finding the right person for organizational needs, the job, the career. The 'retain' is all about career management. Increasingly, it has become crucial to retain employees. People and their human capital are the most critical commodity in any labour market. As an example – when mergers occur, the acquiring company 'buys' people. A typical example would be an IT specialist firm that leases its computers, rents its offices, outsources its services, and does not even have company cars. All the firm's assets, then, lie in the human capital and the brand name. Judged by these criteria, recent acquisitions would suggest that a price of a million dollars per person may well reflect the true worth of a company. Therefore, the most important element following an acquisition is to keep to the people.

But the nature of employment relationships has changed:

- From family organization to team and partnership (you cannot fire a family member, but you can fire a team member).
- From patronising approach to freedom and autonomy, self-managed individuals and teams.
- From structure-based stability to dynamism and flexibility.
- From job security to employability.
- From work-focused career to quality of life and search for work–life balance.

In search of excellence, organizations seek to become enabling, not controlling. They seek for the right promise to make to their employees (e.g. employability) in order to gain a competitive advantage, via creativity and innovation. Career adaptability (Johnston, 2018; Savickas, 1997) is an essential ingredient for survival. The new psychological contracts form a different base for trust and commitment (Baruch & Rousseau, 2019). Multiple commitments (such as commitment to the profession, the team, the self) emerge as substitute for, or additional to, the traditional organizational commitment. The complex contemporary workplace challenges individuals and organizations alike (Rabenu, 2021), generating new career landscapes (Tomlinson et al., 2018), and the work environment is global, for better and for worse, as the COVID-19 pandemic has clearly manifested.

New careers seem to have new meanings and to serve new roles for people (Inkson et al., 2015; Sullivan & Baruch, 2009). Nevertheless, in reality not all have changed, and there is a certain stability and continuity of development, not necessarily via step-changes (Baruch, 2006a). Most people still have a high internal need for work. The major roles work plays in people's lives remain similar to those of a few decades ago. While for many, careers have changed or altered completely, and new professions have emerged, several old-style professions still exist, as well as whole industrial sectors. Mundane work still makes up a large part of the job in many occupations, and companies apply the concept of division of labour to new innovative establishments (see e.g., call centres and modern sweatshops). Trust can be a powerful managerial tool via empowerment, but in many cases so-called empowerment starts and ends with empty words. Even when changes do occur, they take time and the pace is slow, as the case of diversity in the workplace indicates (for women, who still experience a glass ceiling, ethnic minorities, older people, and others from diverse backgrounds who may suffer discrimination).

Future trends

From the perspective of sociology of vocations, the big question is: which new career options will be open to the generation cast out by the service industries? The 4th industrial revolution (Schwab, 2017) and progress in AI pose a threat to careers in the service sector. In the earlier mass movements of workers it was clear where the large majority would go: the farmers and tenant farmers moved to towns and cities and became production workers; production workers who were cast out from the redundant factories moved to the service industries. Now fewer people are needed in the service industries, and the question is: where will they go?

The answer is problematic and complex. With many stakeholders and a variety of influencing factors, responses of individuals, organizations, and societies will be segmented. Some traditional industries and sectors are fairly shielded from its dynamics (e.g. public sector), whereas others are subjected to insecurities, in particular the gig economy – employment on demand (Lobel, 2017). New industries emerge or develop further, while mature labour markets may disappear. Amongst the possible opportunities that are emerging, three come to mind immediately: e-business, the leisure sector, and tertiary education. The leisure sector arises since more people are working fewer hours (the number of working hours per week in Europe are continuing to decrease, getting below the threshold of 40 or 38 at the turn of the millennium), and many are not working (either because they have been made redundant or they are pensioners, with a longer life expectancy). Thus, more facilities are needed in the leisure and entertainment industry. Fitness centres, restaurants, performing arts establishments, and clubs flourish.

Alongside these emerged the idea of a universal basic income (UBI), being suggested as a potential 'buffer' – a social safety net – to the potential impacts of UBI on orientations to work (Perkins et al., 2021). If the idea of UBI materialises, it will present a new type of career path to people – being paid, but not for work. The implication for the management of people at the workplace will be significant; retaining employees when they have a viable alternative of not working could be challenging.

As for the education sector, while a university degree was rare in the early days of the 20th century, by the early part of the 21st century, some one-third of young people in the relevant age group were students, and in some countries the aspiration is to reach 50% at tertiary educational level. Thus, this sector (and associated industries) is rapidly growing.

Technology, e-business careers, and virtual careers

Technology, as has always been the case, influences not just a single occupation, but the whole labour market and society in general. The most significant technological developments influencing careers and employment are concerned with IT. However, the impact is not unidirectional. With continual growth in the number of jobs of people whose work involves extensive use of IT, the skills required to conduct many jobs are *either* increasing *or* decreasing. Evidence suggests that more workers have experienced an increase rather than a decrease in skills as a result of digitization (Cascio, 2000). What is becoming of great importance for future careers is the changing nature of the skills and competencies required, and in particular the role of intellectual capital. Intellectual capital is the knowledge, information, intellectual property, and experience that can be put to use to create wealth and to enhance human welfare (Stewart, 2010). Increasingly, intellectual capital dwells within humans' brains rather than within the system, making knowledge management a field of great importance. Human capital is the source of innovation and renewal, and its management is mediated via career management.

E-business makes a case for fast-growth service companies (while their production sectors took a more traditional approach to e-business at its start) and a new path to employability for a new generation. Embarking on e-business means taking the risk that the operational changes that accompany it could jeopardize existing relationships with both environments – internal (employees) and external (customers). But on average, just a few decades after the introduction of e-business, the early adopters enjoy the significant operational benefits from their e-business commitment, and counting their employees and customers as their biggest supporters. The main benefactors, however, seem to be the shareholders. Companies expect to generate an increasing share of their revenue from e-business, while some businesses have been reluctant to disrupt their traditional ways of working. A word of caution is required too – careers in this dynamic but fragile business segment are at an early stage, and there is no conventional model of an e-career. It will take some time for the emerging pattern of e-careers to take a recognizable form.

To successfully navigate careers in the e-world, people need different skills, the first of which is readiness for extensive change. For customers, the secret lies in their ability to adapt to the availability of new or existing products and services on the Internet. During the COVID-19 pandemic, even firms that rejected online sales had to accept the new reality, and customers changed their shopping habits (Mehta et al., 2020; Eger et al., 2021). For employees, it is that e-business entails a high degree of flexibility and willingness on the part of the people and HR management.

This latest technological development also creates new types of jobs and occupations. Web-page design is one such relatively new profession. The COVID-19 pandemic gave a major boost to low-skilled jobs in the home delivery sector. Many industries are moving a major share of their business to the Internet, in particular sales (certain products such as flight tickets are already dominant in e-businesses).

But it is not just sales that make good Internet business. Another prominent example is recruitment. Job advertising on the Internet has become commonplace, and most recruitment (as well as some selection) occurs online, including CV screening and other selection analysis. Table 10.1 presents the frequently used web pages, some of which are general, others specific for certain fields.

Table 10.1   Finding graduate jobs on the Web

---

1. Target jobs advertise graduate job opportunities across a wide range of sectors including law, engineering, HR, Media FMCG and many more.
2. Milkround allows you to browse through several graduate job vacancies including Design, Education, Marketing and Sports.
3. Save the student has a job search engine for students and graduates. The search engine compiles graduate job vacancies from job sites such as Milkround, Monster, Reed, Target jobs and total jobs.
4. Prospects allows you to search for graduate jobs and filter your search based on salary, location, type of work and sector.
5. GradJobs host career exhibitions and have a job search tool on their site.
6. GraduateLand advertises graduate jobs and career events. If you are looking for a graduate job in Europe, this site may be useful for you.
7. JobsGraduate is part of the CV-Library Group, and advertises job vacancies for graduates across all industries.
8. GetMyFirstJob advertises graduate job vacancies across several sectors including finance, law, marketing and IT.
9. graduatejobs.com allows students and graduates to search for internships, graduate jobs and graduate schemes across all sectors.
10. The Big Choice allows you to search for graduate jobs by industry.
11. Right Network is a network of university students and graduates. They host several networking events every year and have a job board on their site listing graduate jobs in all sectors from accounting to technology.
12. Debut features a job board specifically for graduates. They also have an app that is available on the App Store and Google Play.
13. Graduate Recruitment Bureau (GRB) shares graduate recruitment advice and allows you to search for graduate jobs and internships.
14. GradConnection helps students and graduates to find both internships and graduate jobs.

Job websites for graduates looking for a creative graduate job

1. Fashion Workie advertises graduate opportunities for graduates who want to pursue a career in creative industries such as fashion design, marketing, PR, retail, visual merchandising and more.
2. The Dots lists internship, job and freelance opportunities at graduate and entry-level in creative industries such as design, production, media, product marketing, UX/UI and more.

STEM Graduate jobs

1. Gradcracker is a job website for graduates who studied a STEM-related degree who wishes to find a STEM-related job.
2. STEM Graduates feature graduate job vacancies for graduates who studied a degree related to science, engineering, technology or mathematics.
3. Just Engineers. This job board has a list of jobs specifically for engineering graduates who wish to pursue a career in the engineering field.
4. NewScientist Jobs. Check out this job board if you are looking for a graduate job in scientific fields such as biochemistry, immunology, ecology and more.

Charity jobs

Here are some useful sites if you are looking for a job in the charity sector.

1. CharityJob allows you to browse jobs within the third sector.
2. Thirdsector jobs advertise voluntary, not for profit and charity jobs.

Digital jobs

1. Digital Grads is a platform for those who wish to pursue a career in the digital field. Once you become a member, you will gain access to free online digital marketing courses. You will also be contacted when graduate employers are interested in your profile.
2. DevIT aims to bring more transparency, openness and diversity to the British IT market making the job search process of software engineers more enjoyable.

Source: https://graduatecoach.co.uk/job-websites-graduates

E-business does not start and end with highly prestigious, well-paid jobs. In addition to the IT and professional personnel and the like, the sector requires a new army of employees on call, many delivery people, which may be termed the 'revival of the milkman', but this time delivering the latest book from Amazon.com or veg and fruit boxes direct from farms to individual buyers. These jobs are hardly intellectually stimulating, and form a core of necessary mundane work in the new economy.

Repetitive strain injury (RSI) became quite common for people performing repetitive actions with their limbs (many people suffered wrist and finger problems from operating computers). In new workplaces such as call centres, where employees are required to respond to callers following a prescribed procedure and using the same words, people might suffer from what may be labelled 'repetitive brain injury' (RBI). If people are unable to break away from the rigid routine that calls for no intellectual effort, originality of thinking, or stimulating challenges, their minds become stultified. RBI is a metaphorical parallel of RSI. Similarly, the approach to its cure should be a combination of mind activation, mindfulness, and rest.

Life or working career?

The nature of career systems has also changed. Whereas in the past career systems largely involved planning and managing a relatively passive workforce, modern systems are different. The emphasis is on developmental processes, where the employee is expected and even encouraged to take an active role, while the organization plays the role of facilitator or enabler. Career management is being transformed into a service designed to support managers, professionals, and employees to create and re-create their development path. This can remove them from the organization, but neither side need lament this loss too much.

The organization is not expected to be altruistic and to retain all employees, for example, if there is no need for their outcomes, or if they are not performing to the best of their ability, or if they are unable to achieve a required standard of performance. Moreover, even the best performers may find themselves out of a job due to a competitive market or for other reasons beyond the control of the organization. The implications for people management are given in Table 10.2.

Table 10.2 Career system development implications for people management

From	To
Control and command system	Support and consult system
Organizational manpower planning	Individual career counselling
Monitoring careers	Developing people
Training for a qualification	Lifelong learning
Assigning jobs in succession	Coaching, mentoring, pointing out opportunities
Retirement with pension at 65	Various ways of employment ending, no age boundaries

The creation of wealth via the human asset (Pfeffer, 1998) is an idea representing a shift from financial capital, which was the core key to competitive advantage in the industrial society, to human capital, its concurrent replacement for the information age. Human capital is measured in terms of knowledge, and knowledge management is required from organizations. Sometimes the knowledge is embedded within the system, the technology, the procedures, and regulations. This system of knowledge management somewhat neutralizes the human value. In other cases, the knowledge is embedded within people, forming human capital (and raising legal questions of intellectual properties). Knowledge held by individuals and their competencies become their career asset. The ability to learn is more valuable than formal qualification.

Strategic career or career strategy?

Strategic studies is a relatively new field of studies (Buckley & Ghauri, 2015), with military origins (Baylis, Wirtz, & Gray, 2018). It is a source for business success, and has many practical implications – for organizations (Jarzabkowski & Paul Spee, 2009) and for individuals (Greenhaus et al., 2019) – when developing strategies for growth and progress.

There is a striking similarity between the field of career studies and strategy. First, the study of careers as a specific research area started at about the same time. Moreover, the career area is not the 'property' of a single theoretical discipline (Arthur et al., 1989; Sullivan & Baruch, 2009). It is of interest to note that as in the area of strategy, by the 1980s writing about careers had moved from a primary interest in growth to a focus on competitiveness and renewal.

Putting these strands together, strategic HRM emerged in the late 1980s and 1990s, and is continuing to develop. The strategic HRM approach was introduced by Devanna et al. (1981), continued with the work of Fombrun et al. (1984) and Beer et al. (1984), and is still at the centre of current research (Paauwe & Boon, 2018). According to strategic HRM, the HR strategy should be developed alongside the general strategy of the organization, to acquire a cultural fit within the organization and with the outside environment. HR managers need to be involved in strategic decision-making processes and to link the HR policy and strategy with that of the organization. On the other hand, HRM is a profession that requires the knowledge of a wide range of theories and the skills to apply to a variety of practical programmes, activities, and practices at the operational level (Tzabbar et al., 2017). HR managers are frequently faced with a question of balance between the practical aspect of the HRM roles and the need to be involved in strategic decision making at the organizational level (Baruch, 1998c).

The career ecosystems theory as an over-arching perspective

The career ecosystem theory (Baruch, 2015; Baruch & Rousseau, 2019) offers a theoretical lens through which to explore careers from multiple perspectives and integrate a variety of actors to gain a rich understanding of career systems. The actors are engaged with a labour market; for many it is a global one, where each actor has its own agenda. Individuals may stay or move in their chosen or imposed vocations, organizations, sectors, and locations.

They may work for one or more organizations, sometimes for themselves, and throughout their career they may cross many boundaries, and move in various directions, in what is called a 'flow of talent' across organizations, sectors, and nations. The underpinning constellation involves economy, technology, social forces, legal, and political issues. The eco-system mechanisms of adjustment, expansion, and decline, and the flow of talent, are at perpetual motion of evolution.

As presented in Chapter 1, amongst the characteristics of the labour markets as eco-systems are:

- A constant flow of human capital, prompted and influenced by push/pull factors.
- Spiral learning processes, required for continuous adjustments and adaptation to new situations.
- Ongoing change processes influencing the directions and magnitude of human capital flow.
- Labour markets being global, and influenced by factors at many levels.

The main actors are:

- *Individuals*: competence, needs, values and attitudes.
- *Organizations*: nature of career system – traditional or dynamic, stage of globalization, sector and product type, knowledge management.
- *Nations/societies*: economy, culture, politics, legal.

Overall, this theory offers a useful tool to understand careers at the many levels they operate at.

Lessons and challenges

The new world of careers poses challenges to the traditional ways of thinking and perceiving careers. Let us look at a three-level analysis – individual, organization and society.

Lessons and challenges: Individuals

Navigating uncertainties

If careers are journeys, the main role of the individual is to navigate their way through. The main challenges posed by future career navigating are growing uncertainty, the blurring of boundaries, the diminution of the roles organizations undertake; and the lack of secure, stable employment. With growing individualization in society, people are encouraged to follow their dreams and calling (Hall & Chandler, 2005), which can lead to better career outcomes, including objective outcomes such as higher income and chance of promotion (Cho & Jiang, 2021).

In the past it was assumed that the organizational role was one of command and control. Now the person is in control, or at least there is sharing of it. People should expect no job security, but ensure they have the capacity to acquire new employment should they be made redundant (i.e. develop their employability). They will gain employment via training, skills, and competencies, and a proactive approach towards the labour market. A finger on the pulse is essential for knowledge of employability. Yet, it is acceptable to stay within one organization so long as career progress is being made (not necessarily upward progress, but such that increases competence).

The meaning of career success and measurement is not what it used to be (Spurk et al., 2019). It is less about advancement in a hierarchy or gains in terms of formal power. Career success can be related to professionalism, employability, and work–life balance. It is now less about money making (buying power), and more about the psychological aspects of satisfaction, recognition, esteem, and self-actualization. Internal career success is no less important than external, and careers are looked at in the wider context of life. There are a variety of factors and issues that people may aim at in their career. While some will always strive to climb up hierarchies, others will create different challenges for themselves. Employability is the new currency in the labour market. It can be boosted by acquisition of career competencies (Blokker et al., 2019).

Lessons and challenges: Organizations

Support, challenge, development, flexibility

The role of the organization in planning and management of careers has changed from command and control to the provision of support and guidance, as well as providing the map for the individual to navigate. Flexibility is a key concept. The management of careers may take several forms. A diverse set of career practices exists, and they are directed at a diverse workforce. This diversity is not just demographic, but also relates to the type of contract under which people work (e.g. there is a distinction between core people and contract employees). Introducing alternative work arrangements is an excellent example of what organizations can and should offer. Another form of flexibility may be introduced via the establishment of satellite firms. These can be supported by the core company, and with additional assistance from financial enterprises (e.g. venture capitalists), may be the object of a future management buyout. In this way the people involved will gain control and will be able to build their future careers through good contacts with their former employer.

While redundancies are not a way forward, companies that have no choice but to make people redundant should conduct the process very carefully. Using best practice is advised, following guidelines suggested elsewhere; for example, to make sure that all agree it was inevitable; it was the last action to be taken; it was conducted at all hierarchy levels; and so on (see Bagdadli and Gianecchini, 2019 or Mishra et al., 1998, for examples of how to apply best practice). To equip their employees properly with employability, the type of training that organizations invest in is important. Training improves the employability of the unemployed, but should be labour-market driven, not merely company specific, if organizations put the interests of their employees first.

Lessons and challenges: Society

Demography, globalization, technology, culture – convergence versus divergence

The composition of the population in industrial developed societies is changing. Two tendencies co-exist, which lead to an escalation of the same phenomenon: birth rate is declining, and life expectancy is increasing. An alarming element in business life is the tendency to allow people to leave the active labour market even before normal retirement age. People leave organizations to take early retirement, or are made redundant, at the age of 55, 50 and lower. A crucial source of competence, experience, and creative brainpower is being lost. As a result of the ageing of the population, some one-third of the population will be over 65 early in the 21st century. It is not surprising to hear voices questioning the logic (and the financial viability) of a system that forces people out of the workforce while they are still able to contribute. There are suggestions that the retirement age be raised to 70. This may be a new reality for many, but in contrast, many organizations encourage early retirement for people over 50. This places heavy burdens on pension funds, raises issues of quality of life, and increases the uncertainty and possible stress felt by the employed who watch the process, knowing that their turn will come soon.

Due to the low birth rate there are few options for replacement and ensuring growth. Many developed countries have to rely on cheap labour in the global market, and sometimes this creates sociological and cultural problems (such as the mass attempt of economy-immigration from Africa to Europe or those related to the Turkish community in Germany).

Globalization continues to flourish, but while there is much convergence in management systems and organizational practices, cultural differences have a strong influence and will continue to have an impact on how careers are managed and on the meaning of career and career success. More options for global careers by means of expatriation will develop, but, overall, global careers are not yet the norm, and will probably continue to be the exception in the near future. Similarly, other phenomena such as virtual organizations and careers in the virtual world will be at the leading edge, but will be confined to a few rather than the majority of employees.

Some 20 years ago, Furnham (2000) tried to forecast what the world of work would look like in 2020. Such projections, as he himself admitted, might seem out of balance in terms of the time perspective. However, there is no doubt, first, that the world of work is changing, and second, that certain qualities are to stay with us, perhaps in a modified form. I would predict here, that for the next 20 years the pace of change will continue to grow, and what is certain is that future careers will be dynamic and unpredictable.

'Expect the unexpected' should be the motto for individuals and organizations alike.

DISCUSSION QUESTIONS

LESSONS AND FOOD FOR THOUGHT

For the student: What do you wish your first job to be? Which type of role, which industry? How much do you aim to earn? What level of work–life balance do you wish to have?

When do you plan to start the search? Do not leave it until the month of graduation – use all the last year of study to prepare for an effective job-search. Use career services provided by the university, career fairs, and so on.

For the employee: What do you wish your next job to be? Should it be within the same organization, elsewhere, or does it not matter? Which type of role? What level of increased earnings do you expect, if any? What level of work–life balance do you wish to have?

When do you plan to start the search? Don't wait too long – but also make sure you have enough time in your current job to build experience. Build your networks, consult mentors, colleagues, HR.

References

Abele, A. E., Spurk, D., & Volmer, J. (2011). The construct of career success: Measurement issues and an empirical example. *Zeitschrift für Arbeitsmarktforschung*, *43*(3), 195–206.

Abulof, U. (2017). Introduction: Why we need Maslow in the twenty-first century. *Society*, *54*(6), 508–509.

Adamson, S. J., Doherty, N., & Viney, C. (1998). The meaning of career revisited: Implications for theory and practice. *British Journal of Management*, *9*(4), 251–259.

Agarwal, H., & Vaghela, P. (2018). *Work values of Gen Z: Bridging the gap to the next generation*. In NC-2018-National Conference on Innovative Business Management Practices in the 21st Century, Faculty of Management Studies, Parul University, Gujarat, India (pp. 21–22).

Akkermans, J., Richardson, J., & Kraimer, M. L. (2020). The Covid-19 crisis as a career shock: Implications for careers and vocational behavior. *Journal of Vocational Behavior*, *119*. https://doi.org/10.1016/j.jvb.2020.103434

Akkermans, J., & Tims, M. (2017). Crafting your career: How career competencies relate to career success via job crafting. *Applied Psychology*, *66*(1), 168–195.

Al Ariss, A., & Syed, J. (2011). Capital mobilization of skilled migrants: A relational perspective. *British Journal of Management*, *22*(2), 286–304.

Alcover, C. M., Crego, A., Guglielmi, D., & Chiesa, R. (2012). Comparison between the Spanish and Italian early work retirement models: A cluster analysis approach. *Personnel Review*, *41*(3), 380–403.

Alonso, A. D., Kok, S. K., Bressan, A., O'Shea, M., Sakellarios, N., Koresis, A., ... & Santoni, L. J. (2020). COVID-19, aftermath, impacts, and hospitality firms: An international perspective. *International Journal of Hospitality Management*, *91*. https://doi.org/10.1016/j.ijhm.2020.102654

Altman, Y., Simpson, R., Baruch, Y., & Burke, R. J. (2005). Reframing the 'glass ceiling' debate. In R. J. Burke & M. C. Mattis (Eds.), *Supporting Women's Career Advancement: Challenges and Opportunities* (pp. 58–81). Cheltenham: Edward Elgar.

Altonji, J. G., Kahn, L. B., & Speer, J. D. (2016). Cashier or consultant? Entry labor market conditions, field of study, and career success. *Journal of Labor Economics, 34*(S1), S361–S401.

Alwi, S. F. S., & Kitchen, P. J. (2014). Projecting corporate brand image and behavioral response in business schools: Cognitive or affective brand attributes? *Journal of Business Research, 67*(11), 2324–2336.

Amior, M., & Manning, A. (2018). The persistence of local joblessness. *American Economic Review, 108*(7), 1942–70.

Anderson, A. R., & Warren, L. (2011). The entrepreneur as hero and jester: Enacting the entrepreneurial discourse. *International Small Business Journal, 29*(6), 589–609.

Andresen, M., Al Ariss, A., & Walther, M. (Eds.). (2012). Self-initiated expatriation: Individual, organizational, and national perspectives. London: Routledge.

Andresen, M., Biemann, T., & Pattie, M. W. (2015). What makes them move abroad? Reviewing and exploring differences between self-initiated and assigned expatriation. *The International Journal of Human Resource Management, 26*(7), 932–947.

Angervall, P., Gustafsson, J., & Silver, E. (2018). Academic career: On institutions, social capital and gender. *Higher Education Research & Development, 37*(6), 1095–1108.

Antonacopoulou, E. P., & Güttel, W. H. (2010). Staff induction practices and organizational socialization: A review and extension of the debate. *Society and Business Review, 5*(1), 22–47.

Armstrong, M., & Taylor, S. (2020). Armstrong's Handbook of Human Resource Management Practice. London: Kogan Page.

Armstrong, P. I., Day, S. X., McVay, J. P., & Rounds, J. (2008). Holland's RIASEC model as an integrative framework for individual differences. *Journal of Counseling Psychology, 55*(1), 1–18.

Arnold, J. (1997). *Managing careers into the 21st century*. London: Paul Chapman.

Arnold, J., Coombs, C. R., & Gubler, M. (2019). Career anchors and preferences for organizational career management: A study of information technology professionals in three European countries. *The International Journal of Human Resource Management, 30*(22), 3190–3222.

Artess, J., Hooley, T., & Mellors-Bourne, R. (2017). Employability: A review of the literature 2012 to 2016. A Report for the Higher Education Academy. York: Higher Education Academy.

Arthur, M. B. (1994). The boundaryless career: A new perspective for organizational inquiry. *Journal of Organizational Behavior, 15*(4), 295–306.

Arthur, M. B. (2014). The boundaryless career at 20: Where do we stand, and where can we go? *Career Development International, 19*(6), 627–640.

Arthur, M. B., Claman, P. H., & DeFillippi, R. J. (1995). Intelligent enterprise, intelligent careers. *Academy of Management Executive, 9*(4), 7–22.

Arthur, M. B., Hall, D. T., & Lawrence, B. S. (1989). Generating new directions in career theory: The case for a transdisciplinary approach. In M. B. Arthur, D. T. Hall, & B. S. Lawrence (Eds.), *Handbook of career theory* (p. 7–25.). Cambridge: Cambridge University Press.

Arthur, M. B., Inkson, K., & Pringle, J. K. (1999). *The new careers: Individual action and economic change*. London: Sage.

Arthur, M. B., Khapova, S. N., & Richardson, J. (2016). *An intelligent career: Taking ownership of your work and your life*. New York: Oxford University Press.

Arthur, M. B., & Rousseau, D. M. (Eds.). (1996). *The boundaryless career: A new employment principle for a new organizational era*. New York: Oxford University Press.

Ashforth, B. E., & Mael, F. (1989). Social identity theory and the organization. *Academy of Management Review, 14*(1), 20–39.

Ashkenas, R., Ulrich, D., Jick, T., & Kerr, S. (1995) *The boundaryless organization*. San Francisco, CA: Jossey-Bass.

Ashkenas, R., Ulrich, D., Jick, T., & Kerr, S. (2015). *The boundaryless organization: Breaking the chains of organizational structure*. San Francisco, CA: Jossey-Bass.

Assouline, M., & Meir, E. I. (1987). Meta-analysis of the relationships between congruence and well-being measures. *Journal of Vocational Behavior, 31*(3), 319–332.

Aulack, S., Charlwood, A., Muzio, D., Tomlinson, J., & Valizade, D. (2017). Mapping advantages and disadvantages: Diversity in the legal profession in England and Wales. https://www.sra.org.uk/sra/how-we-work/reports/diversity-legal-profession/

Avelsson M. (1995) *Management of knowledge-intensive companies*. Berlin: Walter de Gruyter.

Avetisyan, E., Baruch, Y., Meschi, P. X., Metais, E., & Norheim-Hansen, A. (2020). Tying the acquirer's human resource management quality to cross-border acquisition divestment probability: Curvilinear connection with slacklining. *British Journal of Management, 31*(3), 568–588.

Aycan, Z. (2001). Expatriation: A critical step toward developing global leaders. In M. Mendenhall, T. M. Kühlmann, & G. K. Stahl (Eds.), *Developing global business leaders: Policies, processes and innovations* (pp. 119–136). Westport, CT: Quorum Books.

Baccaro, L., & Howell, C. (2017). Trajectories of neoliberal transformation: European industrial relations since the 1970s. Cambridge: Cambridge University Press.

Bagdadli, S., & Gianecchini, M. (2019). Organizational career management practices and objective career success: A systematic review and framework. *Human Resource Management Review, 29*(3), 353–370.

Bailey, C., Mankin, D., & Garavan, T. (2018). *Strategic Human Resource Management*. Oxford: Oxford University Press.

Bailyn, L. (1993). Patterned chaos in human resource management. *Sloan Management Review, 34*(2), 77–84.

Baird, L., & Kram, K. (1983). Career dynamics: Managing the supervisor/subordinate relationship. *Organizational Dynamics, 11*(Spring), 46–64.

Bal, M., & Rousseau, D. M. (Eds.). (2015). Idiosyncratic deals between employees and organizations: Conceptual issues, applications and the role of co-workers. London: Routledge.

Bal, P. M., Van Kleef, M., & Jansen, P. G. (2015). The impact of career customization on work outcomes: Boundary conditions of manager support and employee age. *Journal of Organizational Behavior, 36*(3), 421–440.

Bamberger, P. A., Biron, M., & Meshoulam, I. (2014). *Human resource strategy: Formulation, implementation, and impact* (8th ed.). New York: Routledge.

Bandura, A. (1977). *Social Learning Theory*. Englewood Cliffs, NJ: Prentice-Hall.

Bandura, A. (1997). *Self efficacy*. New York: W. H. Freeman.

Bandura, A. (2010). Self-efficacy. *The Corsini encyclopedia of psychology*. https://doi.org/10.1002/9780470479216.corpsy0836

Bankins, S. (2015). A process perspective on psychological contract change: Making sense of, and repairing, psychological contract breach and violation through employee coping actions. *Journal of Organizational Behavior, 36*(8), 1071–1095.

Baptiste, N. R. (2008). Tightening the link between employee wellbeing at work and performance. *Management Decision, 46*(2), 284–309.

Barley, S. R. (1989). Careers, identities and institutions: The legacy of the Chicago School of Sociology. In M. B. Arthur, T. Hall, & B. S. Lawrence (Eds.), *Handbook of career theory* (pp. 41–65). Cambridge: Cambridge University Press.

Barnett, W. P., Baron, J. N., & Stuart, T. E. (2000). Avenues of attainment: Occupational demography and organizational careers in the California Civil Service. *American Journal of Sociology, 106*(1), 88–144.

Barney, J. B. (1991). Firm resources and sustained competitive advantage. *Journal of Management, 17*(1), 99–120.

Barney, J. B. (2001). Resource-based theories of competitive advantage: A ten-year retrospective on the resource-based view. *Journal of Management, 27*(6), 643–650.

Bartel, C. A., Wrzesniewski, A., & Wiesenfeld, B. M. (2012). Knowing where you stand: Physical isolation, perceived respect, and organizational identification among virtual employees. *Organization Science*, *23*(3), 743–757.

Bartleet, B. L., Ballico, C., Bennett, D., Bridgstock, R., Draper, P., Tomlinson, V., & Harrison, S. (2019). Building sustainable portfolio careers in music: Insights and implications for higher education. *Music Education Research*, *21*(3), 282–294.

Bartlett, C. A. & Ghoshal, S. (1989). *Managing across borders: The transnational solution*. Boston, MA: Harvard Business Press.

Bartlett, C. A., & Ghoshal, S. (1992). What is a global manager?, *Harvard Business Review*, 70(5), 124–132.

Bartlett, C. A., & Ghoshal, S. (2003). What is a global manager? *Harvard Business Review*, *81*(8), 101–108.

Baruch, Y. (1995). Business globalization – the human resource management aspect. *Human Systems Management*, *14*(4), 313–236.

Baruch, Y. (1996a). Self performance appraisal vs. direct manager appraisal: A case of congruence. *Journal of Managerial Psychology*, *11*(6), 50–65.

Baruch, Y. (1996b). Organizational career planning and management techniques and activities in use in high-tech organizations. *Career Development International*, *1*(1), 40–49.

Baruch, Y. (1997). Evaluating quality and reputation of human resource management. *Personnel Review*, *27*(5), 377–394.

Baruch, Y. (1998a). The rise and fall of organizational commitment. *Human System Management*, *17*(2), 135–143.

Baruch, Y. (1998b). Empowerment models in organizations. *Career Development International*, *3*(2), 82–87.

Baruch, Y. (1998c). Walking the tightrope: Strategic issues for human resources. *Long Range Planning*, *31*(3), 467–475.

Baruch, Y. (1999). Integrated career systems for the 2000s. *International Journal of Manpower*, *20*(7), 432–457.

Baruch, Y. (2001a). Employability – substitute to loyalty? *Human Resource Development International*, *4*(4), 543–566.

Baruch, Y. (2001b). The status of research on teleworking and an agenda for future research. *International Journal of Management Review*, *3*(2), 113–129.

Baruch, Y. (2002). No such thing as a global manager. *Business Horizons*, *45*(1), 36–42.

Baruch, Y. (2003a). Career systems in transition: A normative model for organizational career practices. *Personnel Review*, *32*(2), 231–251.

Baruch, Y. (2003b). The desert generation. *Personnel Review*, *33*(2), 241–255.

Baruch, Y. (2004a) *Managing careers: Theory and practice*. Harlow: Pearson Education.

Baruch, Y. (2004b). Transforming careers – from linear to multidirectional career paths: Organizational and individual perspective. *Career Development International*, *9*(1), 58–73.

Baruch, Y. (2006a). Career development in organizations and beyond: Balancing traditional and contemporary viewpoints. *Human Resource Management Review*, *16*(2), 125–138.

Baruch, Y. (2006b). Role-play teaching: Acting in the classroom. *Management Learning*, *37*(1), 43–61.

Baruch, Y. (2009). To MBA or not to MBA. *Career Development International*, *14*(4), 388–406.

Baruch, Y. (2014). The development and validation of a measure for protean career orientation. *International Journal of Human Resource Management*, *25*(19), 2702–2723.

Baruch, Y. (2015). Organizational and labor market as career eco-system. In A. De Vos, & B. Van der Heijden (Eds.), *Handbook of Research on Sustainable Careers* (pp. 164–180). Cheltenham: Edward Elgar.

Baruch, Y., & Altman, Y. (2002). Expatriation and repatriation in MNCs: A taxonomy. *Human Resource Management*, *41*(2), 239–259.

Baruch, Y., Altman, Y., & Tung, R. L. (2016a). Career mobility in a global era: Advances in managing expatriation and repatriation. *Academy of Management Annals*, *10*(1), 841–889.

Baruch, Y., Bhaskar, U., & Mishra, B. (2020). Career dynamics in India: A two-wave study of career orientations and employability of graduates. *Personnel Review, 49*(3), 825–845.

Baruch, Y., & Bozionelos, N. (2011). Career issues. In S. Zedeck (Ed.), *APA Handbook of Industrial & Organizational Psychology* (pp. 67–113). Washington DC: APA Publications.

Baruch, Y., Budhwar, P., & Khatri, N. (2007). Brain drain: Inclination to stay abroad after studies. *Journal of World Business, 42*(1), 99–112.

Baruch, Y., & Clancy, P. (2000). Managing AIDS in Africa: HRM challenges in Tanzania. *International Journal of Human Resource Management, 11*(4), 789–806.

Baruch, Y., Dickmann, M., Altman, Y., & Bournois, F. (2013). Exploring international work: Types and dimensions of global careers. *International Journal of Human Resource Management, 24*(12), 2369–2393.

Baruch, Y., & Gebbie, D. (1998). Cultures of success: The leading UK MBOs. *Journal of Business Venturing, 13*(5), 423–439.

Baruch, Y., & Hall, D. T. (2004). The academic career: a model for future careers in other sectors?. *Journal of Vocational Behavior, 64*(2), 241–262.

Baruch, Y., & Harel, G. (1993). Combining multi-source performance appraisal: An empirical and methodological note. *Pubic Administration Quarterly, 17*(1), 96–111.

Baruch, Y., & Hind, P. (1999). Perpetual motion in organizations: Effective management and the impact of the new psychological contracts on survivor syndrome. *European Journal of Work and Organizational Psychology, 8*(2), 295–306.

Baruch, Y., & Hind, P. (2000). The survivor syndrome: A management myth? *Journal of Managerial Psychology, 15*(1), 29–41.

Baruch, Y., Humbert, A., & Wilson, D. (2016b). The moderating effects of single vs. multiple-grounds of perceived-discrimination on work-attitudes: Protean careers and self-efficacy roles in explaining intention-to-stay. *Equality, Diversity and Inclusion, 35*(3), 232–249.

Baruch, Y. & Leeming, A. (2001). The added value of MBA studies – graduates' perceptions. *Personnel Review, 30*(5), 589–601.

Baruch, Y., & Nicholson, N. (1997). Home, sweet work: Requirements for effective home-working. *Journal of General Management, 23*(2), 15–30.

Baruch, Y., & Peiperl, M. A. (2000a). Career management practices: An empirical survey and implications. *Human Resource Management, 39*(4), 347–366.

Baruch, Y., & Peiperl, M. A. (2000b). The impact of an MBA on graduate careers. *Human Resource Management Journal, 10*(2), 69–90.

Baruch, Y., & Peiperl, M. A. (2003). An empirical assessment of Sonnenfeld's career systems typology. *International Journal of Human Resource Management, 14*(7), 1266–1282.

Baruch, Y., & Reis, C. (2016). How global are boundaryless careers and how boundaryless are global careers? Challenges and a theoretical perspective. *Thunderbird International Business Review, 58*(1), 13–27.

Baruch, Y., & Rosenstein, E. (1992). Career planning and managing in high-tech organizations. *International Journal of Human Resource Management, 3*(3), 477–496.

Baruch, Y., & Rousseau, D. M. (2019). Integrating psychological contracts and their stakeholders in career studies and management. *The Academy of Management Annals, 13*(1), 84–111.

Baruch, Y., Sayce, S., & Gregoriou, A. (2014). Retirement in a global labour market: A call for abolishing the fixed retirement age. *Personnel Review, 43*(3), 464–482.

Baruch, Y., Steele, D. J., & Quantrill, G. A. (2002). Management of expatriation and repatriation for novice global player. *International Journal of Manpower, 23*, 659–671.

Baruch, Y., Szücs, N., & Gunz, H. (2015). Career studies in search of theory: The rise and rise of concepts. *Career Development International, 20*(1), 3–20.

Baruch, Y., & Vardi, Y. (2016). A fresh look at the dark side of contemporary careers: Toward a realistic discourse. *British Journal of Management, 27*(2), 355–372.

Baruch, Y., & Winkelmann-Gleed, A. (2002). Multiple commitments: Conceptual framework and empirical investigation in the health services. *British Journal of Management, 13*(4): 337–357.

Baruch, Y., Wordsworth, R., Mills, C., & Wright, S. (2016). Career and work attitudes of blue-collar workers, and the impact of a natural disaster chance event on the relationships between intention to quit and actual quit behaviour. *European Journal of Work & Organizational Psychology, 25*(3), 459–473.

Baumgarten, K. (1995). Training and development of international staff. In A. W. Harzing, & J. V. Ruysseveldt (Eds.), *International Human Resource Management* (p. 214). London: Sage.

Baylis, J., Wirtz, J., & Gray, C. (Eds.). (2018). *Strategy in the contemporary world* (6th ed.). Oxford: Oxford University Press.

Beattie, D. F., & Tampoe, F. M. K. (1990). Human resource planning for ICL. *Long Range Planning, 23*(1), 17–28.

Beer, M. (2015). HRM at a crossroads: Comments on 'Evolution of strategic HRM through two founding books: A 30th anniversary perspective on development of the field'. *Human Resource Management, 54*(3), 417–421.

Beer, M., Spector, B., Lawrence, P. R., Mill, Q. D., & Walton, R. E. (1984). *Managing Human Assets*. New York: The Free Press.

Beigi, M., & Otaye-Ebede, L. (2020). Social media, work and nonwork interface: A qualitative inquiry. *Applied Psychology*. https://doi.org/10.1111/apps.12289

Bell, E. L. J. E., & Nkomo, S. M. (2001). Our separate ways: Black and white women and the struggle for professional identity. Cambridge, MA: Harvard Business Press.

Bender, R. (2004). Why do companies use performance-related pay for their executive directors? *Corporate Governance: An International Review, 12*(4), 521–533.

Benko, C., & Weisberg, A. (2007). Mass career customization: Aligning the workplace with today's nontraditional workforce. Cambridge, MA: Harvard Business Review Press.

Bennett, N., & Lemoine, G. J. (2014). What a difference a word makes: Understanding threats to performance in a VUCA world. *Business Horizons, 57*(3), 311–317.

Berkelaar, B. L., & Buzzanell, P. M. (2015). Bait and switch or double-edged sword? The (sometimes) failed promises of calling. *Human Relations, 68*(1), 157–178.

Bernardin, H. J. (1986). Subordinate appraisal: A valuable source of information about managers. *Human Resource Management, 25*, 421–439.

Bernardin, H. J., Kane, J. S., Ross, S., Spina, J. D., & Johnson, D. L. (1995). Performance appraisal design, development, and implementation. In G. R. Ferris, S. D. Rosen, & D. T. Barnum (Eds.), *Handbook of human resource management* (pp. 462–493). Cambridge, MA: Blackwell.

Berry, D. P., & Bell, M. P. (2012). 'Expatriates': Gender, race and class distinctions in international management. *Gender, Work & Organization, 19*(1), 10–28.

Best, S. L. S. (2020). Career forms: Organizational, gig, and in-between. *The Business & Management Review, 11*(1), 215–221.

Bidwell, M. J. (2013). What happened to long-term employment? The role of worker power and environmental turbulence in explaining declines in worker tenure. *Organization Science, 24*(4), 1061–1082.

Bird, A., Gunz, H., & Arthur., M. B. (2002). Careers in a complex world: The search for new perspectives from the 'new science'. *M@n@gement, 5*(1), 1–14.

Birkinshaw, J. (2000). Network relationships inside and outside the firm, and the development of capabilities. In J. Birkinshaw, & P. Hagstrom (Eds.), *The flexible firm* (pp. 3–17). Oxford: Oxford University Press.

Bishu, S. G., & Alkadry, M. G. (2017). A systematic review of the gender pay gap and factors that predict it. *Administration & Society, 49*(1), 65–104.

Black, J. S., & Gregersen, H. B. (1999). The right way to manage expats. *Harvard Business Review*, 77(2), 52–62.

Black, J. S., Gregersen, H. B., & Mendenhall, M. E. (1992) *Global Assignments*. San Francisco, CA: Jossey-Bass.

Blackham, A. (2015). Managing without default retirement in universities: A comparative picture from Australia. *Legal Studies*, 35(3), 502–531.

Blokker, R., Akkermans, J., Tims, M., Jansen, P., & Khapova, S. (2019). Building a sustainable start: The role of career competencies, career success, and career shocks in young professionals' employability. *Journal of Vocational Behavior, 112*, 172–184.

Bloomberg, J. (2018). Digitization, digitalization, and digital transformation: Confuse them at your peril. *Enterprise & Cloud*, 29 April.

BLS Reports (2020). Labor force characteristics by race and ethnicity, 2019. Report 1088, December. https://www.bls.gov/opub/reports/race-and-ethnicity/2019/pdf/home.pdf

Blundel, R., Lockett, N., & Wang, C. (2017). *Exploring entrepreneurship*. London: Sage.

Boje, D. M., Rosile, G. A., Dennehy, R., & Summers, D. (1997). Restorying reengineering: Some deconstructions and postmodern alternatives. *Communication Research*, 24(6), 631–668.

Bolander, P., Weir, A., & Asplund, A. (2017). The practice of talent management: A framework and typology. *Personnel Review*, 46, 1523–1551.

Bolles, M. E., & Bolles, R. N. (2011). What color is your parachute? Guide to job-hunting online: Blogging, career sites, gateways, getting interviews, job boards, job search engines, personal websites, posting resumes, research sites, social networking. Berkeley, CA: Ten Speed Press.

Bonaccio, S., Connelly, C. E., Gellatly, I. R., Jetha, A., & Ginis, K. A. M. (2020). The participation of people with disabilities in the workplace across the employment cycle: Employer concerns and research evidence. *Journal of Business and Psychology*, 35, 135–158.

Borg, M. (1988) International transfer of managers in multinational corporations. Stockholm: Almqvist & Wiksell.

Borg, M., & Harzing, A. W. (1995). Composing an international staff. In A. W. Harzing, & J. V. Ruysseveldt (Eds.), *International human resource management* (pp. 179–204). London: Sage.

Bothma, F. C., Lloyd, S., & Khapova, S. (2015). Work identity: Clarifying the concept. In P. G. W. Jansen, & G. Roodt (Eds.), *Conceptualising and measuring work identity* (pp. 23–51). Dordrecht: Springer.

Boveda, I., & Metz, A. J. (2016). Predicting end-of-career transitions for baby boomers nearing retirement age. *The Career Development Quarterly*, 64(2), 153–168.

Bowman, N. A., & Bastedo, M. N. (2009). Getting on the front page: Organizational reputation, status signals, and the impact of US News and World Report on student decisions. *Research in Higher Education*, 50(5), 415–436.

Boxall, P., & Purcell, J. (2016). *Strategy and human resource management* (4th ed.). Basingstoke: Macmillan.

Boyatzis, R. E., Stubbs, E. C., & Taylor, S. N. (2002). Learning cognitive and emotional intelligence competencies through graduate management education. *Academy of Management Learning & Education, 1*(2), 150–162.

Bozionelos, N., Bozionelos, G., Kostopoulos, K., & Polychroniou, P. (2011). How providing mentoring relates to career success and organizational commitment. *Career Development International*, 16(5), 446–468.

Bracken, D. W., & Rose, D. S. (2011). When does 360-degree feedback create behavior change? And how would we know it when it does? *Journal of Business and Psychology*, 26(2), 183–192.

Bratton, J., & Gold, J. (2017). *Human resource management: Theory and practice* (4th ed.). London: Palgrave.

Brennen, J., & Kreiss, D. (2016). Digitalization: The international encyclopedia of communication theory and philosophy. *Wiley Online Library*, 23 October, pp. 1–11.

Brewster, C., Houldsworth, E., Sparrow, P., & Vernon, G. (2016). *International human resource management* (4th ed.). London: Kogan Page.

Brewster, C., & Scullion, H. (1997). A review and agenda for expatriate HRM. *Human Resource Management Journal, 7*(3), 32–41.

Bright, H., Pryor, L., & Harpham. L. (2005). The role of chance events in career decision making. *Journal of Vocational Behavior, 66*(3), 561–576.

Briscoe, J. P., Hall, D. T., & DeMuth, R. L. F. (2006). Protean and boundaryless careers: An empirical exploration. *Journal of Vocational Behavior, 69*(1), 30–47.

Brockner, J. (1992). Managing the effects of layoffs on survivors. *California Management Review, 34*(2), 9–28.

Brockner, J., Grover, S., Reed, T. F., & DeWitt, R. L. (1992a). Layoffs, job insecurity, and survivors' work effort: Evidence of an inverted-U relationship. *Academy of Management Journal, 35*, 413–425.

Brockner, J., Tyler, T. R., & Cooper-Schieder, R. (1992b). The influence of prior commitment to institution on reactions to perceived unfairness: The higher they are, the harder they fall. *Administrative Science Quarterly, 37*, 241–261.

Brougham, D., & Haar, J. (2018). Smart technology, artificial intelligence, robotics, and algorithms (STARA): Employees' perceptions of our future workplace. *Journal of Management & Organization, 24*(2), 239–257.

Brousseau, K. R., Driver, M. J., Eneroth, K., & Larsson, R. (1996). Career pandemonium: Realigning organizations and individuals. *Academy of Management Executive, 10*(4), 52–66.

Brown, M., & Heywood, J. S. (2005). Performance appraisal systems: Determinants and change. *British Journal of Industrial Relations, 43*(4), 659–679.

Brunetto, Y., Rodwell, J., Shacklock, K., Farr-Wharton, R., & Demir, D. (2016). The impact of individual and organizational resources on nurse outcomes and intent to quit. *Journal of Advanced Nursing, 72*(12), 3093–3103.

Bryson, A., Ebbinghaus, B., & Visser, J. (2011). Introduction: Causes, consequences and cures of union decline. *European Journal of Industrial Relations, 17*(2), 97–105.

Buchter, L. (2020). Escaping the ellipsis of diversity: Insider activists' use of implementation resources to influence organization policy. *Administrative Science Quarterly.* https://doi.org/10.1177/0001839220963633

Buckley, P. J., & Ghauri, P. (Eds.). (2015). *International business strategy: Theory and practice.* London: Routledge.

Bui, H. T. M., & Baruch, Y. (2012). Learning organizations in higher education: An empirical evaluation within an international context. *Management Learning, 43*(5), 515–544.

Bui, H. T., Chau, V. S., & Cox, J. (2019). Managing the survivor syndrome as scenario planning methodology… and it matters! *International Journal of Productivity and Performance Management, 68*(4), 838–854.

Cameron, K. (2015). Downsizing. In C. Cooper (Ed.), *Wiley encyclopedia of management* (pp. 1–3). Chichester: Wiley.

Campbell, R. J. & Moses, J. L. (1986). Careers for organizational perspective. In D. T. Hall & Assoc., *Career Development in Organizations.* San Francisco, CA: Jossey-Bass.

Cappellen, T., & Janssens, M. (2008). Global managers' career competencies. *Career Development International, 13*(6), 514–537.

Cappellen, T., & Janssens, M. (2010). Characteristics of international work: Narratives of the global manager. *Thunderbird International Business Review, 52*(4), 337–348.

Cappelli, P., & Crocker-Hefter, A. (1996). Distinctive human resource are firms' core competencies. *Organizational Dynamics, 23*(4), 7–22.

Carling, J., & Hernández-Carretero, M. (2011). Protecting Europe and protecting migrants? Strategies for managing unauthorised migration from Africa. *The British Journal of Politics and International Relations, 13*(1), 42–58.

Carson, K. D., & Bedeian, A. G. (1994). Career commitment: Construction of a measure and examination of its psychometric properties. *Journal of Vocational Behavior, 44*, 237–262.

Carson, K. D., & Carson, P. P. (1998). Career commitment, competencies, and citizenship. *Journal of Career Assessment, 6*(2), 195–208.

Cartwright, S., & Cooper, C. L. (2012). *Managing mergers acquisitions & strategic alliances* (4th ed.). London: Routledge.

Carulli, L. M., Noroian, C. L., & Levine, C. (1989). Employee-driven career development. *Personnel Administrator, 34*(3), 66–70.

Cascio, W. F. (2000). New workplaces. In J. M. Kummerow (Ed.), *New Directions in Career Planning and the Workplace* (2nd ed.). Palo Alto, CA: Davies-Black.

Cascio, W. F. (2010). Downsizing and redundancy. *The Sage handbook of human resource management* (pp. 334–346). London: Sage.

Casper, W. J., Wayne, J. H., & Manegold, J. G. (2013). Who will we recruit? Targeting deep- and surface-level diversity with human resource policy advertising. *Human Resource Management, 52*(3), 311–332.

Cassell, C., & Kele, J. (2020). Managing diversity and inclusion. In A. Wilkinson & T. Dundon, *Contemporary human resource management: Texts and cases*. London: Sage.

Castro, A. J., & Bauml, M. (2009). Why now? Factors associated with choosing teaching as a second career and their implications for teacher education programs. *Teacher Education Quarterly, 36*(3), 113–126.

Cattell, R. B., & Kline, P. (1977). *The scientific analysis of personality and motivation*. New York: Academic Press.

Cavanagh, T. (2014). *Sons of the Old Country*. Bloomington, IN: IN Universe LLC.

Chadha, D., & Toner, J. (2017). Focusing in on employability: Using content analysis to explore the employability discourse in UK and USA universities. *International Journal of Educational Technology in Higher Education, 14*(1), 33.

Chakraborty, D., & Biswas, W. (2019). Evaluating the impact of human resource planning programs in addressing the strategic goal of the firm. *Journal of Advances in Management Research, 16*(5), 659–682.

Chatman, J. A., Polzer, J. T., Barsade, S. G., & Neale, M. A. (1998). Being different yet feeling similar: The influence of demographic composition and organizational culture on work processes and outcomes. *Administrative Science Quarterly, 43*, 749–780.

Chatterjee, N., & Das, N. (2015). Key psychological factors as predictors of entrepreneurial success: A conceptual framework. *Academy of Entrepreneurship Journal, 21*(1), 102–114.

Chen, C. C., Choi, J., & Chi, S.-C. (2002). Making sense of local-expatriate compensation disparity: Mitigation by local referents, ideological explanations, and interpersonal sensitivity in China-foreign joint ventures. *Academy of Management Journal, 45*(4), 807–817.

Chen, J., May, D. R., Schwoerer, C. E., & Augelli, B. (2018). Exploring the boundaries of career calling: The moderating roles of procedural justice and psychological safety. *Journal of Career Development, 45*(2), 103–116.

Chen, G., Smith, T. A., Kirkman, B. L., Zhang, P., Lemoine, G. J., & Farh, J. L. (2019). Multiple team membership and empowerment spillover effects: Can empowerment processes cross team boundaries?. *Journal of Applied Psychology, 104*(3), 321–340.

Cheung, M., & Shih, T. L. (2018). From a surgeon to an artist, an integration of medicine and art – Dr. Anthony P. Yim's 'My second career: A collection of artwork'. *Journal of Thoracic Disease, 10*(6), E504.

Cho, Y., & Jiang, W. Y. (2021). If you do what you love, will the money follow? How work orientation impacts objective career outcomes via managerial (mis)perceptions. *Academy of Management Journal*. https://doi.org/10.5465/amj.2020.0841

Christensen, K., & Schneider, B. (Eds.). (2011). *Workplace flexibility: Realigning 20th-century jobs for a 21st-century workforce*. Ithaca, NY: Cornell University Press.

Chudzikowski, K. (2012). Career transitions and career success in the 'new' career era. *Journal of Vocational Behavior, 81*(2), 298–306.

Clair, J. A., Beatty, J., & MacLean, T. (2002). *Out of sight but not out of mind: How people manage invisible social identities in the workplace.* Paper presented at the Academy of Management, August 2002, Denver, CO.

Clark, M., & Zukas, M. (2016). Understanding successful sandwich placements: A Bourdieusian approach. *Studies in Higher Education, 41*(7), 1281–1295.

Clarke, M., & Patrickson, M. (2007). The new covenant of employability. *Employee Relations, 30*(2), 121–141.

Claussen, J., Grohsjean, T., Luger, J., & Probst, G. (2014). Talent management and career development: What it takes to get promoted. *Journal of World Business, 49*(2), 236–244.

Clemense, J. K., & Mayer, D. F. (1987). *The classic touch.* Homewood, IL: Dow Jones-Irwin.

Clutterbuck, D. 1994. *The Power of Empowerment.* London: Kogan Page.

Clutterbuck, D., & Dearlove, D. (1999). *The interim manager.* London: Pitman.

Cocchiara, F. K., Kwesiga, E., Bell, M. P., & Baruch, Y. (2010). Who benefits from graduate degrees? Effects of sex and perceived discrimination on human capital. *Career Development International, 15*(1), 39–58.

Cohen, A. (1991). Career stage as a moderator of the relationships between organizational commitment and its outcomes: A meta-analysis. *Journal of Occupational Psychology, 64*, 253–268.

Cohen, A. (2018). Counterproductive work behaviors: Understanding the dark side of personalities in organizational life. New York: Routledge.

Collings, D. G., Mellahi, K., & Cascio, W. F. (2019). Global talent management and performance in multinational enterprises: A multilevel perspective. *Journal of Management, 45*(2), 540–566.

Collins, C. J. (2020). Expanding the resource based view model of strategic human resource management. *The International Journal of Human Resource Management, 32*(2), 1–28.

Combs, J., Liu, Y., Hall, A., & Ketchen, D. (2006). How much do high-performance work practices matter? A meta-analysis of their effects on organizational performance. *Personnel Psychology, 59*(3), 501–528.

Comfort, M. (1997). *Portfolio people.* London: Century.

Conger, J. A., & Kanungo, R. N. (1988). The empowerment process: Integrating theory and practice. *Academy of Management Review, 13*(3), 471–482.

Conner, J. (2000). Developing the global leaders of tomorrow. *Human Resource Management, 39*(2 & 3), 147–157.

Converse, P. D., Pathak, J., DePaul-Haddock, A. M., Gotlib, T., & Merbedone, M. (2012). Controlling your environment and yourself: Implications for career success. *Journal of Vocational Behavior, 80*(1), 148–159.

Cooke, F. L., Wood, G., Wang, M., & Veen, A. (2019). How far has international HRM travelled? A systematic review of literature on multinational corporations (2000–2014). *Human Resource Management Review, 29*(1), 59–75.

Cooper, C. L., Liukkonen P., & Cartwright, S. (1996). *Stress prevention in the workplace.* Dublin: European Foundation.

Coren, G. (2001) *James Dyson: Against the odds.* London: Texere.

Cornelissen, J. P., Oswick, C., Thøger Christensen, L., & Phillips, N. (2008). Metaphor in organizational research: Context, modalities and implications for research – Introduction. *Organization Studies, 29*(1), 7–22.

Cornell, B., Hewitt, R., & Bekhradnia, B. (2020). *Mind the (graduate gender pay) gap.* Oxford: Higher Education Policy Institute. https://www.hepi.ac.uk/wp-content/uploads/2020/11/Mind-the-Graduate-Gender-Pay-Gap_HEPI-Report-135_FINAL.pdf

Corrigan, P., & Matthews, A. (2003). Stigma and disclosure: Implications for coming out of the closet. *Journal of Mental Health, 12*(3), 235–248.

Costigan, R., Gurbuz, S., & Sigri, U. (2018). Schein's career anchors: Testing factorial validity, invariance across countries, and relationship with core self-evaluations. *Journal of Career Development*, *45*(3), 199–214.

Cox, T. H., & Blake, S. (1991). Managing cultural diversity: Implications for organizational competitiveness. *Academy of Management Executive*, *5*(3): 45–56.

Crabb, S. (1995). Jobs for all in the global market? *People Management*, January, 22–7.

Craig, M. A., & Richeson, J. A. (2018). Hispanic population growth engenders conservative shift among non-Hispanic racial minorities. *Social Psychological and Personality Science*, *9*(4), 383–392.

Cramer, J., & Krueger, A. B. (2016). Disruptive change in the taxi business: The case of Uber. *American Economic Review*, *106*(5), 177–182.

Crant, J. M. (2000). Proactive behavior in organizations. *Journal of Management*, *26*, 435–462.

Crenshaw, K. W. (2017). *On intersectionality: Essential writings*. New York: The New Press.

Cropanzano, R., & Greenberg, J. (1997). Progress in organizational justice. In C. Cooper, & I. Robertson (Eds.), *International review of industrial and organizational psychology*. New York: Wiley.

Crowley-Henry, M., O'Connor, E., & Al Ariss, A. (2018). Portrayal of skilled migrants' careers in business and management studies: A review of the literature and future research agenda. *European Management Review*, *15*(3), 375–394.

Culler, J. (1982). On deconstruction: Theory and criticism after structuralism. Ithaca, NY: Cornell University Press.

Culpin, V., Millar, C., Peters, K., Lyons, S. T., Schweitzer, L., & Ng, E. S. (2015). How have careers changed? An investigation of changing career patterns across four generations. *Journal of Managerial Psychology*, *30*(1), 8–21.

Cuming, M. W. (1986), *Personnel management*. London: Heinemann.

Czarniawska, B. (1997). A four times told tale: Combining narrative and scientific knowledge in organization studies. *Organization*, *4*, 7–30.

Dahlström, C., & Lapuente, V. (2010). Explaining cross-country differences in performance-related pay in the public sector. *Journal of Public Administration Research and Theory*, *20*(3), 577–600.

Dalton, G., Thompson, P., & Price, P. (1977). The four stages of professional careers: A new look at performance by professionals. *Organizational Dynamics*, *6*, 23.

Danziger, K. (2013). Psychology and its history. *Theory & Psychology*, *23*(6), 829–839.

Danziger, N., Rachman-Moore, D., & Valency, R. (2008). The construct validity of Schein's career anchors orientation inventory. *Career Development International*, *13*, 7–19.

Datta, D. K., Guthrie, J. P., Basuil, D., & Pandey, A. (2010). Causes and effects of employee downsizing: A review and synthesis. *Journal of Management*, *36*(1), 281–348.

Datta, N., Giupponi, G., & Machin, S. (2019). Zero-hours contracts and labour market policy. *Economic Policy*, *34*(99), 369–427.

Davidson, M. J., & Burke, R. J. (Eds.). (2011). *Women in management worldwide* (Vol. *2*). Aldershot: Gower.

Davis, E. B. (2017). Everett C. Hughes. In M. H. Jacobsen (Ed.), *The interactionist imagination* (pp. 121–144). London: Palgrave Macmillan.

Day, N. E., & Greene, P. G. (2008). A case for sexual orientation diversity management in small and large organizations. *Human Resource Management*, *47*(3), 637–654.

Day, N. E., & Schoenrade, P. (1995). Staying in the closet versus coming out: Relationships between communication about sexual orientation and work attitudes. *Personnel Psychology*, *50*, 147–163.

De Koeijer, R. J., Paauwe, J., & Huijsman, R. (2014). Toward a conceptual framework for exploring multilevel relationships between Lean Management and Six Sigma, enabling HRM, strategic climate and outcomes in healthcare. *The International Journal of Human Resource Management*, *25*(21), 2911–2925.

De Meuse, K. P., Vanderheiden, P. A., & Bergmann, T. J. (1994). Announced layoffs: Their effect on corporate financial performance. *Human Resource Management, 33*(4), 509–530.

De Pasquale, J. A., & Lange, R. A. (1971). Job hopping and the MBA. *Harvard Business Review*, Nov/Dec, 4–12, 151.

De Stobbeleir, K. E., Ashford, S. J., & Buyens, D. (2011). Self-regulation of creativity at work: The role of feedback-seeking behavior in creative performance. *Academy of Management Journal, 54*(4), 811–831.

De Vos, A., Dewettinck, K., & Buyens, D. (2009). The professional career on the right track: A study on the interaction between career self-management and organizational career management in explaining employee outcomes. *European Journal of Work and Organizational Psychology, 18*(1), 55–80.

De Vos, A., & Van der Heijden, B. (Eds.). (2015). *Handbook of research on sustainable careers.* Cheltenham: Edward Elgar.

De Vos, A., Van der Heijden, B. I., & Akkermans, J. (2020). Sustainable careers: Towards a conceptual model. *Journal of Vocational Behavior.* doi.org/10.1016/j.jvb.2018.06.011

Debebe, G., Anderson, D., Bilimoria, D., & Vinnicombe, S. M. (2016). Women's leadership development programs: Lessons learned and new frontiers. *Journal of Management Education, 40*(3), 231–252.

DeFillippi, R. J., & Arthur, M. B. (1994). The boundaryless career: A competency-based career perspective. *Journal of Organizational Behavior, 15*(4), 307–324.

DeFillippi, R. J., & Arthur, M. B. (1998). Paradox in project-based enterprise: The case of film making. *California Management Review, 40*(2), 125–139.

Delaney, T. J., & Huselid, A. M. (1996). The impact of human resource management practices on perceptions of organizational performance. *Academy of Management Journal, 39*, 949–969.

DeNisi, A. S., & Murphy, K. R. (2017). Performance appraisal and performance management: 100 years of progress? *Journal of Applied Psychology, 102*(3), 421–433.

Derr, B. C. (1986). Managing the new careerists: The diverse career success orientation of today's workers. San Francisco, CA: Jossey-Bass.

Devanna, M. A., Fombrun, C. J., & Tichy, N. M. (1981). Human resource management: Strategic perspective. *Organizational Dynamics, 9*(3), 51–67.

Dewey, J. (1939). *Theory of valuation.* Chicago, IL: University of Chicago Press.

Dickmann, M., & Andresen, M. (2018). Managing global careerists: Individual, organizational and societal needs. In M. Dickmann, V. Suutari, & O. Wurtz (Eds.), *The management of global careers* (pp. 149–181). Cham: Palgrave Macmillan.

Dickmann, M., & Baruch, Y. (2011). *Global careers.* London: Routledge.

Dickmann, M., Suutari, V., & Wurtz, O. (Eds.). (2018). *The management of global careers: Exploring the rise of international work.* London: Palgrave Macmillan.

Dimov, D., & De Clercq, D. (2006). Venture capital investment strategy and portfolio failure rate: A longitudinal study. *Entrepreneurship Theory and Practice, 30*(2), 207–223.

Direnzo, M. S., & Greenhaus, J. H. (2011). Job search and voluntary turnover in a boundaryless world: A control theory perspective. *Academy of Management Review, 36*(3), 567–589.

Dobrow Riza, S., & Heller, D. (2015). Follow your heart or your head? A longitudinal study of the facilitating role of calling and ability in the pursuit of a challenging career. *Journal of Applied Psychology, 100*(3), 695–712.

Docquier, F., & Rapoport, H. (2012). Globalization, brain drain, and development. *Journal of Economic Literature, 50*(3), 681–730.

Doganis, R. (1994). The impact of liberalization on European airline strategies and operations. *Journal of Air Transport Management, 1*(1), 15–25.

Doherty, N. T., & Dickmann, M. (2012). Measuring the return on investment in international assignments: An action research approach. *The International Journal of Human Resource Management, 23*(16), 3434–3454.

Doherty, N., & Horsted, J. (1995). Helping survivors to stay on board. *People Management, 12*, 26–31.

Done, J. & Mulvey, R. (2016) *Brilliant Graduate Career Handbook*. 3rd edition. Harlow: Pearson.

Dougherty, T. W., Dreher, G. F., & Whitely, W. (1993). The MBA as careerist: An analysis of early-career job change. *Journal of Management, 19*(3), 535–548.

Douglas, E. J., & Shepherd, D. A. (2002). Self-employment as a career choice: Attitudes, entrepreneurial intentions, and utility maximization. *Entrepreneurship Theory and Practice, 26*(3), 81–90.

Dowling, P. J., Schuler, R. S., & Welch, D. E. (1994). *International dimensions of human resource, management* (p. 149). Belmont, CA: Wadworth.

Downs, A. (1995) *Corporate executions*. New York: AMACOM.

Drucker, P. F. (1999) *Management challenges for the 21st century* (p. 61). Oxford: Butterworth-Heinemann.

Drucker, P. (2014). *Innovation and entrepreneurship*. London: Routledge.

Dubey, A. D., & Tripathi, S. (2020). Analysing the sentiments towards work-from-home experience during covid-19 pandemic. *Journal of Innovation Management, 8*(1), 13–19.

Dubina, I. N., Carayannis, E. G., & Campbell, D. F. (2012). Creativity economy and a crisis of the economy? Coevolution of knowledge, innovation, and creativity, and of the knowledge economy and knowledge society. *Journal of the Knowledge Economy, 3*(1), 1–24.

Dulewicz, V. (2000). Emotional intelligence: The key to future successful corporate leadership? *Journal of General Management, 25*(3), 1–14.

Dunlop, J. E. T. (1959). *Industrial relations system*. New York: Holt.

Dutton, J. E., & Dukerich, J. M. (1991). Keeping an eye on the mirror: Image and identity in organizational adaptation. *Academy of Management Journal, 34*(3), 517–554.

Earley, P. C., & Ang, S. (2003). *Cultural intelligence: Individual interactions across cultures*. Palo Alto: Stanford University Press.

Eby, L., Allen, T., & Brinley, A. (2005). A cross-level investigation of the relationship between career management practices and career-related attitudes. *Group & Organization Management, 30*(6), 565–596.

Eckhardt, J. T., & Shane, S. A. (2003). Opportunities and entrepreneurship. *Journal of Management, 29*(3), 333–349.

Eden, D. (1984). Self-fulfilling prophecy as a management tool: Harnessing Pygmalion. *Academy of Management Review, 9*(1), 64–73.

Edmans, A. (2012). The link between job satisfaction and firm value, with implications for corporate social responsibility. *The Academy of Management Perspectives, 26*(4), 1–19.

Eger, L., Komárková, L., Egerová, D., & Mičík, M. (2021). The effect of COVID-19 on consumer shopping behaviour: Generational cohort perspective. *Journal of Retailing and Consumer Services, 61*. https://doi.org/10.1016/j.jretconser.2021.102542

Ehiyazaryan, E., & Barraclough, N. (2009). Enhancing employability: Integrating real world experience in the curriculum. *Education+ Training, 51*(4), 292–308.

Eisenberger, R., Fasolo, P., & Davis-LaMastro, V. (1990) Perceived organizational support and employee diligence, commitment, and innovation. *Journal of Applied Psychology, 75*(1), 51–59.

El Haddad, R., Karkoulian, S., & Nehme, R. (2018). The impact of 360 feedback appraisal system on organizational justice and sustainability: The mediating roles of gender and managerial levels. *International Journal of Organizational Analysis, 27*(3), 712–728.

Elbasha, T., & Baruch, Y. (2019). *Celebrity chefs' careers*. Paper presented at the British Academy of Management, Birmingham.

Elley-Brown, M. J., Pringle, J. K., & Harris, C. (2018). Women opting in?: New perspectives on the Kaleidoscope career model. *Australian Journal of Career Development, 27*(3), 172–180.

Elliott, C., & Soo, K. T. (2016). The impact of MBA programme attributes on post-MBA salaries. *Education Economics, 24*(4), 427–443.

Elsbach, K. D., & Kramer, R. M. (1996). Members responses to organizational identity threats: Encountering and countering the Business Week rankings. *Administrative Science Quarterly, 41*(3), 442–476.

Engel, D. M. (2016). *The Myth of the Litigious Society*. University of Chicago Press, Chicago.

Enquist, P. O. (1984). The act of flying backward with dignity. *Daedalus, 113*(1), 61–74.

Esters, L., & Retallick, M. (2013). Effect of an experiential and work-based learning program on vocational identity, career decision self-efficacy, and career maturity. *Career and Technical Education Research, 38*(1), 69–83.

Etmanski, B. (2019). The prospective shift away from academic career aspirations. *Higher Education, 77*(2), 343–358.

Eurostat (2018). How many hours do Europeans work per week? https://ec.europa.eu/eurostat/web/products-eurostat-news/-/DDN-20180125-1

Evans, A. (1993). Working at home: A new career dimension. *International Journal of Career Management, 5*(2), 16–23.

Evans, P. (1986) New directions in career management. *Personnel Management*, December, 26–29.

Fahami, R. (2018). Portfolio careers. *InnovAiT, 11*(10), 583–587.

Fang He, V., Sirén, C., Singh, S., Solomon, G., & von Krogh, G. (2018). Keep calm and carry on: Emotion regulation in entrepreneurs' learning from failure. *Entrepreneurship Theory and Practice, 42*(4), 605–630.

Farber, H. S. (2010). Job loss and the decline in job security in the United States. In K. G. Abraham, J. R. Spletzer, & M. J. Harper (Eds.), *Labor in the new economy* (pp. 223–262). Chicago, IL: University of Chicago Press.

Fares, J., Al Tabosh, H., Saadeddin, Z., El Mouhayyar, C., & Aridi, H. (2016). Stress, burnout and coping strategies in preclinical medical students. *North American Journal of Medical Sciences, 8*(2), 75–81.

Farina, E., Green, C., & McVicar, D. (2020). Zero hours contracts and their growth. *British Journal of Industrial Relations, 58*(3), 507–531.

Farndale, E., Pai, A., Sparrow, P., & Scullion, H. (2014). Balancing individual and organizational goals in global talent management: A mutual-benefits perspective. *Journal of World Business, 49*(2), 204–214.

Feldman, D. C. (1988). *Managing careers in organizations* (p. 24). Glenview, IL: Scott-Foresman.

Feldman, D. C., & Tompson, H. B. (1993). Expatriation, repatriation, and domestic geographical relocation: An empirical investigation of adjustment to new job assignments. *Journal of International Business Studies, 24*(3), 507–529.

Feldman, D. C., & Turnley, W. H. (2004). Contingent employment in academic careers: Relative deprivation among adjunct faculty. *Journal of Vocational Behavior, 64*(2), 284–307.

Festinger, L. (1957). *A theory of cognitive dissonance*. Paolo Alto, CA: Stanford University Press.

Fischlmayr, I. C. (2002). Female self-perception as barrier to international careers?. *International Journal of Human Resource Management, 13*(5), 773–783.

Fishbein, M., & Ajzen, I. (1975). Belief, attitude, intention, and behavior: An introduction to theory and research. Reading, MA: Addison-Wesley.

Fisk, S. R., & Overton, J. (2019). Who wants to lead? Anticipated gender discrimination reduces women's leadership ambitions. *Social Psychology Quarterly, 82*(3), 319–332.

Fitzgerald, L. F., & Cortina, L. M. (2018). *Sexual harassment in work organizations: A view from the 21st century*. In C. B Travis, J. W. White, A. Rutherford, W. S. Williams, S. L. Cook, & K. F. Wyche (Eds.), *APA handbooks in psychology®. APA handbook of the psychology of women: Perspectives on women's private and public lives* (p. 215–234). Washington DC: American Psychological Association.

Flanagan, D. J., & O'Shaughnessy, K. C. (2005). The effect of layoffs on firm reputation. *Journal of Management, 31*(3), 445–463.

Folger, R., & Cropanzano, R. (1998). *Organizational justice and human resource management*. Thousand Oaks, CA: Sage.

Fombrun, C. J., Tichy, N. M., & Devanna, M. A. (1984). *Strategic human resource management* (pp. 19–31). New York: Wiley.

Forbes, J. B. (1987). Early intraorganizational mobility: Patterns and influences. *Academy of Management Journal, 30*(1), 110–135.

Forbes, J. B., & Piercy, J. E. (1991). *Corporate mobility and paths to the top.* New York: Quorum Books.

Form, W. H., & Miller, D. C. (1949). Occupational career path as a sociological instrument. *American Journal of Sociology, 54,* 317–329.

Fortune (2021). https://fortune.com/2020/05/18/women-ceos-fortune-500–2020/

Foss, N. J., Pedersen, T., Reinholt Fosgaard, M., & Stea, D. (2015). Why complementary HRM practices impact performance: The case of rewards, job design, and work climate in a knowledge-sharing context. *Human Resource Management, 54*(6), 955–976.

Foster, K. (2012). Work, narrative identity and social affiliation. *Work, Employment and Society, 26*(6), 935–950.

Frost, R. (1915). The Road Not Taken, in: 'A Group of Poems', *The Atlantic Monthly* (August issue).

Fugate, M., & Kinicki, A. J. (2008). A dispositional approach to employability: Development of a measure and test of implications for employee reactions to organizational change. *Journal of Occupational and Organizational Psychology, 81*(3), 503–527.

Fugate, M., Van der Heijden, B., De Vos, A., Forrier, A., & De Cuyper, N. (2021). Is what's past prologue? A review and agenda for contemporary employability research. *Academy of Management Annals, 15*(1), 266–298.

Furnham, A. (2000). Work in 2020: Prognostications about the world of work 20 years into the millennium. *Journal of Managerial Psychology, 15*(3), 242–254.

Furnham, A. (2005). The psychology of behaviour at work: The individual in the organization. Hove: Psychology Press.

Furnham, A., Hyde, G., & Trickey, G. (2014). The dark side of career preference: Dark side traits, motives, and values. *Journal of Applied Social Psychology, 44*(2), 106–114.

Gabriel, Y. (2012). Organizations in a state of darkness: Towards a theory of organizational miasma. *Organization Studies, 33*(9), 1137–1152.

Ganster, D. C., Rosen, C. C., & Fisher, G. G. (2018). Long working hours and well-being: What we know, what we do not know, and what we need to know. *Journal of Business and Psychology, 33*(1), 25–39.

Garavan, T. N. (2007). A strategic perspective on human resource development. *Advances in Developing Human Resources, 9*(1), 11–30.

Gardner, H. (1983). Frames of mind: The theory of multiple intelligence. London: Heinemann.

Gatzert, N. (2015). The impact of corporate reputation and reputation damaging events on financial performance: Empirical evidence from the literature. *European Management Journal, 33*(6), 485–499.

Gazier, B. (2017). Employability – the complexity of a policy notion. In P. Weinert, M. Baukens, P. Bollerot, M. Pineschi-Gapenne, & U. Walwei (Eds.), *Employability: From theory to practice* (pp. 3–24). New York: Routledge.

Ghasemaghaei, M., Kapoor, B., & Turel, O. (2019). Impact of MBA programs' business analytics breadth on salary and job placement: The role of university ranking. *Communications of the Association for Information Systems, 44,* 892–906.

Ghosh, R., & Reio Jr., T. G. (2013). Career benefits associated with mentoring for mentors: A meta-analysis. *Journal of Vocational Behavior, 83*(1), 106–116.

Ghoshal, S., Bartlett, C. A., & Moran, P. (1999). A new manifesto for management. *Sloan Management Review, 40*(3), 9–22.

Giddens, A. (1997). *Sociology* (3rd ed.). Cambridge: Polity Press.

Gilbert, J. A., & Ivancevich, J. M. (2001). Effects of diversity management on attachment. *Journal of Applied Social Psychology, 31*(7), 1331–1349.

Gill, C., & Meyer, D. (2011). The role and impact of HRM policy. *International Journal of Organizational Analysis, 19*(1), 5–28.

Gilliland, S. W. (1994). Effects of procedural and distributive justice on reactions to a selection system. *Journal of Applied Psychology, 79*(5), 691–701.

Gilpin, D. (2010). Organizational image construction in a fragmented online media environment. *Journal of Public Relations Research, 22*(3), 265–287.

Giménez-Gómez, J. M., Walle, Y. M., & Zergawu, Y. Z. (2019). Trends in African migration to Europe: Drivers beyond economic motivations. *Journal of Conflict Resolution, 63*(8), 1797–1831.

Gioia, D. A., Patvardhan, S. D., Hamilton, A. L., & Corley, K. G. (2013). Organizational identity formation and change. *Academy of Management Annals, 7*(1), 123–193.

Glieck, J. (1988). *Chaos: Making a new science.* London: Heinemann.

Gold, M., & Fraser, J. (2002). Managing self-management: Successful transitions to portfolio careers. *Work, Employment and Society, 16*(4), 579–597.

Goldberg, L. R. (1990). An alternative 'description of personality': The Big Five factor structure. *Journal of Personality and Social Psychology, 59,* 1216–1229.

Goldberg, L. R. (1993). The structure of personality. *American Psychologist, 48,* 26–34.

Goleman, D. (2006) *Emotional Intelligence.* New York: Bantam Books.

Gottfredson, G. D., & Holland, J. L. (1996). *Dictionary of Holland occupational codes* (3rd ed.). Lutz, FL: Psychological Assessment Resources.

Gottlieb, B. H., Kelloway, E. K., & Barham, E. (1998). *Flexible work arrangements.* Chichester: Wiley.

Gough, L. (2011). C. Northcote Parkinson's Parkinson's Law: A modern-day interpretation of a true classic. Oxford: Infinite Ideas.

Gouldner, A. (1957). Cosmopolitans and locals: Toward an analysis of latent social roles. *Administrative Science Quarterly, 2,* 281–306.

Goxe, F., & Belhoste, N. (2019). Be global or be gone: Global mindset as a source of division in an international business community. *European Management Review, 16*(3), 617–632.

GraduateCoach (2020). 24 job websites for graduates. https://graduatecoach.co.uk/job-websites-graduates/

Granrose, C. S., & Portwood, J. D. (1987). Matching individual career plans and organizational career management. *Academy of Management Journal, 30*(4), 699–720.

Grant, D. (2016). Business analysis techniques in business reengineering. *Business Process Management Journal, 22*(1), 75–88.

Grant, R. M. (1991). The resource-based theory of competitive advantage. *California Management Review, 33*(3), 114–135.

Greenberg, J., & Cropanzano, R. (Eds.). (2001). *Advances in organizational justice.* Palo Alto, CA: Stanford University Press.

Greenhalgh, L., & Rosenblatt, Z. (2010). Evolution of research on job insecurity. *International Studies of Management and Organization, 40,* 6–19.

Greenhaus, J. H., Callanan, G. A., & DiRenzo, M. (2008). A boundaryless perspective on careers. In J. Barling (Ed.), *Handbook of Organizational Behavior:* 277–299. Thousand Oaks, CA: Sage.

Greenhaus, J. H., Callanan, G. A., & Godshalk, V. M. (2019). *Career management for life* (5th ed.). New York: Routledge.

Greer, C. R., Youngblood, S., & Gray, D. (1999). HR outsourcing. *Academy of Management Executive, 13*(3), 85–96.

Grimland, S., Vigoda-Gadot, E., & Baruch, Y. (2012). Career attitudes and success of managers: The impact of chance event, protean & traditional careers. *International Journal of Human Resource Management, 23*(6), 1074–1094.

Groves, K. S. (2007). Integrating leadership development and succession planning best practices. *Journal of Management Development, 26*(3), 239–260.

Groysberg, B., Johnson, W., & Lin, E. (2019). What to do when industry disruption threatens your career. *Sloan Management Review, 60*(3), 57–68.

Guan, Y., Arthur, M. B., Khapova, S. N., Hall, R. J., & Lord, R. G. (2019). Career boundarylessness and career success: A review, integration and guide to future research. *Journal of Vocational Behavior, 110,* 390–402.

Gubler, M., Arnold, J., & Coombs, C. (2014). Reassessing the protean career concept: Empirical findings, conceptual components, and measurement. *Journal of Organizational Behavior, 35*(S1), S23–S40.

Gubler, M., Biemann, T., Tschopp, C., & Grote, G. (2015). How career anchors differentiate managerial career trajectories: A sequence analysis perspective. *Journal of Career Development, 42*(5), 412–430.

Guest, D. E. (2017). Human resource management and employee wellbeing: Towards a new analytic framework. *Human Resource Management Journal, 27*(1), 22–38.

Gunnigle, P., Lavelle, J., & Monaghan, S. (2013). Weathering the storm? Multinational companies and human resource management through the global financial crisis. *International Journal of Manpower, 34*(3), 214–231.

Gunz, H. (1989). The dual meaning of managerial careers: Organizational and individual levels of analysis. *Journal of Management Studies, 26*(3), 225–250.

Gunz, H. P., & Jalland, R. M. (1996) Managerial careers and business strategies. *Academy of Management Review, 21*(3), 718–756.

Gunz, H., Mayrhofer, W., & Tolbert, P. (2011). Careers as a social political phenomenon in the global economy. *Organization Studies, 32*(12), 1613–1620.

Guo, C., Porschitz, E. T., & Alves, J. (2013). Exploring career agency during self-initiated repatriation: A study of Chinese sea turtles. *Career Development International, 18*(1), 34–55.

Guo, L., & Baruch, Y. (2020). The moderating role of a city's institutional capital and people's migration status on career success in China. *Human Relations.* https://doi.org/10.1177/0018726720946102

Gutteridge, T. G. (1986). Organizational career development systems: The state of the practice. In D. T. Hall (Ed.), *Career development in organizations* (pp. 50–94). San Francisco, CA: Jossey-Bass.

Gutteridge, T. G., Leibowitz, Z. B., & Shore, J. E. (1993). *Organizational career development.* San Francisco, CA: Jossey-Bass.

Guzzo, R. A., Nooman, K. A., & Elron, E. (1994). Expatriate managers and the psychological contract. *Journal of Applied Psychology, 79*(4), 617–626.

Hajrullina, A. D., & Romadanova, O. A. (2014). Technique of measurement of value of the human capital as intangible asset of corporation. *Life Science Journal, 11*(6s), 518–521.

Hakim, C. (2000). Work–lifestyle choices in the 21st century: Preference theory. Oxford: Oxford University Press.

Hales, C. (2000). Management and empowerment programmes. *Work, Employment & Society, 14*(3), 501–519.

Hall, D. T. (1976). *Careers in organizations.* Glenview, IL: Scott, Foresman.

Hall, D. T. (1996). *The career is dead – long live the career.* San Francisco, CA: Jossey-Bass.

Hall, D. T. (2002). *Careers in and out of organizations.* Thousand Oaks, CA: Sage.

Hall, D. T. (2004). The protean career: A quarter-century journey. *Journal of Vocational Behavior, 65*(1), 1–13.

Hall, D. T., & Chandler, D. E. (2005). Psychological success: When the career is a calling. *Journal of Organizational Behavior, 26*(2), 155–176.

Hall, D. T., & Mirvis, P. H. (1996). The new protean career: Psychological success and the path with a heart. In D. T. Hall (Ed.), *The career is dead – long live the career* (pp. 15–45). San Francisco, CA: Jossey-Bass.

Hall, D. T., & Moss, J. E. (1998). The new protean career contract: Helping organizations and employees adapt. *Organizational Dynamics, 26*(3), 22–37.

Hall, D. T., & Nougaim, K. (1968) An examination of Maslow's need hierarchy in an organizational setting. *Organizational Behavior and Human Performance, 3,* 12–35.

Hall, D. T., Yip, J., & Doiron, K. (2018). Protean careers at work: Self-direction and values orientation in psychological success. *Annual Review of Organizational Psychology and Organizational Behavior, 5,* 129–156.

Hall, J. L., Posner, B. Z., & Harder, J. W. (1989) Performance appraisal systems. *Group & Organizational Studies, 14*(1), 51–59.

Hall-Taylor, B. (1997). The construction of women's management skills and the marginalization of women in senior management. *Women in Management Review, 12*(7), 255–263.

Hamermesh, D. S. (2021). Do labor costs affect companies' demand for labor? *IZA World of Labor.* https://wol.iza.org/articles/do-labor-costs-affect-companies-demand-for-labor/long

Hamilton, L., & Webster, P. (2018). *The international business environment* (4th ed.). Oxford: Oxford University Press.

Hammer, M., & Champy, J. (1993) *Reengineering the corporation.* New York: Harper Business.

Hampden-Turner, C. M., & Trompenaars, F. (2008). *Building cross-cultural competence: How to create wealth from conflicting values.* New Haven, CT: Yale University Press.

Handy, C. (1989). *The age of unreason.* London: Hutchinson.

Handy, C. (2007). Understanding organizations. Penguin UK.

Handy, C. (2012). *The Age of Unreason.* London: Random House.

Harel, G., & Tzafrir, S. S. (1999). The effect of human resource management practices on the perceptions of organizational and market performance of the firm. *Human Resource Management, 38*(3), 185–199.

Harel, G., Tzafrir, S. S., & Baruch, Y. (2003). Achieving organizational effectiveness through promotion of women into managerial positions, HRM practice focus. *The International Journal of Human Resource Management, 14*(2), 247–263.

Harris, C. M., Pattie, M. W., & McMahan, G. C. (2015). Advancement along a career path: The influence of human capital and performance. *Human Resource Management Journal, 25*(1), 102–115.

Harrison, D. A., Price, K. H., & Bell, M. P. (1998). Beyond organizational demography: Time and the effects of surface- versus deep-level diversity on work groups. *Academy of Management Journal, 41,* 96–107.

Harrison, D. A., Price, K. H., Gavin, J. H., & Florey, A. T. (2002). Time, teams, and task performance: Changing effects of surface- and deep-level diversity on group functioning. *Academy of Management Journal, 45*(5), 1029–1045.

Hart, R. (2021). *Positive psychology.* London: Routledge.

Harvey, M. (1997) Dual-career expatriates: expectations, adjustment and satisfaction with international relocation. *Journal of International Business Studies, 28*(3), 627–658.

Harzing, A. W. K. (1995). The persistent myth of high expatriate failure rates. *International Journal of Human Resource Management, 6*(2), 457–474.

Harzing, A. W., & van Ruysseveldt, J. (Eds.). (2017). *International human resource management: A critical text.* London: Sage.

Hasija, S., Pinker, E., & Shumsky, R. A. (2010). OM practice – Work expands to fill the time available: Capacity estimation and staffing under Parkinson's law. *Manufacturing & Service Operations Management, 12*(1), 1–18.

Haslberger, A., & Brewster, C. (2009). Capital gains: Expatriate adjustment and the psychological contract in international careers. *Human Resource Management: Published in Cooperation with the School of Business Administration, The University of Michigan and in alliance with the Society of Human Resources Management, 48*(3), 379–397.

Hassard, J., Morris, J., & McCann, L. (2012). 'My brilliant career'? New organizational forms and changing managerial careers in Japan, the UK, and USA. *Journal of Management Studies, 49*(3), 571–599.

Hatch, M. J., & Schultz, M. (2002). The dynamics of organizational identity. *Human Relations, 55*(8), 989–1018.

Hatch, M. J., & Yanow, D. (2008). Methodology by metaphor: Ways of seeing in painting and research. *Organization Studies, 29*(1), 23–44.

He, H., & Brown, A. D. (2013). Organizational identity and organizational identification: A review of the literature and suggestions for future research. *Group & Organization Management, 38*(1), 3–35.

Healy, G., Kirton, G., Özbilgin, M., & Oikelome, F. (2010). Competing rationalities in the diversity project of the UK judiciary: The politics of assessment centres. *Human Relations, 63*(6), 807–834.

Heenan, D. A., & Perlmutter, H. V. (1979) *Multinational organizational development.* Reading, MA: Addison-Wesley.

Hendry, C. (1995). Human resource management: A strategic approach to employment. Oxford: Butterworth-Heinemann.

Hermelin, E., Lievens, F., & Robertson, I. T. (2007). The validity of assessment centres for the prediction of supervisory performance ratings: A meta-analysis. *International Journal of Selection and Assessment, 15*(4), 405–411.

Herriot, P. (1992). *The career management challenge.* London: Sage.

Herriot, P., & Pemberton, C. (1995). *New deals.* Chichester: Wiley.

Herriot, P., & Pemberton, C. (1996). Contracting careers. *Human Relations, 49*(6), 757–790.

Herriot, P., & Stickland, R. (1999). The management of careers: Introduction. *European Journal of Organization and Work Psychology*, Special issue.

HESE (2020). The Higher Education Statistics Agency (home page). https://www.hesa.ac.uk/

Heslin, P. A. (2005). Conceptualizing and evaluating career success. *Journal of Organizational Behavior, 26*(2), 113–136.

Heslin, P. A., Keating, L. A., & Ashford, S. J. (2020). How being in learning mode may enable a sustainable career across the lifespan. *Journal of Vocational Behavior, 117*. https://doi.org/10.1016/j.jvb.2019.103324

Higgins, M. (2005), Career imprints: Creating leaders across an industry. San Francisco, CA: Josey-Bass.

Hillage, J., & Pollard, E. (1998). *Employability: Developing a framework for policy analysis* (research report rr85). Brighton: Institute for Employment Studies/DfEE.

Hillriegel, D., Slocum, J. W., & Woodman, R. W. (1992). *Organizational behavior* (6th ed.) (p.212). St. Paul, MN: West.

Hochschild, A. (1997) *Time bind.* New York: Metropolitan Books, Holt.

Hochschild, A. R. (2016). *Invisible labor: Hidden work in the contemporary world.* Oakland, CA: University of California Press.

Hofstede, G. (1980). Cultures consequences: International differences in work-related values. Hoboken, NJ: Sage.

Hofstede, G. (2011). Dimensionalizing cultures: The Hofstede model in context. *Online Readings in Psychology and Culture, 2*(1), 2307–2919.

Hofstede, G., Hofstede, G. J., & Minkov, M. (2005). *Cultures and organizations: Software of the mind* (Vol. *2*). New York: McGraw-Hill.

Hogarth, R. M., & Karelaia, N. (2012). Entrepreneurial success and failure: Confidence and fallible judgment. *Organization Science, 23*(6), 1733–1747.

Holbeche, L. (2009). Aligning human resources and business strategy. Amsterdam: Routledge.

Holland, J. L. (1959). A theory of vocational choice. *Journal of Counseling Psychology, 6*, 35–45.

Hölzle, K. (2010). Designing and implementing a career path for project managers. *International Journal of Project Management, 28*(8), 779–786.

Hoskisson, R., Hitt, M., Wan, W., & Yiu, D. (1999). Theory and research in strategic management: Swings of a pendulum, *Journal of Management, 25*(3), 417–456.

Hoynes, H., & Rothstein, J. (2019). Universal basic income in the United States and advanced countries. *Annual Review of Economics, 11*, 929–958.

Hu, Y. S. (1992). Global or stateless corporations are national firms with international operations. *California Management Review, 34*(2), 107–126.

Hughes, E. C. (1937). Institutional office and the person. *American Journal of Sociology, 43,* 404–443. Cited by Adamson, S. J., Doherty, N., & Viney, C. (1998). The meaning of career revisited: Implications for theory and practice. *British Journal of Management, 9*(4), 251–259.

Hughes, E. C. (1958). *Men and their work.* Glencoe, IL: Free Press.

Hull, K. E., & Nelson, R. L. (2000). Assimilation, choice or constraint? Testing theories of gender differences in the career of lawyers. *Social Forces, 79*(1), 229–264.

Huselid, M. A. (1995). The impact of human resource management practices on turnover, productivity, and corporate financial performance. *Academy of Management Journal, 38*(3), 635–672.

Huws, U., Spencer, N. H., & Syrdal, D. S. (2018). Online, on call: The spread of digitally organised just-in-time working and its implications for standard employment models. *New Technology, Work and Employment, 33*(2), 113–129.

Huynh, T. L. D., Hille, E., & Nasir, M. A. (2020). Diversification in the age of the 4th industrial revolution: The role of artificial intelligence, green bonds and cryptocurrencies. *Technological Forecasting and Social Change, 159.* https://doi.org/10.1016/j.techfore.2020.120188

Iansiti, M., & Levien, R. (2004), Strategy as ecology. *Harvard Business Review, 82*(3), 68–81.

Iles, P. (1999) *Managing staff selection and assessment.* Buckingham: Open University.

Inkson, K. (2004). Images of career: Nine key metaphors. *Journal of Vocational Behavior, 65*(1), 96–111.

Inkson, K., Dries, N., & Arnold, J. (2015). *Understanding careers* (2nd ed.). Los Angeles, CA: Sage.

Inkson, K., Gunz, H., Ganesh, S., & Roper, J. (2012). Boundaryless careers: Bringing back boundaries. *Organization Studies, 33*(3), 323–340.

Inkson, K., Heising, A., & Rousseau, D. M. (2001). The Interim manager: Prototype of the 21st century worker? *Human Relations, 54*(3), 259–284.

Jahoda, M. (1982) *Employment and unemployment: A social psychology analysis.* Cambridge: Cambridge University Press.

Jain, P., & Jain, P. (2020). Understanding the concept of HR analytics. *International Journal on Emerging Technologies, 11*(2), 644–652.

Jarzabkowski, P., & Paul Spee, A. (2009). Strategy-as-practice: A review and future directions for the field. *International Journal of Management Reviews, 11*(1), 69–95.

Javidmehr, M., & Ebrahimpour, M. (2015). Performance appraisal bias and errors: The influences and consequences. *International Journal of Organizational Leadership, 4,* 286–302.

Jiang, K., Lepak, D. P., Hu, J., & Baer, J. C. (2012). How does human resource management influence organizational outcomes? A meta-analytic investigation of mediating mechanisms. *Academy of Management Journal, 55,* 1264–1294.

Johns, A., Fook, J., & Nath, V. (2019). Systemic changes to crack the concrete ceiling: Initiatives from the leadership foundation for higher education. *Race, Education and Educational Leadership in England: An Integrated Analysis, 183.*

Johnston, C. S. (2018). A systematic review of the career adaptability literature and future outlook. *Journal of Career Assessment, 26*(1), 3–30.

Johnston, W. B. (1991). Global workforce 2000: The new world labor market. *Harvard Business Review, 69,* 115–127.

Jones, C., & DeFillippi, R. J. (1996). Back to the future in film: Combining industry and self-knowledge to meet career challenges of the 21st century. *Academy of Management Executive, 10*(4), 89–104.

Jones, F., Burke, R. J., & Westman, M. (Eds.). (2013). *Work-life balance: A psychological perspective.* Hove: Psychology Press.

Judge, T. A., Cable, D. M., Boudreau, J. W., & Bretz Jr., R. D. (1995). An empirical investigation of the predictors of executive career success. *Personnel Psychology, 48,* 485–519.

Judge, T. A., Higgins, C. A., Thoresen, C. J., & Barrick, M. R. (1999). The big five personality traits, general mental ability, and career success across the life span. *Personnel Psychology*, *52*, 621–652.

Judge, T. A., & Zapata, C. P. (2015). The person–situation debate revisited: Effect of situation strength and trait activation on the validity of the Big Five personality traits in predicting job performance. *Academy of Management Journal*, *58*(4), 1149–1179.

Kahl, M. (2020, January). What's behind the tens of thousands of auto industry job cuts? *Automotive World*. https://www.automotiveworld.com/articles/whats-behind-the-tens-of-thousands-of-auto-industry-job-cuts/

Kanfer, R., & Heggestad, E. D. (1997). Motivational traits and skills: A person centered approach to work motivation. *Research in Organizational Behavior*, *19*, 1–56.

Känsälä, M., Mäkelä, L., & Suutari, V. (2015). Career coordination strategies among dual career expatriate couples. *The International Journal of Human Resource Management*, *26*(17), 2187–2210.

Kanstrén, K. (2019). The career transitions of expatriate partners and the effects of transitions on career identities. *The International Journal of Human Resource Management*. https://doi.org/10.1080/09585 192.2019.1674356

Kapoor, C., & Solomon, N. (2011). Understanding and managing generational differences in the workplace. *Worldwide Hospitality and Tourism Themes*, *3*(4), 308–318.

Katz, D., & Kahn, R. L. (1966). *The social psychology of organizations*. New York: Wiley.

Katz, L. F., & Krueger, A. B. (2019). The rise and nature of alternative work arrangements in the United States, 1995–2015. *ILR review*, *72*(2), 382–416.

Kaufman, B. E. (2015). Evolution of strategic HRM as seen through two founding books: A 30th anniversary perspective on development of the field. *Human Resource Management*, *54*(3), 389–407.

Kauhanen, M., & Nätti, J. (2015). Involuntary temporary and part-time work, job quality and well-being at work. *Social Indicators Research*, *120*(3), 783–799.

Keller, J. R., Kehoe, R. R., Bidwell, M. J., Collings, D. G., & Myer, A. (2020). In with the old? Examining when boomerang employees outperform new hires. *Academy of Management Journal*. https://doi.org/10.5465/amj.2019.1340

Kelliher, C., Richardson, J., & Boiarintseva, G. (2019). All of work? All of life? Reconceptualising work–life balance for the 21st century. *Human Resource Management Journal*, *29*(2), 97–112.

Kelly, E. L., & Kalev, A. (2006). Managing flexible work arrangements in US organizations: Formalized discretion or 'a right to ask'. *Socio-Economic Review*, *4*(3), 379–416.

Kelly, M. M. (1985). The next workplace revolution: Telecommuting. *Supervisory Management*, *30*(10), 2–7.

Kennedy, D. (2019). Career-derailing discrimination and the duration of compensation for lost wages. *Canadian Labour & Employment Law Journal*, *22*, 47.

Kessler, I. (1994) Performance related pay: Contrasting approaches. *Industrial Relations Journal*, *25*(2), 122–135.

Kessler, I., & Purcell, J. (1992) Performance related pay: objectives and application. *Human Resource Management*, *2*(3), 16–33.

Kets de Vries, M. F. R., & Balazs, K. (1997). The downsize of downsizing. *Human Relations*, *50*(1), 11–50.

Kidd, J. M. (2006). Understanding career counselling: Theory, research and practice. London: Sage.

Kim, Y. H., Jung, Y. S., Min, J., Song, E. Y., Ok, J. H., Lim, C., ... & Kim, J. S. (2017). Development and validation of a nursing professionalism evaluation model in a career ladder system. *PloS one*, *12*(10), e0186310.

Kim, B., Lee, G., Murrmann, S. K., & George, T. R. (2012). Motivational effects of empowerment on employees' organizational commitment: a mediating role of management trustworthiness. *Cornell Hospitality Quarterly*, *53*(1), 10–19.

Kindsiko, E. & Baruch, Y. (2019). Careers of PhD graduates: The role of chance events and how to manage them. *Journal of Vocational Behavior*, *112*, 122–140.

Kinicki, A., & Kreitner, R. (2012). *Organizational behavior: Key concepts, skills & best practices* (*Vol. 1221*). New York, NY: McGraw-Hill Irwin.

Klehe, U. C., Zikic, J., Van Vianen, A. E., & De Pater, I. E. (2011). Career adaptability, turnover and loyalty during organizational downsizing. *Journal of Vocational Behavior, 79*(1), 217–229.

Klein, H. J., Solinger, O. N., & Duflot, V. (2020). Commitment system theory: The evolving structure of commitments to multiple targets. *Academy of Management Review.* https://doi.org/10.5465/amr.2018.0031

Koistinen, P., & Perkiö, J. (2014). Good and bad times of social innovations: The case of universal basic income in Finland. *Basic Income Studies, 9*(1–2), 25–57.

Kolb, A. Y., & Kolb, D. A. (2005). Learning styles and learning spaces: Enhancing experiential learning in higher education. *Academy of Management Learning & Education, 4*(2), 193–212.

Kolb, D. A. (1984). *Experiential learning.* Englewood Cliffs, NJ: Prentice Hall.

Kolb, D. A. (2014). Experiential learning: Experience as the source of learning and development. Upside Saddle River, NJ: FT press.

Konovsky, M., & Folger, R. (1994). Relative effects of procedural and distributive justice on employees attitudes. *Representative Research in Social Psychology, 17*(1), 15–24.

Kontoghiorghes, C. (2016). Linking high performance organizational culture and talent management: Satisfaction/motivation and organizational commitment as mediators. *The International Journal of Human Resource Management, 27*(16), 1833–1853.

Kosinski, N. J. (1970) *Being There*, New York: Bantam Books.

Kossek, E. E., Su, R., & Wu, L. (2017). 'Opting out' or 'pushed out'? Integrating perspectives on women's career equality for gender inclusion and interventions. *Journal of Management, 43*(1), 228–254.

Kossek, E. E., Thompson, R. J., & Lautsch, B. A. (2015). Balanced workplace flexibility: Avoiding the traps. *California Management Review, 57*(4), 5–25.

Kost, D., Fieseler, C., & Wong, S. I. (2020). Boundaryless careers in the gig economy: An oxymoron?. *Human Resource Management Journal, 30*(1), 100–113.

Kotlyar, I. (2018). Identifying high potentials early: case study. *Journal of Management Development, 37*, 684–696.

Kotter J. (1973). The psychological contract: Managing the joining-up process, *California Management Review, 15*(3), 91–99.

Koumenta, M., & Williams, M. (2019). An anatomy of zero-hour contracts in the UK. *Industrial Relations Journal, 50*(1), 20–40.

Koys, D. J. (2017). Using the Department of Labor's 'My Next Move' to improve career preparedness. *Journal of Management Education, 41*, 94–117.

Koyuncu, B., Hamori, M., & Baruch, Y. (2017). CEOs' careers: Emerging trends and future directions. *Human Resource Management, 56*(2), 195–203.

Kraaijenbrink, J., Spender, J. C., & Groen, A. J. (2010). The resource-based view: A review and assessment of its critiques. *Journal of Management, 36*(1), 349–372.

Kraimer, M. L., Seibert, S. E., Wayne, S. J., Liden, R. C., & Bravo, J. (2011). Antecedents and outcomes of organizational support for development: The critical role of career opportunities. *Journal of Applied Psychology, 96*(3), 485–500.

Kram, K. E. (1985) *Mentoring in the work.* Glenview, IL: Scott, Foresman.

Kruger, P. S. (2011). Wellbeing – the five essential elements. *Applied Research in Quality of Life, 6*(3), 325–328.

Krumboltz, J. D., Foley, P. F., & Cotter, E. W. (2013). Applying the happenstance learning theory to involuntary career transitions. *The Career Development Quarterly, 61*(1), 15–26.

Kulik, C. T., Treuren, G., & Bordia, P. (2012). Shocks and final straws: Using exit-interview data to examine the unfolding model's decision paths. *Human Resource Management, 51*(1), 25–46.

Kulkarni, M., Boehm, S., & Basu, S. (2016). Workplace inclusion of persons with a disability: Comparison of Indian and German multinationals. *Equality, Diversity and Inclusion, 35*(7/8): 397–414.

Kumarika Perera, H., Yin Teng Chew, E., & Nielsen, I. (2017). A psychological contract perspective of expatriate failure. *Human Resource Management, 56*(3), 479–499.

Lam, S. S., Ng, T. W., & Feldman, D. C. (2012). The relationship between external job mobility and salary attainment across career stages. *Journal of Vocational Behavior, 80*(1), 129–136.

Larsen, H. H. (1996). Oticon: Think the unthinkable: radical (and successful) organizational change. In J. Storey (Ed.), *Cases in human resource management*. Oxford: Blackwell.

Larsen, H. H. (2002). Oticon: Unorthodox project-based management and careers in a 'spaghetti organization'. *People and Strategy, 25*(4), 30–37.

Larson, R. C., Ghaffarzadegan, N., & Xue, Y. (2014). Too many PhD graduates or too few academic job openings: The basic reproductive number R0 in academia. *Systems Research and Behavioral Science, 31*(6), 745–750.

Latukha, M., Soyiri, J., Shagalkina, M., & Rysakova, L. (2019). From expatriation to global migration: The role of talent management practices in talent migration to Ghana. *Journal of Global Mobility, 7*(4), 325–345.

Laurent, A. (1986). The cross-cultural puzzle of IHRM. *Human Resource Management, 25*(1), 91–102.

Lazarova, M., & Taylor, S. (2009). Boundaryless careers, social capital, and knowledge management: Implications for organizational performance. *Journal of Organizational Behavior: The International Journal of Industrial, Occupational and Organizational Psychology and Behavior, 30*(1), 119–139.

Lee, C. I. S. G., Felps, W., & Baruch, Y. (2014). Toward a taxonomy of career studies through bibliometric visualization. *Journal of Vocational Behaviour, 85*(3), 339–351.

Lee, H. W. (2006). Perceptive of expatriation and cross-cultural adjustment. *Journal of Global Business Management, 2*(1), 22–30.

Lee, H., Hsiao, Y. C., Chen, C. J., & Guo, R. S. (2020). Virtual vs physical platform: Organizational capacity and slack, strategic decision and firm performance. *Journal of Business & Industrial Marketing, 35*(12), 1983–1995.

Lee, S. J., Kim, J., & Park, B. I. (2015). Culture clashes in cross-border mergers and acquisitions: A case study of Sweden's Volvo and South Korea's Samsung. *International Business Review, 24*(4), 580–593.

Legge, K. (2005). Human resource management – rhetoric and realities. Basingstoke: Macmillan.

Leibman, M., Bruer, R. A., & Maki, B. R. (1996). Succession management: The next generation of succession planning. *People and Strategy, 19*(3), 16.

Lengelle, R., Van der Heijden, B. I., & Meijers, F. (2017). The foundations of career resilience. In K. Maree (Ed.), *Psychology of career adaptability, employability and resilience* (pp. 29–47). Cham: Springer.

Lent, R. W., & Brown, S. D. (2013). Social cognitive model of career self-management: Toward a unifying view of adaptive career behavior across the life span. *Journal of Counseling Psychology, 60*(4), 557–568.

Leonardi, P. M., Treem, J. W., Barley, W. C., & Miller, V. D. (2014, July). Attitude surveys. In *Meeting the Challenge of Human Resource Management* (pp. 167–178). Routledge.

Leong, F. T. L., & Hartung, P. J. (2000). Adapting to the changing multicultural context of career. In A. W. Harzing, & J. V. Ruysseveldt (Eds.), *International Human Resource Management* (pp. 212–227). London: Sage.

Leutner, F., Ahmetoglu, G., Akhtar, R., & Chamorro-Premuzic, T. (2014). The relationship between the entrepreneurial personality and the Big Five personality traits. *Personality and Individual Differences, 63*, 58–63.

Levinson, D. J. (1978). *The seasons of man's life*, New York: Knopf.

Levinson, D. J. (1986). Conception of adult development. *American Psychologist, 41*, 3–13;

Levinson, H., Price C., Munden K., Mandl H., & Solley C. (1962). *Men, management, and mental health*. Cambridge, MA: Harvard University Press.

Levitt, S. D., & Dunber, S. J. (2014). *Think like a freak.* New York: Penguin.

Lewin, K. (1951) *Field theory in social science.* New York: Harper & Row.

Lewis, R. E., & Heckman, R. J. (2006). Talent management: A critical review. *Human Resource Management Review, 16*(2), 139–154.

Lewis, S., & Humbert, A. L. (2010). Discourse or reality: 'Work-life balance' flexibility and gendered organisations. *Equality, Diversity and Inclusion, 29*(3), 239–254.

Liguori, E., Winkler, C., Vanevenhoven, J., Winkel, D., & James, M. (2020). Entrepreneurship as a career choice: Intentions, attitudes, and outcome expectations. *Journal of Small Business & Entrepreneurship, 32*(4), 311–331.

Lipman-Blumen, J., & Leavitt, H. J. (1999). Hot groups 'with attitude': A new organizational state of mind. *Organizational Dynamics, 27*(4), 63–73.

Lips-Wiersma, M., & Hall, D. T. (2007). Organizational career development is not dead: A case study on managing the new career during organizational change. *Journal of Organizational Behavior, 28,* 771–792.

Lo Presti, A., Pluviano, S., & Briscoe, J. P. (2018). Are freelancers a breed apart? The role of protean and boundaryless career attitudes in employability and career success. *Human Resource Management Journal, 28*(3), 427–442.

Lobel, O. (2017). The gig economy & the future of employment and labor law. *University of San Francisco Law Review, 51,* 51–74.

Logger, E., Vinke, R., & Kluytmans, F. (1995). Compensation and appraisal in an international perspective. In A. W. Harzing, & J. V. Ruysseveldt (Eds.), *International human resource management* (pp. 144–155). London: Sage.

London, M., & Stumpf, S. A. (1982) *Managing careers.* Reading, MA: Addison-Wesley.

Lord, R. G., De-Vader, C. L., & Alliger, G. M. (1986). A meta analysis of relation between personality traits and leadership perceptions: An application of validity generalization procedures. *Journal of Applied Psychology, 71*(3), 402–410.

Lucas Jr., H. C., & Goh, J. M. (2009). Disruptive technology: How Kodak missed the digital photography revolution. *The Journal of Strategic Information Systems, 18*(1), 46–55.

Lyons, S. T., Schweitzer, L., & Ng, E. S. (2015). How have careers changed? An investigation of changing career patterns across four generations. *Journal of Managerial Psychology, 30*(1), 8–21.

Mack, O., Khare, A., Krämer, A., & Burgartz, T. (Eds.). (2015). *Managing in a VUCA world.* Cham: Springer.

Mackelprang, W. R., & Salsgiver, O. R. (2016). *Disability: A diversity model approach in human service practice* (3rd ed.). Oxford: Oxford University Press.

MacLuhan, M. (1960) *Explorations in communication.* Boston, MA: Beacon Press.

Mainiero, L. A., & Gibson, D. E. (2018). The Kaleidoscope career model revisited: How midcareer men and women diverge on authenticity, balance, and challenge. *Journal of Career Development, 45*(4), 361–377.

Mainiero, L. A., & Sullivan, S. E. (2006). The opt-out revolt: Why people are leaving companies to create kaleidoscope careers. Palo Alto, CA: Davis-Black.

Malik, A., Budhwar, P., & Srikanth, N. R. (2020). Gig economy, 4IR and artificial intelligence: Rethinking strategic HRM. In P. Kumar, A., Agrawal, & P. Budhwar (Eds.), *Human & technological resource management (HTRM): New insights into revolution 4.0* (pp. 75–88). Bingley: Emerald Publishing.

Malone, T. W. (1997). Is empowerment just a fad? Control, decision making and IT. *Sloan Management Review,* Winter, 23–35.

Manchester, C. F. (2012). General human capital and employee mobility: How tuition reimbursement increases retention through sorting and participation. *ILR Review, 65*(4), 951–974.

Mannheim, B., & Dubin, R. (1986). Work role centrality of industrial workers as related to organizational conditions, task autonomy, managerial orientations and personal characteristics. *Journal of Occupational Behavior, 7,* 107–124.

Manyika, J., Lund, S., Robinson, K., Valentino, J., & Dobbs, R. (2015). *A labor market that works: Connecting talent with opportunity in the digital age*. San Francisco, CA: McKinsey Global Institute.

March, J. C. & March, J. G. (1977). Almost random careers: The Wisconsin school superintendency 1940–1972. *Administrative Science Quarterly, 22*, 377–409.

Maree, K. (Ed.). (2017). Psychology of career adaptability, employability and resilience. Cham: Springer.

Markovitch, S., & Willmott, P., (2014). Accelerating the digitization of business processes. *McKinsey Digital*, May, 1–4.

Marlow, S. (2019). Gender and entrepreneurship: Past achievements and future possibilities. *International Journal of Gender and Entrepreneurship, 12*(1), 39–52.

Martin-Alcazar, F., Romero-Fernandez, P. M., & Sanchez-Gardey, G. (2012). Effects of diversity on group decision-making processes: The moderating role of human resource management. *Group Decision and Negotiation, 21*(5), 677–701.

Maslow, A. H. (1943). A theory of human motivation. *Psychological Review*, July, 370–396.

Mayer, A. P., Blair, J. E., Ko, M. G., Patel, S. I., & Files, J. A. (2014). Long-term follow-up of a facilitated peer mentoring program. *Medical Teacher, 36*(3), 260–266.

McClelland, D. C. (1985). *Human motivation*. Glenview, IL: Scott, Foresman.

McCracken, M., Currie, D., & Harrison, J. (2016). Understanding graduate recruitment, development and retention for the enhancement of talent management: Sharpening the edge of graduate talent. *The International Journal of Human Resource Management, 27*(22), 2727–2752.

McGuire, D., Stoner, L., & Mylona, S. (2008). The role of line managers as human resource agents in fostering organizational change in public services. *Journal of Change Management, 8*(1), 73–84.

McKee-Ryan, F. M., & Harvey, J. (2011). 'I have a job, but …': A review of underemployment. *Journal of Management, 37*(4), 962–996.

McMahan, G. C., Bell, M. P., & Virick, M. (1998). Strategic human resource management: Employee involvement, diversity, and international issues. *Human Resource Management Review, 8*(3), 193–214.

McMahon, M. (Ed.). (2016). *Career counselling: Constructivist approaches* (2nd ed.). London: Routledge.

McNulty, Y., & Moeller, M. (2018). A typology of dual-career expatriate (trailing) spouses: The 'R' profile. In M. Dickmann, V. Suutari, & O. Wurtz (Eds.), *The management of global careers* (pp. 257–290). Basingstoke: Palgrave Macmillan.

Mehta, S., Saxena, T., & Purohit, N. (2020). The new consumer behaviour paradigm amid COVID-19: Permanent or transient? *Journal of Health Management, 22*(2), 291–301.

Meiring, D., Becker, J., Gericke, S., & Louw, N. (2015). Assessment centres. In I. Nikolaou, & J. K. Oostom (Eds.) *Employee recruitment, selection, and assessment: Contemporary issues for theory and practice* (pp. 190–206). London: Psychology Press.

Mendenhall, M. E., Arnardottir, A. A., Oddou, G. R., & Burke, L. A. (2013). Developing cross-cultural competencies in management education via cognitive-behavior therapy. *Academy of Management Learning & Education, 12*(3), 436–451.

Mendenhall, M., & Oddou, G. R. (1985). The dimensions of expatriate acculturation: A review. *Academy of Management Review, 10*(1), 39–47.

Mercurio, Z. A. (2015). Affective commitment as a core essence of organizational commitment: An integrative literature review. *Human Resource Development Review, 14*(4), 389–414.

Merrill Lynch (2006). The 2006 Merrill Lynch New Retirement Study: A perspective from individuals and employers. New York: Merrill Lynch.

Meshoulam, I., & Baird, L. (1987). Proactive human resource management. *Human Resource Management, 26*(4), 483–502.

Metzger, W. P. (1987) Academic profession in the United States. In B. R. Clark (Ed.), *The academic profession, national, disciplinary and institutional settings* (pp. 123–208). Berkeley, CA: University of California Press.

Miles, R. E., & Snow, C. C. (1978). *Organizational structure, strategy, and process*. New York: McGraw-Hill.

Milkovich, T. G., & Newman, M. J. (1996). *Compensation* (5th ed.). Chicago, IL: Irwin.

Miller, L. R., & Grollman, E. A. (2015). The social costs of gender nonconformity for transgender adults: Implications for discrimination and health. *Sociological Forum, 30*(3), 809–831.

Miner, J. B., & Miner, M. G. (1985) *Personnel and industrial relations: A managerial approach* (pp. 208–231). New York: MacMillan.

Mishra, K. E., Spreitzer, G. M. & Mishra, A. K. (1998). Preserving employee morale during downsizing. *Sloan Management Review*, Winter, 83–95.

Modise, O. (2016). *Career workshops as a non-traditional research model for enhanced relationships between higher education and the labour market. International Journal of Training and Development, 20*(2), 152–163.

Moen, P. (1989). *Working parents*. Madison, WI: University of Wisconsin Press.

Mor Barak, M. E. (2015). Inclusion is the key to diversity management, but what is inclusion? *Human Service Organizations: Management, leadership & governance, 39*(2), 83–88.

Morgan, G. (1997). *Images of organizations*. Thousand Oaks, CA: Sage.

Morrison, A. M. (1982). *Breaking the glass ceiling*. Reading, MA: Addison-Wesley.

Morrison, A. M., White, R. P., & Van Velsor, E. (1987a). Executive women: Substance plus style. *Psychology Today, 21*, 18–26.

Morrison, A. M., White, R. P., & Veslor, E. V. (1987b). *Breaking the glass ceiling*. Reading, MA: Addison-Wesley.

Morrison, E. W., & Robinson, S. L. (1997). When employees feel betrayed: A model of how psychological contract violation develops. *Academy of Management Review, 22*(1), 226–256.

MOW International Research Team (1987). *The meaning of working*. London: Academic Press.

Murphy, K. R., & Cleveland, J. N. (1995). *Understanding performance appraisal*. Thousand Oaks, CA: Sage.

Murphy, L. R. (1988). Workplace interventions for stress reduction and prevention. In C. L. Cooper, & R. Payne (Eds.), *Causes, coping and consequences of stress at work*. Chichester: Wiley.

Nauta, M. M. (2010). The development, evolution, and status of Holland's theory of vocational personalities: Reflections and future directions for counseling psychology. *Journal of Counseling Psychology, 57*(1), 11–22.

Nelson, D. L., & Quick, J. C. (2013). *Organizational behavior: Science, the real world, and you*. Mason, OH: Cengage Learning.

Ng, T. W. H., Eby, L. T., Sorensen, K. L., & Feldman, D. C. (2005). Predictors of objective and subjective career success: A meta-analysis. *Personnel Psychology, 58*(2), 367–408.

Nicholson, N. (1998). How hardwired is human behavior? *Harvard Business Review, 76*(4), 134–147.

Nicholson, N. (2000). Motivation-selection-connection: An evolutionary model of career development. In M. Peiperl, M. Arthur, R. Goffee, & T. Morris (Eds.), *Career frontiers*. Oxford: Oxford University Press.

Nicholson, N. (2010). The design of work – an evolutionary perspective. *Journal of Organizational Behavior, 31*(2/3), 422–431.

Nicholson, N., & Johns, G. (1985). The absence culture and the psychological contract – who's in control of absence. *Academy of Management Review, 10*, 397–407.

Nijp, H. H., Beckers, D. G., van de Voorde, K., Geurts, S. A., & Kompier, M. A. (2016). Effects of new ways of working on work hours and work location, health and job-related outcomes. *Chronobiology International, 33*(6), 604–618.

Noe, R. A., Hollenbeck, J. R., Gerhart, B., & Wright, P. M. (2017). *Human Resource Management: Gaining a competitive advantage*. New York, NY: McGraw-Hill Education.

Noon, M., & Blyton, P. (1997) *The realities of work*. Basingstoke: Macmillan.

Noon, M., Blyton, P., & Morrell, K. (2013). The realities of work: Experiencing work and employment in contemporary society. Basingstoke: Macmillan.

Nutt, P. C. (1999). Surprising but true: Half the decisions in organizations fail. *Academy of Management Executive, 13*, 75–90.

Nye, C. D., Su, R., Rounds, J., & Drasgow, F. (2012). Vocational interests and performance: A quantitative summary of over 60 years of research. *Perspectives on Psychological Science, 7*, 384–403.

O*NET (2020). O*NET Resource Center (home page). http://www.onetcenter.org/

O'Leary, S. (2015). Integrating employability into degree programmes using consultancy projects as a form of enterprise. *Industry and Higher Education, 29*(6), 459–468.

O'Neil, H. M., & Lenn, D. J. (1995). Voices of survivors: Words that downsizing CEOs should hear. *Academy of Management Executive, 9*(4), 23–34.

OECD (2018). LMF1.5: Gender pay gaps for full-time workers and earnings differentials by educational attainment. *OECD Family Database*. https://www.oecd.org/els/LMF_1_5_Gender_pay_gaps_for_full_time_workers.pdf

Olsen, J. E., & Martins, L. L. (2012). Understanding organizational diversity management programs: A theoretical framework and directions for future research. *Journal of Organizational Behavior, 33*, 1168–1187.

Ones, D. S., & Dilchert, S. (2009). How special are executives? How special should executive selection be? Observations and recommendations. *Industrial and Organizational Psychology, 2*(2), 163–170.

Opstrup, N., & Villadsen, A. R. (2015). The right mix? Gender diversity in top management teams and financial performance. *Public Administration Review, 75*(2), 291–301.

Oshio, A., Taku, K., Hirano, M., & Saeed, G. (2018). Resilience and Big Five personality traits: A meta-analysis. *Personality and Individual Differences, 127*, 54–60.

Osipow, S. H. (1990) Convergence in theory of career choice and development: Review and prospect. *Journal of Vocational Behavior, 36*, 122–131.

Osterman, P. (1996). *Broken ladders: Managerial careers in the new economy*. New York: Oxford University Press.

Ozeren, E., & Aydin, E. (2016). What does being LGBT mean in the workplace? A comparison of LGBT equality in Turkey and the UK. In A. Klarsfeld, E. S. Ng, L. A. E. Booysen, L. Castro Christiansen, & B. Kuvaas (Eds.), *Research handbook of international and comparative perspectives on diversity management* (pp. 199–226). Cheltenham: Edward Elgar.

Paauwe, J., & Boon, C. (2018). Strategic HRM: A critical review. In D. G. Collings, & G. Wood (Eds.), *Human resource management: A critical approach* (2nd ed.) (pp. 38–54). London: Routledge.

Page-Tickell, R., & Yerby, E. (Eds.). (2020). Conflict and shifting boundaries in the gig economy: An interdisciplinary analysis. Bingley: Emerald Publishing.

Paleczek, D., Bergner, S., & Rybnicek, R. (2018). Predicting career success: Is the dark side of personality worth considering? *Journal of Managerial Psychology, 33*(6), 437–456.

Pan, W., Sun, L. Y., & Chow, I. H. S. (2011). The impact of supervisory mentoring on personal learning and career outcomes: The dual moderating effect of self-efficacy. *Journal of Vocational Behavior, 78*(2), 264–273.

Papadaki, V., & Giannou, D. (2021). To be or not to be out of the closet? LGB social workers' visibility management in the workplace in Greece. *Journal of Gay & Lesbian Social Services, 33*(2), 225–249.

Parker, P., & Arthur, M. B. (2000) Careers, organizing and community. In M. A. Peiperl, M. B. Arthur, R. Goffee, & T. Morris (Eds.), *Career frontiers: New conceptions of working lives* (pp. 99–121). Oxford: Oxford University Press.

Parker, S. C. (2011). Intrapreneurship or entrepreneurship? *Journal of Business Venturing, 26*(1), 19–34.

Parker, S. C. (2018). *The economics of entrepreneurship*. Cambridge: Cambridge University Press.

Parry, J., Young, Z., Bevan, S., Veliziotis, M., Baruch, Y., Beigi, M., Bajorek, Z., Salter, E., & Tochia, C. (2021). Working from home under COVID-19 lockdown: Transitions and tensions, *Work After Lockdown*. https://static1.squarespace.com/static/5f5654b537cea057c500f59e/t/60143f05a2117e3eec3c3243/1611939604505/Wal+Bulletin+1.pdf

Parsons, F. (1909) *Choosing a vocation*. Boston, MA: Houghton Mifflin.

Parzefall, M. R., & Jacqueline, A. M. (2011). Making sense of psychological contract breach. *Journal of Managerial Psychology, 26*(1), 12–27.

Pate, J., & Scullion, H. (2018). The flexpatriate psychological contract: A literature review and future research agenda. *The International Journal of Human Resource Management, 29*(8), 1402–1425.

Pattie, M., Benson, G. S., & Baruch, Y. (2006). Tuition reimbursement, perceived organizational support, and turnover intention among graduate business school students. *Human Resource Development Quarterly, 17*(4), 423–442.

Pegg, A., Waldock, J., Hendy-Isaac, S., & Larton, R. (2012). *Pedagogy for employability*. York: Higher Education Academy.

Peiperl, M. A., & Baruch, Y. (1997) Back to square zero: The post-corporate career. *Organizational Dynamics, 25*(4), 7–22.

Perkins, G., Gilmore, S., Guttormsen, D. S., & Taylor, S. (2021). Analysing the impacts of Universal Basic Income in the changing world of work: Challenges to the psychological contract and a future research agenda. *Human Resource Management Journal*. https://doi.org/10.1111/1748–8583.12348

Perlmutter, H. V. (1969). The tortuous evolution of the multinational corporation. *Columbia Journal of World Business*, Jan.–Feb., 9–18.

Pervin, L. A., & John, O. P. (1999). *Handbook of personality* (2nd ed.). New York: Guilford Press.

Pfeffer, J. (1998). *The human equation*. Boston, MA: Harvard Business School Press.

Pogrund, R. L. (2018). Commitment and passion of professionals in the visual impairment field. *Journal of Visual Impairment & Blindness, 112*, 541–542.

Pollert, A. (Ed.). (1991). *Farewell to flexibility*. Oxford: Blackwell.

Pondy, L. R. (1983). The role of metaphors and myths in organization and in the facilitation of change. In L. R. Pondy, J. Frost, G. Morgan, & T. C. Dandridge (Eds.), *Organizational Symbolism* (pp. 157–166). Greenwich, CT: JAI Press.

Popper, M., & Lipshitz, R. (2000). Organizational learning: Mechanisms, culture, and feasibility. *Management Learning, 31*(2), 181–196.

Porter, G., & Tansky, J. W. (1999). Expatriate success may depend on a 'learning orientation': Considerations for selection and training. *Human Resource Management, 38*(1), 47–60.

Porter, M. E. (2011). Competitive advantage of nations: Creating and sustaining superior performance. New York: Simon & Schuster.

Potgieter, I., Ferreira, N., & Coetzee, M. (Eds.). (2019). *Theory, research and dynamics of career wellbeing*. Cham: Springer.

Potočnik, K., & Anderson, N. (2012). Assessing innovation: A 360-degree appraisal study. *International Journal of Selection and Assessment, 20*(4), 497–509.

Powell, A., Dainty, A., & Bagilhole, B. (2012). Gender stereotypes among women engineering and technology students in the UK: Lessons from career choice narratives. *European Journal of Engineering Education, 37*(6), 541–556.

Prahalad, C. K., & Hamel, G. (1990). The core competence of the corporation. *Harvard Business Review, 68*(3), 79–91.

Praskova, A., Creed, P. A., & Hood, M. (2015). Self-regulatory processes mediating between career calling and perceived employability and life satisfaction in emerging adults. *Journal of Career Development, 42*(2), 86–101.

Presser, H. B. (2005). *Working in a 24/7 economy: Challenges for American families*. New York: Russell Sage Foundation.

Pries, L. (2019). The momentum of transnational social spaces in Mexico–US-migration. *Comparative Migration Studies, 7*(1), 1–20.

Pryor, R., & Bright, J. (2011). The chaos theory of careers: A new perspective on working in the twenty-first century. New York: Routledge.

Punnett, B. J. (1997). Towards effective management of expatriate spouses. *Journal of World Business*, *32*(3), 243–257.

Puritty, C., Strickland, L. R., Alia, E., Blonder, B., Klein, E., Kohl, M. T., … & Gerber, L. R. (2017). Without inclusion, diversity initiatives may not be enough. *Science*, *357*(6356), 1101–1102.

Rabenu, E. (2021). *Twenty-first century workplace challenges*. Lanham, MD: Lexington Books.

Ramaswami, A., Dreher, G. F., Bretz, R., & Wiethoff, C. (2010). Gender, mentoring, and career success: The importance of organizational context. *Personnel Psychology*, *63*(2), 385–405.

Ravasi, D., & Schultz, M. (2006). Responding to organizational identity threats: Exploring the role of organizational culture. *Academy of Management Journal*, *49*(3), 433–458.

Reed, M. S., Evely, A. C., Cundill, G., Fazey, I., Glass, J., Laing, A., … & Stringer, L. C. (2010). What is social learning? *Ecology and Society*, *15*(4).

Reis, C., & Baruch, Y. (Eds.). (2013). *Careers without borders: Critical perspectives*. New York: Routledge.

Renwich, P. A., & Lawler, E. E. (1978). What you really want from your job. *Psychology Today*, *2*, May, 53–65.

Riccucci, N. M. (2018). Managing diversity in public sector workforces: Essentials of public policy and administration series. New York: Routledge.

Riketta, M. (2002). Attitudinal organizational commitment and job performance: A meta-analysis. *Journal of Organizational Behavior*, *23*(3), 257–266.

Rivera, L. A. (2012). Diversity within reach: Recruitment versus hiring in elite firms. *The ANNALS of the American Academy of Political and Social Science*, *639*(1), 71–90.

Riyanto, S., Ariyanto, E., & Lukertina, L. (2019). Work–life balance and its influence on employee engagement 'Y' generation in the courier service industry. *International Review of Management and Marketing*, *9*(6), 25–31.

Roberson, Q. M. (2006). Disentangling the meanings of diversity and inclusion in organizations. *Group & Organization Management*, *31*(2), 212–236.

Robinson, S. L., Kraatz, M. S., & Rousseau, D. M. (1994). Changing obligations and the psychological contract: A longitudinal study. *Academy of Management Journal*, *37*(1), 137–152.

Robinson, S. L., & Morrison, E. W. (1995). Psychological contracts and OCB: The effect of unfulfilled obligation on civic virtue behavior. *Journal of Organizational Behavior*, *16*(3), 289–298.

Rodrigues, C. (2009). *International management: A cultural approach*. Thousand Oaks, CA: Sage.

Rodrigues, R. A., & Guest, D. (2010). Have careers become boundaryless? *Human Relations*, *63*(8), 1157–1175.

Rodrigues, R., Guest, D., & Budjanovcanin, A. (2013). From anchors to orientations: Towards a contemporary theory of career preferences. *Journal of Vocational Behavior*, *83*(2), 142–152.

Rokeach, M. (1973). *The nature of human values*. New York: Free Press.

Ronen, S. and Shenkar, O. (1985). Clustering countries on attitudinal dimensions: A review and synthesis. *Academy of Management Review*, *10*, 435–454.

Ronen, S., & Shenkar, O. (2013). Mapping world cultures: Cluster formation, sources and implications. *Journal of International Business Studies*, *44*(9), 867–897.

Rosenbaum, J. L. (1979). Tournament mobility: Career patterns in a corporation. *Administrative Science Quarterly*, *24*, 221–241.

Roth, G., & Kleiner, A. (1998). Developing organizational memory through learning history, *Organizational Dynamics*, *27*(2), 43–59.

Rothwell, A., & Arnold, J. (2007). Self-perceived employability: Development and validation of a scale. *Personnel Review*, *36*(1), 23–41.

Rothwell, A., Herbert, I., & Rothwell, F. (2008). Self perceived employability: Construction and initial validation of a scale for university students. *Journal of Vocational Behavior*, *73*(1), 1–12.

Rothwell, A., Jewell, S., & Hardie, M. (2009). Self-perceived employability: Investigating the responses of post-graduate students. *Journal of Vocational Behavior, 75*(2), 152–161.

Rothwell, S. (1995). Human resource planning. In J. Storey (Ed.), *Human resource management: A critical text* (pp. 167–202). London: Routledge.

Rothwell, W. J. (1994) Effective succession planning: Ensuring leadership continuity and building talent from within. Saranac Lake, NY: AMACOM.

Rothwell, W. J., Jackson, R. D., Ressler, C. L., Jones, M. C., & Brower, M. (2015). *Career planning and succession management: Developing your organization's talent – for today and tomorrow*. Santa Barbara, CA: ABC-CLIO.

Rotter, J. B. (1966). Generalized expectancies for internal versus external control of reinforcement. *Psychological Monographs, 1*(609), 80.

Rousseau, D. (2015). I-deals: Idiosyncratic deals employees bargain for themselves. London: Routledge.

Rousseau, D. M. (1995). *Psychological contracts in organizations*. Thousand Oaks, CA: Sage.

Rousseau, D. M. (1996) Changing the deal while keeping the people. *Academy of Management Executive, 10*(1), 50–59.

Rousseau, D. M., Hansen, S. D., & Tomprou, M. (2018). A dynamic phase model of psychological contract processes. *Journal of Organizational Behavior, 39*(9), 1081–1098.

Rousseau, D. M., Ho, V. T., & Greenberg, J. (2006). I-deals: Idiosyncratic terms in employment relationships. *Academy of Management Review, 31*(4), 977–994.

Rousseau, J.-J. (1762/1974). *The social contract or principles of political right*. New York: New American Library (revised translation in 1974 with notes by C. M. Sheover).

Royle, M. T. (2015). Theoretical drivers of early career success for new entrants to the job market. *International Journal of Management and Marketing Research, 8*(1), 31–56.

Rudolph, C. W., Lavigne, K. N., & Zacher, H. (2017). Career adaptability: A meta-analysis of relationships with measures of adaptivity, adapting responses, and adaptation results. *Journal of Vocational Behavior, 98*, 17–34.

Russo, M. V., & Foults, P. A. (1997). A resource-based perspective on corporate environmental performance and profitability. *Academy of Management Journal, 40*(3), 534–559.

Ryan, M. K., Haslam, S. A., Morgenroth, T., Rink, F., Stoker, J., & Peters, K. (2016). Getting on top of the glass cliff: Reviewing a decade of evidence, explanations, and impact. *The Leadership Quarterly, 27*(3), 446–455.

Sahoo, D. K., & Lenka, U. (2016). Breaking the glass ceiling: Opportunity for the organization. *Industrial and Commercial Training, 48*(6), 311–319.

Salge, C., Glackin, C., & Polani, D. (2014). Empowerment – an introduction. In *Guided Self-Organization: Inception* (pp. 67–114). Berlin, Heidelberg: Springer.

Sanchez, R. (1995). Strategic flexibility in product competition. *Strategic Management Journal, 16*, 135–139.

Sánchez-Hernández, M. I., González-López, Ó. R., Buenadicha-Mateos, M., & Tato-Jiménez, J. L. (2019). Work–life balance in great companies and pending issues for engaging new generations at work. *International Journal of Environmental Research and Public Health, 16*(24), 5122.

Sarfraz, I., Rajendran, D., Hewege, C., & Mohan, M. D. (2018). An exploration of global employability skills: A systematic research review. *International Journal of Work Organisation and Emotion, 9*(1), 63–88.

Savickas, M. L. (1997). Career adaptability: An integrative construct for life-span, life-space theory. *The Career Development Quarterly, 45*(3), 247–259.

Savickas, M. L. (2013). The theory and practice of career construction. In S. D. Brown, & R. W. Lent (Eds.). *Career development and counseling: Putting theory and research to work* (2nd ed., Vol. 1) (pp. 42–70). Hoboken, NJ: Wiley.

Scandura, T. A. (1998). Dysfunctional mentoring relationships and outcomes. *Journal of Management, 24*(3), 449–467.

Scandura, T. A., & Viator, R. E. (1994). Mentoring in public accounting firms: An analysis of mentor-protégé relationships. *Accounting Organizations & Society*, *19*(8), 717–734.

Schein, E. H. (1978). Career dynamics: Matching individual and organizational needs. Reading, MA: Addison-Wesley.

Schein, E. H. (1980). *Organizational psychology* (3rd ed.). Englewood Cliffs, NJ: Prentice-Hall.

Schein, E. H. (1985). *Career anchors: Discovering your real values*. San Francisco, CA: University Associates.

Schein, E. H. (2012). *Career anchors: Participant workbook* (*Vol. 397*). Chichester: Wiley.

Scherer, S. (2004). Stepping-stones or traps? The consequences of labour market entry positions on future careers in West Germany, Great Britain and Italy. *Work, Employment and Society*, *18*(2), 369–394.

Schermer, J. A., Krammer, G., Goffin, R. D., & Biderman, M. D. (2020). Using the 16PF to test the differentiation of personality by intelligence hypothesis. *Journal of Intelligence*, *8*(1), 12.

Schmitt, D. P., Realo, A., Voracek, M., & Allik, J. (2008). Why can't a man be more like a woman? Sex differences in Big Five personality traits across 55 cultures. *Journal of Personality and Social Psychology*, *94*(1), 168–182.

Schneider, F., & Buehn, A. (2018). Shadow economy: Estimation methods, problems, results and open questions. *Open Economics*, *1*(1), 1–29.

Schneider, S. C., & Barsoux, J.-L. (2003). *Managing across cultures* (end ed.). Harlow: Prentice Hall.

Schuler, M. (2004). Management of the organizational image: A method for organizational image configuration. *Corporate Reputation Review*, *7*(1), 37–53.

Schwab, K. (2017). *The fourth industrial revolution*. New York: Crown, Penguin.

Seibert, S. E., Kraimer, M. L., & Crant, J. M. (2001). What do proactive people do? A longitudinal model linking proactive personality and career success. *Personnel Psychology*, *54*(4), 845–874.

Seibert, S. E., Kraimer, M. L., & Heslin, P. A. (2016). Developing career resilience and adaptability. *Organizational Dynamics*, *45*(3), 245–257.

Seligman, M. E., & Csikszentmihalyi, M. (2014). Positive psychology: An introduction. In M. Csikszentmihalyi (Ed.). *Flow and the foundations of positive psychology* (pp. 279–298). Dordrecht: Springer.

Sewell, G., & Taskin, L. (2015). Out of sight, out of mind in a new world of work? Autonomy, control, and spatiotemporal scaling in telework. *Organization Studies*, *36*(11), 1507–1529.

Shackleton, V., & Newell, S. (1997). International assessment and selection. In N. Anderson, & P. Herriot (Eds.), *International handbook of selection and assessment* (p. 82). Chichester: Wiley.

Shantz, A., Wang, J., & Malik, A. (2018). Disability status, individual variable pay, and pay satisfaction: Does relational and institutional trust make a difference? *Human Resource Management*, *57*(1), 365–380.

Sheehan, C., & Cooper, B. K. (2011). HRM outsourcing: The impact of organisational size and HRM strategic involvement. *Personnel Review*, *40*(6), 742–760.

Shen, J., Chanda, A., D'netto, B., & Monga, M. (2009). Managing diversity through human resource management: An international perspective and conceptual framework. *The International Journal of Human Resource Management*, *20*(2), 235–251.

Shirmohammadi, M., & Beigi, M. (2019). *Immigrant employee well-being: A review*. To be presented at the *Academy of Management Proceedings* (*Vol. 2019*, No. 1).

Shore, L. M., Randel, A. E., Chung, B. G., Dean, M. A., Holcombe Ehrhart, K., & Singh, G. (2011). Inclusion and diversity in work groups: A review and model for future research. *Journal of Management*, *37*(4), 1262–1289.

Shore, L. M., & Tetrick, L. E. (1994). The psychological contract as an explanatory framework in the employment relationship. *Journal of Organizational Behavior*, *1*(Trends in OB supplement), 91–109.

Shortland, S. (2016). The purpose of expatriation: Why women undertake international assignments. *Human Resource Management*, *55*(4), 655–678.

Shoss, M. K. (2017). Job insecurity: An integrative review and agenda for future research. *Journal of Management*, *43*(6), 1911–1939.

Silva, P., Lopes, B., Costa, M., Melo, A. I., Dias, G. P., Brito, E., & Seabra, D. (2018). The million-dollar question: Can internships boost employment? *Studies in Higher Education, 43*(1), 2–21.

Simosi, M., Rousseau, D. M., & Daskalaki, M. (2015). When career paths cease to exist: A qualitative study of career behavior in a crisis economy. *Journal of Vocational Behavior, 91*, 134–146.

Singer, P. (1982) *The expanding circle: Ethics and sociobiology.* New York: Farrar, Straus & Giroux.

Singer, P. (1997) How are we to live?: Ethics in an age of self-interest. Oxford: Oxford University Press.

Sisson, K., & Taylor, J. (2006). The Advisory, Conciliation and Arbitration Service. *The Changing Institutional Face of British Employment Relations,* The Netherlands: Kluwer Law International, 25–36.

Sitzmann, T., & Yeo, G. (2013). A meta-analytic investigation of the within-person self-efficacy domain: Is self-efficacy a product of past performance or a driver of future performance? *Personnel Psychology, 66*(3), 531–568.

Skilton, M., & Hovsepian, F. (2017). The 4th industrial revolution: Responding to the impact of artificial intelligence on business. Solihull: Springer.

Smircich, L. (1983). Concepts of culture and organizational analysis. *Administrative Science Quarterly, 28,* 339–358.

Smith, A. (1776, 1982). *The wealth of nations.* Introduction and Notes by A. Skinner. London: Penguin Random House.

Sonnentag, S. (2015). Dynamics of well-being. *Annual review of organizational psychology and organizational behavior, 2*(1), 261–293.

Sonnenfeld, J. A., & Peiperl, M. A. (1988). Staffing policy as a strategic response: A typology of career systems. *Academy of Management Review, 13*(4), 568–600.

Sonnenfeld, J. A., Peiperl, M. A., & J. P. Kotter (1988) Strategic determinants of managerial labour markets: A career systems view. *Human Resource Management, 27*(4), 369–388.

Sparrow, P. R. (2000). New employee behaviors, work designs and forms of work organization: What is in store for the future of work? *Journal of Managerial Psychology, 15*(3), 202–218.

Sparrow, P. R., & Hiltrop, J. M. (1997). Redefining the field of European HRM: A battle between national mindsets and forces of business transitions? *Human Resource Management, 36*(2), 201–219.

Spindler, G. S. (1994). Psychological contracts in the workplace – a lawyer's view. *Human Resource Management, 33*(3), 325–333.

Spokane, A. R. (1996). Holland's theory. In D. Brown, & L. Brooks (Eds.). *Career choice and development* (3rd ed.) (pp. 33–74). San Francisco, CA: Jossey-Bass.

Spreitzer, G. M., Cameron, L., & Garrett, L. (2017). Alternative work arrangements: Two images of the new world of work. *Annual Review of Organizational Psychology and Organizational Behavior, 4,* 473–499.

Spurk, D., Hirschi, A., & Dries, N. (2019). Antecedents and outcomes of objective versus subjective career success: Competing perspectives and future directions. *Journal of Management, 45*(1), 35–69.

Stapley, L. (1995). The personality of the organization: A psychodynamic explanation of culture and change. London: Free Association Books.

Sternberg, R. J. (1998) *In search of the human mind* (2nd ed.). Fort Worth, TX: Harcourt Brace.

Stewart, G. L., & Brown, K. G. (2019). *Human resource management.* Chichester: Wiley.

Stewart, T. A. (2010). Intellectual capital: The new wealth of organization. New York: Doubleday.

Stewart, W., & Barling, J. (1996). Fathers' work experiences affect children's behavior via job-related affect and parenting behaviors. *Journal of Organizational Behavior, 17*(3), 221–232.

Stewart Jr., W. H., & Roth, P. L. (2001) Risk propensity differences between entrepreneurs and managers: A meta-analytic review. *Journal of Applied Psychology, 86*(1), 145–152.

Storey, J. (1995). Human resource management: Still marching on, or marching out? In J. Storey (ed.), *Human resource management: A critical text* (pp. 3–32). London: Routledge.

Straub, C., Vinkenburg, C. J., & van Kleef, M. (2020). Career customization: Putting an organizational practice to facilitate sustainable careers to the test. *Journal of Vocational Behavior, 117.* https://doi.org/10.1016/j.jvb.2019.103320

Strauss, K., Griffin, M. A., & Parker, S. K. (2012). Future work selves: How salient hoped-for identities motivate proactive career behaviors. *Journal of Applied Psychology*, *97*(3), 580–598.

Stuth, S., & Jahn, K. (2020). Young, successful, precarious? Precariousness at the entry stage of employment careers in Germany. *Journal of Youth Studies*, *23*(6), 702–725.

Suifan, T. S., Diab, H., & Abdallah, A. B. (2017). Does organizational justice affect turnover-intention in a developing country? The mediating role of job satisfaction and organizational commitment, *Journal of Management Development*, *36*(9), 1137–1148.

Suleman, F. (2018). The employability skills of higher education graduates: Insights into conceptual frameworks and methodological options. *Higher Education*, *76*(9), 263–278.

Sullivan, S. E. (1999). The changing nature of careers: A review and research agenda. *Journal of Management*, *25*(3), 457–484.

Sullivan, S. E., & Arthur, M. B. (2006). The evolution of the boundaryless career concept: Examining physical and psychological mobility. *Journal of Vocational Behavior*, *69*(1), 19–29.

Sullivan, S. E., Forret, M., Carraher, S. C., & Mainiero, L. (2009). Using the kaleidoscope career model to examine generational differences in work attitudes. *Career Development International*, *14*, 284–302.

Sullivan, S. N., & Baruch, Y. (2009). Advances in career theory and research: Critical review and agenda for future exploration. *Journal of Management*, *35*(6), 1452–1571.

Super, D. E. (1957). *The psychology of careers*. New York: Harper & Row.

Super, D. E. (1980). A life-span, life space approach to career development. *Journal of Vocational Behavior*, *16*, 282–298.

Super, D. E., Savickas, M. L., & Super, C. M. (1996) The life-span, life space approach to careers. In D. Brown, & L. Brooks (Eds.), *Career choice and development* (3rd ed.) (pp. 121–178). San Francisco, CA: Jossey-Bass.

Susskind, D. (2020). A world without work: Technology, automation and how we should respond. Penguin: London.

Sutton, R. I. (1987). The process of organizational death: Disbanding and reconnecting. *Administrative Science Quarterly*, *32*(4), 542–569.

Suutari, V., Tornikoski, C., & Mäkelä, L. (2012). Career decision making of global careerists. *The International Journal of Human Resource Management*, *23*(16), 3455–3478.

Swart, J., Mann, C., Brown, S., & Price, A. (2012). *Human Resource Development*. Elsevier, Amsterdam.

Sweeney, D. S., Haller, D. and Sale, F. (1989) Individually controlled career counselling. *Training and Development Journal*, Aug., 58–61.

Syed, J., & Ozbilgin, M. (2019). Managing diversity and inclusion: An international perspective. Thousand Oaks, CA: Sage.

Szetela, A. (2020). Black Lives Matter at five: Limits and possibilities. *Ethnic and Racial Studies*, *43*(8), 1358–1383.

Tajfel, H. (Ed.). (2010). *Social identity and intergroup relations*. New York: Cambridge University Press.

Tansley, C., Hafermalz, E., & Dery, K. (2016). Talent development gamification in talent selection assessment centres. *European Journal of Training and Development*, *40*(7), 490–512.

Tapscott, D. (1998). Growing up digital: The rise of the net generation. New York: McGraw-Hill.

Tate, W. L., & Bals, L. (2018). Achieving shared triple bottom line (TBL) value creation: Toward a social resource-based view (SRBV) of the firm. *Journal of Business Ethics*, *152*(3), 803–826.

Tavares, A. I. (2017). Telework and health effects review. *International Journal of Healthcare*, *3*(2), 30–36.

Taylor, F. W. (1911). *The principles of scientific management*. New York: Harper.

Taylor, S., & Napier, N. (1996). Working in Japan: Lessons from women expatriates. *Sloan Management Review*, Spring, 76–84.

Ten Brummelhuis, L. L., & Bakker, A. B. (2012). A resource perspective on the work–home interface: The work–home resources model. *American Psychologist*, *67*(7), 545–556.

Terpstra, D. E., & Limpaphayom, W. (2012). Using evidence-based human resource practices for global competitiveness. *International Journal of Business and Management*, 7(12), 107–113.

Theuerkauf, I. (1991). Reshaping the global organization. *McKinsey Quarterly*, 3, 1023–1119.

Thijssen, J. G., Van der Heijden, B. I., & Rocco, T. S. (2008). Toward the employability–link model: Current employment transition to future employment perspectives. *Human Resource Development Review*, 7(2), 165–183.

Thirkell, E., & Ashman, I. (2014). Lean towards learning: Connecting lean thinking and human resource management in UK higher education. *The International Journal of Human Resource Management*, 25(21), 2957–2977.

Thomas, K. W., & Velthouse, B. A. (1990). Cognitive elements of empowerment: An 'interpretative' model of intrinsic task motivation. *Academy of Management Review*, 15, 666–681.

Thompson, P. H., Baker, R. Z., & Smallwood, N. (1986) Improving professional development by applying the four stages career model. *Organizational Dynamics*, 15(2), 49–62.

Thornton III, G. C., & Byham, W. C. (2013). *Assessment centers and managerial performance*. London: Elsevier.

Toffel, M. W., Short, J. L., & Ouellet, M. (2015). Codes in context: How states, markets, and civil society shape adherence to global labor standards. *Regulation & Governance*, 9(3), 205–223.

Toffler, A. (1970). *Future shock*. London: Pan Books.

Toffler, A. (1980). *The third wave*. London: Collins.

Tolentino, L. R., Garcia, P. R. J. M., Lu, V. N., Restubog, S. L. D., Bordia, P., & Plewa, C. (2014). Career adaptation: The relation of adaptability to goal orientation, proactive personality, and career optimism. *Journal of Vocational Behavior*, 84(1), 39–48.

Tomaszewski, W., Perales, F., & Xiang, N. (2017). Career guidance, school experiences and the university participation of young people from low socio-economic backgrounds. *International Journal of Educational Research*, 85, 11–23.

Tomlinson, J., Baird, M., Berg, P., & Cooper, R. (2018). Flexible careers across the life course: Advancing theory, research and practice. *Human Relations*, 71(1), 4–22.

Tornow, W. W., & London, M. (1998). *Maximizing the value of 360-degree feedback*. San Francisco, CA: Jossey-Bass.

Torten, R., Reaiche, C., & Caraballo, E. L. (2016). Teleworking in the new milleneum. *The Journal of Developing Areas*, 50(5), 317–326.

Townley, B. (1994). *Reframing human resource management*. London: Sage.

Townsend, R. (1970). *Up the organization*. New York: Knopf.

Tran, H., Baruch, Y., & Bui, H. T. M. (2019). On the way to self-employment: The dynamics of career mobility. *International Journal of Human Resource Management*. doi: 10.1080/09585192.2019.1640267

Tranowieski, D. (1973). *The changing success ethic*. New York: AMACON.

Travaglione, A., & Cross, B. (2006). Diminishing the social network in organizations: Does there need to be such a phenomenon as 'survivor syndrome' after downsizing? *Strategic Change*, 15(1), 1–13.

Trede, F., & McEwen, C. (2015). Early workplace learning experiences: What are the pedagogical possibilities beyond retention and employability? *Higher Education*, 69(1), 16–32.

Triana, M. D. C., Gu, P., Chapa, O., Richard, O., & Colella, A. (2021). Sixty years of discrimination and diversity research in human resource management: A review with suggestions for future research directions. *Human Resource Management*, 60(1), 145–204.

Triandis, H. C. (1995). *Individualism and Collectivism*. Boulder, CO: Westview Press.

Tsoukalas, G., Belobaba, P., & Swelbar, W. (2008). Cost convergence in the US airline industry: An analysis of unit costs 1995–2006. *Journal of Air Transport Management*, 14(4), 179–187.

Tsui, A. S. (1987). Defining the practices and effectiveness of the human resource department: A multiple constituency approach. *Human Resource Management*, 26(1), 35–69.

Tsui, A. S. (1990). A multiple-constituency model of effectiveness: An empirical examination at the human resource subunit level. *Administrative Science Quarterly, 35*, 458–483.

Tsui, A. S., Egan, T. D., & O'Reilly III, C. A. (1992). Being different: Relational demography and organizational attachment. *Administrative Science Quarterly, 37*(4), 549–579.

Tung, R. L. (1982). Selection and training procedures of US, European and Japanese multinationals. *California Management Review, 25*(1), 57–71.

Turner, P., & Kalman, D. (2015). Make your people before making your products. *Human Resource Management International Digest, 23*, 28–31.

Twenge, J. M. (2010). A review of the empirical evidence on generational differences in work attitudes. *Journal of Business and Psychology, 25*(2), 201–210.

Tzabbar, D. Tzafrir, S. S., & Baruch, Y. (2017). A bridge over trouble waters: Replication, integration and extension of the relationship between HRM practices and organizational performance using moderating meta-analysis. *Human Resource Management Review, 27*, 134–148.

Tziner, A., Kopelman, R., & Joanis, C. (1997). Investigation of raters' and ratees' reactions to three methods of performance appraisal: BOS, BARS, and GRS. *Canadian Journal of Administrative Sciences, 14*(4), 396–404.

US Bureau of Labor Statistics (2020, December). *Labor force characteristics by race and ethnicity, 2019.* Report 1088. https://www.bls.gov/opub/reports/race-and-ethnicity/2019/pdf/home.pdf

US Bureau of Labor Statistics (2021). Persons with a disability: Labor force characteristics – 2020. *News Release.* https://www.bls.gov/news.release/pdf/disabl.pdf

Ulijn, J. M., Duysters, G., & Meijer, E. (Eds.). (2010). Strategic alliances, mergers and acquisitions: The influence of culture on successful cooperation. Cheltenham: Edward Elgar.

Ulrich, D. (1998). A new mandate for human resources. *Harvard Business Review, 76*(1), 124–134.

Unger, J. M., Rauch, A., Frese, M., & Rosenbusch, N. (2011). Human capital and entrepreneurial success: A meta-analytical review. *Journal of Business Venturing, 26*(3), 341–358.

Vaiman, V., Cascio, W. F., Collings, D. G., & Swider, B. W. (2021). The shifting boundaries of talent management. *Human Resource Management, 60*(2), 253–257.

Valcour, M., Bailyn, L., & Quijada, M. A. (2007). Customized careers. In H. P. Gunz, & M. Peiperl (Eds.). *Handbook of career studies* (pp. 188–210). London: Sage.

Valverde, M., Tregaskis, O., & Brewster, C. (2000). Labor flexibility and firm performance. *International Advances in Economic Research, 6*(4), 649–661.

Van De Voorde, K., Paauwe, J., & Van Veldhoven, M. (2012). Employee well-being and the HRM–organizational performance relationship: A review of quantitative studies. *International Journal of Management Reviews, 14*(4), 391–407.

Van der Heijde, C. M., & Van der Heijden, B. I. J. M. (2006). A competence-based and multidimensional operationalization and measurement of employability. *Human Resource Management, 45*, 449–476.

Van der Heijden, B. I. J. M., & De Vos, A. (2015). Sustainable careers: Introductory chapter. In A. De Vos, & B. I. J. M. Van der Heijden (Eds.). *Handbook of research on sustainable careers.* Cheltenham: Edward Elgar.

Van der Heijden, B. I. J. M., De Vos, A., Akkermans, J., Spurk, D., Semeijn, J., Van der Veldek, M., & Fugate, M. (2020). Sustainable careers across the lifespan: Moving the field forward. *Journal of Vocational Behavior, 117.*

Van der Heijden, B. I. J. M., Gorgievski, M. J., & Lange, A. H. (2016). Learning at the workplace and sustainable employability: A multi-source model moderated by age. *European Journal of Work and Organizational Psychology, 25*(1), 13–30.

Van der Heijden, B. I. J. M., Notelaers, G., Peters, P., Stoffers, J. M., De Lange, A. H., Froehlich, D. E., & Van der Heijde, C. M. (2018). Development and validation of the short-form employability five-factor instrument. *Journal of Vocational Behavior, 106*, 236–248.

Van Wingerden, J., Bakker, A. B., & Derks, D. (2017). Fostering employee well-being via a job crafting intervention. *Journal of Vocational Behavior, 100,* 164–174.

Vandenberghe, C., Landry, G., Bentein, K., Anseel, F., Mignonac, K., & Roussel, P. (2021). A dynamic model of the effects of feedback-seeking behavior and organizational commitment on newcomer turnover. *Journal of Management, 47*(2), 519–544.

Vecchio, R. P. (1995). *Organizational behavior* (3rd ed.). Fort Worth, TX: Dryden Press.

Veiga, J. F. (1981). Plateaued versus nonplateaued managers: Career patterns, attitudes, and path potential. *Academy of Management Journal, 24,* 566–578.

Veld, M., Paauwe, J., & Boselie, P. (2010). HRM and strategic climates in hospitals: Does the message come across at the ward level? *Human Resource Management Journal, 20*(4), 339–356.

Venkataraman, S. (2019). The distinctive domain of entrepreneurship research. In J. A. Katz, & A. C. Corbett (Eds.). *Seminal ideas for the next twenty-five years of advances.* Bingley: Emerald Publishing.

Vermunt, R., & Törnblom, K. Y. (2016). Introduction distributive and procedural justice. In K. Törnblom, & R. Vermunt (Eds.). *Distributive and procedural justice* (pp. 17–28). London: Routledge.

Vesa, M., den Hond, F., & Harviainen, J. T. (2019). On the possibility of a paratelic initiation of organizational wrongdoing. *Journal of Business Ethics, 160*(1), 1–15.

Vinkenburg, C. J., & Weber, T. (2012). Managerial career patterns: A review of the empirical evidence. *Journal of Vocational Behavior, 80*(3), 592–607.

Virtanen, M., & Kivimäki, M. (2018). Long working hours and risk of cardiovascular disease. *Current Cardiology Reports, 20*(11), 1–7.

Von Glinow, M. A., Driver, M. J., Brousseau, K., & Prince, J. B. (1983). The design of a career oriented human resource system. *Academy of Management Review, 8*(1), 23–32.

Voss, Z. G., Cable, D. M., & Voss, G. B. (2006). Organizational identity and firm performance: What happens when leaders disagree about 'who we are'? *Organization Science, 17*(6), 741–755.

Walker, J. W., & Gutteridge, J. G. (1979). *Career planning practices: An AMA survey report.* New York: AMACOM.

Walsh, L. C., Boehm, J. K., & Lyubomirsky, S. (2018). Does happiness promote career success? Revisiting the evidence. *Journal of Career Assessment, 26*(2), 199–219.

Wanberg, C. R., van Hooft, E. A., Liu, S., & Csillag, B. (2020). Can job seekers achieve more through networking? The role of networking intensity, self-efficacy, and proximal benefits. *Personnel Psychology, 73*(4), 559–585. https://doi.org/10.1111/peps.12380

Wanous, J. P. (1992) Organizational entry: Recruitment, selection, orientation, and socialization of newcomers (2nd ed.). Reading, MA: Addison-Wesley.

Warhurst, C., & Nickson, D. (2020). *Aesthetic labour.* London: Sage.

Warren, T., & Lyonette, C. (2018). Good, bad and very bad part-time jobs for women? Re-examining the importance of occupational class for job quality since the 'great recession' in Britain. *Work, Employment and Society, 32*(4), 747–767.

Waterman Jr., R. H., Waterman, J. A., & Collard, B. A. (1994). Toward a career-resilient workforce. *Harvard Business Review, 72*(4), 87–95.

Watson Wyatt (1999). WorkUSA 2000: Employee commitment and the bottom line. Bethesda, MD: Watson Wyatt.

Weber, M. (1905). The Protestant Ethic: *Archiv fur Sozialwissenschaft und Sozialpolitic* (Vol. *20 & 21*). Cited by Giddens, A. (1971). *Capitalism and modern social theory.* Cambridge: Cambridge University Press.

Weber, Y., & Tarba, S. Y. (2012). Mergers and acquisitions process: The use of corporate culture analysis. *Cross Cultural Management: An International Journal, 19*(3), 288–303.

Weick, K. E. (2001). *Making sense of the organization.* Oxford: Blackwell.

Wellbeing People (2017). Google's secret to workplace wellbeing. https://www.wellbeingpeople. com/2017/08/28/googles-secret-workplace-wellbeing/

Wernerfelt, B. (1984). A resource-based view of the firm. *Strategic Management Journal*, *5*, 171–180.

Whyte, W. H. (1956). *The organization man*. New York: Simon & Schuster.

Wickman, J., & Vecchi, A. (2009). The importance of business travel for industrial clusters – making sense of nomadic workers. *Geografiska Annaler: Series B*, *91*, 245–255.

Wikström, K., Artto, K., Kujala, J., & Söderlund, J. (2010). Business models in project business. *International Journal of Project Management*, *28*(8), 832–841.

Wilensky, H. L. (1961). Careers, life-styles, and social integration. *International Social Science Journal*, *12*, 553–558.

Wilensky, H. L. (1964). The professionalization of everyone? *American Journal of Sociology*, *70*, 137–158.

Wilhelm F., & Hirschi, A. (2019) Career self-management as a key factor for career wellbeing. In L. Potgieter, N. Ferreira, & M. Coetzee (Eds.), *Theory, research and dynamics of career wellbeing*. Cham: Springer.

Wille, B., & De Fruyt, F. (2014). Vocations as a source of identity: Reciprocal relations between Big Five personality traits and RIASEC characteristics over 15 years. *Journal of Applied Psychology*, *99*(2), 262.

Williams, G., Blackstone, T., & Metcalf, D. (1974). *The academic labour market: Economic and social aspects of a profession*. Amsterdam: Elsevier.

Wilton, N. (2008). Business graduates and management jobs: An employability match made in heaven? *Journal of Education and Work*, *21*(2), 143–158.

Wolfe, A. (1998) One nation, after all: What middle-class Americans really think about God, country, family, poverty, racism, welfare, homosexuality, immigration, the left, the right, and each other. New York: Viking.

Wong, K., Chan, A. H., & Ngan, S. C. (2019). The effect of long working hours and overtime on occupational health: A meta-analysis of evidence from 1998 to 2018. *International Journal of Environmental Research and Public Health*, *16*(12), 2102.

World Economic Forum (2020). *Insight report: Global gender gap*. Geneva: WEF. http://www3.weforum. org/docs/WEF_GGGR_2020.pdf

Wright, M., & Coyne, J. (2018). *Management buy-outs*. London: Routledge.

Wright, M., Thompson, S., Chiplin, B., & Robbie, K. (1991). *Buy-ins and buy-outs*. London: Graham & Trotman.

Wright, P. M. & Snell, S. A. (1998). Toward a unifying framework for exploring fit and flexibility in strategic human resource management. *Academy of Management Review*, *23*(4), 756–772.

Yakoboski, P. J. (2016). Adjunct views of adjunct positions. *Change: The Magazine of Higher Learning*, *48*(3), 54–59.

Yao, A., Duan, Z., & Baruch, Y. (2020). Time, space, Confucianism and careers: A contextualised review of career research in China – current knowledge and future research agenda. *International Journal of Management Review*. doi: 10.1111/ijmr.12223

Yarnall, J. (2008). *Strategic career management*. Amsterdam: Elsevier.

Zaccaro, S. J., Dubrow, S., & Kolze, M. (2018). *Leader traits and attributes*. In J. Antonakis, & D. V. Day (Eds.), *The nature of leadership* (pp. 29–55). London: Sage.

Zapf, D., Kern, M., Tschan, F., Holman, D., & Semmer, N. K. (2020). Emotion work: A work psychology perspective. *Annual Review of Organizational Psychology and Organizational Behavior*, *8*.

Zell, D. (2003). Organizational change as a process of death, dying, and rebirth. *The Journal of Applied Behavioral Science*, *39*(1), 73–96.

Zhu, X. S., Dalal, D. K., Nolan, K. P., & Barnes-Farrell, J. L. (2021). Understanding the role of organizational personality and social identity concerns on initial recruitment outcomes. *Journal of Vocational Behavior*, *124*. https://doi.org/10.1016/j.jvb.2020.103518

Zikic, J. (2015). Skilled migrants' career capital as a source of competitive advantage: Implications for strategic HRM. *The International Journal of Human Resource Management, 26*(10), 1360–1381.

Zimmerman, M. A. (2000). Empowerment theory. In *Handbook of Community Psychology* (pp. 43–63). Boston, MA: Springer.

Index

Page numbers in *italics* refer to figures; page numbers in **bold** refer to tables.